A History of Television's
The Virginian, 1962–1971

A History of Television's
The Virginian, 1962–1971

PAUL GREEN

FOREWORD BY FRANK PRICE

McFarland & Company, Inc., Publishers
Jefferson, North Carolina, and London

The present work is a reprint of the library bound edition
of A History of Television's *The Virginian*, 1962–1971,
first published in 2006 by McFarland.

LIBRARY OF CONGRESS CATALOGUING-IN-PUBLICATION DATA

Green, Paul.
A history of television's *The Virginian*, 1962–1971 /
Paul Green ; foreword by Frank Price.
p.   cm.
Includes bibliographical references and index.

ISBN-13 978-0-7864-4680-3
softcover : 50# alkaline paper ∞

1. Virginian (Television program)   I. Title.
PN1992.77.V56   2010   791.45'72—dc22   2006019835

British Library cataloguing data are available

Front cover—Cast of *The Virginian* from left: Lee J. Cobb, James Drury,
Doug McClure(Photofest); background ©2010 Shutterstock

Manufactured in the United States of America

*McFarland & Company, Inc., Publishers
Box 611, Jefferson, North Carolina 28640
www.mcfarlandpub.com*

To my wife Bev
and my mother, father and sister,
who shared in the joy of watching *The Virginian*
every Friday evening on BBC 1 in the 1960s.

Acknowledgments

Writing this book has been a huge task, impossible to accomplish alone. I've often relied on the expertise and kindness of others to help me with difficult research. In no order of preference I'd like to thank the following.

Frank Price for his continued support throughout the entire project and for sharing his knowledge of the creative process. His expert knowledge of *The Virginian* from his years as executive producer helped fill in many blanks and provided a more rounded perspective of the show. His wife Katherine Crawford has also been a great help in sharing her memories of working on three episodes and of the everyday working life of an actress.

Western author Kirby Jonas for introducing me to James Drury and setting up my first interview. James Drury for kindly agreeing to answer my questions and arranging interviews with Gary Clarke and Roberta Shore. Gary Clarke for his humor and honesty and quick response to my request for personal photos. Roberta Shore for her interview and arranging for me to speak with Randy Boone. Randy Boone for his detailed recollections. Tané McClure, BarBara Luna and Diane McClure for their insightful memories of Doug McClure. Pippa Scott for describing her time as Molly Wood. Sara Lane, in the eleventh hour, for being so friendly and cooperative with her recollections.

Thanks to Barbara Townsend for providing so much information on the show, specifically on Doug McClure and Trampas, and Alice Munzo for her expert knowledge of Owen Wister. Actor John Saxon for sharing his recollections of his three guest star appearances and putting me in contact with producer Joel Rogosin. Joel and Deborah Rogosin for sharing memories. Writer Roland Kibbee's daughter Meredith and Elizabeth Perry, daughter-in-law of the late director Abner Biberman. Renata Casser, former neighbor to Sara Lane, and Topanga Canyon poet Pablo Capra for arranging the interview. Mila Blurton for her assistance in locating Sara Lane when I'd given up hope. Bill Halvorsen, Martin Grams Jr., Dick Shane. And a special thanks to my wife Bev for her patience, kindness and hard work when I've been tied to my desk for hours on end.

In attempting to contact surviving cast members of *The Virginian*, I found it interesting that the actors most willing to talk belonged to the early seasons. Regular cast members from later seasons were either unavailable or didn't respond to requests to contribute. Actress Katherine Crawford had her personal viewpoint on why this was the case.

"I think that the original actors in any series feel like the legitimate children, and later actors, replacements or additions, feel like the stepchildren. They don't have such a sense of belonging or ownership."

Table of Contents

Foreword

by Frank Price

In the fifth season of *The Virginian,* my wife and I were at our house watching an episode of the show as it aired. Suddenly, the unfolding drama took a startling turn. The picture jumped to scenes just before the end of the episode and skipped the intervening scenes. I realized that the NBC technician responsible for switching from one reel to another had switched to the wrong reel, and the episode would now make no sense at all. I called NBC Burbank, where the broadcast feed originated, to get them to fix the problem, but the switchboard was busy. The flood of calls made it impossible to get through. Finally, the technician became aware of the problem and switched back to the proper reel, but by then, of course, the audience was totally confused.

By the next morning, though, I realized what an important audience our show had. One complaint call did get through that switchboard. The call was from a thoroughly annoyed regular viewer, former President Dwight D. Eisenhower, calling from his home in Palm Springs. His White House–trained staff knew how to get through even jammed switchboards.

I was executive producer of *The Virginian* for a number of seasons, including some of the most crucial. What is an executive producer? Today they use the term "show runner" to explain it. As executive producer I made decisions about which producers, directors and writers to hire or, in some cases, to fire. I made the final decisions on which stories to develop into teleplays and which teleplays to commit to film. I made the final decisions on casting the actors who appeared each week in support of our continuing stars. It was my responsibility to make sure the episodes were produced for the amount of money that had been budgeted by the studio. If Jim Drury had a complaint about his role in the latest script, I was the one who had to handle it. I either had to persuade him he was wrong or else agree that he had a solid complaint and I would then order rewrites until we fixed the problem.

Since I saw my job as making sure that our leading players had acting roles that showed them in a flattering and favorable light, my relationship with actors was generally good. They knew I wanted to make them look good, whatever flaws might exist in a proposed script. I've always liked actors and I have great respect for what they do. Writers, producers and directors use their talents and skills to make a show, which may turn out well or badly. When it's bad, they are all somewhat anonymous. An actor, however, is right there on screen, personally memorialized forever in a photoplay that didn't work. It's not just his work that looks bad. He or she can come off dreadfully in person. Some of the finest actors, however, have such talent they can survive almost any turkey. They have such truth in their own performances that they come off well regardless of the script.

We were fortunate in *The Virginian* to have several actors of that caliber. Lee J. Cobb and Charles Bickford, for instance. But James Drury and Doug McClure were also in that category. Jim's deep-seated belief that he was the Virginian, that he was the actual foreman of Shiloh Ranch, gave his performances a consistent reality that surmounted most script deficiencies. And Doug had a natural acting talent that I found truly amazing. His instinctual approach always added dimension and humor to anything that appeared on the written page. Both Jim and Doug were consistently underrated by critics. They made it look so easy that their talent and skills weren't fully appreciated.

I played my own role in our *Virginian* offices far away from the stages or locations where episodes were shot. Located in offices next to mine were the producers such as Winston Miller, Cy Chermak and Joel Rogosin. Pat Betz, the NBC programming executive, would call with his notes and comments on our latest script. Or he might be calling to give his opinion on an outline that had been submitted to the network. Pat was involved from the beginning with *The Virginian* and was a great fan of the show. He was a down-to-earth Midwestern guy who was also a tough critic. Another executive, Dwayne Ratliffe, was the NBC censor who looked for gratuitous sex or excessive violence. He read every script carefully before it was shot and saw every episode before it went on air and had the authority to insist on changes.

Many crafts contribute to the making of a television show or movie. Actors, writers, directors and producers are more publicly known, but it takes a huge variety of skills and talents to make up a film. Cinematographers, lighting experts, makeup and hair experts, sound experts, art directors, set designers, prop men, wranglers (handling animals from horses to snakes and rats) and special effects people (fires, explosions). There are also the carpenters, the painters, the plumbers, the lawyers, the accountants and the insurance people.

All of these people love show business. They will put in long hours under somewhat unpleasant circumstances while shooting a film. Twelve-hour days are common for shooting television episodes. There's a joke about a man working in a circus. His job is to follow behind the elephants with a shovel and bucket to pick up the elephant dung. When he complains about his job, someone suggests he quit and get another job. "What? And get out of show business?" is his response.

Filming an episode of *The Virginian* required a disciplined attention to detail. Shooting a Western in the environs of Los Angeles meant that, in all outdoor shooting, the sky had to be watched so that our camera didn't pick up condensation trails from passing jets. These "con" trails, while cloud-like, were something not present in the Wyoming skies of 1886.

People wear wristwatches. They wear them so much they forget they wear them. That's a problem if the person wearing a wristwatch is an actor portraying a cowboy in 1886. If no one spots that wristwatch, generally concealed by a shirt cuff, and it's revealed by the camera in a particular shot, well, it just might escape the attention of the film editor, the producers and all the potential checkers down the post-production line because they are used to seeing wristwatches on people and they are concentrating on the actors' performances. Then it finally shows up on television. Some eagle-eyed viewer will spot it, of course. And then all of us on the show are embarrassed.

But, even if the wristwatch is taken off, we may still have a problem. People who regularly wear wristwatches develop a light band around their wrist where the skin has been shielded from the tanning sun. When the cowboy reaches out and exposes his wrist in that film set back in 1886, lo and behold, there is evidence that he wears a wristwatch when not shooting period Westerns. So it is up to the body makeup people (they're a different group from those who do facial makeup) to check wrists for those tell-tale pale bands.

The Virginian benefited from a large pool of experienced writers, directors and technicians that existed in the Hollywood of that time. They were people who had learned their crafts in the center of the world's entertainment capital. They had done every kind of Western conceivable and had shot them under every circumstance.

I was young, energetic and full of ideas. I loved the legend of the West and the actual history of those days. I had grown up watching everything from Johnny Mack Brown, Hopalong Cassidy and Gene Autry to *Red River, High Noon* and *Giant.* I increasingly hired young and talented writer producers like Cy Chermak and Joel Rogosin. They had the energy to keep the enthusiasm and the standards

Frank Price, executive producer and writer of the original format for *The Virginian* (courtesy Frank Price).

up on episode after episode. But we all depended on those people who had gone through the years that gave them incredible experience. When we handed a script to a Bill Witney, Don McDougall, Abner Biberman or Earl Bellamy, we knew they would have the expertise to put the scenes that existed only on paper onto film and do it in precisely eight days.

We benefited from the existence of a central wardrobe institution called "Western Costume." The studios had partnered on a separate company so that each studio didn't have to maintain its own Western clothes. Our wardrobe people could fit most of the leading characters out of our own wardrobe department. But available to us was the endless racks of Western clothing, including cowboy hats and boots, U.S. Cavalry uniforms, sunbonnets and dresses and everything you'd encounter in the West. The studios sold it off years ago.

Jean Holloway and Carey Wilber were two of our reliable and outstanding writers. Jean wrote very strong women and idealized but somewhat weak men. Carey, on the other hand, would write strong men but weak women. I once tried to get them to collaborate on a script. I had visions of what wonderful scenes could result from a relationship between Jean's strong woman and Carey's strong man. I arranged for a meeting in my office so they could get to know each other. The meeting turned into a disaster. After only a few minutes of conversation, they could not stand being in the same room together. So much for that good idea.

When we started on *The Virginian,* we didn't know that producing a series of weekly 90-minute movies that dealt with the same characters in the same setting was nearly impossible. So we managed to get the job done. And I am particularly pleased that the series created a spot for itself in the tastes and minds of a discriminating, intelligent audience, including Dwight D. Eisenhower.

The Virginian played a key formative role in my life. I got on-the-job experience in running a high-profile show business enterprise, learning to coordinate business and creative endeavors. It was that experience that prepared me to run Universal Television for five years. It also prepared me to run a famous motion picture studio, Columbia Pictures, and then return to Universal to head Universal Pictures and the MCA Motion Picture Group. The jobs were all similar. Develop entertaining scripts, choose good directors, assemble good casts and produce the pictures within the proper budget limits. That was the job, whether it led to making *The Virginian*'s "Felicity's Spring" or Universal Pictures' *Out of Africa.*

The Virginian also led to my meeting my future wife, a young actress from the Royal Academy of Dramatic Art in London. She was also Roy Huggins' daughter. He suggested that I use her in a small role in an episode titled "Say Goodbye to All That." I did and thought she did a good job. But it wasn't until nearly two years later that our romance began. I saw her in a brilliant show called "The End of the World, Baby" on *Kraft Suspense Theatre* and I thought she was terrific. I was executive producer of two shows at that time, *The Virginian* and the short-lived *Destry.* I called Katherine's agent and offered her starring roles in upcoming episodes of both. In my mind, she was perfect for both. In *The Virginian* she played the role of a Swedish mail order bride in an episode titled "A Bride for Lars." It was on that show that our romance began. It has lasted over 43 years since then.

Preface

The Virginian was a major television Western series from 1962 to 1971. Throughout its nine-year run, it maintained high production values and employed quality talent. This book documents *The Virginian* from Owen Wister's 1902 novel, *The Virginian: A Horseman of the Plains,* to the 1957 Screen Gems pilot starring James Drury and the Revue–Universal TV series in 1962.

The main focus of this book is the 1962–1971 television series, documenting, with the help of personal interviews, creative personnel including actors, producers, directors, writers and cinematographers and an extensive episode guide covering all 249 episodes.

The Virginian was the third longest-running television Western, with only *Gunsmoke* (1955–1975) and *Bonanza* (1959–1973) having longer lives. Yet the series has had relatively little written about it. It is the intention of this book to redress the balance and to provide a permanent record of an influential and important series.

Introduction

The Virginian was a huge gamble for NBC back in 1962. A 90-minute television Western was a new format and the show went straight to air without a pilot to test audience response. Nobody knew if viewers would get bored and switch channels. The budget was huge compared to *Cheyenne, Maverick* and *Wagon Train* and the shooting schedule was hectic, with actors rushing between sets to work on two or three episodes in the same day.

But the gamble worked. After a lukewarm start, *The Virginian* attracted an audience that would see the show finally break into the top ten Nielsen ratings in 1967. *The Virginian* attracted outstanding talent in actors, directors, writers and composers. Actors Lee Marvin, Robert Redford, George C. Scott and Charles Bronson went on to international stardom. Writer Borden Chase and producer Winston Miller had scripted two classic Westerns, *My Darling Clementine* (1946) and *Red River* (1948). Directors William Witney and John English had helmed movie serials for Republic Pictures, that are now being acknowledged by director Quentin Tarantino as masterful examples of kinetic direction. Burt Kennedy went on to a successful movie career directing *Support Your Local Sheriff* (1969) and Samuel Fuller has attracted cult status for his often controversial work in movies such as *The Big Red One* (1980) and *White Dog* (1982).

Executive producers Roy Huggins and Frank Price created the vision that sustained the show in its early years following the departure of Charles Marquis Warren. Radio veteran Norman MacDonnell, famous for his work on *Gunsmoke,* steered it through its later seasons. Seasoned actors Lee J. Cobb, Charles Bickford, John McIntire and Stewart Granger had the maturity and experience necessary to convincingly portray the owners of Shiloh Ranch.

The rotating format was an essential ingredient in the success of *The Virginian.* Unlike shows that relied on one lead character to sustain their popularity, *The Virginian* could highlight different characters from Shiloh Ranch each week. Not only did it prove a successful formula, it prevented actor "burnout" and audience fatigue. James Drury and Doug McClure were the only actors to stay the course. Not only were they very effective in their roles as the Virginian and Trampas, they were also the best of friends away from the camera.

When *The Virginian*'s ratings slumped in the eighth season, the bosses at NBC and Universal decided to give it a makeover. *The Virginian* attempted to reinvent itself with a change of name and a new, stylish theme by acclaimed "Spaghetti Western" composer Ennio Morricone. It was reborn in 1970 as *The Men from Shiloh.* That particular gamble failed. Despite good ratings, the show was cancelled in 1971 after nine years on the air. It was one of 35 prime time shows to be cancelled that year.

In the course of the nine-year run of *The Virginian,* America had lived through the assassinations of President Kennedy, Robert Kennedy, Martin Luther King and Malcolm X and the horrors of Vietnam. Heroes couldn't be counted on to save the day and the anti-heroes of Sergio Leone's "Spaghetti Westerns" had replaced traditional role models. Clint Eastwood's cynical, amoral character struck a chord with audiences at a time when television was cutting back on violence.

Advertisers were looking to attract a younger demographic. Television had always been a partnership between corporation and sponsor. To sponsors the show was the entertainment that filled the gap between the commercial breaks that advertised their product.

The passing of *The Virginian* marked the beginning of the end for the TV Western. Only *Gunsmoke* would survive into the mid–1970s and new attempts at reviving the genre were short-lived.

The Virginian was in many ways the culmination of the Western invasion of television in the 1950s. NBC decided to go bigger and better. The series had its detractors who found the 90-minute format padded and the stories boring and long-winded. Many thought the episodes were just an extension of the old "B" movie Western. But the 90-minute color show was in a different league than the vast majority of TV Westerns on the air in 1962.

The success of *The Virginian* also paved the way for the birth of the TV movie in 1964. When *The Virginian* ended in 1971, not only had it sustained a change of name but the entire TV landscape had undergone a transformation. It would be claiming too much to say *The Virginian* was responsible, but its new, bold format had proved to network executives that viewers were willing to watch a 90-minute filmed series and it opened up new possibilities in a medium that was often too timid to take creative leaps of faith.

1

Owen Wister

"I do not believe there ever was any life more attractive to a vigorous young fellow than life on a cattle-ranch in those days."
—Theodore Roosevelt, 1883

The Virginian was born out of Owen Wister's travels to the West, in particular Wyoming. Wister first visited Wyoming in the summer of 1885, staying at Major Wolcott's Deer Creek Ranch. His doctor had ordered a "rest cure" to help him recover his fragile health. He was 25 years old and would return regularly to the West over the next 15 years. His experiences from these many visits provided material for his novel *The Virginian: A Horseman of the Plains,* published in 1902.

Owen Wister was born July 14, 1860, at 5103 Germantown Avenue, Philadelphia, the only child of Owen Jones Wister and Sarah Butler Wister. His father was a well-respected physician and his mother the daughter of famed English Shakespearean actress and writer Fanny Kemble.

Harvard-educated Wister majored in music with intentions of becoming a composer. Graduating *summa cum laude* in 1882, he studied music composition the following year at the Paris Conservatoire under Ernest Guiraud and was introduced to composer Franz Liszt while staying in Bayreuth. Upon his return to New York in 1883, Wister abandoned any thought of a musical career and took temporary employment as a bank clerk before entering Harvard Law School in 1885. Wister graduated three years later and was admitted to the bar in 1889. He took up office space in the Philadelphia law firm of Francis Rawle. But his experiences in the West had dulled his senses to a life spent engaged in law. He made the bold decision to become a writer and abandoned his second career choice.

While at Harvard, Owen Wister met Theodore Roosevelt, who was two years his senior. They formed a friendship that would shape Wister's future writing career. Roosevelt's journeys to the West had inspired Wister to take his first trip to Wyoming.

A man named Walter Furness provided him with the impetus to write his first short stories about the West. Wister recalled how, one autumn evening in 1891, he was dining at the Philadelphia Club with Furness, where they discussed, "why wasn't some Kipling saving the sagebrush for American literature...." Wister decided there and then to begin writing on his first short story. *Hank's Woman* was the result. It was published in issue 36 of *Harper's Weekly,* dated August 27, 1892. Throughout the 1890s Wister continued to contribute to *Harper's* and *The Saturday Evening Post.*

A meeting with painter and sculptor Frederic Remington on an 1893 visit to Wyoming developed into a strong friendship and the article *Evolution of a Cow-Puncher* (1895) in which Wister compared the European medieval knight and the cowboy, claiming they were "the same Saxon of different environments." Remington provided illustrations for the *Harper's New Monthly Magazine* article.

The novel *The Virginian* would find its roots in the short stories *Em'ly* (1893) and *Balaam and Pedro* (1894). The character of the Virginian in these early stories was secondary to the central characters of Pedro the pony and Em'ly the hen. Wister had even considered abandoning the Virginian character until the managing clerk from his law office threatened to never speak to him again if he did so. The Virginian returned from the woods he disappeared into at the conclusion of *Balaam and Pedro* and never looked back. The lack of a name for the Virginian was explained by the original secondary aspect of the character, who didn't require a name. Wister said the Virginian "remained anonymous through habit."

Wister began compiling *Em'ly* and *Balaam and Pedro* with later published stories from *Harper's* including *Where Fancy Was Bred* (1896), *Grandmother Stark* (1897) and *The Game and the Nation* (1900), plus *Superstition Trail* (1901) from *The Saturday Evening Post,* into one book shortly before the Wister family left for summer vacation in Saunderstown in 1901. Work on the book, including new material to create a more coherent structure, continued during a three-month winter visit to Charleston, South Carolina. Wister finally completed his manuscript in March 1902.

First published in April 1902, *The Virginian* was reprinted 15 times in the first year following publication. Wister's mother expressed her dislike for it, claiming the "doubtful morality" of the "hero's conduct" in a controversial lynching scene.

But Wister's mother was one of few dissenting voices. Theodore Roosevelt praised the novel and the general public and critics agreed. *The New York Times* book review dated June 21, 1902, read:

Owen Wister, author of *The Virginian: A Horseman of the Plains* (courtesy Alice Munzo; photograph first published in *World's Work* magazine, November 1902).

Owen Wister has come pretty near to writing the American novel ... Mr. Wister has set forth a phase of life which is to be found only in the United States, and has pictured it with graphic delineative force, with picturesqueness and with brilliant narrative power. The Virginian ought to live as an artistic embodiment of a man fast passing into a remembrance ... The Virginian in a broad sense is a historical novel. It rings true, and we believe it to be a faithful study.

The Virginian was unique in that the hero was a "cowboy." Cowboys were usually portrayed in a negative light. But Wister did make one concession: His cowboy wasn't from the West but from the "civilized" East. Throughout the novel we never learn the Virginian's real name. He is a classic hero figure. Revealing enough about himself to enable the reader to identify with him, but keeping enough back for the reader to remain intrigued by his mysterious past.

The novel centers on the Wyoming town of Medicine Bow, situated 263 miles from Sunk Creek Ranch and owned by Judge Robert Henry. The Virginian acts as foreman of the ranch. Wister called *The Virginian* a "colonial romance." And throughout the novel the Virginian wins over the affections of Vermont school-marm Molly Stark Wood.

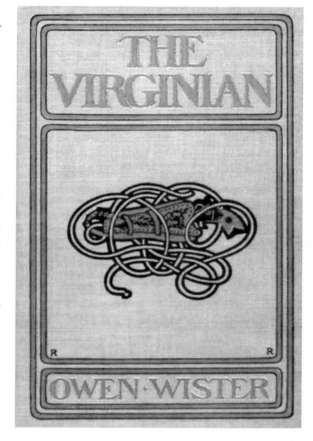

The Virginian: A Horseman of the Plains, 1902 **first edition (The American Treasures of the Library of Congress).**

Wister describes the villainous Trampas as "sullen" and "ugly." His meeting with the Virginian across a poker table resulted in the most quoted line of the novel, "When you call me that, smile!" The Virginian ultimately faces his enemy in what is arguably the first shoot-out in Western literature. The stranger from the cultured East has ventured to the uncivilized West and demonstrated his ability to survive in a hostile environment. The taming of the West was just around the corner.

Vivid descriptions of life in Wyoming are based on personal experiences of Wister and the no-nonsense approach of the Virginian mixes the sensibilities of East and West into a compelling portrait of an individual. It is this realism that set the novel apart from the cheap dime-novel pulp fiction of the period.

Wister was born at the start of the Civil War. His grandmother, Fanny Kemble, had described her time spent in Darien, the Georgia plantation owned by the Wister family, in her 1839 book *Two Years on a Georgia Plantation.* The young Wister had divided loyalties; novelist and family friend Henry James best summed up his mindset as "a Northerner of Southern descent." Wister transplanted his inner conflict into an East-meets-West

Panorama of Medicine Bow, Wyoming (courtesy Alice Munzo; published by Sanborn Souvenir Company, Denver, Colorado, in the 1940s).

drama in *The Virginian*. Years earlier, Wister's poem *Brothers Again*, written in 1877, expressed his wishes for eternal peace between soldiers from North and South.

Wister adapted his novel for a "five-act version" in collaboration with Kirk La Shelle. Dustin Farnum played the Virginian and Frank Campo portrayed Trampas, singing "Ten Thousand Cattle," a song composed and written by Wister. A successful 138-performance run in New York's Manhattan Theatre began on January 5, 1904. Farnum toured the country with the production and starred in the first filmed adaptation in 1914.

The Virginian: A Horseman of the Plains was Wister's first and last Western novel. He continued the genre in his short prose but abandoned it in long form for stories of aristocratic Southerners in Charleston following the Civil War in *Lady Baltimore* (1906). His last major work was a biography of Theodore Roosevelt, *Roosevelt, the Story of a Friendship, 1880–1919* (1930).

In 1898, Wister married his younger second cousin Mary Channing Wister from Boston. They had three sons and three daughters. His wife died giving birth to their sixth child in 1913. Wister died of a cerebral hemorrhage at North Kingstown, Rhode Island, on July 21, 1938.

Many people asked Wister if the Virginian was based on a real-life person. The answer is, the Virginian was the product of the assimilation of a number of people Wister met on his travels.

A major influence on Wister's Virginian was Corporal Charles Skirdin of the Second Cavalry, from Fort Bowie, Arizona, who was detailed to accompany Wister on his travels. Wister became a close friend of Skirdin, who had been abandoned by his family as a child in Arizona and was badly wounded in the Philippines, suffering a crippled arm and hand. Commenting in his 1928 preface to *The Virginian*, Wister wrote, "He, more definitely than any other frontier character I had met, continually realized and ratified my imaginary portrait."

Other influences, admitted by Wister in his 1928 preface, were two Kansas boys he met at Las Playas, New Mexico, and Dean Duke, the foreman of a ranch at Apache Tejo, who "did and said many things which reminded me of the Virginian."

Another admitted influence was George West, one of Wister's hunting guides in Wyoming. He possessed many of the qualities Wister later transferred to the Virginian. The infamous lynching scene, where the Virginian hangs his best friend Steve, could have been inspired by a letter West wrote to Wister where he described how he was going to hunt horse thieves and hang them. Plans for horse ranching and a hunting lodge with Wister evaporated after Wister sensed that West would be financially dependent on him.

Wister's Harvard classmate, Guy Waring, has also been cited as a source of inspiration. Four years after a fire destroyed his general store in Winthrop, Washington, in 1893, Waring returned to the Methow Valley and built a sturdy log cabin for himself and his wife. In 1898 Wister spent his honeymoon at the cabin, known as "Waring's Castle." Claims that *The Virginian* was inspired by Waring and the people of the Methow Valley may have some basis in fact, but any such claims have to take into account that the novel was, in part, composed of a number of short stories written many years earlier. It is possible the honeymoon chapter could have been inspired by his stay in the beautiful Methow Valley in Washington state.

Another inspiration for the Virginian character was "Mr. Morgan from Virginia," whom Wister recalled meeting at a stage station on Chugwater Creek called "Point of Rocks." In a letter to his mother, Wister recounted how Mr. Morgan cared for Mrs. Morgan, who was sick with malaria, "he making the beds and being more gentle to her and us than words can say..."

The desire for fame led to many questionable claims. Milton Storey and his wife staked their claim of being the models for the Virginian and Molly Stark in a Methow Valley newspaper article in 1922. Wister received at least half a dozen letters claiming knowledge of the "original" Virginian within six months of publication of *The Virginian*. Wister dismissed such claims, saying none of the people mentioned were known to him.

Edwin B. Trafton appeared to have more substantial proof of his claim when a special agent of the U.S. Department of Justice signed a letter stating he was the model for the Virginian. Wister failed to reply to a wire from the *Los Angeles Times* asking for his comments, but once again he dismissed the claim in private.

Yet another claim named Charles Sturgeon, who married Molly, a local schoolteacher from Little Medicine Bow River. However, details of Sturgeon meeting Wister on his arrival at Medicine Bow by train fail to match Wister's personal account of his arrival by wagon, accompanied by Frank Wolcott.

Perhaps the most enigmatic influence, having a genuine claim to authenticity, was Everett Cyril Johnson. The source of the story comes from Johnson's daughter-in-law Jean Lamont Johnson (1899–1992). In her 1967 biography of Everett C. Johnson she claims Owen Wister first met him at the Cheyenne Club in Cheyenne, Wyoming, in 1885. He maintained a correspondence with Johnson and sent him an autographed copy of *The Virginian* in 1904. They met in person for the final time in 1911 in Calgary, Canada.

Born in Richmond, Virginia in 1858, Everett Cyril Johnson, a cattle driver, rancher and butcher, moved to Wyoming and settled in Medicine Bow before moving on to Montana and Alberta, Canada in the late 1880s. His tombstone reads, "*In Loving Memory of Dad—Everett C. Johnson 1858–1946. The Virginian.*"

Literary influences on Wister include James Fenimore Cooper, whom many credit as the founder of the Western tradition with his 1826 novel *The Last of the Mohicans*. Natty Bumppo is one of the first frontier heroes in American literature and possesses similar virtues to the Virginian. But the Virginian is unique in speaking with one voice and thus creating an ideal of the lone hero so prevalent in subsequent Western novels.

Bret Harte was writing tales about contrasting characters and environments in his short stories for *Overland Monthly*. The contrast of cultures and backgrounds evident in Harte's work, going back as early as the 1860s, would be one factor in the influences that shaped "cowboy literature." Other writers of note from that period included Edward Eggleston, Hamlin Garland, Andy Adams and Alfred Henry Lewis.

Wister's novel managed to capture the mood of the time. The West was opening up through the railroads, and trade between the East and the West was lively. By 1893 five railroads crossed the West. The Virginian of Wister's imagination had escaped the confines of genteel society, based in Old World values, and was transformed into a "new" American, stripped of social pretensions. The concept of the lone hero fighting injustice in a lawless land captured the public's imagination and a new genre was born.

2

Beginnings

"Owen Wister was not the first to write about the cowboy. Nevertheless he probably did more than any other writer to popularize the cowboy as folk hero."
—T.A. Larson, *Wyoming* (1977)

Owen Wister lived to see three movie adaptations of his work. In 1914, Cecil B. DeMille filmed a silent 50-minute feature based on Wister's novel and the play by Kirk La Shelle and Wister. Dustin Farnum reprised his Broadway role as the Virginian, with uncredited roles for William Elmer playing Trampas and Jack W. Johnston as Steve.

A longer (84-minute) silent version directed by Tom Forman followed in 1923. Douglas Fairbanks expressed a strong interest in playing the Virginian but the part went to Kenneth Harlan. Russell Simpson portrayed Trampas, with Pat O'Malley as Steve and Milton Ross as Judge Henry. Writers Louis D. Lighton and Hope Loring adapted Wister's novel.

But it was the 1929 sound version from Paramount that would have the greatest success, and to this day it is still considered the best movie adaptation of Wister's novel. The laconic Gary Cooper was cast as the Virginian, with Walter Huston making a suitably villainous Trampas. Richard Arlen played Steve and E.H. Calvert was Judge Henry. Directed by Victor Fleming with an uncredited Henry Hathaway as assistant director, the film boasted a host of writers claiming credit, including Howard Estabrook, Grover Jones and Keene Thompson.

A 1946 Paramount remake directed by Stuart Gilmore and starring Joel McCrea as the Virginian, Brian Donlevy as Trampas, Sonny Tufts as Steve Andrews and Minor Watson as Judge Henry received lackluster reviews. It would prove to be the final theatrical movie release of Wister's novel before the Golden Age of television dawned and TV Westerns caught the public imagination.

The Virginian first hit black-and-white TV screens via a Screen Gems production that was broadcast as part of NBC's *Decision* (1958). The short-lived anthology series highlighted a different pilot show every Sunday evening with "The Virginian" marking the debut episode of the series on July 6, 1958. Leslie Stevens' script gave the Virginian a tangible past, informing the viewer he studied veterinarian medicine and was part of Jeb Stuart's Cavalry in the Civil War. It also introduced us to a Virginian dressed in clothing that suggested an educated Easterner and a gentlemanly manner that disguised an uncompromising individual.

The Screen Gems production attempted to follow the rudiments of the Wister novel, introducing us to a wayward Steve, in debt to foreman Ben Stocker, played by Andrew Duggan. The Virginian literally drops in on a poker game, through a barn window, and uncovers Stocker's marked deck to all present. A customary gunfight ensues and a repentant Steve confesses his gambling debt to his father, Judge Henry.

A young up-and-coming actor out of New York was cast as the Virginian. James Drury gave a credible performance, complete with Virginian accent and a questionable fashion sense.

"We had the 1958 character costumed in a frilly shirt and front and lace cuffs," recalled Drury. "The silver filigree handle on the pistol. Kind of an effete look to him. Not in the character but in the costume. He was kind of a fop actually. Although that wasn't the problem with the character. The costume was very fussy."

A young Frank Price, working as a story editor and analyst for Columbia Pictures' television subsidiary, Screen Gems, had recommended the Wister novel as a suitable project for a possible series.

"I noticed that *The Virginian* had gone beyond its copyright date, which consisted of two periods of 28 years. So it had gone into the public domain. That is why I was able to recommend the property as a possible Screen Gems series a couple of years before the pilot was made. Once a property went into the public domain, every studio in town could make a version of it, all at the same time."

Despite the limitations of a short format, writer Leslie Stevens managed to convey the essence of the Virginian as a man of peace who preferred to talk first and shoot later. Although the pilot failed to sell, Drury made a good enough impression on NBC executives for them to reconsider him for the role four years later, in 1962. The National Broadcasting Company was undergoing change in the mid to late 1950s. Former ABC president Robert Kintner took over programming at NBC in 1956 and became NBC president in 1958. Together with Robert Sarnoff they instigated changes within the network, including the decision to cut back on in-house production and to increase their links to outside film companies. MCA–Universal would become a major source of filmed programming for the network.

"There was a very close relationship between MCA and NBC that long predated 1958," recollected Frank Price. "MCA represented all those radio comics like Jack Benny and Fred Allen who were the backbone of NBC's network programming. One year MCA made a deal with CBS that took all those comics away from NBC, and sold them to CBS. NBC, after that, was always careful to stay close and loyal to MCA."

MCA was the Music Corporation of America. President and chief executive Lew Wasserman wanted the talent agency to move into film production after they were given a waiver by the Screen Actors Guild which prohibited agents from hiring actors for productions.

"The waiver has been given a lot of negative publicity since it was attributed to the relationship between Lew Wasserman and Ronald Reagan, later president of the SAG," commented Price. "I think Walter Pidgeon was the president when the waiver was given. It was intended to create jobs for actors since the movie business had been shattered by the advent of TV."

In 1943, MCA incorporated Revue Productions, producing live programs for television. Revue moved into filmed television series production in 1952 with early hits such as *The Adventures of Kit Carson* (1952) and *City Detective* (1953). Studio space was leased from Republic Studios. But there was one major problem. Republic didn't own a back lot.

Wasserman needed to expand. Contrary to the prevailing trend of movie studios selling land and property to developers who in turn demolished back lots to make way for real estate, MCA, under Wasserman, bought the 367-acre Universal back lot on December 18, 1958, for $11.25 million to use for film production. MCA recovered their investment by leasing out the back lot to Universal for $1 million a year for the next decade. Wasserman had convinced the Universal chiefs that the deal would be of great benefit to them under the existing tax code. Revue Productions became Revue Studios, the television production unit of Universal. In 1962, MCA acquired Universal's parent company, Decca Records, and merged with Universal.

Jennings Lang was promoted to vice-president of MCA-TV and a place on the company's board of directors in 1950. Throughout the 1950s Jennings worked with Universal studios and began creating, developing and selling new shows for network programming.

"Jennings was a big, handsome, larger-than-life guy," fondly recalled Frank Price, "who lived life in a larger-than-life way. Women loved him and he loved them. He was a bold, visionary salesman who was afraid of nothing and I really liked him. He had been a great agent before he took on the job of product development. He was famous for having been caught in an affair with Joan Bennett. Her husband, Walter Wenger, shot Jennings while Jennings was in a parking lot at a restaurant where he'd lunched with Joan Bennett. He shot him in the groin. Jennings lost a testicle. Wanger served a short prison term.

"Jennings drank like a fish, but normally held it well. He had been able to drink and keep up with ad agency people back in New York in those days. That was way back in the days of the three-martini lunch. Jennings sometimes made deals with network executives and ad agency executives where everyone had sufficient to drink that no one could quite remember what the deal agreed to was on the following morning. That's why Sid Sheinberg was added to Jennings' operation. Sid, after such a deal was made, was the guy who had to follow up with the other companies and pin down exactly what the deal was."

The deciding factor in the birth of the *Virginian* TV series was MCA's decision to move the successful *Wagon Train* from NBC to ABC in 1962. NBC needed to fill the void and producer-writer Frank Price was asked to write a format for the proposed replacement, *The Virginian,* by Jennings Lang.

"Jennings was in many respects my mentor," continued Price, "and the mentor of Sid Sheinberg. We both worked for Jennings on his New Projects team. Sheinberg was a young lawyer helping him with deals. And I was a young writer, fresh off producing *The Tall Man.* My job was to write formats for new series while I was waiting for a new series to produce. That's how I came to write the *Virginian* format."

The Virginian would be a major departure for NBC and Revue—and a huge gamble. Filmed in color, with a running time of 90 minutes with commercials, each episode would be a self-contained feature with continuing weekly characters. Tests were done on high quality 16mm film but the quality wasn't deemed high enough and 35mm was chosen as the film format for the series.

James Drury was chosen to play the Virginian. Price commented, "A lot of actors were considered, but others dropped by the wayside and Jim was the one left standing at the end. I think Steve Forrest was one that was considered.

"Doug McClure had the role of Trampas from the beginning. Doug was under contract to Revue Productions and was considered a great asset. He was originally cast in *Over-land Trail* with William Bendix. While the series didn't succeed, the studio and the network really liked Doug's performance. Doug was a great favorite of us all. At the time I wrote the original format, I didn't envision Doug in the role. However, the first time his name was mentioned, it seemed like a perfect idea.

"Regarding a story that says Tony Young was up for the role: Perhaps Charles Marquis

Warren wanted him tested and the studio humored him. But since Doug was one of our contract players, the fix was in."

Price viewed the Gary Cooper and Joel McCrea film versions of *The Virginian* but decided Owen Wister's book was the best base to start from for a series format.

"I checked out two previous versions of motion pictures that had been done, but they were not as useful in creating a series format as the book, which is a marvelous book. Judge Henry was the judge and I kept that name. Later Lee J. Cobb wanted to change the name, which is how he became Judge Henry Garth.

"I created the character of Betsy because I felt the young girl's presence would add a lot. It helped make the family work. It gave Judge Garth a family. It also made for a connection with our young leading men who gained a sisterly figure in their lives.

"I modified Trampas so that he had some rebellious colors, but removed the elements that led him to become a bad guy. Steve was the least defined. I figured I'd get to that later. I had an interesting American Indian character as the cook in the main house, but that got dropped—probably by Charles Marquis Warren. My reasons for having an American Indian at Shiloh were varied. I did not want a standard Gabby Hayes cook for humor, or an invisible Chinese cook. I liked the idea of a sympathetic Indian character at Shiloh Ranch. Indians of course had been in this land before the white men and had a great attachment to it. I wanted to acknowledge this. Also I wanted to show that the West was changing as modern times were approaching. Indians were not over the horizon waiting to attack.

"He and Judge Garth had met in the early days before Garth owned Shiloh. He had been a strong warrior in his Crow tribe, and he saved Garth's life. He had great dignity and a depth of wisdom out of his own culture. The Crows worked with the Army and for a time he had been a scout. He had a particular interest in cooking and a talent for it that was developed while he was attached to officers at the U.S. Army fort.

"That's what I remember now of what I sketched out years ago. I never got motivated to add him back after he was dropped, probably because casting the right actor would not have been easy then."

Price had definite views on the background of the Virginian that would serve as a back story for producers and writers.

"The Virginian, as I saw him, was a man torn from his life of considerable wealth and refinement by the Civil War, which—similar to Robert E. Lee—he chose to fight for his state of Virginia, though he personally opposed slavery. He, like many upper-class Southerners, was a great horseman and a great shot.

"Everything he had in the world, including his family, was destroyed by the war and its aftermath. He went through soul-searing experiences. I think there is a truism that those who have experienced great tragedy become either very bitter and vengeful or exceedingly gentle. It was no longer possible for him to complete his schooling at William and Mary or Princeton.

"Reduced to nothing and becoming a wanted man for specious reasons, he heads West as so many did. His name? If it were Pendleton or Lee or Byrd, that would tell strangers in the West too much about his background, which he didn't wish to reveal. If he were possibly wanted for a justifiable homicide, then the name would be a giveaway. In the West it was acceptable to be Tex or The Texan or some such. Since Owen Wister chose not to detail his former life, I didn't presume to either.

"I have ancestors who were Virginia planters. Next door neighbors of James Madison in the Virginia Piedmont. I drew on some of that to sketch in the Virginian's background."

Sunk Creek, the original ranch in the Wister novel, underwent a name change to Shiloh. The Civil War battle was a deciding factor in the choice of the revised name for Frank Price.

"Shiloh was chosen because neither side scored a victory and the losses made it a tragic battle. In writing the format, I decided that Sunk Creek was less than euphonious and I preferred giving the ranch a name with some possible significance."

Executive producer Charles Marquis Warren had just left a very successful stint as writer, director and executive producer on TV's *Rawhide*. With a background of working on numerous 1940s and 1950s "B" Westerns, he seemed a perfect fit for *The Virginian*.

James Drury recalled working with Warren. "I was very fond of Warren. He'd been a producer at *Gunsmoke* when I'd worked there. We'd been friends for years. He was a very sweet man."

Despite being credited in the first half of season one as executive producer, he relinquished his position before the first episode was broadcast. Frank Price explained the complicated sequence of events that led to Warren's premature departure.

"Dick Irving was going to be executive producer and I was going to be producer on it. And we started to move forward and then it turned out NBC wanted a 'name' executive

Roy Huggins, executive producer of *The Virginian* in 1962–63 (courtesy Frank Price).

producer and 'name' producers. So Dick and I were off the show and Charles Marquis Warren came in.

"Nothing had aired when Roy Huggins took over. Long before the fall air date on the first season of *The Virginian*, the top executives of NBC and Universal Television became concerned about the film footage they were seeing. Actual filming began in late May to early June 1962. They were disappointed in the early rough cuts that Charles Marquis Warren showed them. Since the whole project, television's first 90-minute Western, was a huge gamble for NBC and the studio, they felt they had to act early to save the series from possible disaster. MCA Universal executives Lew Wasserman and Jennings Lang and NBC executives Mort Werner and Robert Sarnoff did not like the work Warren was doing and they did not like his explanations.

"MCA Universal brought in a very, very expensive consultant, Roy Huggins. He had a phenomenal track record with creating and producing series, including *Maverick*, *Cheyenne* and *77 Sunset Strip*. Roy screened all the available footage and read scripts in work. He agreed that a great deal needed to be done to prevent the whole enterprise from becoming a disaster. He made a deal with Universal to fix the existing episodes. Charles Marquis Warren was removed from the series."

With the early departure of Warren, before the first episode went to air, Roy Huggins had a major task ahead of him, reshaping the existing Warren material into a form both acceptable to NBC and the studio.

3

The Virginian

Season One

"My father [Roy Huggins] and Frank Price shared the same high values and love of literature and great stories. I think that's what set *The Virginian* apart. It's not a 'standard' Western. It's literature set in the West."
—Katherine Crawford

"Roy Huggins was at that time going to U.C.L.A. working off his Ph.D in Political Science. He was about 15 years older than me," explained Frank Price. "Roy did not wish to stop going to U.C.L.A. but the network and the studio were very happy with what he was doing and they wanted him to continue and not just fix these episodes. Because that's what the initial deal had been. Come in, fix those episodes, help us out. He did that and now they wanted him to continue. And he was saying, No I can't do this. I have this other commitment. He became executive producer and I became supervising producer. That varied because on some episodes I produced them, so I took a producer credit."

Price described the problems NBC and Universal saw with Warren's original footage.

"The Charles Marquis Warren shows had a number of serious problems. The scripts, and therefore the episodes, tended to concentrate on the guest stars instead of building our continuing stars, the Virginian, Trampas and Judge Garth. Much more needed to be done to make them central to the episodes and to show them in a favorable light. They were not supposed to be background players to the important guest stars.

"There was a problem of simple logic in many of the episodes. Things just didn't make sense and weren't logical. Correcting that took patching and explanations. There were also dramatic situations that just didn't work and weren't believable. Those were the kind of problems that NBC and Universal wanted addressed.

"The first problem, the one of lack of emphasis on the continuing stars, could have been the most fatal one. Audiences get involved with your continuing characters and that's what brings them back week after week, even when individual episodes may vary in quality. Our main job as producers was to create scripts that made our continuing stars look good, regardless of what other flaws the show might have."

Price took charge of duties during the day, screening the previous day's shooting with other producers to see if anything needed correcting or to be reshot. He was available by phone to address any problems that might have occurred before the shooting company or companies began at 8 a.m. Arriving at his office at 9 a.m., Price met with writers, producers, casting agents and production managers and handled NBC executives, noting their suggestions for improvement. Decision making on any problems during the day was the

The first-season cast of *The Virginian*. Left to right: Gary Clarke (Steve Hill), Roberta Shore (Betsy Garth), Lee J. Cobb (Judge Henry Garth), James Drury (The Virginian), Doug McClure (Trampas).

responsibility of Price unless he considered it serious enough to defer to Roy Huggins when he took over duties at 5 p.m.

Price briefed Huggins on his arrival at the studio, before they worked jointly through the evening hours. Huggins assumed his executive producer role, making decisions about filmed footage and meeting with writers and directors. Huggins and Price would work until 8–10 p.m. screening first or second cuts of existing episodes that needed editorial work.

"Roy and I carefully scrutinized each scene and then gave notes to the film editor on the changes needed to be made," said Price. "Sometimes we would wrap up work as late as 2 p.m. It made for a very long day for me. Fortunately I was young and could survive such a grueling schedule."

Joel Rogosin, former producer on TV's *77 Sunset Strip,* also served as a Roy Huggins assistant.

"They needed someone to cover bases while Roy was taking classes," said Rogosin. "At that time, he was executive producer of *The Virginian.* I wasn't hired initially to work on *The Virginian* specifically, but just to act as his assistant."

The debut episode ran on Wednesday, September 19, 1962, at 7.30 p.m. "The Executioners" (1:01) guest-starred Hugh O'Brian and Colleen Dewhurst. In an unremarkable episode we are introduced to all the regular characters—the Virginian, Trampas, Judge Garth, Steve Hill and Betsy. O'Brian played Paul Taylor a.k.a. Newcome, arriving in Medicine Bow to investigate the hanging of his father. Dewhurst played Celia Ames, a local schoolmarm who lets Taylor's father hang rather than admit to being with him the night a woman was murdered.

The second episode, "Woman from White Wing" (1:02), proved to be superior to the first, concentrating on the relationship between Judge Garth and Betsy. We learn that Betsy is Garth's adopted daughter from a doomed relationship with her mother, Annie Dawson, who died three months after giving birth to Betsy at "White Wing." Roy Huggins and Frank Price, however, did not like the episode.

"Roy and I did not like the fact that Burt Kennedy altered the format and changed Betsy to an adopted daughter," recollected Price. "Charles Marquis Warren should have prevented that. There was nothing that could be done to change that since it was buried into the basics of that episode. I decided to let time go by and by ignoring it forget it. That's what we did.

"That episode closed off some possible approaches to a Garth story I would probably have done. Once Betsy was established as his adopted daughter, that made it difficult to tell a story that treated her as his real daughter."

"Throw a Long Rope" (1:03), the first episode to be assigned a production number, guest-starred Jack Warden as an alleged cattle rustler who is supported by the Virginian, despite protests from Judge Garth and local ranchers. This intelligent episode highlights the bond of trust between the Virginian, Judge Garth, Trampas and Steve Hill and the Virginian's commitment to pursuing the truth in spite of peer pressure to change his mind. Drury gave one his best performances of the season, working with a script that strongly delineates his character and provides insight into his Virginia background in the opening narration. Although we learn the Virginian was born in Fairfax County, Virginia, this wasn't included in Frank Price's original format.

"The Brazen Bell" (1:05) featured George C. Scott as cowardly schoolteacher Arthur Lilley, who is forced to confront his fears when his schoolchildren are held hostage by two outlaws at Medicine Bow School. Roland Kibbee wrote and produced the episode. His daughter Meredith described filming the hostage scenes.

"The school was on the Universal back lot. Ten kids on our block were extras, including my two brothers and me. I was the girl in purple with a light-colored headband. We were hostages and I can recall my best friend, Jaime Hanna, another kid in the classroom, who sat next to me on my left, was extremely shy. And when they needed a kid to cry in close-up, the director picked Jaime and not me. I was so jealous, but amazingly enough, I held my tongue. I was only eight at the time. The girl to the left of Jaime was another neighbor, Eileen Eshelman.

"Lee J. Cobb and my father were very close friends and we were neighbors, so I knew him very well. The red-headed kid who Lee looks at sternly in the classroom is his real-life stepson, Tim Hirsh. Another point of interest, it was my mother who actually did the printing on the chalkboard."

"Big Day, Great Day" (1:06) featured Judge Garth, Trampas and Steve in a story about an Italian bed, a wrestling championship and a feud between Trampas and Steve over Steve's plans to marry a saloon girl. Fine interplay between Trampas and Steve was offset by a lack of focus in the script. Only six episodes into the series we find Steve Hill preparing to marry and buy a ranch in Texas. The premise has little emotional impact with a character only introduced a month earlier.

Roland Kibbee in his study, 1980 (courtesy Meredith Kibbee).

"When NBC replaced Warren with Roy Huggins, it was a very radical step," Price said. "It told the world that there was big trouble on this show that was so important to NBC's new season. If *The Virginian* failed, it would make the NBC top brass look like the worst of fools, buying another expensive, bloated Western from the studio that sold *Wagon Train* away from them to another network. NBC was desperate or they never would have taken such a public move. But nobody could understand what Warren was doing with the series. Clearly you aren't seeing the whole picture, because everything you are seeing has been changed and recut by Roy and me.

"There's no particular significance to the fact that Warren has producer and not executive producer credit on this particular episode. All the Warren episodes got the careful redo. If memory serves me, some of the redo had to be done while it was still shooting."

Early reviews of *The Virginian* weren't encouraging. Writing for the October 27–November 2, 1962, edition of *TV Guide,* Gilbert Seldes remarked,

High-minded principles are announced by Lee J. Cobb ... and in the background, coming forward on occasions for a word or a fight, is a character called "Virginian" in whom it is impossible to be interested.

"Riff-Raff" (1:07) was another example of misjudgment by Warren, with the Virginian, Trampas and Steve all enlisting with the Rough Riders and fighting in Cuba, spending five months away from Shiloh Ranch. While the story was entertaining, the premise was highly unlikely and undermined credibility in the *Virginian* format.

"This was one of the episodes that drove the studio and the network crazy," recalled Price. "Why would any producer do something this far afield from the basics at the very beginning of establishing the series and its characters? I suspect that with all the other troubled episodes, this one probably made them decide to replace Warren. Disaster loomed before them."

"It Tolls for Thee" (1:09) was memorable for Lee Marvin's performance as an escaped convict who kidnaps Judge Garth and tests his moral character. Noted movie director Samuel Fuller wrote and directed the episode. But, as with all footage shot during Warren's short time in charge, it needed help from Huggins.

"This required a lot of time and alteration from Roy," remembered Price. "I helped him with some added scenes but he was in the cutting room for many nights trying to correct inconsistencies in the logic and the plot line. He did a great job of remanufacturing the episode. Sam Fuller could shoot some good scenes but they didn't always tie together well."

"West" (1:10) was written, produced and directed by Doug Heyes, a friend of Huggins from his time on *Maverick.* It was quickly put into development by Huggins and enabled Huggins and Price to catch up on their badly delayed schedule. Heyes' handling of a scene involving a gun battle with an outlaw gang required re-editing and shooting inserts.

Price explained, "Doug did a terrible job of shooting the gun battle. It was impossible to edit so that it looked dangerous and exciting. We were too close to air date and it was too expensive to reshoot the sequence. I decided to shoot inserts. These are very tight shots that could be easily shot on a small sound stage with a minimum crew. Just a cameraman and an assistant.

"I shot tight shots of pistols being pulled, rifles cocked, guns firing, horses hooves pawing, horses heads rearing, etc. I took the basics of the scene Doug had shot and used the inserts to create excitement and pace. It worked. The gunfight was no longer an embarrassment. I was hoping no one had noticed how much we cheated.

"Lo and behold, a terrific review of *The Virginian* appears—I think from the U.K.—which cited that gunfight as outstanding and a consciously artistic choice to avoid violence and create a surrealistic depiction and battle. I basked in the glory of the review, not having previously known just what great artistic intentions I'd had. Of course, the reviewer meant to credit that sequence and artistic achievement to Doug Heyes who screwed it up to begin with."

Even though Huggins had been creatively involved in the show since the first episode, he wasn't credited on screen until halfway into the season. Price was likewise uncredited until late into the first season. Huggins' first credited episode as executive producer, "The Accomplice" (1:13), centered on Trampas being charged with a bank robbery, but was essentially a vehicle for Bette Davis.

"In the first year of *The Virginian*, we cast Bette Davis in an episode," recollected Price. "This came about because she put an ad in the trades as an actress looking for work, causing a scandalous stir in Hollywood. We responded by offering her the guest star role in one of our shows. She accepted and did the job well. In subsequent interviews she referred to it as 'shit' as I recall. No good deed ever goes unpunished. But it was always fun dealing with the idols of my childhood."

"The Man from the Sea" (1:14) was notable for a number of reasons. It featured the final screen credit for Charles Marquis Warren, Lee J. Cobb calling the script "shit" in a script reading in front of guest stars Tom Tryon, Shirley Knight and Carol Lynley, and a script that originally included a birth name for the Virginian. Price described the controversy surrounding the name.

"This episode was about to film when Roy and I took over. A decision had to be made immediately about the matter of giving the Virginian a name, since it had happened in the script. Roy agreed with my argument that it was insane to give a name to a character who had benefited for many decades from the mystery surrounding his background. Owen Wister, his creator, deliberately chose not to reveal his name, so what did we have to gain by naming him? It would only reduce the stature of this fictitious character. Roy was easily persuaded because he saw the advantages to the mystery.

"Additionally, I found the choice of name to be outrageous. To name the Virginian 'Jefferson Davis Beaumont' was to name him after the symbol of Confederate racism and hate. Either it was stupidity or a deliberate attempt to undermine the show. That name would identify the Virginian's parents as admirers of an unrepentant slave holding diehard. I had felt that the proper family background for the Virginian was that of Robert E. Lee. Lee was opposed to slavery and was opposed to secession, but he was loyal to Virginia and felt it was his duty to support his state.

"Having a name like Lee would be a key reason that the Virginian would be reluctant to use his name. People would ask too many questions and the name Lee would create both unsought love and unsought dislike. He was certainly not on the run from the law. If he were, then he'd have been better off using an assumed name.

"I hated the choice of Jefferson Davis Beaumont. Beaumont was just weak and not the kind of name for the Virginian. Fate arranged it so that I was there at the proper time to kill the idea."

Episodes of note under Huggins' total control included "Duel at Shiloh" (1:15), which served as an introductory story for Steve Hill and his arrival at Shiloh Ranch.

"Brian Keith did an incredible job of acting. The scene where he's teaching Steve to shoot was mostly Brian improvising and he did it brilliantly," said Price. "Gary was never better. That episode was based on a Universal Pictures screenplay titled *Man Without a Star*, which starred Kirk Douglas. We got the screenplay out of Universal's files when we were desperate for scripts to shoot so we could stay on the air.

"We rewrote it, but it was still pretty close to the original. What we didn't realize is how little time had elapsed between the release of the movie and our lifting of the screenplay. *Man Without a Star* was still playing in some parts of the world, perhaps even in the U.S. We were pretty nervous when we learned all this, but nothing bad happened.

"I think the television show turned out to be different enough from the movie, particularly with Brian Keith's performance, that no one recognized what we had done. What complicated our lives was that we were still Revue Productions and didn't own Universal yet. The deal was made but wasn't closed. So we sweated a bit."

Thomas Fitzroy contributed stories to "The Exiles" (1:16), "If You Have Tears" (1:20), "The Golden Door" (1:24) and "Strangers at Sundown" (1:27).

"All four of these are Roy Huggins stories," explained Price. "Thomas Fitzroy was an early pseudonym. When we took over the show, one of the immediately identifiable problems was the scary lack of development. That's why Roy plunged into creating stories and putting dependable writers to work immediately.

"When Roy created a story, he dictated a complete treatment of the story, scene by scene, so that the writer's job was to flesh that treatment with additional dialogue. Generally Roy included quite a bit of dialogue in his treatments.

"Roy's stories tended to be plotted melodramas. He started as a detective story novelist so that's how he thought as a writer. I was pleased with 'The Golden Door' because we had a chance to do something of an educational piece about American democracy. We needed these stories badly because we were under tremendous air date pressure."

"The Judgment" (1:17) marked the first appearance of Clu Gulager in the series as outlaw Jack Carewe, seeking revenge on the people of Medicine Bow and Judge Garth for the hanging of his brother.

"I modeled this particular episode on the career of Judge Parker, a tough judge who kept order in the territory," recalled Price. "Roy Huggins was upset with me for making this episode. He opposed the death penalty and he felt the show advocated it. It was something of a *High Noon* show."

Katherine Crawford, the daughter of Roy Huggins, made her debut film appearance in "Say Goodbye to All That" (1:18). After attending the Royal Academy of Dramatic Art in London alongside friend Anthony Hopkins, she decided to change her family name on her return to Los Angeles, feeling her father's name was too well-known in Hollywood. Taking the stage name Crawford from her grandmother's maiden name, she met her future husband, Frank Price, when she visited Universal with Roy Huggins.

"Being the child of a prominent person in this industry can create animosity," commented Katherine Crawford, "and resentment in others. My plan to remain anonymous worked for about three hours before seemingly everyone knew. We should have known that would happen. I would have kept my own name.

"'Goodbye to All That' was my first job after returning from London. I was 18 years old during that show. I had to spend several weeks losing the British accent I had so diligently acquired there. It was a basic requirement at RADA that the English as well as six American students that attended each year master the British accent perfectly. Removing it proved harder than expected. But a career in America with an English accent would be too limited, so it had to be done. Remnants of it are still apparent in that episode and my father had a line written into the script to explain why I spoke that way.

"When my father found that role for me, it was something of a thankless one. It was the old standard of the hapless girlfriend or wife of the man who has to go out and subject himself to danger for some reason. She was the classic 'please don't!' character. But it would provide me with film, and therefore an agent ... hopefully. So I was happy.

"As an interesting side note, the first audition they sent me on after *The Virginian* was for the role of an English girl on *The Alfred Hitchcock Hour*. So I had two hours to quickly revert back to 'British.' The producer, Joan Harrison, who was English herself, obviously believed I was a true English girl and hired me, which resulted in Revue Studios' [MCA] talent division asking me to become a contract player for them. I accepted their offer and had a very good career thereafter. So I am very grateful for what this *Virginian* episode did for me."

Katherine Crawford fondly recalled working with Fabian on "Say Goodbye to All That." "He was a sweet, kind, gentle, truly nice person. No ego or attitude. No entourage or protectors, in spite of his rock star status. But he was also shy, as was I, so we had a sweet, quiet relationship. We never got to know each other well but I liked him very much.

"I also think he was somewhat scared. This was a big risk he was taking. He was a singer, not an actor, and his performance would be watched by every young girl in America, so he had to do well. And I don't think he felt confident at all. That's just my personal observation. I felt for him during shooting. Roberta Shore admired Fabian, and praised him, and lifted the spirits of the set. I liked her a lot.

The episode featured a bear that was terrorizing the local ranchers. "What a problem that bear was! There was a real bear and a bear suit with a man in it. But to do it right in TV-time was a real bear of a problem," Crawford joked.

Although Huggins expressed a desire to make the Virginian, Trampas, Judge Garth and Steve central characters in storylines, he occasionally fell into Warren's trap of highlighting the guest star. "The Money Cage" (1:23) was essentially a showcase for Steve Forrest's talents with little interaction from *Virginian* regulars.

Joey Heatherton in a 1960s publicity pose.

"I think this one got made because we had to catch up on our air dates," remarked Price, "and this was one that didn't require much of our series leads who were working elsewhere. We didn't like to do this, but by the end of the season we had to."

"A Distant Fury" (1:25) featured Ida Lupino and Howard Duff in a tale about fear and greed, when an ex-convict (Duff) returns to Medicine Bow to reclaim stolen money. The episode was notable for Joey Heatherton's rather stilted performance and a flawed script by Howard Browne and Roy Huggins (credited under another Huggins pseudonym, John Francis O'Mara), involving an unlikely suicide attempt and an erratic Sheriff Abbott.

"Howard Browne was an old friend of Roy's and his first editor," Price said. "Howard was an adequate, tending-to-pedestrian writer, but their working relationship brought pluses and minuses. The plus was that they communicated quickly and understood each other because of their detective story backgrounds. The minus was that the pulp fiction kind of over-plotting sometimes made for over-complicated, non-emotional stories.

"That was the problem with 'A Distant Fury.' I, as supervising producer, could do little to improve that kind of storyline since it was so intricately plotted that it's hard to change just one or two elements. Winston Miller did his polish on the script, but didn't fix all the plot inconsistencies. This was a case of everyone doing the best they could with some basically flawed material."

"I was never drawn to the heavily plotted pulp fiction type of story, so we did very little, if any, after the first season. Roy was extremely good at that kind of story, but this is not one of the good examples. I found the step-by-step plotting heavy going, and I was much much more comfortable with more character-driven stories, rather than plot-driven."

Casting for any episode always involved a number of factors, chief among them being big-name stars who could generate publicity. Price explains.

"I thought we scored a coup in getting Ida Lupino and Howard Duff to do this episode. That guaranteed newspaper publicity. Since Joey Heatherton had a young teen image and was a hot number, she also guaranteed us some visibility with a different segment of the audience.

"Joey Heatherton was very strange. It was like dealing with a mannequin. She had a scene where she had to cry. But she became known as the girl with the iron eyeballs on this episode. When the time came for her to cry, she could not do it no matter how long the director waited or how much she tried. A solution was placed in her eyes to bring artificial tears on. No tears resulted though they made several attempts. I think they finally just put drops on her cheeks."

"The Mountain of the Sun" (1:28) sees the Virginian accompanying three female missionaries into Yaqui Indian territory. Excellent location photography and a memorable music score by Sidney Fine, Morton Stevens and Sydney Shores highlights strong performances by Dolores Hart, Jeanette Nolan and James Drury in a story of love and forgiveness.

"Working with Dolores Hart was a pleasure," commented Price. "She was such a genuinely nice person, and of course very beautiful. The screenplay was written by Harry Kleiner, a writer who had worked with Roy Huggins for many years. Harry was a dependable professional, whose fault could be that he might write in a pedestrian way. However, under Roy's supervision and guidance, he turned in first-rate material. And he did it fast.

"Warren Duff was the producer on record but he didn't contribute enough in his assignment for me to bring him back in the second year. Bernie McEveety was a good quality action director that I used whenever he was available. I believe we shot the episode in Southern California desert country down near Indian Wells."

Dolores Hart retired from acting shortly after the episode was filmed and joined the Benedictine Regina Laudis convent in Bethlehem, Connecticut.

"Run Away Home" (1:29), an episode featuring the Virginian and Steve, involved the return of $40,000 in cash to Medicine Bow. The story by Gene Roddenberry and Howard Browne was adapted in 1971 for the *Alias Smith and Jones* episode "The Girl in Boxcar #3."

"The Gene Roddenberry-Howard Browne script had an interesting history," recalled Price. "The story was Roy Huggins'. Gene turned in a terrible draft of the script and Roy fired him after berating him for turning in non-professional work. Roy put Howard Browne on to do a new draft."

At the season's conclusion, Huggins moved on to Universal's *Kraft Suspense Theatre*. Joel Rogosin followed, with Frank Price taking over as executive producer on *The Virginian* when the second season premiered on September 18, 1963.

"Working on *The Virginian* had reignited my father's love affair with show business, and he never returned to his studies," declared Katherine Crawford.

4

Early Seasons
Seasons Two and Three

"In the effort to constantly make things better, the writers would continue working on the script until the show was finished shooting. The 'new' pages sent down to the set would be a different color so you would know the newest version. Our scripts had many differently colored pages in them."
—Katherine Crawford

The first half of season one of *The Virginian* had been a mix of patchwork episodes, rescued by Roy Huggins and Frank Price. Charles Marquis Warren had set the stories in the 1890s, in a time of change, with encroaching civilization making its presence felt. New executive producer Price had also envisioned a late 1890s timeline in his original format, but having worked on the many problems caused by Warren's footage and approach, Price decided to revise his original decision.

"In my original format, I had wanted to deal with the West in the transitional period," said Price, "as new technologies like electric lights and telephones were coming into use. But, as used in some of the Warren episodes, these things seemed like tacked-on anachronisms so we cut most, if not all, of them out in the re-editing. It's possible such a time period would have worked, but it would have taken much more attention and careful execution so that the audience understood what we were doing and didn't think we'd made some mistake.

"For the series as a whole, I assumed an approximate date of 1886. That was before the Great Blizzard of 1887. Up until that blizzard, the English investors were making handsome profits in cattle. The production rate of cattle was phenomenal, leading to jokes about all the cows having twins. That's why I was always fairly specific about the year 1886. The cattle boom was still on."

The second season got off to a strong start with an episode recalling how Trampas first arrived at Shiloh Ranch. "Ride a Dark Trail" (2:01) gives us a glimpse into the young, headstrong Trampas and his often impetuous nature. Seeking revenge for the death of his father in El Paso, Texas, Trampas arrives at Shiloh to discover the killer is closer than he imagined. But when he's confronted with a choice between revenge and forgiveness, the reaction of the person he considers guilty makes him realize choices aren't always black and white.

A seemingly simple tale of revenge escaped the normal clichés of the genre by concentrating on character rather than violence to resolve the conflict. Writers E.M. Parsons and Arthur Browne, Jr., had taken aspects of Trampas from the original Owen Wister

31

novel and toned down his villainy to a lighter shade. A tendency to cheat at gambling and an aversion to honest work were characteristics of his pre–Shiloh personality. His often shady former acquaintances had a habit of catching up with him when they arrived in Medicine Bow. Conflicts from his past often tugged at Trampas throughout the series and was one element that made him such an interesting character. This episode provided the backdrop to understanding the personality of Trampas and established a strong bond between Judge Garth, the Virginian and Trampas. Their trust in him gives Trampas room to heal from his emotional scars and provides him with a new family following the death of his father. Forgiveness and healing becomes the main theme of the episode.

"The studio and the network fought with me over the choice of Sonny Tufts as Trampas' father. They felt he was too tarnished a figure and Doug would be harmed by the association. I thought he was perfect casting for the role and that we would get great publicity." recalled Price. "Other than Sonny Tufts, there was no other star name possible for that role. It was a small role that most stars would not even consider. But Sonny needed a job and was perfect as Frank Trampas, his first name being a reference to me."

Price commented on the creative team behind the episode.

"John Peyser had talent as a director, but was difficult to work with and wouldn't give me the kind of coverage I needed to edit the show properly. So it was a running battle as I forced him to give me editing alternatives.

"Arthur Browne, Jr., came up with some good background material for Trampas. Much of it came from me in our story meetings, but he wrote a poor screenplay that needed major work. We had a very difficult time getting that script done. I recall rewriting quite a bit of it myself since we had to have the script and had run out of time. I don't recall E. M. Parsons, so it's possible we tried Parsons, found out that it didn't work and just took it the rest of the way. I had a major advantage in that I knew pretty much exactly what I wanted Trampas' background to be.

"Trampas had been a character with charm and humor, but also one with some character flaws, some dark tones in his makeup. We wanted to do a story to reveal to us what his life was like before coming to Shiloh, so we understood what factors in his life shaped his character. His father was key to this. Once we had created a life for him that could produce someone with Trampas' characteristics, then our next dramatic invention was to deal with how this flawed guy came to be part of Shiloh Ranch and tell that story in an interesting way."

Broderick Crawford guest-starred in "Killer in Town" (2:04) as a bounty hunter feared by Trampas. Price recalled Crawford's heavy drinking from his time working with him on *Highway Patrol* for Ziv Television.

"Brod Crawford was a real alcoholic. But he could be a fine actor and he'd been a big star, so I readily set him to star in this episode. To make sure his drinking didn't cause problems, we arranged to shoot his scenes as early as possible in the day, since the problems showed up the later you were past lunch. Our strategy worked and we got the film we needed from him."

Another interesting Trampas-centric episode from season two was "Man of Violence" (2:14). The story finds Trampas tracking his uncle's killer, accompanied by an alcoholic doctor, the killer's wife and an outlaw searching for gold. DeForest Kelley and Leonard Nimoy shared scenes three years before they starred together again in *Star Trek*. The episode was adapted from a screenplay by James Patrick and boasted fine location photography and direction by William Witney and an excellent performance by Kelley as the drunken doctor.

Frank Price said, "'Man of Violence' was, as I recall, a script out of Universal's library that we hastily rewrote and put into production, when we were falling behind on scripts. It had been a Universal picture under another title. That must be the only credit James Patrick had on our show. Since it was directed by Bill Witney and took place in the desert, I'm reasonably sure the location was near Bill's ranch in Mojave. The area has beautiful desert scenery and Bill knew every foot of it. We could afford to make the entire episode on distant location because of careful planning, but also because of Bill Witney's ingenuity and knowledge."

Price recalled an interesting visit from a member of the Senate committee investigating violence in television.

"That episode caused me trouble with the U.S. Senate. At that time, Thomas Dodd headed a Senate committee investigating violence in television. The title attracted his attention and suddenly one day my office files were sealed by Senate staffers. They examined the episode and pored through my files of correspondence with NBC and internal studio memos. They came up empty. I gave it the title 'Man of Violence' to promise more action than the film delivered. I was afraid it would be boring. The staffers were hoping to find in my files memos where the network asked us to put in more violence. There were no such memos. Also, I acquired a habit from Lew Wasserman. I rarely wrote memos. And certainly never wrote self-incriminating memos.

"In fact, however, *The Virginian* was notable for its lack of gunplay and violence. One of my basic principles that I tried to enforce was that a shooting in Medicine Bow must be a major event, because Medicine Bow was on its way to being a civilized community, not a rowdy Western shoot-'em-up town. If a gun was fired in Medicine Bow, the sheriff would investigate.

"The production office estimators in the first years also allowed far too much money in our budget for ammunition. I used a tiny fraction of that budget. The estimators were basing their figures on previous Westerns like *Laramie*. Anyway, after huffing and puffing and finding nothing, the Senate moved on its way and not long afterwards Senator Dodd, father of today's Senator Chris Dodd, went to prison for some malfeasance."

The Virginian was given a storyline describing *his* introduction to Shiloh Ranch and Medicine Bow in "The Drifter" (2:19). His personal integrity and dedication to people he respects and trusts is highlighted in an episode that helps explain the special bond the Virginian and Judge Garth share. Involved in a personal feud between ranch owner Miles Peterson and Judge Garth, the Virginian falls for Peterson's daughter (Mariette Hartley) much to the anger of Peterson's foreman, who plans to take control of the ranch through marriage. When the Virginian is critically wounded, Judge Garth is blamed, but the Virginian soon learns the truth behind the shooting.

In a scene where Garth cares for the badly injured Virginian, we see the beginning of a relationship built on trust. In a delirious state, the Virginian reveals secrets about his past to Garth. Secrets Garth promises to keep to himself.

Price was responsible for creating the background details for the characters of the Virginian and Trampas.

"In doing 'The Drifter' and 'Ride a Dark Trail' I set out to fill in the back story on these characters. I wanted to do my own fill-in because I wanted a guide for other writers so that they didn't come up with wildly inappropriate back stories in other episodes they were doing. With the Virginian's story, I had to fill in his background but still leave the mystery behind why he was called only the Virginian.

"With Doug, I wanted to establish why Judge Garth and the Virginian put up with the sometimes difficult or headstrong Trampas. I spent a lot of time and a lot of creative energy and thought on those episodes."

Another second season episode of note involving the Virginian was "No Tears for Savannah" (2:03). A chance meeting with former girlfriend Savannah reignites buried feelings for the Virginian. Gena Rowlands was perfectly cast as the tough yet vulnerable Savannah who ends up fighting for her life as Judge Garth defends her in a murder trial.

"I was delighted to get Gena Rowlands for the lead. I thought she was very beautiful and an actress of great depth and skill," recalled Price.

"A Portrait of Marie Vallone" (2:08) starred Madlyn Rhue in Dean Reisner's story of a mysterious female missing in New Orleans.

"This episode was way off format because I took the Virginian into the rococo New Orleans and did a mystery melodrama love story. Dean Reisner was one of my favorite writers and subsequently wrote *Dirty Harry* and the entire script of the ten-hour *Rich Man, Poor Man* miniseries," commented Price.

Other Virginian-centered episodes in season two included "Stopover in a Western Town" (2:10) with Joan Freeman, "The Fatal Journey" with Robert Lansing (2:11), "Another's Footsteps" (2:24) with Sheree North as the Virginian's love interest in a tale about a bank robbery leading to murder and the Virginian's search for justice, and "The Long Quest" with Ruta Lee (2:27).

A second season episode of special interest featured the brief return of Molly Wood, a character who provided a love interest for the Virginian in the Charles Marquis Warren first season episodes. Loosely based on the Owen Wister schoolmarm Molly Stark Wood, from the original novel, Molly Wood was transformed into the *Medicine Bow Banner* newspaper editor for the television series. A strong female character with a job of influence was rare for TV Westerns of the period.

But Frank Price and Roy Huggins saw Molly Wood as unnecessary to the series and a hindrance for the Virginian. Price explained, "In the first year, Roy and I decided to eliminate the Molly Wood character immediately when Roy took over. Both of us agreed that we preferred the Virginian not to have a regular romantic interest. We wanted him to be available for the romances that a good Western hero must have. If the women in the audience thought he was two-timing his regular love interest, they wouldn't like him. So we regarded her character as a format flaw. We stopped using her.

"I remember how Roy hated the name Molly Wood. 'Hollywood' came to his mind. I said, 'Well, Owen Wister wrote that book before Hollywood existed.' But the audience didn't know that."

Pippa Scott decided to leave the show shortly before the character of Molly Wood was being phased out, frustrated with the lack of development of what began as a strong, independent female character. Wood met her demise in "The Fatal Journey" (2:11). Scott failed to reprise her first season role, with the viewer seeing only the silhouette of Molly Wood moving behind the window of the *Medicine Bow Banner* office before she is gunned down by a gang of outlaws.

"I think I decided to portray her death in the second year for the benefit of those members of the audience who wondered what happened to her. I was cleaning up an oversight," commented Price.

Under Price's supervision, storylines were generally more character-centered with the Virginian, Trampas, Steve, Judge Garth and Betsy all featuring in episodes that emphasized them. Lee J. Cobb featured in "Make This Place Remember" (2:02) alongside Joan Blondell and John Dehner.

"The writer, Howard Bud Swanton, used the script as a writing sample to get other jobs, but would never work for me again because I made him work too hard. He did think it was his best work," recollected Price. "I like this episode because of the intellectual challenge of it. I was intrigued by the storyline because it was about a man of great integrity who does everything right and for the right reasons, given the circumstances, but he finally crosses the line by taking the law into his own hands, still with good motivation.

"I offered the John Dehner role to a prominent actor who had worked a lot for Universal. Ronald Reagan. He thanked me for the offer, but he did not care to play bad guys, even if they seemed right for most of the show. Dehner was probably my last choice to play it, but he was the only one I could get at the last minute. It was not a favorite with the network. They asked me not to do more like that."

"A Time Remembered" (2:12) involved a rewrite and new casting following a dispute between Price and James Drury over Drury's insistence on replacing his Appaloosa with a Paint horse.

"There was a big clash where Jim at one point decided he was going to change his horse. He was going to go from the Appaloosa that he had ridden in all the episodes prior, to a Paint horse. Jim got very stubborn about it and I said, 'No way. I've got over a year of stock footage here that you're destroying. Why do you want to change?'

"I believe that it was Robert Horton's stunt double, who joined Jim as one of his hangers-on, who persuaded Jim he would stand out better from the rest of the cast if he rode a Paint horse, as Horton did on *Wagon Train*. Often I needed something when I was doing a show where if Jim was on a journey somewhere, at least we had in our library footage where he's on a horse. I don't necessarily have to shoot that again.

"It was around that time I was doing a romance that was Jim Drury and a leading woman. Jim was refusing the thing with the horse so I said. 'Okay, it's going to be Doug McClure in this role.' And Doug had been persuaded by Jim to stand with him. So he wouldn't do the role. So I said, 'Okay, it's going to be Gary Clarke.' Gary Clarke stood with them.

"I then decided I couldn't let that happen or these guys would have had me. They would have had control. So then I decided I would make it Lee J. Cobb's romance. Figuring Lee would not stand with them because Lee really wanted to do a romance. So I rewrote the script and I think I made it Lee and Yvonne DeCarlo. Part of the reason that Lee was delighted to play in the episode was that Yvonne DeCarlo was a real genuine movie star leading lady. Lee, deep down, saw himself as a romantic figure and here I was casting him opposite a woman whose screen persona was that of a very sexy lady. He couldn't have been happier. And neither could I. I loved her! I had been a fan of hers since many years before when I saw a picture she did with Alec Guinness called *The Captain's Paradise.*"

Meanwhile, the dispute with Drury and his horse continued.

"Jim was still refusing to ride the Appaloosa. I had the scripts written so if he was in the show, he either walked into the shot or he came in on a buckboard. I had warned him I would do this. If he refused to comply, he would be suspended and sued. I warned his agent about this. We were at an impasse for about three shows and then Jim finally conceded and went back to the Appaloosa. I thought Gary was talented and interesting but tended to be quite difficult. And that, kind of, was the straw that broke the camel's back. I decided to drop him from the series and replace him."

Clarke's refusing to step into the lead vacated by the dispute with Drury had put him in breach of contract.

"His contract, "continued Price, "specified that he would perform in the roles offered him on the series. I could have suspended him immediately and had the studio legal department institute a suit against him. I did not do that, because I hoped Gary would help me out of the bind I was in. I also understood he was under a lot of pressure from Jim and Doug to support Jim's position. But while I was understanding, it showed me that in any conflict between the producers and Jim, Gary was on Jim's side and therefore was of no use to us as a backup leading man. That knowledge removed one key reason for having Gary on the series, where he suffered from being the third young leading man in the pecking order. He didn't get the roles the other two did and now that he was offered a good one, he wouldn't take it. "

Steve Hill–centered episodes included "Run Quiet" (2:09), featuring Clu Gulager as a deaf mute, on the run after being accused of murder, "Roar from the Mountain" (2:16) and "Rope of Lies" (2:26).

"Clu enjoyed the acting challenge of this role. I thought he was terrific in it and was very sympathetic. I like stories that suggest a strong moral lesson," remarked Price.

A personal favorite of Gary Clarke, "Roar from the Mountain" starred Jack Klugman as a homesteader out to prove his worth to his wife after she falls for the charms of Steve Hill.

"Before I could take such an action to replace Gary, I needed the network and the studio to agree. That took time. We were successful and no one wanted to rock the boat. He appeared in the main title, so that would have to be addressed and possibly redone to eliminate him, at some considerable expense.

"The role of Steve was never well-defined. The Virginian was clear. Trampas was clear. Who was Steve? In the book he got hanged, so he garnered sympathy. He didn't get that in our scripts. So Gary was low man on the totem pole, the third man.

"When he got time on film, he often tried too hard to make an impression, so he sometimes came across as forced and pushing. I always liked Gary as a person and never took any difficult behaviour personally. With me, it was all about getting the best *Virginian*'s that could be done. He was in a difficult position. He was competing for roles and screen time," concluded Price.

Lee J. Cobb featured in "The Fortunes of J. Jimerson Jones" (2:17). Set in Chicago, and starring Pat O'Brien as a gold prospector who attracts con artists trying to swindle him out of his newly acquired fortune, the episode was a departure from the usual format. Price recollected the inspiration for the story.

"J. Jimerson Jones was based on some of the reports about a prospector in the West who hit it big and, as a newly rich man, went to Chicago. When the bellhop took him in the elevator on the way to his room, the prospector thought this was his room. Of course, it was thin stuff and way off format, but I get drawn to comedy, witness *Tootsie* and *Ghostbusters,* and sometimes can't resist. The opportunity to do this with Pat O'Brien was one I couldn't pass up, feeling that because it was Pat O'Brien our audience would forgive us. But I felt we barely got away with it at the time and I suspect age has done it no good. Plus our pacing on *The Virginian* was always deliberate and that's not always compatible with comedy."

Randy Boone was introduced to viewers as Randy Benton in "First to Thine Own Self" (2:20). Accused of the murder of a gold miner, Randy hides out with the miner's young daughter Melanie, a situation that presents Betsy with a moral dilemma when she is torn between keeping her promise to Randy to keep his hiding place secret or telling the Virginian where he is.

"When I brought in Randy Boone," recalled Price, "he added something a little different. Actually when I was looking for somebody at that same time I had seen a guy that I really liked. He was a singer at Leadbetters which was in Westwood at that point. They did folk music there. I brought our casting people over. I couldn't get much support. I don't know if that I could have wound up with the guy in the show. He became a huge country-western hit singer. John Denver. But I couldn't get the casting people to agree with me at that point. I didn't feel like overruling them."

The introduction of the teenage Randy Benton to the series was good news for Betsy Garth, who now had a person of her own age to confide in. Actress Roberta Shore was also relieved when Boone joined the cast as she often felt an outsider among a cast of older men. Betsy Garth featured in "The Evil That Men Do" (2:05), "The Fortunes of J. Jimerson Jones" (2:17), "First to Thine Own Self" (2:20), "The Intruders" (2:23) and "The Secret of Brynmar Hall" (2:26) starring Jane Wyatt as a woman who invites Betsy and a group of friends to Brynmar Hall, blaming them for her daughter's death in a fire.

Said Price, "With 'The Secret of Brynmar Hall' I needed an episode to catch up on production time. An episode that didn't require much, if anything, of our key characters Jim, Doug and Cobb. So I decided to try something different featuring Betsy. One of the great things about the Western format is that any kind of scary story can be plausibly told in the Western background. I was putting my theory to the test."

"The Evil That Men Do" (2:05) was written by Frank Chase and featured Robert Redford in an early role.

Price said, "Frank Chase worked for me a lot. He is the son of Borden Chase, who wrote one of my all-time favorite Westerns, *Red River.* One of his best scripts was "The Evil That Men Do" that had a young Robert Redford as the star. Many years later, while we were shooting *Out of Africa,* Redford explained to me he had his sights set on higher targets. Motion pictures, specifically. However, he needed some money to buy some available acreage near Provo, Utah. So the $10,000 that he received from *The Virginian* enabled him to buy the first parcel of land that became Sundance. But for that need to buy the property, he would not have done any television show."

The majority of season two was produced by 53-year-old Winston Miller. Price has fond memories of working with him.

"Winston Miller was a terrific writer. Exactly the kind of writer you wanted to put the final polish on a script. Winnie tended to rewrite every script that he produced. He had a realistic, spare style that led him to eliminate overwrought dialogue and long speeches. He wrote the screenplay for one of my favorite movies, *My Darling Clementine.*"

Many episodes from seasons two and three were the result of two or more writers collaborating on a script with "teleplay" and "story" credits split. Price explained the reasons behind the often convoluted writing credits.

"The Writers Guild regulated the screen credits and used an arbitration procedure to determine who received what credit. A writer who wrote the complete script, and where no other writer, such as a producer, sought credit, would receive a 'written by' credit. Then it got complicated. We might buy a published story or buy a story from a freelance writer. The writer would get a 'story by' or 'based on a story by' credit. Or we might hire a writer to do an original, but when he finishes his work, we are not satisfied with it; we hire a new writer to do a new script based on the first writer's work.

Producer Winston Miller in his Universal Studios office, 1965 (courtesy Frank Price).

"The rewritten script and all earlier drafts are then sent to the Writers Guild, where a committee of writers judges the work and votes on the credits. Writer number one might get a 'story by' credit, and writer number two 'teleplay by.' Or writer number one and two could split the 'teleplay by' credit, with writer number one still getting 'story by' credit.

"We, as producers, had no influence over the credit arbitrations and often the arbitrations were distinctly unfair. If a production executive, such as Winston Miller or Cy Chermak, totally rewrote a script and put in for a credit, he would be most unlikely to receive it. The arbitration system was prejudiced against anyone on the production staff, no matter how good a writer or how illustrious his previous credits may have been. Unemployed freelance writers bore some resentment toward writers who were also producers on these shows."

"A Bride for Lars" (2:28) featured Katherine Crawford as a Swedish bride-to-be, escorted by Trampas to meet her middle-aged fiancé. The sexual suggestiveness of the script was unusual for *The Virginian* and 1964 prime time TV. But the light comedic interplay between Doug McClure and Crawford ensured that nobody would be offended.

"Did I know it was suggestive? Well, yes! And I never considered doing it otherwise," recalled Katherine Crawford. "No one guided me against doing it that way. In TV you don't usually get a director's guidance, and actors don't often discuss their roles with each other. So it's up to you to work it out yourself. But I had no doubts about the flirtatiousness of that role. It was so well-written. She was a spirited girl and Swedish!"

Crawford found McClure easy to work with. "He was wonderful in his reactions and it seemed effortless. We never discussed it. We just did it. In series TV you rehearse once or twice for blocking, then shoot. He was such a wonderful actor. Some actors make other actor's jobs easier. Doug was one of those. And no, Doug and I didn't have a flirtation off screen, though we got along easily. He always seemed to have something else going on that he was off to do, off the set."

During filming, Crawford hurt her back when she lost control of a horse racing down a hill.

"Doug's horse, which I was riding in the scene where I was running away from the bad guys, went totally out of control in a runaway," recalled Crawford. "He went at full speed toward the camera and under the limb of a tree that would have cut me in half. My back had 'gone out' some time back up the hill during my strain to pull him in. The horse came to a jolting sudden stop in front of the camera, and there I was, stuck in place, grasping his neck. After that, for a couple of days, they used a double to do my action shots, and put me in the close-ups."

A talking point of the episode was the heavy Swedish accents employed by the American actors.

"My RADA background had instilled in me a deep respect for doing things right!" Crawford recalled. "The producers found me a Swedish woman to talk to, and she spoke a few paragraphs of the dialogue into my tape recorder, and we discussed the correct pronunciation of some of the harder sounds. After that I just mimicked what was there, and tried to adapt that 'sound' to the rest of the dialogue. And we began shooting the next day!

"In a way it frees you up when things are so crazily imperfect. I wish I could have done a milder version of it now though, after seeing it. But that would've taken more time. The other actors who also spoke in the accent didn't shoot until the end, so we couldn't confer or compare. I don't remember any of the other actors really. We weren't together enough."

Hair and makeup for the character reflected Hollywood tastes of the 1960s, as it did with most female characters throughout the series.

"Back then, they did it that way," remarked Crawford. 'I was young and didn't tell them how to do it. And looking back, I gasp at the stiff hair and heavy eye makeup. Eyeliner, arched brows, poofed hair and an old-fashioned concept of 'elegance.' The method they used to curl hair was the curling iron. It was the kind that has an electrically heated 'box,' which was an oval metal tube that the iron itself was placed into to heat. The iron would lose heat when removed from the heater so it was always put back in between curls. We also used to 'tease' hair then a lot. A dreadful act.

"The character should have been more 'natural' in my opinion. I'm wondering now why we didn't just do braids. Very Swedish, and natural and easy. But we mustn't judge then by now. It seemed good at the time."

Season three was a time of change for *The Virginian*. Fans of Gary Clarke were shocked to find him missing from the opening "ride-in" credits. Clarke would appear in only three episodes of the season before disappearing into the sunset without any explanation for his absence from Shiloh Ranch. Randy Boone would take his place on a regular basis, with another new cast member, Clu Gulager as Emmett Ryker, being introduced in the premiere episode of the third season. Steve Hill became the first of many regular characters to leave the show, throughout its run, without any sense of closure. Frank Price clarified the reasoning behind this decision.

Katherine Crawford on location on "A Bride for Lars" (courtesy Katherine Crawford).

"Logistics are probably what makes us not do closure episodes. We were well ahead in shooting so by the time a cast member was leaving, we had already shot their last segment. Also, I think I preferred to just let it happen and not necessarily alert the fans of that particular player until they've learned to do without him or her. I think my first explanation applies to Steve leaving."

The departure of Gary Clarke resulted in a new filmed title sequence for season three. The familiar "ride-in" credits were replaced by a mixture of action shots, "ride-ins" and the singing duet of Randy Boone and Roberta Shore. A large letter V zoomed toward the viewer as each cast member was introduced. The new dynamic approach was at the request of Jennings Lang, who felt the opening credits needed to evoke a feeling of excitement.

Clu Gulager had worked with Price on *The Tall Man* (1960–62). He joined the cast of *The Virginian* in 1964, having appeared in individual episodes in season one and two as an outlaw and a deaf mute, respectively.

"I added Clu Gulager to the *Virginian* cast because I wanted to keep him working," Price explained, "and I thought he had a very good chance to develop into a major star. I also felt that we used the Medicine Bow sheriff so frequently that we ought to cast his role with someone with the potential to draw more of an audience."

"Ryker" (3:01) introduced viewers to Emmett Ryker, a contradictory character with a shadowy past. Offered work as a hired gun by landowner John Hagen (Leslie Nielsen), Ryker helps Sheriff Abbott (Ross Elliott) bring the murderer of a local rancher to justice. Ryker decides to stay in Medicine Bow and is hired as deputy sheriff.

The episode featured an early appearance of Raquel Welch. Jennings Lang had suggested to Price he could get added publicity for the new season if he cast "sexy young women as saloon girls" and send photographs of them to newspapers. Price launched an extensive search for the girls and included them in certain episodes, but decided to eventually drop the idea because it didn't fit in with the character of the show.

"These young ladies stood out like sore thumbs," joked Price.

Writer Frank Fenton provided an intelligent script, despite personal problems that affected his output.

"Frank Fenton was one of my favorite writers," recalled Price. "His work was erratic, but he wrote dialogue that was spare and cryptic, and carried meaning beyond the words. His plotting could leave big holes in any story, but we tried to fix that. Frank didn't work for me much, but I tried to get him whenever I had a suitable story. He was a character out of Old Hollywood, back in the real movie days. He hung out at a watering hole called the Cock and Bull on Sunset Boulevard and consumed a lot of alcohol while he was writing. Frank had a problem making delivery dates. He died much too young."

"Felicity's Spring" (3:05) would become the highest-rated episode of the season. A simple love story between the Virginian and Felicity Andrews (Crawford) takes on added emotion when the viewer shares a secret kept from the Virginian until the episode's final scenes. The success of the episode, filmed on location at the Disney Ranch, was a testament to the power of good acting. Years later, James Drury confessed to not getting along with Crawford throughout the filming of the episode. Crawford recalled her account of the strained relationship.

"Jim and I did not get along during the shooting. Jim was very focused and serious. He wasn't a talker. He would speak to the director if he had a problem and didn't stay around the camera when not needed. During the wedding rehearsal scene, on my close-up, Jim was gone and the script girl read his lines. I looked at a square they put there for me that substituted for Jim. I was young and very insecure and shy. Jim and Mariette Hartley became friends instantly, and were together a lot. With her he relaxed, and even laughed. They were both older than I, and were very established actors, and seemed very confident and in control. None of which I was. My insecurity created separation. I would go back to the makeup area and sit there, with the people I felt safe with, or I would sit somewhere by myself and review the scene.

"The sad thing is that I liked them both very much and wished it could be different. I admired them. They both had a wonderful quality of heart and warmth which I loved. I felt they were both very good actors and good people and I would love to have been able to be friends, but I was unable to be myself with them, so it couldn't happen. Fortunately we grow out of many of our insecurities, as I did my shyness, finally."

Any personal issues disappeared during the filming of scenes between Crawford and Drury and once in character Crawford "believed he loved me, and I him."

"I remember the long shot of us riding toward camera together before the Virginian proposed by the river. I was an expert rider on my own, and loved that very long gallop into the close-up. They didn't use a stunt double for my riding shots and it was a joy for me. It was as beautiful as it looked on film. Maybe even better. I was impressed by Jim's tenderness and love and vulnerability in those scenes.

"We became friends later. After Frank and I were married, Jim and his wife came to our house for social occasions. We never discussed the shooting of 'Felicity's Spring' though. It had been a wonderful episode and that's what we remembered."

Price provided some insight into the writing on "Felicity's Spring."

"I got the idea from *Dr. Kildare*. They did a powerful episode on the 'dying girl' romance premise. I believed women controlled the television set dial. This was before multiple sets and remote controls. So I tried to do stories that would appeal to that vast woman's audience. If women wanted to watch the show, the men would agree.

"Winston Miller produced 'Felicity's Spring' which was written by Jean Holloway. Winnie, however, did the final and uncredited draft. Jean was a good love story writer, but her original background was soap opera and the dialogue could get pretty purple."

"Big Image ... Little Man" (3:07) focused on insolent rich kid Paul Leland, who is rescued in the desert by the Virginian after he is pushed off a train by an angry secretary. Unwilling to help out with chores on the cattle drive, Leland is given an ultimatum: do his share of the work or starve. The episode featured strong direction by veteran William Witney. Price often used his talents on *The Virginian*.

"'Big Image ... Little Man' was my version of *Captains Courageous*. Our director, Bill Witney, was a solid pro. He and John English had done serials, which had been done on even tighter schedules than ours.

"Bill could shoot action involving horses in the most exciting way I've ever seen. He knew exactly where to put the camera to make the action look great. He could make the simple act of the star mounting a horse and riding off look exciting. I told Bill he should open a school to teach the new directors coming out of live television how to shoot action."

A young Kurt Russell starred in "A Father for Toby" (3:08). The episode features interesting interplay between Toby Shea (Russell) and Trampas, when Toby proudly claims Trampas as his father to friends at his orphanage. Trampas plays along, reluctantly, until the boy's real father (Rory Calhoun) appears on the scene, but prefers to remain anonymous.

Although Steve Hill appeared in three episodes in the third season, only the third centered on the character.

"The Girl from Yesterday" (3:09), broadcast on November 11, 1964, featured one of Gary Clarke's stronger performances. Asked to go undercover to find out when how and when a gold shipment is going to be stolen, Steve is reluctant to accept the job due to the fact his childhood sweetheart Jane Carlyle (Ruta Lee) may be implicated.

Another director to make his presence felt in season three was Don McDougall. He directed 11 episodes. Price liked to surround himself with professionals he could trust to do a good job.

"Doing *The Virginian* on an eight-day schedule was an always difficult task. To do it, I needed professionals with great experience who could cope with any surprises that came up during production, whether that was weather or difficult actors, etc. Don McDougall was that kind of a director. He had a good sense of humor and was easy to work with."

"A Slight Case of Charity" (3:21), a Trampas-centered episode featuring Kathryn Hays, was based on a story by Howard Browne and a teleplay by Browne and True Boardman. Price explained the reasoning behind the credits.

"True Boardman was put on to rewrite Howard Browne. True placed more emphasis on writing character and emotionally moving scenes, so the choice meant that Howard's draft was deficient in those areas."

The final episode of the season, "We've Lost a Train" (3:30) served as a pilot for a the comedy Western series *Laredo* (1965–67). The practice of introducing and testing the idea for a new show on an existing successful series was cost-effective. If the network didn't think the concept strong enough to carry a series, they still had a show they could broadcast.

Price explained, "'We've Lost a Train' was the *Streets of Laredo* pilot, which we did as a segment of *The Virginian,* utilizing Doug McClure to legitimatize it as a *Virginian.* As I recall, we had wraparound scenes at Shiloh to deal with Trampas' departure and his return after his business down in Texas. We dropped those from the pilot, of course. I had suggested the opening to Borden Chase; it was a steal from *The Three Musketeers.*

"Universal owned a picture titled *Streets of Laredo* which is why I used the title, but the network shortened the series title to just *Laredo.* I always liked the Western song 'Streets of Laredo' so I presumably would have stuck with the title. Not that it mattered that much. I presume they removed it from *The Virginian* in syndication because they were able to make more money selling it in a different package. Maybe they categorized it as a 'movie.'"

Price was correct in his observation. The episode was used, in part, in *Backtrack* (1969), edited with scenes from "Ride a Dark Trail" (2:01).

In the episode, Trampas becomes involved with a group of Texas Rangers out to recover stolen gold in Mexico. Borden Chase provided the script with Earl Bellamy directing. Price described Bellamy as "a pro with great experience and easy to work with. His son Earl, Jr., was an assistant director, then a production manager for us."

Borden Chase was a veteran writer whose *Saturday Evening Post* story "Blazing Guns on the Cimmaron Trail" was adapted by Chase for the classic Howard Hawks Western *Red River* (1948). Price had worked with Chase on *The Tall Man,* but had been let down when a screenplay he provided turned out to contain exact duplicated dialogue and scenes from his original screenplay for the movie, *Winchester '73.* Price had to rewrite the scenes overnight in time for shooting the following morning.

"My job was to change the script enough so we wouldn't be legally liable, but not so much that new production problems were created for the shooting company," explained Price.

Price never worked with Borden Chase again until he needed him for "We've Lost a Train."

"*Laredo* was a coming together again for Borden and me," commented Price.

Price decided to leave *The Virginian* at the conclusion of the third season.

"At the end of season three, our ratings were very strong. I, the young executive producer, was the 'star' producer at Universal TV. In addition to running the highly successful 90-minute series, I had produced pilots for *Convoy* and *Streets of Laredo*. Both sold. I made the decision that I would not try to produce all three series at once, since that would have been a killing task.

"One thing that worried me at that time was that I was becoming known as an expert in Westerns. People in the industry were referring to me as someone in the category of David Dortort, Norman MacDonnell and Charles Marquis Warren. I was about 20 to 30 years younger than those guys. I realized once you get that 'tag' it's very difficult to shake it. And if Westerns ever faded in popularity, which I knew they would, it would limit my employment chances. So I decided it was best to leave *The Virginian*. I declined to do *Laredo*, another Western.

"I opted to take on *Convoy* because it wasn't a Western. It was a very difficult show to do from a production viewpoint. And it would be the only NBC show not broadcast in color, because of the lack of available stock footage in color from World War II Navy footage."

Veteran radio and TV producer Norman MacDonnell would replace Frank Price. But the fourth season included a major upheaval of the Shiloh family—an upheaval that affected ratings and threatened the show's future.

5

Change of Direction
Season Four

"You know, I used to not even watch *The Virginian.* This was one of the things that really piqued my agent and my manager. I didn't own a TV set."
                                                                    —Randy Boone

Norman MacDonnell found himself on a very short list of people to replace Frank Price following his departure. The initial choice, however, was Joel Rogosin, whose brief stint as executive producer went uncredited.

"I was not comfortable being an executive," explained Rogosin. "That was a period of time that didn't last too long. It was a kind of a transitional thing and I was happy to hand over control to Norman MacDonnell and return to working on the show as a producer."

An imposing figure with silver hair, MacDonnell brought his own unique vision to *The Virginian* in season four. Abandoning many of Price's creative staff, MacDonnell worked with colleagues from his days as a producer and director at CBS radio in the 1940s and 1950s, including actor John Dehner from *Have Gun Will Travel* (1958) and *Frontier Gentleman* (1958) and director and writer Anton (Tony) Leader from *Murder at Midnight* (1946) and *Suspense* (1948). Arthur H. Nadel and James Duff McAdams were new additions to the *Virginian* production staff, replacing Winston Miller for the majority of the season.

MacDonnell joined *The Virginian* following ten years (1955–65) as associate producer and producer on *Gunsmoke.* Prior to that he had worked on the original radio version of *Gunsmoke,* on which William Conrad provided the voice for Marshall Matt Dillon. *The Virginian* was undergoing change when MacDonnell replaced Price. Roberta Shore had decided to leave the show at the end of the third season; her new husband wanted Shore to devote herself to raising a family and living a Mormon lifestyle in Salt Lake City, away from the corrupting influences of Hollywood.

Price tried to persuade Shore to stay with the show at the end of the third season.

"Roberta—Jimmye—Shore was something of a country singer before she started acting," explained Price. "She was more singer than actress, so she basically played herself. And that was terrific for us. She had a sincere, honest character. I thought she was the ideal daughter for our ranch. I think her family background and her Mormon background gave her lots of inner problems, but it didn't show in her work. I think it showed in her personal and romantic relationships.

"In modeling Betsy I used Elinor Donahue, the daughter on *Father Knows Best.* I knew

Joel Rogosin, 1965 (courtesy Frank Price).

her at Screen Gems and liked the character she played on the show. Roberta Shore was perfect casting. She was the ideal younger sister, possessing a warmth and a wholesomeness. A more overtly sexual young actress would have undercut the family feel. The bonus with Roberta Shore was that she was a singer and that I was able to use with Randy Boone added to the cast."

"My relationship with her was very pleasant but I never got to know her well. She had something of a wall around her. We only had one disagreement that I recall. She wanted to get rid of her ponytail and I was totally against it. In my judgment, that ponytail look helped her to keep looking young. She tended to gain weight in the hips disproportionately and we had to work on that.

"I tried very, very hard to persuade Roberta to stay with the show, even if she limited her appearances to only a few each year. But I think her mindset was to go to Utah and become a real Mormon. She visited me a couple of times in the years afterwards and I felt she realized she had made a mistake in leaving the series to go to very Mormon Utah. I think she found she was less Mormon than she thought. She was a big loss."

In what proved to be a wise move, MacDonnell invited Shore back to film a farewell episode. "The Awakening" (4:05) turned out to be one of the season's best.

Shore was credited as a guest star in an episode that sees her fall in love with jaded minister David Henderson (Glenn Corbett). At the episode's conclusion, Judge Garth marries Betsy and Henderson and they leave Shiloh Ranch for the final time. A fine script by Robert Crean provided Betsy Garth with time to reflect on her decision to leave Shiloh as she listened for the final time to Randy Benton singing in the bunk house from her bedroom window. An era at Shiloh had ended with more upheaval to follow.

Lee J. Cobb wanted out of the series. Price had known how to handle him. Cobb had claimed he wanted to quit since the first season, but Price recognized his complaining as integral to Cobb's personality. He simply liked to complain.

Said Price, "Lee was a consummate actor. He brought so much to each scene that he appeared in and was always outstanding on film. He almost never liked a script, however. So I concluded we would never be able to give him a script that he liked and I told him so. We did conclude by making a deal. Once he read a script that I sent him, he would tell me specifically what his problems were and I would address those problems by rewriting and sending the revised pages for his further comment.

"The system worked very well. I remember how much Lee hated a script that I cast Lloyd Nolan in opposite Lee. I tried to address all Lee's expressed concerns, but frankly I just thought he was biased against the script. He did this show, protesting as we started. However, once he saw how well it was working with Lloyd Nolan, his protest faded and he began to really like the episode.

"It turned out quite well and Lee had a good time enjoying his work opposite Lloyd. Frankly, it was a joy for me to watch those dailies, seeing these old pros playing opposite each other."

Producer Joel Rogosin recalled, "Lee Cobb always wanted to do 'King Lear' and he always felt television, in general, was a step down from his ambition. He sort of had a love-hate relationship with *The Virginian* because television was not the quality material he wanted to do."

MacDonnell gave in to Cobb's demands before his five-year contract had expired. Cobb won the day and made a hasty retreat from *The Virginian*.

"The unexpected event was that Norman didn't know how to handle Lee J. Cobb, Price revealed. "Lee was something of a bluff. The bluff needed to be called at times. Lee told Norman he was leaving the show and Norman took him seriously. I'm sure Lee didn't believe he'd actually be able to get out of his contract. He certainly wouldn't have, had *I* been running the show. I would have dismissed his threats, as I sometimes had in the past, and reminded him that he had a firm contract and why would he want us to force us to sue him for everything he had in the world? I would have said it with a smile, but Lee would have understood that we dearly wanted him to stay.

"The loss of Lee was a terrible event for the show. Roberta had already left. But I think Norman liked the opportunity to redo the show more to his personal taste. When he encountered trouble with Lee, he undoubtedly should have called me to find out my take on Lee. I had handled him for three years and I certainly would have explained Lee to him."

Judge Garth left Shiloh to become territorial governor of Wyoming. But unlike Betsy, Judge Garth wasn't given a farewell episode. His final episode, "Nobody Said Hello" (4:16), is a tale of a former Confederate officer's (James Whitmore) attempt to extort money from

Judge Garth. The show had lost two of its most popular characters in quick succession.

Betsy Garth's replacement made her debut in "Jennifer" (4:07). Jennifer Sommars arrives at Shiloh following the death of her parents. Blaming their death on her uncle, Judge Garth, she forms an attachment to a fugitive (James MacArthur) and becomes a victim of misplaced trust.

Jennifer Sommers was in direct contrast to Betsy Garth. An attempt to give the new young woman at Shiloh some depth was offset by the lackluster delivery of actress Diane Roter. Roter had practically no film experience and seemed an unusual choice for a replacement.

"I'm not sure that MacDonnell understood the underlying reasons that such a character was necessary for Shiloh. I saw no evidence of that," remarked Price.

Lee J. Cobb's replacement was equally contentious. John Dehner was a fine actor, particularly suited to authoritarian figures and villains. Norman MacDonnell had formed a friendship with him during his time with CBS radio, casting him in many of his shows, including *Fort Laramie* (1956), *Have Gun Will Travel* (1958) and *Frontier Gentleman* (1958). His deep, resonant voice was particularly suited to radio.

"Morgan Starr" (4:21) introduced viewers to the new boss at Shiloh Ranch. The Virginian takes a dislike to Starr which is aggravated further by the latter's plan to deal with a plague of locusts threatening Shiloh grazing land.

The episode was one of the stronger entries in season four, with the conflict between Starr and the Virginian particularly compelling. However, Starr lacked warmth. Coupled with Jennifer Sommars' equally lukewarm persona, the new residents at Shiloh Ranch failed to register with viewers and the ratings started to slide.

The Virginian had previously relied on a formula that emphasized a family atmosphere. With the arrival of Morgan Starr, a strict, formal atmosphere replaced the geniality so evident in the first three seasons.

Series continuity was another problem evident in season four. "The Claim" (4:04) featured William Shatner in an effective episode about greed and friendship. It also included the unexpected return of Alex the cook (E.J. Andre)

"Norman MacDonnell and his casting agents must have been unaware the cook had been murdered in 'The Intruders.' That's the problem with changing producers. 'Show memory' gets lost," commented Price.

Despite the season's faults, it did contain some good episodes. "The Horse Fighter" (4:13) sees Randy Benton become a close friend to an aging bronco buster, who blames himself for the death of his wife and unborn child. A particularly fine aspect of the episode is Randy's relationship with the Virginian, highlighting Randy's immaturity and the Virginian's common sense.

"One of the episodes we did starred Harry Guardino," recalled Randy Boone. "It was called 'The Horse Fighter.' Harry is from around New Jersey. He said, 'Hey guys, I have to come up with some kind of accent the way you guys are talking.'"

"I went to him and said, 'Harry, don't change your accent at all. Just suit your inflection to match the scene. Talk the way you talk. Because, look Harry, in any history book you read you'll find these cowboys came from all over the country and even from other countries. They talked the way they talked. They didn't all have Southern accents or some kind of Western drawl. You're just fine with the way you talk. So all you have to do is imagine this person from wherever you are, who talks this way and is a cowboy.' And that's why he just used his normal accent. To me, that was realism.

"That particular episode got both of us an award. 'The Wrangler Award' is from the Western Heritage Center and Cowboy Hall of Fame in Oklahoma City. It's their award for actors they feel did the best realistic portrayal of the American cowboy in a film or a movie that year and is very prestigious. It's kind of considered the cowboy Oscar. A lot of cowboys haven't ever received it and they don't give it every year."

Boone recalled working on a scene in the Shiloh bunkhouse.

"This particular scene required some rehearsal because it was a card game. It was in the bunkhouse and it had all three principals in it. I was in it with Doug McClure and James Drury. I remember it because James Drury as the Virginian was going to fire the horse fighter guy and I got mad and slugged him. But before that took place, we were at the card table and there was a fly that kept buzzing around. The director was getting ready to shoot it and the grips had rolled up newspapers. One of them had a fly swatter and they were all trying to get the fly so the director could shoot the scene.

Finally the director said, 'All right, c'mon, let's roll.' And I looked at the camera director, the guy who's responsible for all the lighting and making sure the camera has the right lens on it. and I said, 'What are you gonna do about the fly?'

"He replied, 'We won't light the fly!'"

Another bunkhouse scene, involving Randy Boone, resulted in a stuntman going to the hospital.

"Me and a fellow playing an Indian were in a scene. He was supposed to come and grab me and we'd fall on this table. The table would break and we'd smash through the table and fall down on the floor. So I told him, when he grabbed hold of me, that first I was going to try and fling him around.

"I said, 'Hold tight because first we gotta hit this table and smash it down. If you let go of me, you're liable to roll over against the wall and hit yourself. If you hold tight I'll make sure we hit the table and smash you down.'

"Well, the old guy did just what I told him. He grabbed me and pushed me and we flung ourselves on this table top. But they didn't saw deeply enough and it didn't break. We sailed right across the top of it and came down, the both of us, head first. He had my arms pinned so I couldn't put my arms out in front of me and he had his arms around him. So we both hit right on our heads. I mean, I've got a pretty hard head and I was woozy after we hit. They took him to the hospital with a concussion."

Randy Benton made his final appearance in "A Bald-Faced Boy" (4:29). An unsatisfactory episode, it featured an over-familiar tale of an ex-convict (Andrew Duggan) seeking revenge on Randy for his part in sending him to prison. A mix of badly timed comedy, romance and drama resulted in a weak farewell episode for Boone.

The final segment of the fourth season, "The Mark of a Man" (4:30), featured the Virginian sewing socks with a darning egg and an animated Sheriff Ryker in a tale that touched on social prejudice. Moody photography by Ray Flin added to the story of family tension, and Tony Leader's direction (with an emphasis on close-ups and low angled viewpoints) created a feeling of apprehension that reflected young Johnny Younce's (Barry Primus) mental state. It was a creative conclusion to Norman MacDonnell's first stint on *The Virginian*. Earlier in the season, in an interview with Peter Bogdanovich for *TV Guide*, MacDonnell had expressed his desire to make the characters more human, but James Drury told MacDonnell it didn't fit his image to be seen darning socks. Clearly, by the season's conclusion, MacDonnell finally persuaded Drury to change his mind.

Despite some interesting attempts at varying the formula of the show, MacDonnell's first season on *The Virginian* proved to be a failure. John Dehner, Diane Roter and Randy Boone were replaced when Frank Price was asked to return for season five.

Randy Boone was approached by Norman MacDonnell with the idea for a new series.

"There was talk of a spin-off show," recalled Boone. "I'd be married and running a small ranch. It had a *Little House on the Prairie*–type premise but it came to nothing."

Commenting on season four, Price explained why he was asked to return.

"The fourth season of *The Virginian* did not go well. Lee J. Cobb was released. Tired replacements arrived at Shiloh Ranch. The audi-

Frank Price in his office, photographed by Katherine Crawford, 1965 (courtesy Frank Price).

ence watched a different *Virginian*. Some episodes were very well done, but they weren't *The Virginian* the audience wanted. The drop in the ratings was precipitous. It was critical to the financial success of the show that it get a fifth season. About 100 episodes were needed for successful syndication. A fifth season would bring *The Virginian* to about that number.

"NBC was pressed hard for renewal. I was asked to return and take it over. That was an inducement for them to renew. I agreed to do that and they, reluctantly, renewed. They believed the show was dead. I learned that when I came up with ideas to revitalize the show and received little or no support from the network executives."

Price only met MacDonnell briefly a few times and was never aware of how the experience of season four affected him. But it hurt Price, as he explained.

"I had invested a lot of blood, sweat and tears, working long, long hours, in order to build a successful series. Norman seemed oblivious to what had been done. I got the impression that he felt his shows were vastly superior to what we had done before."

Season five would be seen as a make-or-break year for *The Virginian*. The responsibility placed on Frank Price could be viewed by some as a burden, but Price saw an opportunity to restore the balance and to return *The Virginian* to its roots.

6

New Beginnings

Season Five

"Season four came close to destroying the show. Had season five been in the
same vein, *The Virginian* would have ended, probably by mid-season."
—Frank Price

The new owner of Shiloh Ranch had to be a figure of stature and authority. Frank
Price was dismayed with the casting in season four.

"John Dehner was just a dreadful mistake. It's hard to believe they could do something that dumb. He had no characteristics to recommend him for the role."

In veteran actor Charles Bickford, Price saw the qualities needed to convince viewers he could successfully run Shiloh Ranch.

"When I persuaded Charlie's agent to get a meeting for me with Charlie, the agent told
me that Charlie was dead set against doing the series," Price recalled. "The meeting was for
lunch at his house. We started talking at 12 noon and continued talking until after 6 p.m. He
enjoyed the meeting and I did too. He asked lots of questions and I answered them, making
the best pitch to him that I could. He finally and enthusiastically agreed to do the series."

Not everyone agreed with Price's judgment. NBC executives thought Bickford was
too old and refused to promote him, preferring to broadcast generic *Virginian* promos featuring James Drury alone. Bickford had originally been considered in 1962 for the role of
Judge Garth and was rejected *then* because of his age. So it was no surprise to Price when
he met with a negative reaction from the network.

"I bulldozed and bludgeoned the studio and the network into running what I called
Virginian 'Milestones' in the summer repeats. No fourth year shows were repeated. And I
selected star vehicles with Robert Redford and Hugh O'Brian and outstanding shows from
the first three years for repeats. This was not an easy thing to accomplish because it cost
money to lose those free fourth season repeats and then take third runs on the first three
years shows, which had to be paid for in residuals.

"However, by the time September rolled around, *The Virginian* ratings were moving
back into good territory, thanks to our repeats. People were seeing the old *Virginian* and
liking it.".

Not only had Morgan Starr and Jennifer Sommers departed the show, Price also
decided it was time to replace Randy Benton with a new youthful male character. He
solved the problem by giving John Grainger a family. Granddaughter Elizabeth Grainger
and grandson Stacey Grainger provided the young female and male characters so necessary to attract a younger audience.

"Creatively, I analyzed what I wanted to achieve. I wanted what I once had in Lee J. Cobb and Roberta Shore. Reality told me that Charles Bickford was too old to have a teenage daughter (not biologically, but psychologically). But I wanted a teenage girl in the show, to help bridge the relationships with the Big House and the bunkhouse, and I wanted the kind of family feel that Lee and Roberta had given the show. So I decided that the girl would be his granddaughter. Betsy is a nickname for Elizabeth so choosing Elizabeth was our little private bow to the former daughter at Shiloh. I didn't want to look as though I was just copying what we had done before, so to make it different, I decided he had two grandchildren and the other was a young man. The young man I felt should be something of a rebel, a James Dean.

"We were up against a highly touted new show called *The Monroes*, with Michael Anderson, Jr., and Barbara Hershey, which everyone in the industry and the critics felt was so good it would destroy us. It was about a bunch of orphans in the West. Since orphans seemed to be all the rage, I decided these grandchildren would be orphans. I was pleased with what I did, from a creative standpoint. I had a new family installed in Shiloh.

"It was headed by a powerful, respected patriarch. I had the wholesome, fresh young woman that all the cowhands wanted to protect. And I had a young man who could inherit the place someday, if his rebellious temperament didn't destroy him. There was a lot of appeal in the situation of a grandfather caring for his orphaned grandchildren."

Price discussed his new approach with his reassembled team of Joel Rogosin, Cy Chermak and Winston Miller. Rogosin created a "bible" on the family, fleshing out the Stacey and Elizabeth Grainger characters.

"A bible described the characters in terms helpful to episode writers, providing the background history of the character up until their first episode," said Price. "The basic psychology of the characters. It would be a few pages long. One of the reasons I asked Joel to write a bible was to make sure Universal TV owned the continuing characters. If a freelance writer wrote a script based on what I told him about the Graingers, that writer would be entitled to a royalty for creating those characters every time they subsequently appeared in a *Virginian* episode. By making sure that were documented the creation of the characters in such a bible, we avoided any such claims. Since Joel, Cy, Winston and I were under contract to Universal TV, anything one of us wrote automatically was owned by the studio."

Price had high hopes for Sara Lane and Don Quine, seeing potential for their characters to grow. Lane had some of the qualities of Roberta Shore. Youthfulness, naiveté and charm.

"I was looking for a girl with Roberta Shore's kind of appeal," commented Price. "The wholesome, fresh, girl-next-door, sisterly type. Our casting directors saw plenty of candidates and I interviewed quite a number in the search. Sara Lane was not an obvious choice and we considered others seriously. I wasn't totally satisfied with the choice of Sara, but she seemed to be the best person we found during that particular search. We ran out of time and had to make a decision. One reason I cast Sara's character, Elizabeth Grainger, young was that I wanted at least two or three seasons before she outgrew the younger sister age category.

"I thought she was at best okay, so I was fundamentally disappointed in my choice. She turned out to be limited as an actress and didn't have the natural ebullient personality that Roberta Shore had. She filled the role adequately enough to suit the purposes of our format, but brought nothing extra to the role."

One aspect of Sara Lane that Price didn't anticipate was the effects riding a horse had on her well-rounded figure.

"One thing I remember in particular was that I had to have a special brassiere designed for her after I saw the dailies on her from one of her first episodes. She rode into the scene with gusto and since she was a well-built young lady, there was a lot of chest movement that was just not appropriate for *The Virginian.*

"I learned from wardrobe that a normal bra wouldn't dampen the effect which is why I got involved with designing something that would prevent unusual bouncing. This may sound somewhat prudish on my part, but you had to see the film to really understand the visual impact of her entrance on horseback."

Quine had an edge, missing from the laid-back Randy Boone—a rebelliousness that always attracted teenage viewers. Price explained his decision to replace Boone.

"Unfortunately, Randy didn't fit into the newly revamped version of the show. I needed screen time to establish the new owner and to round off who he was and how he related to the Virginian and Trampas. Would he keep the Virginian as foreman? Could he put up with Trampas' darker moments? I had a new character in Don Quine that had potential. And, of course, I wanted Sara to succeed as Roberta's replacement, so she needed screen time. I didn't have a need for Randy Boone or room for him for that matter."

Price decided on casting Don Quine after an extensive search.

"Not all the potential candidates were available. After all, this was a role in a four-year old Western that would probably get cancelled after the next season. (Actor's agents stay informed about the business.) The role would be the fourth male lead after Drury, McClure and Bickford, so that means some actors wouldn't even allow themselves to be considered. I thought there was a possible James Dean quality about Don that would emerge."

The Graingers were introduced on September 14, 1966, in the opening episode of season five, "Legacy of Hate" (5:01). Arriving at Shiloh Ranch, Grainger is greeted with hostility by a neighboring rancher (Jo Van Fleet) who blames Grainger for the death of her husband.

The new owners of Shiloh boosted the ratings. The warm family atmosphere had been successfully restored and *The Virginian* was back on track. Price once again worked with creative staff he trusted to do a good job. Winston Miller had worked on season four to a limited extent. Price gave him greater responsibility and brought back producer Cy Chermak. Don McDougall and Abner Biberman directed 20 episodes of the fifth season between them. Biberman was new to *The Virginian* but would assume an increasing role as the seasons progressed. Price discussed his preferences for McDougall and Biberman.

"Clearly I liked using both directors. Both men were highly experienced professionals. McDougall was better at action and with macho male stories. He was more comfortable directing men than women. Abner was probably the better director of actors and I tended to use him more on dramatic material that relied less on action. These rules were not written in stone."

"Don directed 'Felicity's Spring,' certainly a woman's picture, and did a great job. In that case, however, I made sure that the two lead actresses were strong enough to need little direction. Both men were easy to work with."

"Don McDougall was a wonderful, sweet man," recalled Katherine Crawford. "I enjoyed him so much. He was a good director. A director makes all the difference. Frank used him frequently and I would see him sometimes when he came to see Frank."

As well as new opening credits that included Bickford, Lane and Quine, season five saw a change in the end credit titles, with an overhead view of Shiloh Ranch replacing the Virginian astride a chestnut horse.

"Sometimes changes happened for trivial reasons," said Price. "Perhaps Jim got annoyed with the chestnut horse shot. So we eliminated it ... and him for good measure. We had plenty of high shots of the ranch available. And one of them made a better background for the end credits than Jim on his horse."

Episodes of interest in the fifth season included "The Captive" (5:03) starring Susan Strasberg. A white girl raised by Indians, Strasberg denies she was abducted as a child when confronted with the prospect of meeting her birth parents,

"I was drawn to this episode because I found the situation of the white girl preferring to remain with the Indians intriguing. That did happen not infrequently in history. And the story provided good moral and emotional conflict," said Price.

In "The Challenge" (5:06), Trampas suffers amnesia and is accused of robbery and murder. The episode introduced a striking young actress called Barbara Anderson, who would find fame a few years later as Eve Whitfield on *Ironside* (1967–75) playing alongside Don Galloway, who also featured in this segment. A fine music score by Leo Shuken and Jack Hayes and a good supporting cast (including veteran actor Dan Duryea, in one of his final performances, and youngster Michael Burns) added to a satisfying episode.

"Dan Duryea's relationship with Charles Bickford was key to him doing our show," recalled Price. "Actors had great respect for Bickford."

"Trail to Ashley Mountain" (5:08) was notable for featuring African-American actor Raymond St. Jacques. African-Americans rarely featured on TV Westerns in roles of any substance. St. Jacques played a bounty hunter pursuing a murderer into mountain country.

Joel Rogosin, Frank Edmunds, Don McDougall and Frank Price in the "Black Tower" (Universal offices, 1965; the building was named for its black glass exterior; courtesy Frank Price)

Writer Sy Salkowitz had previously scripted the fourth season episode "Long Ride to Wind River" (4:18), but this was his first script for Price.

"That script led us to make Sy one of our regulars," recalled Price. "He wrote good dramatic and emotional situations well. He continued on to *Ironside* with us. I decided we were going to integrate the show. I think it was in the fifth year. Westerns were very white shows and in the fifth year I figured I wanted to do that. I think we had a number of terrific episodes that integrated the show and were very interesting dramatically. There was one involving Raymond St. Jacques who starred as this bounty hunter who was dangerous. There was an overtone that he really liked hunting down and killing. And he was a fast shot. Bernie Hamilton was in one where he had twins, and that was very successful.

"One of the big civil rights things in the '60s was when the African-Americans had gone into the dining establishments and sat at the lunch counter and insisted they be served. *Bonanza* did an episode like that. And I thought, that's so silly, because it wasn't happening then. What I did was try to tell stories that worked well dramatically that could have black cast members.

"You had to inform the Extras Guild and say, 'We are going to have blacks on the streets of Medicine Bow. They should be there.' Now, that means you have to deal with the Extras Guild and make sure that they have such people and they are going to look appropriate to walk around the streets of a Western town. It required attention to every area. We were one of the first shows to do that as a Western."

Memorable segments featuring the Virginian from season five include "Ride to Delphi" (5:02), "High Stakes" (5:10), "Linda" (5:12), "Requiem for a Country Doctor" (5:18), "The Gauntlet" (5;20) and "Bitter Harvest" (5:25).

The Virginian also featured in the light-hearted "Deadeye Dick" (5:09), about a young girl's (Marjorie Hammond) infatuation with the Virginian, seeing in him the qualities of her dime novel hero "Deadeye Dick," much to the annoyance of a young suitor (David Macklin). Joseph Hoffman provided the script. Price had worked with Hoffman at Screen Gems, when Hoffman was a producer and Price a young story analyst for *Ford Theatre*.

"Nearly a decade later, when I was running *The Virginian*, Joe Hoffman submitted for our consideration a feature script he had written in the past. It was somewhat away from our preferred approach, but both Winston Miller and I thought it had charm and could be made to work. I was pleased because Joe had always treated me well and I wanted to reciprocate. Winston did his usual professional job of polishing Joe's script and that raised the quality level even more.

"I would not have wanted to make many that were quite that soft. And it was short on compelling plot elements. But I think we were right in our belief we could get away with it because of its charm and humor."

Pernell Roberts, fresh from quitting *Bonanza*, gave a strong performance as a man attempting to reform his life in "The Long Way Home" (5:13). An intelligent and thoughtful script by Ken Finley and Andy Lewis addresses issues of loneliness, idol worship, responsibility, ambition, jealousy and self-control. Michael Burns was featured as Jim Boyer's (Roberts) son, looking for a role model in his wayward father.

Said Price, "I liked Pernell. He was temperamental, but he was talented. He made a terrible decision to leave *Bonanza*, but I think he felt he had no choice. He didn't present any problems to us during shooting. He liked the script. It was a good publicity coup to get him on our show. The network, however, was mad at him and nearly vetoed the idea. Had we not been stubborn (and successful), I think they would have."

A continuing problem posed to writers on Virginian-based segments was the need to limit scenes where the Virginian's birth name might be called into question. Price commented on the difficulties posed by certain situations.

"Romantic involvements were not a problem to handle. The limitation probably improved the dialogue so that we avoided the 'John' and 'Marcia' back-and-forth lines. However, checking in at a hotel was tricky. Or when a strange sheriff stopped him and wanted information. As tricky as these situations were, the value of having such a mystery about this character outweighed any reasons to hang a name on him.

"Almost every freelance writer that worked for us wanted to give him a name. I'm sure that every freelance writer that was hired for *Superman* wanted to do the story of Clark Kent marrying Lois Lane. In one episode you blow apart your basic appeal. I would patiently explain this was our format and we wanted them to use their writerly skills so we skillfully could avoid such awkward scenes.

"Don't put him at the check-in desk at the hotel, signing in. Start him walking into the hotel, then cut to the clerk ushering him into his room. Think and avoid the necessity of giving him a name. Owen Wister did not give the Virginian a name for very good reasons. The concept created the Western as we know it and I saw no reason to try to improve on Owen Wister's thinking by suddenly tagging a name on his character. Instead of the Virginian, he's Fred Jones. Somehow it doesn't ring the same.

"The mystery was an overall advantage, not a drawback. I wanted the audience to always wonder why he didn't use a name. What was Shane's full name? Pete Shane? Romance and mystery are good elements, not elements to eliminate."

James Drury could often be as elusive as the Virginian's name. Price recalled an episode on the set at Universal.

"Jim could be difficult at times, mostly with other people. When the studio tour was developed and the trams started coming too close to where the company was shooting, I would get a call that Jim had left the lot and no one could find him and it was impossible to shoot. I would then leave the lot, go to where I thought he might be, find him there and talk out the problem with him. I would promise to take up the problem with the highest authorities on the lot—Lew Wasserman—to make sure the tram people stopped this. With my assurances, Jim would return. All would go well for a few weeks until the stupid tram people would make the same mistake. And we'd do the routine all over again."

Sara Lane was given a chance to show her acting talents in "Beloved Outlaw' (5:11) where she attempts to train a white stallion in time for the Founder's Day race.

"Bill Witney shot that one in Mojave. I think Red Rock was one of the locations," Price recalled. "That was really about a girl and her horse. Sort of *Black Beauty*. Notice that we had a white horse, in case anyone thought we were ripping off an old chestnut. Sure fooled them."

The segment included scenes of horse whispering, decades before it reached the public consciousness in the best-selling novel and movie *The Horse Whisperer*. Although True Boardman's original script featured scenes of horse whispering, Sara Lane and William Witney, both lovers of horses, added to and refined material.

"Sara did a terrific job," continued Price. "As, of course, did Bill Witney. He identified with and understood the emotion of this story so he was able to give good character direction to Sara. Bill deserves the lion's share of the credit for everything in this episode—excluding the music and post-production, of course. Bill knew and loved horses. I've never met a director who could shoot footage involving horses better than Bill."

The episode featured another outstanding music score by Leo Shuken and Jack Hayes, whose work was one of the highlights of the fifth season.

Don Quine's talents were highlighted in "Vengeance Trail" (5:15), with Stacey Grainger becoming the target of a friend's revenge, and "Yesterday's Timepiece" (5:17), where a pocket watch provides clues to Stacey's tragic past.

A character missing from the first half of season five was Emmett Ryker. The always temperamental Clu Gulager was in a financial dispute that wouldn't be resolved until midway through the season. He finally made his first appearance of the season in "Sue Ann" (5:16), starring Patty Duke.

"The Modoc Kid" (5:19) starred John Saxon as the leader of a group of bank robbers holding the Graingers hostage at the ranch. John Saxon recalled working on the episode, one of two he starred in, directed by Abner Biberman.

"The first role I ever played in a movie was in *Running Wild* directed by Abner Biberman, who also directed the two shows I did of *The Virginian*. In between those roles, Abner Biberman became something of a mentor to me. I remember, on 'The Modoc Kid,' I 'bent' a line of dialogue to suggest more about the mind of the character I was playing than the written line itself intended to imply. Biberman chuckled at this.

"I had worked with Charles Bickford in 1958 on *The Unforgiven*. One small story sticks in my mind. Returning from the *Unforgiven* location in a car to town, Charlie sat in the front passenger seat of respect. After a long quiet ride, he turned to me sitting in the back of the car and, with a glint in his blue eyes, and unrelated to anything, said with a tone of multiple inferences, 'So, you want to be a character actor!'

"On the *Virginian* set I remember Bickford saying that, with TV and *The Virginian*, he was reaching a larger audience than he had ever done in his film career. Charlie's *Virginian* contract gave him the right to finish work at 6 p.m. So after finishing his close-ups in the scene in the parlor where I lean over a chair talking to him, Charlie said, 'Good night,' and up and left. Abner Biberman, anxious to do my close-up and finish the scene, commiserated that the woman doing continuity would read Charlie's lines to me. I told Abner no, I would do it myself.

"He was apprehensive about this. But I knew Charlie's dialogue, and his attitude and tones, better in my mind than any continuity woman reading dialogue in rote off the page. Her reading would have been a hindrance and a distraction to listen to. And I did it, looking left off-camera at my imagined Charlie Bickford, and probably did it as well as if he were there."

Price had negotiated the provision that Bickford leave at 6 p.m. each day in deference to his age.

"Anyone who knew Charlie knew you couldn't bluff him. To him, a deal was a deal. Louis B. Mayer learned how tough Charlie Bickford could be. Charlie lived up to his word and he demanded you live up to yours. The reality is that Bickford, at his age, knew how much energy he could expend. He didn't want to have to plead with an assistant director or a director to let him go because he was tired and desperately needed the rest. And if he didn't get that rest, he might not feel up to reporting for another hard day's work the next morning."

The episode also introduced a young Harrison Ford to viewers. John Saxon met up with Ford again, over a decade later, in the first-class seats of a plane and introduced himself. Ford had, in the meantime, become a major star, thanks in part to *Star Wars* (1977).

"I engaged Harrison by telling him I hadn't seen him since we'd worked together in

Mexico on a *Virginian*. He shook his head. He didn't know what I was talking about. I persisted a little further but it seemed that he was becoming annoyed so I dropped the subject and there was no more conversation," recalled Saxon.

"Very recently, while watching the 'Modoc Kid' episode, I realized I'd mixed up Harrison Ford with Randolph Mantooth, with whom I'd worked on a *Men from Shiloh* starring Stewart Granger, which was filmed in Mexico. Quite possibly Harrison Ford never remembered working with me or in 'The Modoc Kid,' where he was billed as 'Introducing Harrison Ford.'"

In a story reminiscent of "Felicity's Spring" (3:05), Trampas' plans to marry are doomed to failure because of a tragic secret in "Melanie" (5:22). Newcomer Susan Clark starred as Melanie. Toronto-born Clark was a graduate of the Royal Academy of Dramatic Art in London. Her RADA–trained accent is in evidence throughout the episode and has a slightly jarring effect given her father (Victor Jory) has a strong American drawl. The romantic story by Stephen Lord includes a flawed and unsatisfactory denouement which sees Trampas humiliated in front of his friends.

The ill-fated love affair was a familiar and overused plot device in TV Westerns. Characters in Westerns must remain single or be widowers. A hero figure cannot have a wife and therefore all relationships are doomed to failure.

"Since 'Felicity's Spring' was such a great success with our audience, there was a desire to duplicate that success with another love story. It was too close an imitation," commented Price.

TV Guide reviewer Martin Maloney wasn't impressed. In the August 19, 1967, edition he commented,

> *The Virginian* generally sets up a nice gloopy love story which always ends badly. In Medicine Bow, nobody ever seems to get the girl, which may explain why Wyoming is largely unpopulated, even to this day.

Another repeating theme of ranch-based TV Westerns from the 1960s was their reliance on a strong father figure such as Judge Garth, Ben Cartwright (*Bonanza*), John Cannon (*High Chaparral*) and Murdoch Lancer (*Lancer*), leading some commentators to view a these Westerns as morality tales with an underlying Biblical base. Price denied making script decisions based on any religious theme.

"Certainly there was no conscious effort to instill Christian values into our heroes. I'd add there was also no attempt to instill Jewish values. What I wanted to do in these backstories was to tell how each of these men came to Shiloh Ranch and how they bonded with each other. I wanted to tell a good story in each case and tell a story that had emotional content that the audience could identify with.

"Since we have a Judeo-Christian society, I'm sure these values will generally be reflected in our storytelling since that's what our audience responds to. *The Virginian* was strong in the U.K., but always somewhat weak in Japan since they loved shoot-'em-ups like *Laramie*. Maybe *Laramie* also had better Shinto values.

"We were a major program on BBC 2, which was relatively new and was regarded as the more intellectual channel of the BBC. I was always pleased that the British critics recognized the quality of our series and its difference from other Westerns. Most U.S. critics lacked the acumen to discern the difference. To many of them, one Western was the same as any other. So I always enjoyed reading our reviews out of the U.K.

"One of my maxims to all was that our goal was to make our shows for the critical ten percent of the audience. Ninety per cent of the audience will be entertained by almost anything you do if they like the actors and the concept of the series. But ten percent have a higher threshold of approval. And those were the people we were trying to please. We didn't always succeed but we were always trying. As opposed to settling for that dreadful thing, 'Good enough.'

"That viewpoint was something I learned from my fairly brief experience in working with Roy Huggins. It was basic to his approach, and when he voiced it I recognized that that was the only personally satisfying approach to any creative work. So that reinforced my instincts and became my defined tactic from there on in. He made tangible something I already felt."

While newcomers Sara Lane and Don Quine required direction for their still evolving characters, James Drury and Doug McClure often dictated how the Virginian and Trampas should be portrayed. Price explained the relationship between actor, character, writer, director and producer on a weekly TV series.

"A good actor knows his own character better than most of the writers or directors who work on the show. Writers generally move from show to show, so they may be involved with only one episode or a few at most. Their interest often goes little beyond the fictional characters they have created in the episode they write. Directors in television have little time for much character work with actors, particularly the leads. Sometimes directors in television are referred to derisively as 'traffic cops.' They need to keep things moving.

"Individual writers and directors did not have the overall picture of the series in mind, which is why they could make mistakes. The individual producers tended to know only their own episodes. That is why I, as the only other person who had responsibility for every episode, had to do my best to protect the image of each character."

Price depended on Drury and McClure to pick up on anything that felt out of character. This sometimes led to conflicts with the director and telephone calls to Price to resolve matters without wasting valuable time on set. Price tried to catch any errors at the script stage, but mistakes could escape notice until the dailies or first rough cut was screened. If an out-of-character or negative trait got this far, it involved either re-shooting part of a scene or editing out the material.

"Any good actor learns what he and his character can do well," concluded Price, "and what looks most attractive. It is a rare director that can add much to that."

"Lady of the House" (5:28) starred Myrna Loy in a story contrasting trust and deception.

"The idea for this episode was suggested by Dale Eunson's 1942 play *Guest in the House*. Never forget, even Shakespeare had no qualms about lifting good stories from other sources," says Price.

"I tried to do one for absolute minimum budget at one time and decided to see what we could do it for. So it was specially written. I did it with Bickford and Myrna Loy for $188,000. That was under circumstances where I wanted no exterior shooting at all. Only using stock footage and shooting on our standard sets. That was the minimum the show could be made for. It was not an exercise, but a means of making up for overages that we had run up in that season so far. It made us come in under budget for the season. The frosting on the cake was that the show was so well-received by the audience and by the critics.

"Myrna Loy was an absolute delight to deal with. She loved working with Charles Bickford. They got to do something of a romance and that was infrequent for actors of their age. Leslie Stevens was a master at handling actresses. He helped deliver her for the role. Abner Biberman's creative approach was always appreciated by serious actors. And in this episode he had only actors to deal with and no horses."

With ratings soaring by the end of season five, a bidding war for broadcast rights to *The Virginian* began.

Price recalled, "The newly revamped *Virginian* got terrific ratings in spite of lack of promotion. We handily crushed *The Monroes*. I personally never believed that their premise of orphans in the West was a good idea. What's good about watching vulnerable kids in jeopardy? That created sympathy but anxiety also. My orphans had a grandfather and some darn good cowboys to look after them. We won and they lost.

"We became so successful that year that CBS entered into negotiations to air the series commencing with the sixth year. Bill Paley was personally involved in trying to get *The Virginian* on his network. NBC had ordered *The Virginian* at a bargain price originally. The standard network deal gave the networks options to renew a series through its fifth year. After that amount of success, the series could be sold to a different network or, if its ratings were strong, it was a wonderful opportunity to renegotiate the terms and get a much better financial deal for the studio. This is what happened with *The Virginian*. NBC made a rich new offer to keep its newly revitalized hit. They wound up paying a huge price to keep *The Virginian*. Had CBS bought the show, their deal with MCA would have required that I remain as executive producer of the show, so my career would have taken a different path."

James Drury, Frank Price and Doug McClure relaxing at *The Virginian*'s 5th-season wrap party, 1967 (courtesy Frank Price).

The traditional end of season "wrap party" would be the last attended by Price. The party was traditionally held on the stage that was used on the final day of the shoot. As soon as the last shot was filmed, the party would begin. As the last day normally involved an interior shot, it was easy to set up the party, situated a distance from the last set to be shot. In attendance at Price's final wrap party were Drury, McClure, Clu Gulager, Sara Lane and Don Quine, with McClure's good friend Robert Fuller also present.

"Generally, wrap parties were limited in the amount of time that everyone could spend on stage," recollected Price. "It was an occasion for conviviality for a while and then everyone splits. The studio wouldn't keep the stage occupied and lit for long. Serious drinkers undoubtedly headed off the lot for one of the nearby bars where they could get in trouble on their own. There was the 'Rickshaw Boy Restaurant and Bar' directly across Lankershim Blvd. More drinking than was wise went on there. Eventually the studio bought the land and wouldn't renew the lease for the restaurant."

Price left *The Virginian* at the conclusion of season five to take over production duties, from Collier Young, on *Ironside* (1967) starring Raymond Burr. Norman MacDonnell would return to guide *The Virginian* through season six and beyond.

7

MacDonnell in Charge
Seasons Six to Eight

"That sense of family is what makes shows successful, and I think that's certainly what made *The Virginian* successful."

—Joel Rogosin

Given the failure of MacDonnell's first tenure on *The Virginian* (season four), the decision to hire him again following Frank Price's departure appeared a strange one. Price explained the decision.

"Norman was well-liked and was a good producer. It was agreed he had learned from the fourth-year experience what not to do, and that he would try harder to follow the established format that I had put back in place. And finding a replacement for me at a reasonable price, someone who had respect, ability and stature, made Norman a good choice.

"Very little was communicated between us that involved the series. He had his taste in stories and it was not necessarily the same taste that I had. Also, I think Norman prized his own professional independence and wanted to take the show his own way, improving on it. He had attempted that on season four and failed. This time he took over the show with a full complement of scripts already prepared. I think the studio executives explained to him that his job now was to continue on the path I had set forth."

The opening episode, "Reckoning" (6:01), was a good start with a strong performance by Charles Bronson in the role of outlaw Harge Talbot and an atmospheric music score by Bernard Herrmann. The episode would later be released as part of a clumsy and poorly conceived compilation movie, *The Meanest Men in the West* (1967), that attempted to create a new story by adding footage from "It Tolls for Thee" (1:09) starring Lee Marvin.

Price explained the reasoning behind the theatrical releases.

"There was a man named Harry Tatelman on the lot at Universal, a producer who specialized in scavenging episodes which he would edit into theatrical releases for foreign markets. Sometimes he'd edit two or more of the episodes together, invent some kind of connective tissue, and call it a movie. The resulting pictures were not good, but Harry was widely praised by the financial people for his ability to turn otherwise useless film into money.

"Tatelman did this work for quite a long time without many of the producers on the lot being aware of what he was doing. By the time anyone learned what had happened with the old episodes, it was pretty much too late to change anything. I don't think I ever saw any of the pictures Tatelman crafted together. It was enough that someone described what he'd done. I didn't care to see it since I couldn't stop it."

Joel Rogosin, producer of "Reckoning," described his shock on seeing his name credited on *The Meanest Men in the West.*

"I saw my name credited to a movie I had not done. Tatelman had taken two *Virginian* episodes starring Charles Bronson and Lee Marvin. It's distinguished by the fact that the two lead characters never appear together in a scene. And that's because it's intercut from two different episodes. I did the Bronson episode. On its own it was a very good episode and I was horrified when I saw it. I don't want that credit. It's a terrible disservice to everybody who was involved in doing the two good shows. It was awful."

David Hartman made his first appearance on *The Virginian* as George Foster in "The Masquerade" (6:06), playing a timid man who poses as the sheriff of Medicine Bow to please his father. Although Hartman worked exclusively in the MacDonnell seasons, the person responsible for hiring him was Price.

"I had discovered David for a pilot I did called *I Love a Mystery*. A *World Premiere* movie starring Ida Lupino, which introduced David Hartman. It was a poor comedy, filmed in 1967 and not broadcast until 1973, that didn't sell. But I thought David could be a star so I needed a place to park him where I could put him under contract and salary. I added David to *The Virginian* and passed him along to Norman along with a substantial number of the scripts of that sixth season."

MacDonnell and the network saw enough potential in Hartman's performance to hire him as a permanent member of the cast the following season.

The sixth season was going well for MacDonnell until Charles Bickford was taken ill and passed away only a few months into filming. His final appearance was in "Ah Sing vs. Wyoming" (6:07), which aired on October 27, 1967. Bickford died a few weeks later, on November 9, 1967.

"He was a very thinking actor. As an example, his character John Grainger called Elizabeth 'Lib' or 'Libby.' This was his subtle way of personalizing the relationship between him and his granddaughter. It was his own touch that he undoubtedly worked out in his own mind—the parts of the relationship that we hadn't told and that he drew on as a performer in scenes with her.

"One remarkable thing about Bickford. When he was shooting, he could seem frail and worn down, his voice a whisper before a scene. But when he walked into the scene to shoot, suddenly strength flooded through him. The frailty was gone and the voice became powerful. It was amazing to watch. I think he really felt most alive when he was working. He was a tough old guy. He survived a fall down the long stone steps before the ranch house when he tripped, and was not injured by it.

"I was really distressed by news of his death. I think, given a choice, he would have preferred to be an actively working actor when he died, as he was. I doubt stress contributed to his death. He derived too much pleasure from his work. Maybe working extended his life," declared Price.

In a situation reminiscent of season four, MacDonnell was forced to look for a new owner of Shiloh Ranch. Veteran actor John McIntire was the consensus choice. McIntire was a veteran of movies going back to 1948, mainly a character actor in Westerns such as *Winchester '73* (1950) and *The Tin Star* (1957). The decision to feature him as the new ranch owner met with some criticism. Former executive producer Price disagreed with casting McIntire, considering him to be lacking in authority compared to his predecessors Lee J. Cobb and Charles Bickford. He commented on the decision to cast him.

"John McIntire was miscast. He was a supporting player by virtue of his persona. I would have cast him as a sod buster, a down-on-his-luck farmer. That's how I saw him. So when Norman, with the network and studio agreeing, cast McIntire in *The Virginian*, I made no secret of my opinion that they'd made a terrible mistake.

"They compounded the mistake by putting his wife, Jeanette Nolan, in Shiloh Ranch. The lack of an adult female was an essential part of the underlying psychology of our show. It created tension that worked for us with the women's audience.

"Jeanette Nolan and John McIntire were really terrific people. When I felt they didn't belong at Shiloh Ranch, some people interpreted that as meaning that I didn't like them. My feeling had nothing to do with not liking them. It had to do with the two of them being wrong for *The Virginian*. Clearly Jeanette was a good actor so anyone seeing her on film could say they liked her. That doesn't mean that she would make the series succeed. Just the opposite. Her fine presence changed the character of the whole series."

McIntire and Nolan made their entry on "Bitter Autumn" (6:08) as John Grainger's brother Clay and his (Clay's) wife Holly. A multi-layered story featuring diseased cattle, an accidental death, revenge and deception won the 1968 Western Heritage Award for "Best Fictional Drama." Bickford's sudden departure meant that many scripts, already prepared with John Grainger in mind, had to be modified to accommodate Clay and his wife. Charles Bickford continued to be featured in the opening filmed credits until the end of the year, with John McIntire credited as "Special Guest Star."

"I thought McIntire and Nolan were a wonderful mix," commented Joel Rogosin, producer of "Bitter Autumn." "It changed the complexion of the show. I liked them very much. They were wonderful people, they were terrific actors and they were professionals. New cast members were almost always a consensus effort between Monique James, who was the vice-president in charge of talent, the vice-president of television Jennings Lang and Norman. Usually the studio had somebody they wanted to recommend and there was usually no reason to object to that."

"Execution at Triste" (6:13) featured a story about jaded gunfighter Lee Knight (Robert Lansing) looking for a final confrontation with Trampas in a ghost town called Triste. A familiar tale was aided by excellent cinematography by Walter Strenge and a moody uncredited music score combining the talents of acclaimed composers Leonard Rosenman and Bernard Herrmann.

MacDonnell's use of Rosenman created an atmosphere in marked contrast to earlier seasons, which often depended on a traditional approach to background music. Rosenman's style was distinctive, creating a sense of unease and tension. MacDonnell also employed Herrmann, famous for his long association with Alfred Hitchcock. The use of these two accomplished musicians along with the introduction of distinctive new talent such as Ralph Ferraro, Dave Grusin and David Shire gave the latter seasons of *The Virginian* a contemporary feel.

"Norman's approach to the show was softer. Frank had a little tougher attitude toward the show. Norman's attitude became more modern," commented Rogosin. "It was more sophisticated. In the very early days it was a little elemental. I've caught some of the early shows on cable and I didn't think they were as good as the later shows. There was a distinction between the very early shows and the ones where Frank and Roy took over. I think I was lucky enough to be involved when we were doing the best shows."

Rogosin, having worked for both Price and MacDonnell, contrasted the styles of the two *Virginian* executive producers.

"Frank was laid-back, but very dynamic and forceful and extremely bright. He was very unusual as an executive because his background was writing. He had specific likes and dislikes and was very articulate in expressing them. Frank was one of a kind. He was extremely competent, extremely capable, extremely articulate and extremely focused. Frank was more actively involved and was an excellent creative administrator.

"Norman was milder, softer and gentler. Very capable in other ways. He was very distinguished-looking and looked like a movie actor. He had steely gray hair and a mustache and was quite handsome. Very warm and kind and gentlemanly. Kind of old school, I thought."

John McIntire finally replaced Charles Bickford in the opening title credits on "Jed" (6:17), broadcast January 10, 1968, in a ride-in sequence filmed on the Shiloh Ranch back lot.

"With Help from Ulysses" (6:18) starred Shaggy the dog as Ulysses (a.k.a. Fred) in an enjoyable, light-hearted comedy featuring Trampas and written by True Boardman, about two women claiming to be the niece of an old gold prospector.

The sixth season also saw the introduction of new, young acting talent such as Peter Deuel, Ben Murphy, Don Stroud, Burr DeBenning and Steve Ihnat.

"The Good-Hearted Badman" (6:20) featured Deuel as an outlaw recuperating from wounds at Shiloh Ranch. In the first of two guest star roles, he was perfectly cast as the charming Thomas Baker, hiding his true identity from a smitten Elizabeth Grainger. Deuel would later find himself playing another good-hearted badman in *Alias Smith and Jones* (1971), as Hannibal Heyes. After a change of name to Pete Duel, the talented but troubled young actor ended his life on December 31, 1971, at the young age of 31.

Price recalls, "Pete was a wonderful actor. He was great to work with and certainly improved any role that he undertook. My contact with him was mostly on the pilot for *Alias Smith and Jones*. Unfortunately, Pete suffered from depression and it got him."

"The Handy Man" (6:24), starred Mel Tormé, who also provided the script, in a flawed episode. Mediocre acting by Tormé and an inconsistent story that relies on the viewer believing the Medicine Bow townsfolk and Sheriff Abbott would trust two troublemakers in favor of Trampas stretches belief. Tormé adapted his 1950s Western novel *Dollarhide*, written under a pseudonym, for the segment and in doing so failed to take into account the continuity of the *Virginian* series.

The final episode of season six, "Seth" (6:26), produced and directed by Rogosin, featured Michael Burns as a youngster torn between his old life and a new beginning at Shiloh Ranch. The conclusion of the story led many viewers to believe that Burns would become a regular on the show the following season, but MacDonnell had another actor in mind.

Season seven saw yet more changes for *The Virginian* with the unexplained absence of Stacey Grainger. A temperamental and unsettled Don Quine was replaced by David Hartman as David Sutton.

"David was under contract to Universal and I don't think Universal and Don Quine were particularly happy with each other," recalled Rogosin.

A new title sequence featured Hartman in the ride-in with a fresh arrangement of the title theme. Another absentee was the equally temperamental Clu Gulager as Emmett Ryker, who left the show after a run of five years.

David Sutton, was introduced in the premiere episode of season seven. "The Saddle Warmer" (7:01), acquainted the viewer with the greenhorn veterinarian student from Pennsylvania, given a tough time by Trampas and the Shiloh ranch hands after he ropes and tames a wild horse meant as a gift for Elizabeth Grainger from Trampas.

"Vision of Blindness" (7:04) featured John Saxon as an escaped convict guiding a blind Elizabeth Grainger back to Shiloh Ranch with the intention of getting revenge on Trampas for the death of his brother. Filmed on location in Los Padres National Forest, the episode also starred the Irish Rovers, who made appearances throughout the season. An aspect of the segment that lacked continuity to previous episodes was the fact that Shiloh Ranch appeared to be in easy walking distance of mountain territory.

"I seem to remember that Sara Lane and I got along very well," Saxon says. "I also remember Ben Johnson's speech to me in 'Vision of Blindness' about vengeance, and getting even. I remember telling the director Abner Biberman that it reminded me of Iago taunting Othello. Biberman thought that was an interesting approach and directed Johnson to do that ... in his own way ... of course. Seeing it on-screen, I don't think it came off as vividly as I imagined, but it was still good."

Biberman's daughter-in-law, actress Elizabeth Perry, remarked on Biberman's qualities.

"Abner, who I called Papa, directed numerous *Virginian*'s. Doug McClure was often a guest at his house. At that time he was married to his third wife, Sibil, and they had a young son together, Thor, and an Australian shepherd dog called Shep. Papa Biberman was a fascinating man and could quote, years later, lines he had learned in his first Broadway plays. He had been a young man in the Group Theatre with Strasberg and Cluman. He said he had brought Clifford Odets, the great American writer who wrote *Golden Boy* and *Waiting for Lefty* and many other wonderful plays, into the group. He was particularly fond of quoting from Maxwell Anderson's *Winterset*.

"Other people are not aware when someone makes a name in film or television, that there were years of struggle and successes in the theater that preceded national recognition. Abner loved classical music and did much more than listen to it. He was enormously informed about the performing artists and composers. He was an old-fashioned raconteur and loved recounting stories of his experiences.

"As regards *The Virginian*, I know he enjoyed directing it, and one segment of *The Virginian* features his son Tony, but I don't think Abner directed that one. I was directed by Abner once on *Voyage to the Bottom of the Sea*.

"He became incapacitated by kidney failure and diabetes at too young an age and died when he was just 64 years old. His first wife, Helen, my ex-husband's mother, remained my friend until her death in 2000 at 93. His son Thor resides in San Diego. His mother Sibil died a few years ago. Thor is a journalist and creative writer."

Director Abner Biberman in the Universal offices, 1965 (courtesy Frank Price).

The war in Vietnam and the Civil Rights Movement was having

an effect on the average person's perception of America's role in the world. *The Virginian* attempted to address the issues of minorities and indigenous peoples in episodes such as "The Wind of Outrage" (7:05) and "The Heritage" (7:07), concentrating on the plight of the Canadian Metis Indians and Native American Indians, respectively. Folk singer Buffy Sainte-Marie, who guested on *The Virginian,* was a Cree Indian from Saskatchewan, Canada, who insisted that only Native American actors be employed in Native American roles in "The Heritage." Thus *The Virginian* became the first Western, in TV or movie history, to employ an all–Indian cast. Thirty-seven actors American Indian actors were employed from among various tribes including Hopi, Cree, Apache, Ute, Nez Pierce, Blackfoot, Yuma, Mohawk, Shawnee, Kickapoo, Navajo, Chumash, Winnebago, Ponac, Oneida, Creek, Mission and Sauk and Fox. Seven of the 37 played speaking parts, with the remainder acting as extras.

Casting presented a problem as the Screen Actors Guild and Screen Extras Guild had relatively few American Indians among their members. Producer Joel Rogosin also had to contend with Sainte-Marie's continued demands for authenticity regarding the portrayal of the Indians throughout the story. The general public had a stereotypical view of the Indian based on Hollywood movies that viewed them as primitive savages. Movies such as *Broken Arrow* (1950) attempted to provide a sympathetic view, but always insisted on a white actress starring as the "beautiful Indian squaw." Sainte-Marie decided it was time to redress the balance.

The story focuses on the Shoshone tribe and a dispute over the right of way of a cattle herd over Shoshone reservation land. An intelligent script by Stephen Lord and a fine performance by Sainte-Marie highlights the Shoshones' plight as they cling to their identity amid changing times. The presence of Jay Silverheels in the cast highlighted for the viewer the groundbreaking nature of the episode in attempting to break through stereotypes perpetuated in Silverheels' famous role as Tonto on TV's *The Lone Ranger.*

"Big Tiny" (7:13) teamed Trampas and David Sutton in an enjoyable comedy in which Sutton agrees to become engaged to a young woman he's just met in order to discourage the attentions of a persistent suitor. McClure and Hartman made a good comedy team, with the tall, lanky Sutton serving as the fall guy to the handsome, streetwise Trampas.

"Death Wait" (7:15) featured Trampas and Sutton in a story that shows McClure and Hartman's dramatic acting skills to good effect. An oft-told tale of a father seeking revenge for the death of his son includes Sutton feeling remorse and guilt over the shooting of the son in self-defense. Fine photography by Robert Wyckoff and sturdy direction by Charles S. Dubin do justice to a thoughtful script by Gerald Sanford.

The family element had always been vital to the success of *The Virginian.* MacDonnell had learned the hard way when season four's ratings plummeted due to a general lack of warmth and family atmosphere in the episodes from that season.

Frank Price always insisted that the centrality of the family was a major factor in the show's continuing success. MacDonnell took this one step further by giving the owner of Shiloh Ranch a wife. Unlike *The High Chaparral* (1967–71) which featured the young and beautiful Victoria Cannon, wife to ranch owner Big John Cannon, Clay Grainger's wife Holly was near his own age. Jeanette Nolan conveyed a full range of emotions as Holly. Her despair over the fate of Elizabeth in "Storm Over Shiloh" (7:23), desperation in the face of fear for her husband's life in "Sins of the Father" (8:22) and her forthright manner and honesty concerning Clay's friend in "The Orchard" (7:03) revealed a character of substance.

Female characters in TV Westerns often tended toward the sexually attractive, with seasoned actresses usually playing widows, spinsters or faithful wives in guest spots. It was unusual to see a recurring role for a veteran actress. Only *The Big Valley* (1965–69) provided a strong, mature female role model with Barbara Stanwyck as matriarch Victoria Barkley.

While MacDonnell's decision to include an elderly wife at Shiloh Ranch was welcomed by many viewers, others felt it disturbed the format of the show which relied on the widowed owner of Shiloh Ranch shuffling the demands of a successful working ranch with those of his teenage daughter or granddaughter.

Trampas and David Sutton were teamed up again in "Crime Wave in Buffalo Springs" (7:17). Boasting a large guest cast including Yvonne DeCarlo, Tom Bosley. Carrie Snodgress, Ann Prentiss and James Brolin, with music from the Irish Rovers, the story is a mixture of broad comedy, slapstick and drama. Not as restrained as "Big Tiny" (7:13) and lacking believability, "Crime Wave in Buffalo Springs" is harmless fun with an interesting scene in which Trampas and Geraldine (Prentiss) share chicken. Quite risqué for family viewing in 1969.

Joel Rogosin recalled, "Each of the producers tended towards a slightly different style. At the time, they thought some of the producers' shows were a little softer than others. Some were a little more comedic, some were a little more heavy drama. I remember that there was generally comment about that, that involuntarily the producers brought a certain personality to the episodes that they produced. I think I did 52 episodes over the years. If you look

Hand-signed photograph of Sara Lane on the set of *The Virginian* (courtesy Sara Lane).

at a body of group of shows of each of the producers, I think you would recognize that there's a difference among them. The ones I did tended to be on the more dramatic side."

Peter Deuel returned to Shiloh for his second guest appearance in "The Price of Love" (7:18). Deuel played a troubled young man, unable to handle any criticism of Clay and Holly Grainger, who cared for him as a child, without resorting to violence. Deuel gives a discerning performance as a man who considers love and loyalty of prime importance, even to the point of death.

"Storm Over Shiloh" (7:23) vividly illustrated the bond between the Virginian, Trampas and the Graingers. A strong family drama featuring Elizabeth Grainger, trapped in a mine shaft, the script by Frank Chase addresses themes of loyalty and self-sacrifice in one of the stronger episodes of the season. Sara Lane and Doug McClure give fine performances, reflecting on the true value of friendship and family.

The Grainger family history and series continuity was seriously compromised in "Girl in the Shadows" (7:24) when Clay Grainger revealed he had two brothers, neither of them John Grainger. A serious oversight that ignored Charles Bickford's contribution to the series, this spoiled an otherwise entertaining episode featuring Brenda Scott as a mind reader who plots to swindle Elizabeth Grainger out of half her inheritance.

"Fox, Hound and Widow McCloud" (7:25) was a rarity in that it served as a sequel to the previous season's "A Bad Place to Die" (6:09) with veteran actor Victor Jory reprising his role as Luke Nichols, now a fugitive from the law.

A Virginian-centered episode, "The Stranger" (7:26), in which he sets out to prove the innocence of a ranch hand (Shelley Novack) sentenced to hang for robbery and murder, rounded off the season.

More changes occurred at Shiloh Ranch at the start of season eight. David Sutton was gone. Although Hartman and McClure worked well together, Sutton was relegated to a minor role for the latter half of the seventh season. Hartman had an offbeat persona that wasn't ideally suited to *The Virginian*. Still under contract to Universal, he was transferred to the contemporary drama series *The Bold Ones: The New Doctors* (1969). A young up-and-coming actor named Tim Matheson replaced him.

Casting for new talent was an ongoing process on *The Virginian* with a steady turnover of cast members throughout the nine seasons. The auditioning process involved seeking out talent in local theater groups, on Broadway and Off-Broadway, West End theaters in London and the movies.

"We believed in putting promising young actors under contract and then developing their careers," explained Frank Price. "Rather than pay top prices for outside talent, we felt we'd do better growing our own. A woman talent executive named Monique James had the job of spotting such people, putting them under contract, and then insuring that they appeared in our series. Katharine Ross, Susan Clark, Katherine Crawford, Kent McCord and Martin Milner were some that readily come to mind. Later we had Tom Selleck. We put Selleck in five pilots before one finally clicked."

The eighth season got off to a promising start with "The Long Ride Home" (8:01) introducing Jim Horn (Tim Matheson) to Shiloh. The teenage sidekick of drifter Ben Stratton (Leslie Nielsen), who served as Horn's guardian and mentor, go their separate ways when Horn decides to stay at Shiloh Ranch.

Matheson was only 21 when he joined the cast and added a much-needed young face to Shiloh. His self-assured and easygoing manner was transferred to his Jim Horn character and mixed with the enthusiasm of youth.

"Tim Matheson is likable, has warmth and humor and is an excellent actor. Great comedy talent. He could have played Trampas had there not been a Doug McClure years earlier," remarked Frank Price.

"A Flash of Blindness" (8:02) highlighted a defenseless Virginian. Following a fall from his horse, the Virginian is blinded. Finding refuge in an isolated homestead, he must fight for his life when he discovers the owner of the homestead and his two sons have been rustling Shiloh-branded horses. Joseph Pevney's direction, Enzo A. Martinelli's photography and Leonard Rosenman's score combined to make this a memorable if flawed segment.

The story could be faulted for eroding the strength of character that the Virginian displayed throughout the seven previous seasons. His vulnerability, exposed through blindness, veered toward helplessness as the Virginian stumbled, like a lost child, through the countryside. In marked contrast, a blind Elizabeth Grainger displayed a greater sense of calm in the previous season's "Vision of Blindness."

John Dehner made a brief return to *The Virginian* as Marshall Teague in "Halfway Back to Hell" (8:03). This Trampas-centered episode sees him become head of a prison rehabilitation ranch following the death of a prisoner who was due to teach the other prisoners about ranching.

Tim Matheson's talents were highlighted in "The Family Man" (8:05) in which his affection for a pregnant young lady (Darleen Carr) turns to love when he delivers her baby in the absence of her husband (Frank Webb), who is running from the law.

James Drury starred as a frustrated suitor in the Joseph Pevney–directed segment "A Love to Remember" (8:07). Diane Baker featured as an artist-reporter from Boston who is more interested in a businessman, for reasons not linked with romance.

"A Touch of Hands" (8:11) saw Trampas doomed to yet another failed romance in a predictable story by John Dunkel. The story might have had more impact with the youthful Trampas of earlier seasons, but Doug McClure looked too mature for a young Belinda Montgomery. Frank Price was aware of the problems connected with aging actors.

"I realized early on that, as a producer, I had to reevaluate my judgment on the age of actors every so often. I decided to make a point of it every five years. If you are paying attention to the age issue, you realize there are certain stories you can no longer do credibly, but there are others that may be more appropriate that Doug could have done when younger. I always liked the episode with Doug and Katharine Ross, where her father tried to get Doug to marry the handicapped girl. That might still have worked, even with an older Doug.

"From the beginning I made a big point of age on *The Virginian*. I wanted the supporting players and the extras cast young. I insisted on the point that my approach was more authentic, historically. The West was settled by young people. I wanted the general store to have an enterprising young guy who'd just started his first store. It wasn't always possible, since some roles required older people and I had nothing against them being old if they were stars. But I didn't want the Medicine Bow street populated with the old 'Gower Gulch' ancients."

"You Can Lead a Horse to Water" (8:15) was a broad comedy in the style of season seven episodes that paired Hartman and McClure. Strother Martin and Elizabeth Hubbard provide the comedy relief along with McClure in a tale of horse thieves, robbery and romance. The comedy ranges between amusing and farcical in a story by Lois Hire that often forces the humor rather than letting it flow naturally. Joan Crawford made a rare

TV appearance in "Nightmare" (8:16), playing a woman beset by ill fortune: Her home is destroyed in a fire and she finds herself accused of manslaughter.

"Holocaust" (8:17), one of the last classic Shiloh-centered episodes, sees the ranch burned to the ground and rebuilt after a ruthless businessman tries to buy the place. Special effects master Albert Whitlock created the illusion of the destruction of the Shiloh house in an episode that was broadcast in certain markets as the final episode of the season. The story served as a fitting conclusion to the original series with all the cast members gathered for one final time to raise their glasses and say "cheers" to Shiloh.

"The Gift" (8:24) would be the final NBC episode under the title *The Virginian*. Broadcast March 18, 1970, the tale about an outlaw (Tab Hunter) looking for hidden loot, and a romantic entanglement involving Jim Horn and a former Trampas girlfriend (Julie Gregg), was an enjoyable if unremarkable conclusion to the season.

Although season eight contained good episodes, the ratings continued to fall. *The Virginian* would be renewed for another season but the classic format would be missing. The ninth season would involve major changes, not all for the better, and along with the changes would go the name of the series that had sustained the show for eight years.

8

The Men from Shiloh

Season Nine

"There was a different dynamic as the owners of Shiloh Ranch changed, but the spirit and the style of the show remained essentially the same. When it became *The Men from Shiloh*, it tended to become more anthologized. It didn't work."

—Joel Rogosin

Season nine heralded a new look for *The Virginian*, devoid of its former title and music. In effect, the ninth season had the look and feel of a completely new show. Frank Price was asked to supervise the revamped *Virginian* under its new name *The Men from Shiloh*. The name and revised format had been the joint decision of Sid Sheinberg, head of Universal TV, and Herb Schlosser, NBC program head. The format was directly influenced by their successful TV series *The Name of the Game* (1968), with rotating stars taking the lead on alternate weeks.

Besides the name change, the classic *Virginian* theme by Percy Faith would be dumped in favor of a new theme by Italian composer Ennio Morricone. Famous for his work with director Sergio Leone on a series of "Spaghetti Westerns" starring Clint Eastwood, Morricone had reinvented the traditional approach to scoring Westerns with a heavy use of chorus and unusual instrumentation, including the bullwhip.

Graphics, as used on *The Name of the Game* and *The High Chaparral*, would replace the traditional filmed "ride-in" credit sequence. Jack Cole's montage of photo images included Indians, milk churns and cattle but neglected Shiloh Ranch and set the tone for the new non–Shiloh-centered approach. *The Men from Shiloh* would emphasize "from" and very few episodes would take place at Shiloh Ranch.

Another key change: For the first time in its nine-year history, the show would be missing any feminine influence. Newcomers Stewart Granger and Lee Majors joined the cast, replacing the Grainger family and Jim Horn from season eight.

Frank Price commented on his role and the new approach:

"I was a vice-president of MCA Universal and was given responsibility for overseeing *The Men from Shiloh*. I was fully in charge but I took no screen credit, partially because I didn't want to. I was making the transition from being a producer to being an executive. Also, I undertook the project with grave doubts about the decision that was made to remake *The Virginian* into *The Men from Shiloh*. I thought it was a bad idea. I tried to get Herb Schlosser of NBC and Sid Sheinberg of MCA Universal to change their minds, but they were in love with patterning this revamped show after *The Name of the Game*.

Doug and Tané McClure share a horse on *The Men from Shiloh* set (courtesy Tané McClure).

"I said that the core strength of the show was always the family and this would hurt our ability to get a family feel to the show. They said to do it as *The Men from Shiloh*, with all the separate units to do individual star episodes. They had made deals with two new stars, Stewart Granger and Lee Majors. They didn't agree with my protest and wanted me to make sure it got done in accord with their new approach, but that I was free to add all the 'family' elements that I could. Not the most satisfactory answer, but that's what I attempted to do. The key component of the family—a Betsy—was gone."

Yet another major change involved the costumes of the Virginian and Trampas. The classic red-brown corduroy shirt and black leather vest was replaced with a heavy brown corduroy jacket and blue-striped cotton shirt. Trampas' appearance was altered even further with the addition of a mustache and a new costume that included boots worn over his trousers.

"Doug McClure and Lee Majors had been given considerable authority over their costuming," commented Price.

Production duties were split between four executive producers, each handling different characters. Herbert Hirschman and Edward J. Montagne would be in charge of Col. Mackenzie and Roy Tate episodes, Leslie Stevens and Glen A. Larson worked on Trampas episodes and Norman MacDonnell produced episodes featuring the Virginian.

Price hired proven and upcoming talent on the new show. "Norman MacDonnell was already in place and under contract. I brought in some favorite working partners: Leslie Stevens, Herb Hirschman, Glen Larson and Ed Montagne, who I used to work for on *The Tall Man*. Leslie Stevens and I partnered on the *It Takes a Thief* pilot. Somewhere around this time I put a promising young writer named Glen Larson with Leslie to break him in as a producer. Then later, Glen Larson and I partnered on the *Alias Smith and Jones* pilot.

"Leslie and Glen were the right choices to handle the Trampas episodes. I used Glen and Leslie on *McCloud* episodes when that series got in trouble. They were both excellent writers who were particularly good at humor.

"Herb Hirschman was a terrific guy. A gentleman who had excellent taste and was respected by all. He had a good record of quality and success in his work and his character and personality made him the right person to handle that tough, exacting English gentleman Stewart Granger. Herb was unflappable."

Price had reservations about the best way to introduce the characters of Col. Mackenzie and Roy Tate into *The Men from Shiloh*.

"The more challenging task was to introduce Stewart Granger and Lee Majors into this new format. Had I had the choice, I would have handled these introductions in a similar manner to the way I'd handled introducing Charles Bickford four years earlier. But the new format didn't permit that. Verbal guarantees had been made to Jimmy and Lee, so that separate producing units had to be set up for each actor."

Mackenzie's backstory told of time spent in Africa and with Gen. Gordon in the Crimea and Khartoum. Mackenzie returned to India to find his wife ill with malaria. Following her death, he refused to send his men into what he considered a suicidal battle and left Her Majesty's service. His path ultimately leading to Wyoming and Shiloh Ranch.

The premiere episode, "The West vs. Colonel Mackenzie" (9:01), broadcast on September 16, 1970, was atypical of the episodes to follow in that the story centered on Shiloh Ranch and included the Virginian, Trampas and Col. Mackenzie. A cold reception, by the Virginian and Trampas, to the new owner of Shiloh Ranch gives way to respect for the Englishman in charge by the episode's conclusion.

A good opener was followed by another episode of quality, "The Best Man" (9:02). This episode gave a hint of things to come, taking place on the Mexican border many miles from Shiloh Ranch. The episode also included the song "Take a Look Around." The song would feature again in the final Trampas episode, "The Legacy of Spencer Flats" (9:17), and in two more Glen A. Larson productions, *McCloud* (1970) and *Alias Smith and Jones* (1971).

Trampas appeared in six solo episodes in the ninth season, with "The Best Man" (9:01), "With Love, Bullets and Valentines" (9:04) and "Hannah" (9:13) among the most successful.

"With Love, Bullets and Valentines" (9:04) featured Jack Albertson and Tom Ewell as members of the aging Valentine Gang, planning one final robbery. A sharp script by Glen A. Larson and excellent performances by Albertson, Ewell and Art Carney make this an enjoyable episode.

Veteran actress Greer Garson starred in "Lady at the Bar" (9:08) as a lawyer defending Trampas on a murder charge. A solid, if unremarkable, courtroom drama benefited from a rare TV appearance by Garson, who was persuaded out of semi-retirement in Texas by Leslie Stevens.

"Hannah" (9:13) featured Lisa Gerritsen in a story written by her grandfather True Boardman. Of interest to trivia buffs is the fact Trampas can be seen reading the same dime novel used in "The Good Hearted Badman" from season six.

The integrity of Trampas in *The Men from Shiloh* was occasionally called into question when a mean-spirited streak and a certain dimwitted attitude surfaced.

The Virginian's character, by contrast, remained intact, in his first solo segment "Jenny" (9:03), guest starring Janet Leigh as ex-girlfriend Jenny Davis. Excellent location photography by Enzo A. Martinelli and good acting from Leigh lifts a familiar storyline of outlaws seeking hidden loot.

The Virginian's six solo episodes also included the interesting and thoughtful "Experiment at New Life" (9:10), starring Vera Miles as a woman caught up in communal marriage and the Virginian's attempts to stop it.

Roy Tate was introduced in the fifth episode, "The Mysterious Mr. Tate" (9:05), which also featured Col. Mackenzie. The episode sees Mackenzie rescue Tate from a lynch mob and offer him a job at Shiloh Ranch.

Katherine Crawford worked with Lee Majors on "The Animal" (9:16) in a story about a deaf-mute Indian being pursued over an alleged murder. Crawford recalled, "Lee Majors was a good friend of Frank and myself when I worked on that episode. Lee is very good to work with. He's always a gentleman, and is fun and funny. He's a fine actor and a good guy. The actor, Rudy Ramos, who played the young Indian boy was very impressive. He was bright, philosophical and interesting offscreen."

"I liked Lee as an actor," Price adds. "*The Men from Shiloh* was not something Lee wanted to do, but he went along with the strong desires of Sheinberg and Schlosser who wanted him in their new concept. They assured him he'd get top notch 'star treatment' and have his own unit."

Tate also featured in "The Price of a Hanging" (9:09) by *Virginian* regular Frank Chase. The somber, well-told tale sees Tate attempting to uncover the truth behind a murder in order to save a doctor from the gallows; Mackenzie's life also hangs in the balance. The episode featured one of Tom Tryon's final screen appearances before he retired from acting to concentrate on a successful writing career.

Stewart Granger as Col. Mackenzie, the new owner of Shiloh Ranch, had an imposing presence, his distinguished English accent giving him the necessary authority to make Mackenzie convincing. Granger initially approached his first venture into regular work on a television series with enthusiasm, but soon had second thoughts. Granger was at odds with the fast production schedule and the lack of development in his character over the course of the series. In an August 1970 interview for the *Los Angeles Times*, he commented:

> You'd see him buy the ranch, then the growth with sometimes setbacks of his relationship with Doug and Jim—their suspicions of this bloody Briton ... But they say it can't work that way. There won't be any progression where you could see any growth in the character.

Frank Price had fond memories of working with Granger.

"Stewart Granger and I got along particularly well, possibly because I was familiar with and liked his movies. In college, I saw and loved *King Solomon's Mines* [1950]. Then I got to know Stewart Granger well when we did *The Men from Shiloh* and we had fun discussing the movie. At Columbia Pictures, I developed the script for *Out of Africa*, partially out of my long love for *King Solomon's Mines*. I finally got *Out of Africa* made when I ran Universal Pictures, so for me it was a bit of an homage to one of my favorite old movies.

"I was saddened when Jimmy* died. I last saw him at a Royal Film Premiere we had in London for *Gandhi*. As I recall, Queen Elizabeth was the Royal attendee. Jimmy looked great, of course, and we reminisced about *The Men from Shiloh* and I got to tell him again how much I loved him in *King Solomon's Mines*. He had a larger-than-life presence and commanding persona. Most of the great old Hollywood stars had that. Charlie Bickford certainly did. Maybe MGM gave them special vitamins."

Two episodes of the final season were filmed outside of the U.S., near Mexico City.

James Drury wearing his hat from *The Men from Shiloh* (courtesy James Drury).

Stewart Granger's real name was Jimmy Stewart, which was changed for obvious reasons.

"We never left Southern California except in the ninth year because of, I think, tax problems, " recollected James Drury. "Stewart Granger elected to have two segments shot in Old Mexico in Durango so he could get out of the country. He had to leave the country for a certain amount of time every year to maintain his tax status. I was not involved in those shows. I did not go with him."

"I made a trip to Mexico City to meet with Stewart Granger," said Price. "He was unhappy about various things connected with the production and I had to fly down and do some spreading of oil on troubled waters."

One of the problems concerned fellow actor John Saxon, who recalled working on "The Regimental Line" (9:21).

"The most interesting *Virginian* guest starring role for me was in *The Men from Shiloh*. First of all, it was a unique matter to receive a television script a whole month before the start of shooting. The reason for this was that in a manner of speaking I had a dual role with dual accents. The character first appears as a rough-and-tough Irishman in the U.S. Cavalry who speaks with an Irish brogue until Granger observes him under a microscope and declares he is an upper class, Sandhurst-educated English officer who fled from the field of battle against the Pathans (in Afghanistan I presume) and, in doing so, disgraced the family and regiment.

"Which is why the officer assumed a new identity in the U.S. and, when confronted by Granger, confesses he is the English officer in his upper class Sandhurst accent. And why I was chosen to play the role and given a month to work those accents.

"Granger insisted doing those accents was impossible to do. And, no doubt, that was why the producer came to my hotel suite with the recommendation that I not even try. I answered with, 'Tell me how else can an upper class Englishman who pretends to be Irish be played.'"

"I was asked to try to play it that way. I replied that I'd rather fly from Mexico City back to home, and they could ask someone else to try.

"The short of it was I did the accents quite well. So well that Granger, annoyed with that fact, attempted to throw me off stride by mocking me from the sidelines and I knew I had won my point. Near the end of filming, I came nose to nose with Granger, and he turned and left the set."

Frank Price recounted his version of events.

"To understand my meeting with Jimmy, I must tell you something of the art of dealing with stars. First, you can never flatter them too much. Second, you can never flatter them too much.

"You must remember that stars in a successful series have all the power. If they don't like a scene or a script, they can maintain they can't say the lines. If they don't like the executive producer or producer, they can bar him from the set, as the *Bonanza* guys did to David Dortort.

"In dealing with stars, I saw my role as roughly equivalent to the role of the lion tamer in a circus. The stars are the lion or the tiger. I, the lion tamer, enter the cage. I carry a whip and a chair. These can make noise and be swung around, but they are only puny devices to intimidate the beasts. If the lion really decides to go for you, these devices offer no protection and the lion will get you for lunch. So it is very important to make the lion believe you are more powerful than he is.

"When I met Jimmy in that hotel, I had taken the first step to controlling him. I, the top executive connected with the show, had flown to Mexico City to deal personally with his complaints. That massaged his ego. I wasn't handling it by telephone. Had I tried to handle this matter on the phone, he would have felt free to lose his temper, to make irrational demands and possibly hang up in a fury.

"By meeting with him, listening to his complaints and engaging him in conversations that flattered him, I was able to reason with him. It helped that I genuinely liked Jimmy. I enjoyed his company and his movie career tales. He had an aura about him in dealing with the Mexican hotel staff that commanded immediate attention and obedience. He expected them to cater to his exacting demands. And they did. He knew how to handle Colonials. In him, I saw how the English were able to rule the world.

"He covered his various complaints, including the one about John Saxon, but he sort of talked himself out of making anything more out of the matter. I explained to him what a nice guy John Saxon was and how Jimmy, as an important and admired star, had to give him a chance. Jimmy seemed pacified, so I said goodbye and returned to L.A."

The episode was written by Price's good friend Gene L. Coon, who had worked with him previously on the third season episode "Showdown" (3:29) and the espionage series *It Takes a Thief* (1968).

"He was a complete pro, a writer with great talent and a good producer. Gene was one of those rare writers who could handle action adventure and humor well," recalled Price.

The final episode of the series, "Jump-Up" (9:24) found Roy Tate serving hard labor for a murder he didn't commit. A rambling script by Ron Bishop included some good scenes for Lee Majors, but overall the episode didn't serve as a fitting conclusion to the series. James Drury made an appearance in the final scenes of the episode and the series. The Virginian and Col. Mackenzie, arms around each other's shoulders, walk into the Shiloh house for the final time.

Despite good ratings, *The Men from Shiloh* was cancelled by NBC in May 1971 and television's first 90-minute Western was laid to rest.

"I think the show had maybe burned itself out a little bit. It's tough to keep a show on the air for nine years," remarked Joel Rogosin. "Even with multiple producers and rotating actors. In nine years, the climate in the industry changes considerably. So it had its moment in the sun and it was very successful. And when it was good, it was very good, and when it was bad, it was ordinary. You have to take into account the hours of entertainment that were provided. You could never do a Broadway show that would have as much demands on it as a television series."

Price expressed his feelings on *Men from Shiloh*'s demise: "I think the format got in the way of our making the show as good as we could have. But we did get a substantial 34 share for the season in our ratings. Generally enough for a renewal. So we succeeded in our mission. Schlosser, though, was tired of the show and did not renew it. As with all long-lived shows, the demographics were older. It took years before NBC achieved ratings that good again in that time slot.

"Everyone did the best job they could and we made good episodes. But demographics led to our demise. Our average audience age was too old and Herb Schlosser never really understood or liked the show. William Paley at CBS kept *Gunsmoke* on the air 19 years, I think, and their demographics got well up there. So off we went. No scripts were prepared for the following season since renewal was such an iffy proposition all along. I would not have stayed with the series had it been renewed.

"I did feel that if I had been able to redo the show as *The Virginian* I could have caused the series to generate substantially higher ratings than we did and have done a better, more entertaining show. I would have given Stewart Granger a family."

9

Production and Location

"Shiloh Ranch was a beautiful location. The heart and soul of the show was the location."

—Joel Rogosin

Producing a weekly show for television is always a pressurized environment. When that show is a 90-minute prime time Western series, the pressure becomes that much more intense. Westerns involve location work with horses and cattle added to the mix, and production can be halted by injury or bad weather. Budgets and deadlines must be met and excuses for failing to meet these must be kept to a minimum.

Frank Price explained the filming and production process used on *The Virginian*. It began with the writer.

"All the producers on the show were familiar with the professional writers in the community. New writers joined that community constantly, but the working pros tended to be the same people, although we were always hoping to nab terrific new writers. We all, each producer, made our individual judgments on these writers, judging some excellent for our show and some unacceptable.

"Each producer would recommend writers that they wanted to work with and I would either veto or approve the choice. The producers and I all came up with ideas that we would like to do and we would discuss those ideas with writers to see who inspired them with which idea. Or writers might come up with ideas of their own that we either liked or didn't like. Sometimes we would like the idea and give them an assignment. Sometimes we might say to the writer that we have an idea to pitch to them and we would explain the story we wanted to do. If the writer got stimulated by the idea, then we'd make a deal with him or her to write an outline for us.

"We never gave an outline to a writer. I came up with a number of stories and also did rewrites on a lot of scripts, but I had a policy of never seeking credit for this work. It made my relationship better with the freelance writer if they didn't think I was competing with them."

Production numbers were assigned after a writer's idea or outline for an episode was deemed good enough to hire them. A production number for an episode enabled an accounting place to charge to that episode the money the writer was paid. All charges incurred during writing and pre-production would be placed against the number.

Writers didn't work to a character guide but were expected to have knowledge of past episodes. Individual producers were responsible for "series memory" with Frank Price or Norman MacDonnell taking control of final checking.

The script would then go to the production manager who would determine the best approach to shooting, based on the budget available. The production manager would break down the script, listing every requirement in every scene. If a script demanded location filming, costs would take into account travel to and from location for cast and crew, accommodations at the location including special provisions for the star players, and fees and permission requirements to film in restricted areas or national parks. Exotic locations would generally be represented by local locations and/or stock footage.

A good writer would take into account the limitations of a television budget when writing his script, thus making the job of the production manager that much easier.

"I, and the producers, stayed in close communication with our production manager, often credited as the unit manager," Price explained. "I would give George Santoro, who handled this job in our early years, a verbal description of a story that was being written, detailing the general nature of the episode and anything unusual that might be called for, so he could begin the budgeting process early and anticipate those special requirements.

"Perhaps he would send location scouts out to find the kind of terrain that would be called for. Once I could give him a first draft, with verbal notes on what might change in future rewrites, he could do a real budget. The production or unit manager worked out of his office, which was located in the main physical production office. The man in overall charge of physical production on the Universal lot was Paul Donnelly. He had an overall responsibility to supervise all productions, from physical production and cost standpoint through the unit manager.

"Once we had a director signed to the episode, he then went over the production plan with the production manager. In addition to consulting with the production manager, the director would meet with the art director, location manager and cinematographer to scout possible locations before making a final decision in consultation with them. The decision to use existing sets or build new ones was also taken into account by the production manager. The process proceeded with the completed shooting script.

"A script provides a combination of exterior and interior scenes, and it provides action and dialogue sequences. Once we had a reasonably complete shooting script in hand, we would time it by reading it aloud and estimating the timing of action sequences. We also kept a scene-by-scene timing as we shot. I always preferred to shoot 'long'—to have more footage than we needed—so that we had flexibility in editing and could get rid of stuff that didn't work."

Pre-production preparation required a minimum of eight or nine days for a skilled director familiar with the show, such as Don McDougall or Abner Biberman. A longer period of three to four weeks or longer was usually preferable for a director new to the series.

Another aspect of pre-production, wardrobe, was handled by department head Vincent Dee, with assistance from Burton Miller.

"I worked closely with Vince on all costuming," commented Price, "since I had to approve it all. If any of our continuing cast wanted to change any part of their wardrobe, I had to be consulted to approve it. The wardrobing of guest stars had to be approved. Vince Dee was a good friend. I still have my *Virginian* cowboy boots, which Vince gave me out of the wardrobe stock."

"Burton Miller became a good friend. He designed my wedding dress," recalled Katherine Crawford. "I was very fond of him. The wardrobe building was fun. They kept a large number of period costumes there. I loved to walk through the aisles and look at them all. I'd often spot ones I had already worn in one show or another, as had others!"

With color relatively new to TV in the early 1960s, Universal employed a color consultant to check color coordination and the manner in which certain colors transferred to the television screen. Price considered the consultants, Alex Quiroga and Robert Brower, to be more of a hindrance than a help.

"I considered the 'color consultant' work as a scam. At Universal, we were restricted to certain basic colors for years. There was a particularly annoying green that was used as background for many sets. I suffered through the color consultant on *The Virginian*. But when I made the *It Takes a Thief* two hour pilot, the director Leslie Stevens and I challenged the color restrictions. After a lot of internal studio fighting, the post of color consultant was done away with. If there ever had been a real reason to have such a consultant, that reason had disappeared over the years. And those ideas tended to make our shows look drab. *It Takes a Thief* revolutionized Universal's color approach. And we got rid of that green for good."

Frank Edmunds served as casting director, checking out local legitimate theater and movies for new and promising talent. He would arrange for interviews and readings with directors, producers and Frank Price. Although he chose the talent to be interviewed, he didn't have the power to pick actors. His job was to suggest possibilities for various roles on *The Virginian*.

A continuing problem with the casting process was the possibility that the actors might be lying about their abilities to ride and handle a horse.

"Actors, before being hired, would assure the casting directors and our directors that they knew how to ride, " explained Price. "Once on location, when they had to get on a horse and perform, it would become apparent that they lied to us. But it was too late to replace them so a double might be used in their place, or they could be given some rudimentary instructions that sufficed for minimal action in the saddle.

"Poor riders look terrible as they bounce on their saddles riding into a scene. Most times I was able to cut away from actors who rode like amateurs. It was embarrassing for us to show working ranch hands in the West riding like rank tenderfeet. There was no simple, inexpensive way to learn whether or not these actors could actually ride. They would want the job and their agents would swear to the truth of their lies."

Price often insisted in cutting unessential dialogue from the script before the shoot began, preferring minimum dialogue to tell the story.

"I was encouraged in this by Lee J. Cobb in the first season. He complained to me when the dialogue said too much of what his attitude was or what he was thinking. He preferred to act those things, not state them. It made for harder writing, but it was worth it because it made for better scenes."

With pre-production complete, all was prepared and ready for the shooting of an episode.

"There was no requirement for a specific amount of footage for any one day," described Price. "That would not be a practical approach. *The Virginian*'s 90-minute format actually required 75 minutes of dramatic film, including the opening and end credits and title. Exterior action scenes generally require much more shooting time for the same amount of screen time. Interior dialogue scenes eat up a lot of screen time with much less shooting.

"I tried to develop scripts that could be shot with a basic approach. In general, in order to get a show done on budget, we devoted one or two days to nearby locations to get visual scope. It might be the Bell Ranch, Iverson Ranch, Albertson Ranch, Corriganville, Vasquez Rocks or the Disney Ranch. There was also the Conejo Ranch at a greater distance that we went to if we needed greater scope. Conejo was where *Wagon Train* had shot its big scope shots.

"The drawback to Conejo was that it took more time to travel there and that ate into our crew time. Crews went on the time clock when they left the studio on their way to a location and continued to get paid while they worked and for all the time traveling back to the studio. So getting to and from location was costly.

"Cattle, which we rarely used, were rented from ranchers where we shot or at least nearby. Often, in a trail drive episode, we would rent a small number of cattle that matched the cattle in stock footage of big cattle drives. We would wardrobe our players to match the small figures seen in the stock footage. So, by using the big cattle drive footage, then cutting to closer shots of our main players with some of our rented cattle milling around them, we could create scenes of much greater scope than we could afford to shoot, had we needed to actually shoot giant herds against *Big Country* scenery. Matching all these shots takes careful attention and skill, but done well the effect is great. Done poorly, it all looks fake."

"We filmed at Iverson's Ranch and where Westlake Village is now, with $2,000,000 homes out there. We chased cattle all over that country. That was all open range land at the time," added James Drury.

Actors and actresses arriving at the studio for the day's filming first had to go into makeup, hairstyling and wardrobe. Jack Barron and Florence Bush served as department heads with Bud Westmore and Larry Germain in charge of makeup and hairstyles respectively. Michael Westmore joined Universal in 1961 on an apprenticeship and often worked uncredited applying makeup to guest stars such as Katherine Crawford.

Crawford says, "Actresses usually had 6:30 a.m. calls, meaning they were to appear in makeup at 6:30, to be ready for the first shot at 8:00. However, if the company was going on location that day, it might be earlier, 6:00 or 5:45, depending on the drive time to the location. Makeup, hair and wardrobe usually took 90 minutes for actresses. The actors would usually arrive 45 minutes later for their makeup. 'Body Makeup' was required for exposed necks, arms, legs and bodies. The series leads had their own trailers where makeup was applied. A series lead 'perk.' A mini-home.

"I remember Bud Westmore as a very warm, sweet man. He would assign the makeup people to the shows. His son, Mike Westmore, was my makeup man, and he was wonderful. Also Leo Lotito. I really liked him. He was special to me. Larry Germain was the one who finally cut my hair when I got brave enough to do it. It was an 'event.' He grabbed my hair at the base of my neck and just cut and held out my pony tail in his hand! He was good and very nice to me. He had a lot of charm. The people in makeup and hair deserve more recognition than they get.

"My memory of the makeup room, or the make-up area on the set, is of the dark stage away from the bright set you were working in, with the little table set up among the debris of cables and fake walls and lighting hardware. And the lights that came from the table that would shine on the makeup and the hair people, like a fireplace, as they sat around it. They were always there, and happy to see you. It was like having a home, where you knew you would be fine again, no matter what. My memory isn't of me in the mirror, or what problems we might have had regarding the show. Just them, and their wonderful faces, and how I felt with them.

"They did a lot of hair work on men in *The Virginian*. By hair work I mean the kind where you glue on sideburns, beards, mustaches and baldness! They would use makeup for beard stubble, though. Just stipple it on with a little sponge or brush."

Lee J. Cobb, Roberta Shore, Charles Bickford and John McIntire all wore hair pieces or attachments. James Drury, although balding, didn't wear a hair piece for almost five years.

"He grew his hair very long in the back where he had hair and he combed it forward to conceal his bald pate," said Price. "He once rode into a scene without a hat and, under those conditions, his hair flapped up and down. I had to cut away from him in editing the film so that this hair action didn't show. I urged Jim to get a hair piece. I finally persuaded him to let us do a test. We would test it, confidentially on film. But he insisted that his girlfriend make the final decision. She was an intelligent woman, so I agreed to the condition. However, when we saw the test, she sided with Jim against having the piece.

"Later in the season, however, Jim asked for a private meeting with me and he showed up wearing a cap. When we were totally alone, he took off the cap, revealing that he was now totally bald. He explained that he had just returned from a rodeo appearance in Calgary, Canada, where he and a stuntman friend had a disagreement that led to a fight. The stuntman had grabbed Jim's longish black hair and it came out by the roots. So Jim now wanted a wig quickly. We were about to shoot. This time we raced against our production deadline to get him an acceptable hair piece. We kept the hat on until the piece was ready."

Another vital aspect of production involved stuntmen, wranglers and doubles. The Virginian employed many, including Bill Babcock, Chuck Courtney, Gary Combs, Harper Flaherty, Dick Shane, Bill Raymond, Monty Laird, Jerry Summers, Fred Carson and Clyde Howdy. Stagecoach work demanded the best stuntmen. Price described the work.

"The stuntmen I used regularly for difficult stagecoach work were Joe Yrigoyen and Boyd Stockman. Joe was the best and if I couldn't get him, I'd get Boyd. Stagecoaches look best when they have six horses pulling them. That's called a 'six-up.' And you always see that in 'A' Westerns. 'B' Westerns used 'four-ups.' That doesn't give you the great look. I preferred always to use a six-up. Bringing a stagecoach with six galloping horses into our Western Street and making the turn to stop at the saloon was a tricky and tough assignment. But it looked great on film. And it added energy and excitement to something fairly routine. Joe and Boyd were the only ones that could handle six horses under those conditions. If neither was available, we eliminated the shot. It was too dangerous."

Stunt doubles Dick Shane and Harper Flaherty became regulars in the Shiloh bunk house in the later MacDonnell seasons. A Universal Studios press release on Shane described him as doing "dangerous" stunt work for James Drury, John Dehner and Stewart Granger in addition to "portraying himself" on *The Virginian*.

"The stunt doubles on TV series became the retinue of the series stars," Price explained. "They were stand-ins and doubles for the actors, so they became best buddies with the actors, whose favorable attitude toward them could result in the double or stuntman getting a bump in his pay. It was a hierarchal world of its own. The stunt men were generally highly skilled, athletic and daring people who knew their business well. It was in their own interest to maximize any contribution they might make to the action on an episode. The more they did, the more money they received."

Two or three days of the schedule would be devoted to back lot locations, including Shiloh Ranch, Falls Lake (which had a lake and waterfall that could be turned on), the Western Street (with another lake and a riverboat), the Mexican Street and the Medicine Bow street (which included the train).

Price: "Our train could only arrive in town or depart. We had no open country in which to run the train. Therefore an actual train sequence, such as we used only occasionally, required us to go to a very distant location. There was a suitable train with mountain country scenery up by Bishop."

Guest stars would usually be interviewed and hired only two or three days prior to filming. Katherine Crawford described the filming process from the viewpoint of an actor on an average working day on *The Virginian*.

"When you start work on a show, there is not a day where all the actors rehearse, as there is in theater. You arrive the first morning and meet the other actors in the set for the first scene. If the first scene shot is the last one of the show, and perhaps the key moment, and you have never met the other actors before, that's par for the course. The schedule is set up by the production office based on locations first. You stay in a place or on a particular stage until all the scenes for that area are done.

"Then they schedule based on who is in the scene. They like to use actors for the fewest days, so they clump certain actors' scenes together. That doesn't apply to guest actors who usually work every day. So your scenes are scrambled around, relative to their placement in the script. In the first run-through, problems are worked out and your 'marks' are put on the floor. Then the camera and lights are moved into place, which takes 10 to 20 minutes. During that time you meet with the script girl who tells you what you have to 'match' from any scenes that have been shot. When the camera is ready the assistant director calls, 'Actors on set!' Then there's another 'rehearsal,' or two, and then shooting begins.

"You always begin with the master shot, showing the whole scene and all the actors together. Then the camera is moved around to get smaller groups or the individual actors' shots. There are 'over the shoulder' shots, meaning the camera faces you from behind the other actor's shoulder, showing his back and your face. And there are individual close-ups.

"All of these shots had to be done for each scene. If they weren't, then the editor might not have coverage on an actor for a certain moment that was important. So they always shot all the different camera positions for every scene for each actor. Five or six 'takes' is common. So a simple four-person scene would require many camera moves and repeated 'takes' before being done.

"One result of repeating the scene so many times is that the energy can go out of the scene. So actors usually do a deliberately flat or underplayed performance when they are behind the camera, so as to be fresh and energized for their shot on camera. That's not selfish. It's necessary. Actors are all okay with it. Once during a large scene, at the beginning of my career, when my close-ups were not going to be done until after several other actors' close-ups, the director said to me, 'Katherine, save it,' because he knew I was doing a full performance each time. I was grateful to him.

"The set is filled with people. The grips are in the rafters, balancing on skinny boards and setting up the lights for each actor and the whole scene. They stay up there, all day. The script girls stand behind the camera and watch everything you do. They have to be able to tell you when you flicked your hair off your shoulder, or crossed your arms, or whatever, in the master shot so that you will do the same thing in the close-up and over-the-shoulder shots. You learn quickly not to be fidgety in a scene.

"A working day can go on for 12 hours, or more. The only rule is that you have to have 12 hours between calls. A Screen Actors Guild rule. So if you worked until midnight, you wouldn't be called until noon the next day."

The eight-day schedule for each episode involved much forward planning, as Price explained.

"Once we started a season and were in production, our intention was to start a new show immediately on the day after we finished shooting an episode. The new show would have an entirely different crew and director. We shot Monday through Friday, with Saturday and Sunday off. The overtime charges for shooting on Saturday were not worth it. Also, since the cast and crew basically worked 12-hour days, they needed the weekend to recover."

Shooting on a Saturday occasionally took place when the cast and crew were at a distant location and it made sense to use their time rather than just waste the weekend. The problem of cast and crew suffering the lingering effects of an over-indulgent weekend resulted in the decision to try and avoid starting new episodes on a Monday.

Shooting two episodes simultaneously or overlapping them in order to meet deadlines was normal practice. Price continued.

"Our scripts had to be created with the objective of keeping ahead of air dates in mind. If we had Jim or Doug starring heavily in one episode, then we had to use him lightly, perhaps in only a scene or two, in an episode that shot simultaneously. The overlapping was something that happened constantly, but there wasn't a specific pattern to it. Our objective with our leading actors was to use them together enough to keep the family feel and the relationships alive, but then follow the one or two leads through their own starring roles in a particular episode."

The Shiloh Ranch set was an integral component of *The Virginian* that served as a focus for the Shiloh "family" and ranch hands. Built specifically for the show on a plot of land on the Universal back lot, the standing set was situated off the U.S.101 Hollywood Freeway.

Price recalled, "We took over that area from that huge historical epic that Stanley Kubrick directed, *Spartacus*. That's where they had all the crosses up in the end scene. The set wasn't so close to the freeway that we could pick up freeway noise. One of the good things

Dick Shane, stunt double for James Drury (courtesy Dick Shane).

Tané McClure hugs father Doug on the Shiloh Ranch set. Note the buggy parked outside the bunkhouse (courtesy Tané McClure).

about the ranch set was that we could shoot in any direction and see no signs of civilization other than our ranch."

Price described his drive to the Shiloh Ranch set.

"Almost everyone had to be driven back to the set because of teamster rules. Since I was executive producer, I could drive my car to the set by special exemption from the union. I would drive from the Black Tower to where a road went up the hill to the right. I would proceed up that road, past the fire station, then past Laramie Ranch, continuing on to crest the hill.

"At that crest you looked down at the ranch and its little valley. The Big House was to the left and the bunkhouse was to the right. Behind them, as I recall, was possibly a barn, corral and other outbuildings."

Like all standing sets on *The Virginian,* Shiloh Ranch and its buildings were facades. The appearance of weight and structure was illusory as the walls and roofs were of a very light construction and held up by long wooden braces on the inside. Actors would enter the house through an exterior door to be greeted by a bare wooden platform that barely sustained their weight.

Interior scenes would be filmed on a sound stage where various rooms of the Shiloh house and bunkhouse had been erected. Interior sets had thin, removable walls to allow for different camera angles, with sets and actors being lit by overhead lights. Sound stages were soundproofed to eliminate outside noise and facilitate a smooth shoot. Our final four or five days would be shot on sound stages, where we could generate a lot of screen time with dialogue scenes that were far easier to shoot than outdoor scenes and much more controllable than outdoor dialogue scenes. We tried to do a segment in eight days. Sometimes we had to go nine, even ten days, if a show was just too difficult or we encountered unexpected problems. I think by the time we reached *The Men from Shiloh* years, we were customarily doing them in nine days.

"There were always exceptions to our pattern of shooting. As I recall, Bill Witney came up with a production plan for the 'Beloved Outlaw' script that allowed him to do much of the shooting for the picture up in Red Rock country with a tiny, and therefore cheap, crew. They shot all the horse action footage with Sara Lane and her stunt double (the double doing most of the work on horseback). So he was able to do practically the whole show on a fairly distant location for the same cost that we incurred under our normal schedule."

Price often applied a method of using alternating directors on episodes, but it had its limitations. Filming an episode involved the major part of production, but it still needed much work before it was ready for screening. Post-production completed the process.

"Basically, post-production was done in the amount of time available to get it done," continued Price. "That meant we had much more time at the beginning of each season and less time as we made each episode and got closer to season's end. The shot film had to be edited by the film editor. Various editing changes were made in subsequent versions of the assemblage."

Editing is one aspect of post-production that is often vital to the success of a particular segment, but is overshadowed by the work of the director, who may not be creatively involved with the editing process on a television production.

Price: "Generally the editing process is taken for granted and ignored. It is truly amazing what skillful editing can do to improve or even save a picture. I place great, great emphasis on editing which goes well beyond pacing. The film editor makes creative, artistic choices in how he puts the individual shots together in the proper sequence to make a film. Once an assemblage has been created, then the work starts on editing the film.

"In training the producers who worked with me, I explained always that they must treat the editing process just as they would if they were starting a script. They must start fresh, without preconceived ideas about what they intended to accomplish through the script. They must see in the assembled film what they actually have.

"All put together, the film and its many scenes may vary greatly from what they intended. They must look at it dispassionately and spot everything in it that doesn't work. That material must then be fixed or removed. Perhaps it can be fixed by editing changes or tricks. Perhaps something needs to be reshot. But at this stage, the film must be treated like a first draft and you are writing a revised draft using film instead of a typewriter.

"I got on-the-job training from Roy Huggins in editing film. He was brilliant at it and I felt he taught me a lot. I asked him where he learned it so well. He said Bill Orr taught him. Bill Orr was Jack Warner's son in law. And where did Bill Orr learn? Jack Warner taught him, said Roy."

"David O'Connell was, for years, head of editorial, so all film editors, their assistants and any related functions, such as the stock library, came under his administrative control. For the studio as a whole, David hired and fired editors. He sought out good ones that were capable of working under our fast-paced system. Dave assigned editors to the various series, in consultation with the producers.

"If you were a strong executive producer, you got what you wanted. If not, you got who Dave had available. Post-production was therefore his responsibility, although the Music Department, under Stanley Wilson, functioned as its own entity, with separate budgets and controls."

Pacing in the editing process dictates the way we view the finished episode or film. Action sequences, comedy and drama all require different approaches. Price explains the pacing he preferred to use on *The Virginian.*

"Perhaps because of the quick cutting and fast pacing that starts in their lives with *Sesame Street*, young audiences today are addicted to the type of film seen on MTV music videos. Staccato action, jump cuts, etc. On *The Virginian* I preferred not to try to dazzle the audience with stylistic tricks. I played it straightforward. We were deliberate. If I had the Virginian ride through the countryside, I would take the time to see beauty shots of the country. I might well cut to shots of the wildlife as he rode past to give the audience an idea of what the land was like. I loved to see a stagecoach traversing the great open spaces of the American West and I would allow time for the distant image of a tiny stage pulled by six horses to pass by, underlining how small we humans are against these vast lands. Comedy requires pacing that is faster and moves the story along."

Picture, dialogue, effects and music were synchronized together at the dubbing stage.

"In exterior shooting, it was generally judged more effective to record the actors' voices and the existing effects, such as horses' hooves, as a temporary track while the scenes were being photographed. It would be too difficult to wait for perfect silence before shooting, so various minor sounds were tolerated. Once the picture had been edited, actors reported to the looping stage to rerecord the lines they spoke on location. At Universal, we had a simpler and lower cost process that we used for looping. We did not run the picture track for the actors so they could see their lips moving, as well as hear their voices through headphones on their ears. We only used the headphones and depended on the skills of the actors under the supervision of a looping editor, to match their spoken words. If they didn't succeed in matching their mouth movement exactly, then their lips would stop moving before their voice finished, or vice versa. A mismatch created a rubbery look to lip movement."

Katherine Crawford described the looping process from her personal viewpoint as a guest star on *The Virginian*.

"Looping was something done by every actor that had a single line that was spoken outside. Everything recorded outside had to be redone later, to remove any extraneous sounds, or just to achieve better sound quality. Looping was done after there was a final cut of the show, so it was done two or three weeks after shooting.

"They call you into the looping room, which is soundproof, and you stand in front of a microphone and listen to a 'loop' of a line you spoke in the scene and you repeat it precisely as you heard it. Then it comes around again and you keep hearing and repeating until the two looping guys nod and say, 'Next.' They are in a room on the other side of a soundproof window and they speak through a speaker to you.

"All the lines shot in exteriors are looped. I repeat that because it's amazing to think of all those lines spoken outside on *The Virginian*. And they usually look pretty natural by the time you see the finished show. That's a credit to the sound men. And the actors too. It's a hard job to reproduce part of a cry out or a laugh that was perfect in the original version. You have to duplicate it a little bit at a time. Then the next bit in the next loop with the same emotion and sense of continuity. You have to keep the bits short, no more than one normal sentence at a time, or you won't be able to get the timing right. But it's not always that hard. Lots of easy lines are there too.

"Jim and Doug and all the regulars would have spent a good bit of their lives in that little room. So next time you watch an episode of *The Virginian*, watch out for the exterior scenes. All the sound is mixed in and put together. However, some 'exterior' scenes were shot inside. The shots in 'A Bride for Lars' with me and Doug at night by a campfire hearing the wolves were shot inside. But you usually can tell. The love scene where the Virginian proposes by the river in 'Felicity's Spring' was looped because it was shot outside at the Disney Ranch."

With looping completed, the new voice track was cut together from the dubbed lines to match the picture track. A separate effects track that included horses' hooves, footsteps, etc., was created and the final mix of voice, sound effects and recorded music blended together in a soundproof recording chamber, referred to as a dubbing stage.

"It was important that the music not drown out the voices and the sound effects sound real and not overpowering. This step was critical and was done under the supervision of the producer."

The final stages of post-production involved the lab, negative cutting, trial prints, color timing and final print to deliver to the network.

"Post-production was all a matter of managing the number of hours and the overtime costs," concluded Price.

Following the demise of the TV Western in the mid–1970s the Shiloh Ranch set was demolished, to make way for the continuing expansion of the Universal Studios tour.

10

Lee J. Cobb

Judge Henry Garth

Lee J. Cobb was a character actor with range. He could play villains and men of high principles with equal conviction. The heavy lips inevitably turned to a scowl in times of deep thought or moral indignation. His role as Judge Henry Garth on *The Virginian* gave rise to much scowling, both on set and behind the scenes.

A native of New York City, Cobb was the adopted stage name of Leo Jacoby. As a child he displayed a talent for music and was an accomplished violinist and harmonica player.

Following an unsuccessful attempt at finding acting work in Hollywood, Cobb returned to New York and studied accounting at City College of New York. He kept his acting ambitions alive with the college dramatic society, the Curtain Club. Three years at the Pasadena Playhouse in California followed before he returned yet again to New York, making his Broadway debut in Dostoyevsky's *Crime and Punishment* in 1935. That same year he joined the left-wing Group Theatre, appearing with Elia Kazan in Clifford Odets' political drama *Waiting for Lefty*.

Cobb's rapidly disappearing hairline and burly physique resulted in him regularly playing characters much older than himself. Born December 8, 1911, Cobb was only 37 years of age when he was approached to play Willy Loman in Arthur Miller's Broadway production of *Death of a Salesman* in 1949. Cobb excelled as the tragic Loman and sealed his reputation as an actor of stature, receiving the Donaldson Award for his portrayal. He reportedly studied the movements of an elephant to achieve the effect of the downtrodden Loman who had "the weight of the world on his shoulders."

Cobb's movie career had been steady, if unremarkable, until 1954 when he received a Best Supporting Actor Academy Award nomination for the role of Johnny Friendly in *On the Waterfront*. The 1950s saw Cobb's best work in movies such as *The Three Faces of Eve* (1957), *Twelve Angry Men* (1957) and *The Brothers Karamazov* (1958), for which he received his second Best Supporting Actor Academy Award nomination.

The early 1950s saw Cobb's career teetering on a precipice. His involvement with Group Theatre members and fellow alleged Communists Elia Kazan, Clifford Odets and actor John Garfield dragged Cobb into the field of vision of the HUAC. The House Un-American Activities Committee had charged him with "being or having been a Communist."

Established in 1938, the HUAC originally targeted subversive individuals, groups and organizations, but following World War II it enlarged its scope to include the Hollywood film industry and Communist sympathizers. Blacklisted individuals found their careers ruined.

Cobb reversed his initial decision to remain quiet, in part due to his wife's poor health and the negative effect on his career. In 1953, Cobb appeared before HUAC and named 20 people as former members of the Communist Party. The change of heart saved his career and kept him out of the penitentiary. But his personal life suffered, with his marriage to actress Helen Beverly ending in divorce a few years later. This was followed by a massive heart attack in 1955. The road to recovery began with marriage to elementary school teacher Mary Hirsch in 1957 and the birth of Tony and Jerry Cobb adding to a son and daughter from his previous marriage.

In 1962, Cobb was approached to appear in a new 90-minute Western television series that would highlight his talents. *The Virginian* was sold to NBC on the premise it was Cobb's show. He signed to a five-year contract playing Judge Henry Garth, a stern yet fair-minded patriarch. Television was not held in high regard by theater and movie actors and actresses of the day. Cobb had been tempted by a large salary and the security of regular work. But the reality of working on a weekly television series proved to be more of a grind than a creatively fulfilling exercise for Cobb.

Frank Price had personally experienced the potentially destructive effects of Cobb's complaining at script readings and asked him to keep any disagreements and grievances between him and the producers. The morale and enthusiasm for the show had to be maintained. Cobb obliged. But he couldn't disguise his feelings for *The Virginian* to the media and told Peter Bogdanovich he "was ashamed of it."

Cobb's past history with HUAC was always lurking in the background and he felt particularly sensitive about it. Price recollected having to calm him down regarding a *TV Guide* article.

"Early one Sunday morning, I received a call at home from Lee. He was panicked and frightened and needed to talk with me. He wanted to stop *TV Guide* from publishing an article about him. I met with him to get the full story. Lee had ignored our standard advice about dealing with reporters, which was to deal with them only through our own publicists. Lee had been approached by a reporter writing a piece for *TV Guide* and Lee felt he had developed a trusting relationship with that reporter, so he spent quite a bit of time with him.

"The reporter was at his house, bringing the interviews to an end when suddenly he started grilling Lee about his membership in the Communist party and his role as a witness in the House Un-American Activities Committee hearings. Lee tried to cut off the interview but could not resist continuing to answer questions. With the reporter out of the house, Lee spent a sleepless night, worrying that a big story in *TV Guide* about his past could destroy his career. Lee had spent quite a bit of time unemployed during those Red scare days. He was in a terrible state when he called me."

Price considered what strategies he could use to alleviate Cobb's growing anxiety.

"I told him I would have to figure out how to handle this. I told him there was no way we could pressure *TV Guide* through Universal or NBC threats to them about advertising etc. That would only stiffen their determination to publish whatever they pleased. I said I would do everything possible to help him.

"At the studio I conferred with our publicity people. I consulted with Lew Wasserman. We explored the various approaches to dealing with the problem. We decided there was no way we could kill it.

"When I got back together with Lee, I suggested to him my idea, that the best approach I could think of was for him to call the editor in chief of *TV Guide,* Merrill Pannitt. If Lee made a personal plea to Merrill not to dredge up all this material from the past and destroy his career, he stood the best chance of influencing the tone of the article. I thought if it was just a contest between companies, Lee would get ground up. A personal appeal might be hard to turn down. Lee agreed to try this. I furnished Merrill Pannitt's phone number to him and he made the call. Pannitt took the call, listened to Lee but gave no reaction.

"We waited anxiously until the article was published. The article was generally positive about Lee and there was only a brief and bland reference to the controversial material toward the article's end."

Cobb stayed with *The Virginian* for three and a half years before leaving in late 1965. Price was annoyed that, in his absence, the producers had let Cobb talk himself out of his contract. He still had one and a half years remaining. Price had spent much time appeasing Cobb and knew how to handle him. Price's successor Norman MacDonnell had given in to his demands and noted, "I don't think anybody is going to change Mr. Cobb."

Following his departure, Cobb reprised his role of Willy Loman in a 1966 television version of *Death of a Salesman.* He also resumed his movie career, starring in the spy spoofs *Our Man Flint* (1966) and *In Like Flint* (1967) with James Coburn and Don Siegel's *Coogan's Bluff* (1968) with Clint Eastwood. Surprisingly, he returned to television series

Lee J. Cobb and his wife at Frank Price and Katherine Crawford's wedding reception in the Crystal Room of the Beverly Hills Hotel, May 15, 1965 (courtesy Frank Price).

work as attorney David Barrett in the short-lived show *The Young Lawyers* (1970–71). Two of his late movie roles of note were in the controversial *The Exorcist* (1973) and *That Lucky Touch* (1975).

Price recalled the time he rescued Cobb from a sinking sailboat at sea.

"This was after he and I had left *The Virginian,* around 1966. He had learned how to sail and had his sailboat berthed in nearby Marina Del Rey. I also decided to learn to sail. One Saturday morning, my wife and I were with our sailing instructor as we sailed out of the jetty leading into Marina Del Rey. We were in the final stages of our instruction so we could handle this boat reasonably well.

"As we made our way up the channel we spotted a sailboat in distress. The boat had failed to tack properly coming up the channel and had gone aground against the rocks at the sides of the channel. A lone person was clinging to the mast as waves banged the hull against these rocks and rocked the boat back and forth.

"Our sailing instructor immediately headed toward the boat in distress, telling me to take the tiller and swing alongside the boat so he could leap aboard and help out. I had to make sure that we didn't *also* go aground in making this maneuver.

"As we got close to the distressed sailboat, suddenly I could see that the lone person aboard was Lee. That sight doubled my concern because I knew Lee had a mild heart condition. Anyway, I was able to come close enough for the instructor to successfully leap aboard. And I didn't go on the rocks.

"The instructor dropped Lee's sail, which was the force keeping Lee's boat against the rocks, and managed to shove the boat out into the channel. We all headed back to the main docks and spent a little time with Lee. He was shaken, but had no new heart trouble."

In his final episodic television appearance (December 1974), Cobb starred with his actress daughter Julie Cobb in the *Gunsmoke* episode "The Colonel."

Lee J. Cobb died of a heart attack on February 11, 1976. He was 64. The inscription on his tombstone in Mount Sinai Memorial Park, Los Angeles, reads, "Ay, Every Inch a King."

11

James Drury

The Virginian

Born April 18, 1934, in New York City, James Drury had an early taste of ranch life at his mother's ranch near Salem, Oregon. His father was professor of marketing and advertising at New York University. Dividing his time between New York and Oregon, Drury was struck down by polio at ten years of age. He spent his time acting out characters from the numerous books he read while recovering. Intent on becoming an actor, Drury studied drama at New York University, receiving straight As, and signed his first contract for MGM in 1954.

His initial MGM career consisted of small roles in films such as *The Tender Trap* (1955) and *Forbidden Planet* (1956). He fared better at 20th Century-Fox, performing alongside Elvis Presley in *Love Me Tender* (1956) and Pat Boone in *Bernardine* (1957). Suspension from the studio for refusing to accept parts led him to Walt Disney and his first real screen success in *The Nine Lives of Elfego Baca* (1959), *Toby Tyler* (1960), *Pollyana* (1960) and *Ten Who Dared* (1960). Drury also appeared in guest spots on TV Westerns such as *Gunsmoke*, *Wagon Train*, *Sugarfoot*, *The Rifleman*, and *Rawhide* and two unsold pilots, *The Virginian* (1958) and *The Yank* (1961), the latter about a surgeon venturing West after the Civil War.

In 1962, Sam Peckinpah cast Drury in a supporting role in *Ride the High Country* starring Randolph Scott and Joel McCrea as aging cowboys. One of Drury's best performances to date, it would be his final movie appearance for quite some time. *The Virginian* would keep him busy in the years ahead.

The role of the Virginian was a perfect fit for Drury. As the foreman of Shiloh Ranch he was friendly and polite to people he respected and trusted, and stern and often angry with people who crossed him. Preferring not to use a gun or resort to violence unless necessary, the Virginian expected others to respond to his authority and leadership.

In April 1966, Drury entertained troops in Vietnam with his band the *Wilshire Boulevard Buffalo Hunters*. Drury performed 54 shows in 21 days for the USO (United Service Organizations) "Hollywood Overseas Committee"; Drury's show included singing and dancing girls in Indian squaw costumes.

Drury made two movies during summer hiatuses, *The Young Warriors* (1967) and *Breakout* (1970), as well as guesting on *It Takes a Thief* (1968) and *Rowan and Martin's Laugh-In* (1969) with Doug McClure. In 1970 he appeared as Sheriff Lom Trevors in a pilot for a new comedy Western, *Alias Smith and Jones* (1971). When *The Men from Shiloh* was cancelled in 1971, Drury starred in the TV Western movie *The Devil and Miss Sarah* (1971) and guested on *Alias Smith and Jones'* third season premiere.

James Drury (courtesy James Drury).

Firehouse (1974), a 30-minute show focusing on the LA fire department, marked Drury's return to weekly TV. Drury played Capt. Spike Ryerson in a series influenced by the success of the series *Emergency!*. The show suffered in comparison and only lasted 13 episodes before it was cancelled in mid-season.

Drury retreated from Hollywood and acting following the failure of *Firehouse,* trying his hand at various business ventures, including hotel renovation, before returning to the small screen in the 1983 *The Fall Guy* episode "Happy Trails," reprising his role of the Virginian alongside Doug McClure, in a homage to TV Western stars. *The Gambler Returns: The Luck of the Draw* (1991), starring Kenny Rogers, was based on a similar homage format and saw Drury teamed up again with McClure.

Recurring roles on early episodes of *Walker: Texas Ranger* (1993) and *The Adventures of Brisco County Jr.* and two guest starring roles on *Kung Fu: The Legend Continues* followed. Drury's longtime connection with the Virginian continued in 2000 when he was cast in a brief cameo role in a TV movie adaptation of Owen Wister's *The Virginian*, starring Bill Pullman in the title role.

Drury continued to be active through 2005, appearing in the Western *Hell to Pay* with Lee Majors, William Smith, Andrew Prine and Stella Stevens. He was inducted into the Hall of Great Western Performers of the National Cowboy and Western Heritage Museum in 1991.

PAUL GREEN: Can you describe auditioning for *The Virginian?*

JAMES DRURY: I had been put under contract for seven years to Universal Studios at some point in 1962. I remember there was a big, very well-known search at Universal to find a man to play the Virginian and it's my understanding that over the course of time they tested about 70 people. They ran them through short, ten-minute screen tests with proposed scenes from the show. In some cases we did scenes by ourselves and in some cases we did scenes with other actors that were also auditioning for the parts of Trampas and Steve. And of course, Doug and I kept auditioning.

I think they pretty much picked Doug for Trampas before the audition. And I also think they had the Virginian part in mind for me when they signed me to a contract, but they did not inform me of that. I still had to go through the auditioning process. We did a screen test and they called me and told me I had to lose weight. So I started losing weight. In a 30-day period I lost 30 pounds. I just ran it off and worked it off and starved it off. I did an awful lot of exercise. Then they called me in for a second screen test and they told me I still had to lose weight. This was before I lost the 30 pounds.

But to cut a long story short, in the 30 days when I lost 30 pounds they did a third screen test and found that acceptable. They informed me and Doug both, on the Friday night before the Monday morning we had to shoot, that we had the parts. We didn't have any real preparation time in terms of getting ready. I think they'd pretty much made up their mind but they didn't let us know until the last minute.

PG: So you were the first to be chosen?

JD: With the exception of Lee J. Cobb. We knew he was going to be in it because it was his name recognition and clout and star quality that actually sold the show to NBC and made it possible for us to proceed into production without a pilot. We just started making episodes. He was getting top billing and getting a great deal of money to do the show for the time.

PG: Did you read the Owen Wister novel to get a handle on the character?

JD: No. I had read the book when I was in high school. I had played in a lot of Westerns before I ever got to Universal. Episodic television westerns. And of course *Ride the High Country* (1962), *Ten Who Dared* (1960) and *Good Day for a Hanging* (1959). All those pictures I made were pretty good training for the Western genre. As far as the specific character goes, I wanted to make him into a man of the West and put into him some of the elements of the pioneers, including my maternal grandfather who I grew up with. I gave the Virginian a lot of my grandfather's character elements and others I thought would be worthwhile. And of course it was an evolving thing.

An acting characterization is not something like a painting that you paint and paint and paint on and finally it's finished. You just don't do that. You keep evolving as time goes on and you use things that you think will work.

PG: Did Universal provide you with a back story for the Virginian character?

JD: Yes, to some extent. The producers discussed the concepts of where they thought he came from and we were all in agreement on that. A lot of his elements were necessarily vague because the character written by Owen Wister in his original book in 1902 was purposely left somewhat vague. The fact he never gave him a name was an indication that the author expected him to be viewed as somewhat of a man of mystery. That was an element that I always thought was a great plus for the Virginian and for any actors who are playing the Virginian because you don't have to do anything to achieve that mystery. It just simply follows you on stage when you make an entrance. Because people whisper "Oh, that's the Virginian." He never uses his right name. Immediately, everybody's suspicious, of course. If he rises above that suspicion, that's how he becomes accepted.

PG: How did your approach to the character differ from the 1958 pilot?

JD: We obviously had a bigger canvas to work on. We were dealing with a 90-minute format as opposed to a 30-minute format. So we made him a larger character with more responsibility and more substance perhaps. But the 1958 costume was fussy. We made the costume in 1962 to be very practical and down-to-earth.

PG: Did you have any input into the 1962 costume?

JD: Oh, absolutely. I made suggestions and we looked at a lot of sketches that they'd come up with and chose elements from different ones. And we put it together so that it was comfortable. Everybody agreed on it.

PG: Did you share sets and bump into cast members with other Universal shows of the time? For example, *Laramie* and *Wagon Train?*

JD: Absolutely. And sometimes we were shooting virtually elbow to elbow out there. We all of course knew each other. I had appeared in a *Wagon Train* so that's probably when they first saw me and thought of me as the Virginian.

PG: In the first season it seems many scripts were built around the guest star with the cast almost being incidental to the story. I understand Lee J. Cobb wasn't happy with this. Did you have any input into making the stories more Virginian-, Trampas- or Steve-centered?

JD: First of all, because of its format, our writers always had the opportunity to write a major guest star role. To my knowledge, that didn't change throughout the nine years. We would always have a guest star, somebody to create conflict and to be a major part of the story we could react against and go into conflict with. That was the plan all along. Lee J. Cobb was a wonderful, wonderful man to work with. Very co-operative and very helpful and very kind. But he felt the show was beneath his dignity to some extent, and perhaps it was. I know he made a comment one time to the press that I felt was really hilarious.

He said, "If I had the money, I'd buy all the prints of this show and turn it into banjo picks."

He left the show after the first three years and of course we went on for six more. We were all sad to see him go but he was really very unhappy having to do it every week. He didn't like the schedule. He didn't like a lot of things about it. Now that I think about it, he probably did make a comment about some of the segments being away too much. And there were a few that didn't seem to involve a lot of the people of the show or the ranch. But I think that was necessary to get some variety. They did anything they could to make it work. At any rate, all of us were very proud to work with him and loved him all the rest of his life. I went to see him on Broadway a couple of times. But he was happy to be out of the show.

PG: Did you find not being able to refer to yourself by a birth name awkward?

JD: They certainly took great pains to make it not necessary for me to introduce myself all the time. I was always referred to as the Virginian when I was not present and as the boss or the foreman or the ramrod when I was present. And that's how we avoided the embarrassment of that thing. You never saw me register for a hotel. I was so charismatic it just became a moot point. Just kidding [*laughter*].

PG: Were you aware of budget restrictions after Charles Marquis Warren left?

JD: Up to a point I was aware of them. As I remember in the second or third year I went to war about that. They had a patterned budget. They agreed to spend a certain

A bespectacled James Drury and Frank Price at *The Virginian*'s 5th-season wrap party, 1967 (courtesy Frank Price).

amount of dollars per episode and it was a ridiculously low amount. It was something like $330,000 for a 90-minute series. After Warren left, the cost did drop to a certain extent down to that level. Then when the show was a hit, they wanted to shave that every week by $30,000. It was putting 30 grand in their pockets a week. I absolutely dug in my heels and kicked and screamed and went all the way to Lew Wasserman's office about that and they restored the budget.

That's what people do in the restaurant business. They start a big restaurant with top quality foods and a great chef and as soon as they're a success they fire the chef and hire a cook and drop the cost of the food and people stop coming. People don't want to eat there any more. It's plain stupid to do that. And I fought a lot of battles and I think we maintained that budget.

About that time I was beginning to throw my weight around because I was the only one who'd been there, outside of Doug, from the beginning and I knew what the character had done in the past and I knew what would be in and out of character for him. I started getting involved in script conferences and all that kind of thing much to the high disapproval and high chagrin of the producers. They didn't want my input and they didn't want to hear from an actor. They didn't want anything to do with my coming to story conferences and telling them what to write and what to do.

I got along fine with executive producer Frank Price, up to a point. But the show producers, the guys like Cy Chermak and people like that, I got into conferences with them. And they, quite naturally, resented that. It didn't bother me in the least that they resented it. I went ahead and did it because it was important to keep the continuity going with the character. You didn't want him doing something in one episode he just wouldn't have done in another episode. I was about the only one that was keeping track of that. That's what got me into a lot of contention with the studio and caused a lot of heavily held feelings of resentment that I felt they had against me.

PG: Were you ever in danger of being fired?

JD: No, they couldn't get rid of me. Power corrupts and absolute power corrupts absolutely and when I had absolute power I was absolutely corrupt. In the sense I had no particular care or concern about the sensitivities or the feelings of the people I was working with. I did throw my weight around and got real nasty and mean and just impossible to live with.

PG: Do you regret that now or would you do it again?

JD: I'd do it again in a heartbeat because we had nine years of a show that kept its quality up all the way. And I, in my own mind, take a lot of credit for that. I guess if I hadn't watched the continuity, no one else would have. That's how I felt at the time and I still feel quite justified in having done it.

PG: *The Virginian* entered a strange phase when Lee J. Cobb left and Morgan Starr (John Dehner) took over at Shiloh. Many fans say these episodes have a dark feel. What's your opinion?

JD: We had to shoot the scripts as they came down the pipe and we didn't suddenly read a 90-minute script and turn to each other and say "I say old chap, this has a dark feel." It never occurred to us. We shot the episodes as they came along and if the perception of the audiences now is that John Dehner episodes had a dark feel, then so be it. It wasn't anything we were reaching for, I can assure you of that.

It may have been intentional on the part of some producer without telling me, but it wasn't something that was apparent to me and I was extremely alert and aware of the elements that went into every story. Probably the most famous episode I remember with John Dehner was the one with the locusts where we had to fight the fire. He had a very authoritarian, "military bearing" take on the character and was very firm and kind of a distant figure compared to the chumminess we had with Lee J. Cobb. Although it was only distant in effect.

PG: Similar to Stewart Granger

JD: It was somewhat similar in that his look at the character was somewhat more removed from his employees than Lee J. Cobb, who treated us like a family. In Dehner's case at least, over time I thought he became much more friendly and the characters became much closer in effect. We all enjoyed working with him and we all got along famously. I was happy when he came and puzzled when he left. And I was also very, very happy with his replacement.

Charles Bickford was absolutely fabulous to work with. A wonderful man and he carried on a very humanistic tradition as leader of the ranch. He certainly became as much of a father figure and as much of a friendly figure as Lee J. Cobb's character had been. Of all the people that I've worked with, I think Charles was one of the finest and admired him immensely as time went on.

PG: The Charles Bickford years introduced the Graingers. Don Quine had quite a following but again was written out. Was he easy to work with?

JD: I have no idea why he was written out and he was just fine to work with. I had no problem with him at all. He didn't give me any trouble. I was not aware of any problems behind the scenes. As you can imagine, I had a very full plate. I was extremely busy.

PG: When Bickford died, was John McIntire first choice to replace him? Did they take long in casting a replacement?

JD: I don't know if John was the first choice but he certainly would have been my first choice. It did not take long to replace Charles Bickford. He came in quite soon. John had been working for the studio for a long time in *Wagon Train* and he was very well liked and known here and I think they just said, "Well, why don't we get John McIntire and we'll get Jeanette Nolan while we're at it." And so the two of them came over. They were wonderful years. Great people to work with.

You know Jeanette had been in the original pilot in '58 and I had worked with John several times in other shows and as a result we were close friends. All of us were. We just loved them. That was a great time in the show. They were quite a suitable replacement for Charles Bickford. Had the family feel. When we came to the set, it was like family because we'd all been friends for years.

PG: Sara Lane was in many ways similar to Betsy, but more reserved. What was she like to work with? I know she loved horses.

JD: Just wonderful. The sweetest little girl you ever met. A beautiful girl. She did love horses. She owned horses and rode some personal horses of mine. She was crazy about my old lean appaloosa mare, Easter Ute. I remember at one time she lived in Topanga Canyon on the beach side and back in an area of almost shantytown lean-tos that had been there for 60 to 80 years. Dilapidated houses that came from the [early] 1900s back in there. When the big rains came one time, she got flooded out and I personally went in with a four-wheel drive truck and got her and her cats and dogs and belongings out and got her into a hotel. I don't think they even had a phone. I haven't stayed in touch with her. I wish I had. She was a wonderful lady.

PG: Tim Matheson was a fine young actor who starred in the final season of the original format. Why wasn't he carried over into the *The Men from Shiloh?*

JD: I had very good relations with him and got along great with him. I think the concept of *The Men from Shiloh* was that there would be four stars: myself, Doug McClure, Stewart Granger and Lee Majors. And out of 24 shows we'd each do six. I ended up doing eight or nine and I think Lee did about four and Doug did about seven or eight and the other guy did the others. It was a whole new take on the idea. We all went off and did our own shows. If there were four stars in the thing, I guess there wasn't room for a fifth. That's speculation. I don't have any idea and I had no input into it.

PG: *The Men from Shiloh* was something of a departure from *The Virginian.* Did you like the change in title music and credits?

JD: At the time, everybody thought it was a good idea. We all said it'd be great to give the show a new look and get it back up in the ratings.

PG: When you were told the series was going to be revamped, did you think it marked the end?

JD: No. I thought it marked a new beginning. It obviously was the end. I heard from many people that they tuned in to find *The Virginian* and couldn't find it anywhere in *TV Guide* and had no idea what *The Men from Shiloh* was. So they just went on to watch other things.

PG: Only yourself and Doug McClure lasted the entire nine seasons. Did you have a special bond with Doug? You worked so well together.

JD: We absolutely had a special bond. From the very first moment that we actually met. We had gone to University High School of West Los Angeles together but he was, I think, a year behind me. I'd see him around the campus but I never knew him well. Maybe I knew what his name was, and that was about it. I went to Beverly Hills High for the first year and then we moved over to West Los Angeles. I enrolled there and did the second two years of high school at University High School. But we were not friends in high school. We just knew each other to nod to.

I'd seen him in some things before we worked together. But we'd actually met when we were testing for *The Virginian.* We talked and got to know each other and then we called each other and got together when it looked imminent we were going to start. And that was the Friday night before the Monday morning we started shooting.

We had our first one-on-one meeting about the show and talked about it. We were both excited about working with each other and thought we could really do well with it. We obviously had no problem getting along. Then we became really close friends. He was like a brother to me and I hope I was to him as well. I think it came across on the show. There's a real magnetism between us and about us that I think was palpable. And I always enjoyed it so much. If you talk to a guy three times a week for 30 years, you really miss him. And I miss him terribly since he's been gone.

PG: Were you happy with the way the series evolved through the seasons? Do you have a favorite cast?

JD: I was happy with the way the series evolved through the seasons. I'd have to say the Charles Bickford and the John McIntire years were probably the ones I felt most comfortable in. Or maybe more of a complete unit with the family. Just on a personal level. But I had no problem with any of them. I was very comfortable with those years. I perhaps enjoyed myself more during those times than other times in actually doing the show and getting satisfaction out of it.

PG: When the series ended, did you feel relieved or sad? Or both?

JD: I felt very sad. No relief involved. I had no need of relief. I would have gone on for another ten years. I certainly would have been in favor of it but the ratings just did not sustain it. We never were able to attract an audience to the final year. I mean an audience in sufficient numbers to make it worthwhile. That's the way it goes. Everything runs its course but I was certainly not happy to see the show end and I doubt if I ever will be.

PG: Did you manage to keep any of your costumes or props?

JD: A few elements I have here. A hat from *The Men from Shiloh*. I don't have one from *The Virginian*. We changed hats. In fact, I think there's a couple of copies of that hat available somewhere. I have some of the jackets and some of the pants and maybe one of the suits. I have a pair of boots I think that I wore on the show. Everything was from the costume department, except for things like the belt buckle that was made up for me. The shirt was made out of upholstery corduroy. It looked great on film but it was certainly extremely heavy. When it got hot, it was just like being in a steam bath. We struggled through with it.

PG: Was your horse Joe ever injured during the filming of the show?

JD: He had a chronic injury which was a quarter crack on his left front hoof. We had to really baby him along at times because a quarter crack is like a crack in the cuticle and if you work it too hard it gets worse. But we treated it and put all kinds of salves and unctions on it. At one point we gave him leather protection for his horseshoe to keep him from reinjuring or rubberizing the foot or damaging it. We didn't use him for a lot of fast chases over hard ground for a while. The injury was something he kind of had before he came on the show. It's something that the horse will get and it'll last for the whole life. They can work fine but you can't work them too hard on the front end. We had several double horses for him, virtually identical, and we used them for various things like fast chases and to get him to fall, which could be dangerous. So we kept him out of harm's way as much as possible.

We called him Joe D or Joe. But most of the time I just called him Jo. He was seven-eighths American quarter horse and [one-eighth] Appaloosa. Sometimes they're spotted all over, which is called a leopard spot, and sometimes they're spotted on the back, which is called a blanket spot. Joe D had some spots on his rump but he had a lot of red on his ankles and he had the white sclera around the eye which is characteristic of the breed. When you saw him up close, he looked a lot redder.

He lived to be 37 years old. Retired in the tall grass of Mariposa County with Del Combs, the man who found him for me and took care of him. I used to go visit him every once in a while and he'd always be ready to work, right up to the end. Thirty-seven is an old, old age for a horse but it's not unknown. I've ridden 37-year-old polo horses who were still out there playing polo. It's an age they can certainly attain if they're well taken care of and kept in condition.

PG: I know you don't recall individual episodes because of the hectic filming schedule, but does anything stand out in your memory from your time on the show?

JD: An impossible question to answer. Nothing I want to get specific about at this time. My reticence in a large part is based on the fact there are still many people alive who were involved. I am not a man who carries tales. My memories are almost universally good of my time on the show and the bad memories I have, I would never mention.

PG: Were you ever approached for a "reunion" movie and would you have liked the idea of an updated *Virginian?*

JD: We never had a chance to get a reunion with any of the original cast members. No one ever came up with a concept. Of course I did appear in the Bill Pullman version of *The Virginian* for TNT in a cameo. There was a novel written called *The Virginian Returns.* It's a fine book and a well-written novel. It's a look at the Virginian some 20 years later and kind of explains where his name came from and postulates all kinds of different theories and Owen Wister appears as an actual character in the book. It would have made a fine film and at one point I told Bill Pullman about it. In fact, I got a copy of it to him but I never heard he did anything with it.

James Drury (courtesy James Drury).

Owen Wister's book was the writing style of the day but is somewhat obscure and obtuse. It's quite stilted but the conventions of the time required that's what people thought of when they thought of cowboys. They kind of talked in that highfalutin manner which of course is not the case. But it may have been the case in Owen Wister's time. Who am I to say? Language is constantly evolving. New words are added to the dictionary every year by the thousands. Language is something we have no real control over. It evolves whether we like it or not.

As far as some of my evasiveness and my flat-out refusal to answer some questions, I'm reminded of a saying I once heard that was attributed to Orson Welles: "The mystery and power of a star or a performer to convince people of the veracity of his performance is directly proportionate to his distance from his public."

PG: A lot of today's stars are just too much in your face and there's no mystery.

JD: They're simple made up by a public relations agent. And their closest, most intimate parts of their lives are examined in great detail by a voracious public. Apparently the public has an unending appetite for that kind of detail about people's personal lives that they admire and watch on the screen. And I think the whole process just sucks. So I have adopted Orson Welles' principle throughout my life and I answer very few questions. I've tried to give you factual answers.

12

Doug McClure
Trampas

Doug McClure possessed a youthful exuberance well into his fifties. It was only when cancer struck that his features aged demonstrably and the effects of hard living took their toll. McClure's premature death, at age 59, came as a shock to everyone who remembered him as the fun-loving Trampas on *The Virginian*.

Born May 11, 1935, in Glendale, California, McClure and his brother Reed grew up in Pacific Palisades. His mother, Clara McClure, an English emigrant from Canterbury, wrote her own column for *The Santa Monica Evening Outlook*.

"Doug's mother was a remarkable and wonderful woman and the very best mother-in-law one could have. We had great affection for each other," said Diane McClure.

Summers spent working on a Nevada cattle ranch made Doug comfortable around horses and he became a highly skilled rider at an early age.

Attending University High School of West Los Angeles, Santa Monica City College and UCLA, McClure excelled in athletics but preferred drama. Early work modeling for record covers and a TV commercial for Zest soap led to his first uncredited roles in two high-profile movies, *Friendly Persuasion* (1956) and *The Enemy Below* (1957).

McClure's first featured role cast him opposite Burt Lancaster in *The Unforgiven* (1960). Lancaster formed a lasting friendship with McClure and recommended him to Lew Wasserman at Universal.

A seven-year contract with Universal followed and in 1960 McClure appeared in his first weekly television series, alongside William Bendix. *Overland Trail* (1960) would only last 17 episodes, but McClure made a good enough impression as Indian-raised Frank "Flip" Flippen for executives to immediately cast him in his second series the same year. *Checkmate* (1960) co-starred Sebastian Cabot. Set in a San Francisco detective agency, the show was a moderate success, lasting 70 episodes.

When *Checkmate* was cancelled in 1962, McClure once again went directly into another weekly series. *The Virginian* would keep him employed for the next nine years and make him an international star.

In the Owen Wister novel, Trampas was a villain who met his death at the hands of the Virginian. McClure's Trampas would be a lovable rogue. Coming from a shady past, Trampas was impetuous and often petty but at heart a decent person who gradually learned to accept responsibility and trust people. McClure was so popular as Trampas that he would be the only leading cast member, apart from James Drury, to survive all nine seasons.

McClure enjoyed many busy summer breaks over the nine years of the show's run, appearing in five feature films and one TV movie. His most successful movie would be the Civil War drama *Shenandoah* (1965) starring James Stewart. Other films included *The Lively Set* (1964), *Beau Geste* (1966), *The Longest Hundred Miles*, a 1967 telemovie, *The King's Pirate* (1967) and *Nobody's Perfect* (1968).

Following the cancellation of *The Men from Shiloh* in 1971, McClure continued his hectic work schedule and in 1972 began starring in his fourth TV series, *Search*. Like *The Men from Shiloh*, the series featured a weekly rotating star format, much favored by Universal at the time. The show was interesting in its theme of "bio-electronic implants" being used to track down missing persons and artifacts. But characterization

Doug finds joy at home with his young daughter Tané (courtesy Tané McClure).

was secondary to the hi-tech gadgetry and it was cancelled after one season.

McClure continued to work in TV movies and was cast in his fifth TV series in 1975. Set in a San Francisco casino, *Barbary Coast* co-starred William Shatner. McClure and Shatner played nineteenth century government agents in a light-hearted show that failed to gain an audience. It was cancelled after only 14 episodes.

McClure turned to England, where he appeared in a string of successful Edgar Rice Burroughs adaptations filmed at Shepperton and Pinewood Studios and on location in the Canary Islands and Malta: *The Land That Time Forgot* (1975), *At the Earth's Core* (1976), *The People That Time Forgot* (1977) and *Warlords of Atlantis* (1978). It was during his time in England that he met his fifth wife. Diane McClure grew up in London with her twin sister, watching *The Virginian* on the BBC. She first met Doug while working for producer John Dark on *The Land That Time Forgot*.

"Doug loved working in England and felt totally comfortable living in London," recalled Diane. "Doug would talk passionately about his memories working on *The Virginian* with Jim Drury. They were like brothers. Whenever we were in Los Angeles at the

Doug McClure as Frank "Flip" Flippen in *Overland Trail* (1960) (courtesy Tané McClure).

same time, we would get together with Jim and his wife. I remember traveling to Washington together for a political event and spending New Year's Eve in Las Vegas."

Diane recalled her husband's love of painting. "Doug had great satisfaction with his watercolor paintings. They were all in the Western theme and he had a number of very successful art shows and donated many pieces to charity events. He was commissioned by Wilford Brimley to do an oil painting from a photograph. Doug was really pleased with the result and delighted that Wilford was so very happy with the piece. He mostly did watercolors."

Heavy drinking became a problem for McClure in the late 1970s.

"As was quite common with many people in the entertainment community, drinking was an integral part of the social fabric of their personal and professional lives," commented Diane. "We were married in 1979 and during the first few years of our marriage, Doug decided to lead a healthier lifestyle and gave up drinking and smoking and joined a gym."

Returning to America, McClure became typecast in horror and sci-fi movies.

"Doug loved to work and realized as he got older that there were not as many opportunities as a 'leading man' available to him and he sometimes accepted less quality movies," explained McClure.

In 1987 he starred in his sixth and final TV series, the sitcom *Out of This World.* McClure's character, Mayor Kyle Applegate, was peripheral to the main star of the show, Maureen Flannigan as a half-alien with special powers.

In 1991, McClure teamed up with James Drury again in *The Gambler Returns: The Luck of the Draw* (1991) and featured briefly in *Maverick* (1994) starring Mel Gibson. McClure was diagnosed with lung cancer on August 1, 1994.

"Doug was very optimistic about his condition and after going through all the chemo and radiation therapy, he really believed he had survived the cancer," recalled Diane.

He continued to guest in TV shows such as *Burke's Law* (1994) and *Kung Fu: The Legend Continues* (1994). His final feature was the Western *Riders in the Storm* (1995) with actress-daughter Tané McClure. On the set of the TV series *One West Waikiki* (1995) McClure was taken ill and passed away a few days later, February 5, 1995, in Sherman Oaks, California. He was 59.

James Drury was a pallbearer at his funeral in Pacific Palisades, California. Five hundred people attended

Doug McClure, 1994 (courtesy Tané McClure).

the funeral service at St. Matthew's Episcopal Church, including his wife Diane and two daughters Tané and Valerie. Friends Burt Reynolds, Clint Eastwood, Connie Stevens, Jamie Farr, Loni Anderson and Mel Brooks were also in attendance.

A few months earlier, on December 16, 1994, McClure received a star on the Holly-wood Walk of Fame with the help of a longtime friend, actor Robert Fuller. Three of his five wives attended, including Diane McClure, BarBara Luna and Faye Brash.

Frank Price and Katherine Crawford paid their personal tributes to Doug McClure.

Frank Price: "I found him to be an amazingly talented actor. His approach to each role was to make it his own. He could take an otherwise ordinary straight line and make it humorous. And his riding skills were top-notch. No one else in the cast could ride like Doug. I think Doug brought a greater range of acting ability to the role than I could have envisioned. He had great comedic talent, but also could handle whatever dramatic situations you threw at him. And he did it all effortlessly."

"Doug was a wonderful, delightful, distracted, fidgety person," Crawford recalled. "Warm and friendly, and funny! His humor was often self-deprecating, making everyone laugh. We got along well, and laughed a lot, and he was also very helpful with me."

Diane McClure remembered a husband who was "extremely sensitive, likable, fun-loving and had a great sense of humor."

"He loved attending celebrity tennis tournaments and playing tennis with his friends Dick Van Patten, Bernie Kopell, Robert Fuller and Patrick Wayne. Doug also enjoyed team

Doug McClure and friend Robert Fuller at *The Virginian*'s 5th-season wrap party (courtesy Frank Price).

roping and cutting and was a strong swimmer who liked to ski. In his youth, Doug had a real passion for surfing. Family was extremely important to him and he just loved his daughters, Tané and Valerie. They meant everything to him. Doug would always talk about his past with great nostalgia. Most of all, he had a great passion and joy for his days on *The Virginian*. Those days, for Doug, were the most memorable."

Tané McClure was born June 8, 1958, to Doug McClure's first wife Faye Brash. She starred with her father in the *Virginian* episode "The Small Parade" (1:21) as a young child.

PAUL GREEN: Do you have memories of working with your father in "Small Parade"? I know you were only four years old when it was filmed.

TANÉ MCCLURE: You know what's funny? I remember it so well. I shouldn't say everything, but so many things. My favorite part was the song "Skip to My Lou My Darling." In fact my father after shooting that used to sing it to me all the time. I loved that. I had a hard time differentiating reality...

PG: Between that and reality?

TM: Well, when I was four I'd sometimes forget. Apparently they had a couple of outtakes because I'd say "Oh, Dad" in a take.

PG: So you weren't referring to him as Trampas, but Dad.

TM: I did a couple of times. And I messed up. I definitely remember my favorite part was singing the song. The funny part is, there was a scene where we were all eating breakfast and I remember asking if the eggs were real. Because I was still trying to figure out the difference between reality and fiction.

I've just always remembered all the scenes with my father quite well. I remember so much of it. Pulling the big log across the room. For a child that age, it's like playing a big game of pretend.

PG: Even if the viewer isn't aware you're Doug's

Doug and Tané McClure on the set of "Small Parade" (courtesy Tané McClure).

real-life daughter in the scene, you can see there's a connection and he's really proud of you.

TM: Yes, he was really cute.

PG: I understand you spent most of your summers in Hawaii with your mother.

TM: Other way around, actually. I went to Punahou School in Hawaii from September until June. I spent my summer vacations with my father, and often my Christmas and spring breaks as well. Then right before I turned 17, I moved in with my father. And I have to admit I missed every minute, because I was always looking forward to being with my father. Not that I didn't like being with my mother in Hawaii … don't get me wrong. But I missed my father.

PG: Was he a fun type of father?

TM: Oh! Honestly. I'm not just saying this, he was the best. Super good fun. And when I would be with him, I used to spend most of my days on the set. He worked so much, I'd just hang out on the set with him. Myself and Cindy Mayberry, the director Russ Mayberry's daughter. She and I used to hang out quite a bit and we used to play pretend.

Doug and a teenage Tané McClure poolside in the 1970s (courtesy Tané McClure).

PG: So you were about the same age?

TM: Yeah. And also Chris Drury who is James Drury's son. And we're all still friends today. We used to play pretend all the time. My horse was actually boarded at the time on the Universal lot. When I think about it now, I feel terribly spoiled. But when you're young, you don't know better. As far as I knew, everyone had a playground the size of Universal Studios' back lot. Chris Drury, Cindy Mayberry and myself used to play bank robbers and we'd gallop our horses on different lots. If they were shooting in one area, we would go and play bank robbers on another Western lot. We'd go galloping down and jump off our horses and pretend we were robbing the bank. It was so amazing. And then the directors, would yell, "Can't those kids be quiet?" (Laughter)

PG: Was your horse ever used in the show?

TM: I was recently told that my horse Shiloh, a gray Arabian, was used in one episode.

PG: Did you like the mustache your father wore in *The Men from Shiloh?*

TM: No.

PG: I understand it was your father's idea to have the mustache.

TM: Probably. I don't remember that it was. But I think he thought it looked cool.

PG: I suppose if you've spent eight years in the same role you want a change.

TM: Yeah, you want to look cool with the look back then. What I remember off-screen is the guys were wearing bell bottoms, for crying out loud.

PG: Were you particularly friendly with any members of the cast?

TM: Roberta Shore was always very nice to me. She was always very sweet.

James Drury was, of course, very friendly because Jim and my dad and I and his boys used to do the rodeo circuit on the off-season. I was awfully young. But we'd go on the little rodeo circuit and they'd come out and shoot. I think some of it was paid and some of it was charity. It was just being themselves and dressing in character.

They wouldn't do a show necessarily. Sometimes my dad would sing and once in a blue moon goof around. It was basically just public appearances.

PG: Do you recall working with Gary Clarke and Lee J. Cobb?

TM: Yeah I do, but I don't remember anything specific. I just remember Roberta Shore being very sweet. What I remember specifically about her back then is how I thought she was so beautiful. Of course, [me being] a young child, she just seemed so amazing. To me as a kid playing make believe, I loved all those long dresses.

PG: Around 1964, your father was missing from *The Virginian* for about half a season. When he reappeared he had a big scar on his chin. Do you recall him having a bad accident around that time?

TM: I don't remember what it was, but I do remember he had an accident and he got smashed up and had a scar underneath. But he was also working on other movies too. He worked on *Beau Geste* and *Shenandoah.* He got really hurt on *Beau Geste.* He injured his back. There was a scene in the film where he was required to climb up a ladder, get shot and then fall backward. During one of the takes, he hurt himself quite badly as he fell backward. I remember when I went to the screening and saw him die on screen, I cried and cried and cried. I knew it wasn't real but I was so young. It was hard to see my father hurt on camera.

He had a couple of injuries including the one where he had a big old scar under his chin. Eventually he had to get that scar removed. Kind of like John Wayne, my dad sometimes had a bad back. Not a really bad back, but he had hurt it.

PG: He was a physical guy, anyway.

TM: Yeah. He did a lot of his own stunts.

PG: Was James Drury athletic as well?

TM: Yeah, they both were.

PG: And they used to socialize together?

TM: Yeah! (Laughter) In those days, things were different. Hollywood was different.

It was very common for executive producers to say at lunchtime, "Okay, Doug, let's go have some cocktails." There was a place next door to Universal. Everybody went there. It's literally right across the street. But you've got to understand. That was the norm. In fact, you were supposed to be able to have a cocktail or two with the executives and go back to work. But nobody does that any more.

PG: No. They do it in private instead.

TM: Yeah! My father used to drink but he quit 16 or 17 years before he passed away. I think my father only had a drinking problem for three years.

PG: Was that during *The Virginian* or after?

TM: No. Long past. Probably 1979 to the early 1980s. It was only a period of time that he didn't do so well. Then he quit and was fine after that. He'd gone through a divorce and things like that. People go through that.

PG: He was paying alimony all over the place.

TM: Exactly. And that gets hard, you know. During *The Virginian* years he was fine. He didn't seem to drink that much.

PG: I get the impression that was his favorite period as an actor.

TM: Yeah, I think it was probably one of his favorites. He did very well.

PG: Is it true your father was working on a Trampas script during his *Virginian* years?

TM: That sounds like my dad. Those are the sort of things I don't remember specifically. But I can tell you this: My father, for years, did want to produce. That's for sure. He had a production company that, very sweetly, he named after me, Tané Productions. So that's definitely what he had wanted to do.

I ended up producing an independent film and a pilot that didn't go anywhere. I now produce commercials here and there and whatever else I can grab. But I returned the favor. My production company is called Trampas.

PG: Have you never though of putting together a new Trampas movie?

TM: No, but it's a really good idea, now that you mention it to me.

PG: A major factor that was good about *The Virginian* was the fact you cared what happened to the characters.

TM: That's the biggest problem with a lot of shows. You have to have likeability in the character.

PG: If you don't like them, you couldn't care less and turn off.

TM: You are probably telling the story about my dad's character, right? The fact that the Trampas character in the Owen Wister book was really not a good guy. And that my father helped to persuade the studio to change the character...

PG: It was Doug's input?

TM: Yes. Because of his personal character and the way he played the role and the way he came across, likable. Kind of like a bit of a scamp, if you know what I mean.

PG: Yes. A rogue.

TM: Exactly. But he has a quality that makes you want to like him. Do you know what I'm looking at right now? I'm sitting in my office and have a framed picture of a *TV Guide* with my dad on *The Virginian*.

PG: Was your father nostalgic for *The Virginian* days in his later years or did he think it was just part of his past and time to move on?

TM: I haven't thought about it that way but I'd have to say yes, he was nostalgic.

PG: When *The Men from Shiloh* began, did you get the impression your father knew it was approaching the end?

TM: Yes. I remember that.

PG: Was he depressed about it?

TM: No. He kind of had an "Oh, well" attitude. He'd been doing it for awhile so he had an "I don't know if this is going to work" approach. We used to have a house in Encino [California] and we used to have a pool table. All the guys used to come over and play pool. And he had buddies back then like James Franciscus, James Drury, Bill Cosby and Frank Sinatra.

Doug and Tané in 1994, shortly before he was diagnosed with lung cancer (courtesy Tané McClure).

PG: Burt Reynolds was his friend wasn't he?

TM: Oh, Burt Reynolds was over there all the time. Basically they'd talk about changes and things like that and what was happening. My father had a real good attitude about change overall.

PG: So he was ready to move on.

TM: I mean, not that he wanted to.

PG: When the series ended, did he feel a mixture of relief and sadness?

TM: I don't know if relief is the word. But I think he was looking forward to new opportunities.

PG: He went into two series that failed. *Search* and *Barbary Coast*, and then he found his niche in the Edgar Rice Burroughs movies in England.

TM: That's right. He met his last wife Diane Furnberg in London and truly loved and honored her.

PG: Did he manage to keep any of his Trampas props or costumes?

TM: Yes. He had some of them. Holsters and guns.

PG: Do you have any of them now?

TM: I have hats and cowboy boots. His gun went to his stuntman, Chuck Courtney. He did a lot of stunts with my Dad. So did Harper Flaherty.

In the overall life, from beginning to middle to end, I'm really proud of my father. The thing is, we all make mistakes and we do things we think we shouldn't exactly do in our life. But it's the overall life that really what counts. Because you learn from your mistakes.

I could never be more proud of my dad. I'm sure I probably sound incredibly biased, but he was really a good guy.

BarBara Luna

Doug McClure's second wife BarBara Luna was born in New York City on March 2, 1939. Early work on Broadway in Rodgers & Hammerstein's *South Pacific* and *The King and I* and a national touring company production of *Teahouse of the August Moon* ultimately led to her playing opposite Frank Sinatra in *The Devil at Four O'Clock* (1961). A guest starring role on *Overland Trail* (1960) introduced Luna to future husband Doug McClure. Following their divorce, Luna worked on series such as *The Big Valley, Star Trek, The High Chaparral, Hawaii Five-O* and *Buck Rogers in the 25th Century*.

Luna maintained her presence on Broadway in *West Side Story* as Anita and appeared in her own nightclub act. In the 1980s Luna starred in the soap operas *Search for Tomorrow* and *One Life to Live* and, following a time-out from her career, returned to TV on *Sunset Beach*.

Luna is a member of the Thalians, a charity foundation at Cedars Sinai Hospital, and is active on the *Star Trek* convention circuit.

PAUL GREEN: Can you describe your first meeting with Doug?

BARBARA LUNA: Dougie and I met when I guest starred on his first series *Overland Trail*. Our chemistry was undeniable. We were probably like Ben Affleck and Jennifer Lopez except we followed through with marriage, and perhaps with the complications of Brad Pitt and Angelina Jolie.

PG: Did Doug celebrate with you after being chosen for Trampas?

BL: Yes, we had many celebrations. I knew from the start he had the role but he was uncertain. How did I know and he didn't? Dougie was under contract to Uni-

BarBara Luna attending the *Twilight Zone–Star Trek* convention at the Beverly Garland Hotel, Los Angeles, 2005 (courtesy BarBara Luna).

versal and the only actor they tested. He was completely hoodwinked! It was of course a money game they played with contract players.

PG: Did Doug ever invite other *Virginian* cast members to your home?

BL: We were close with Jim and Phyllis Drury. I often cooked at home and they were always welcome.

PG: If Doug had a bad or difficult day at work, did he sulk or take it out on you by being antisocial? Or did he leave his work behind him when he arrived home?

BL: One of Dougie's better qualities was his willingness to share his feelings with me no matter what that involved. I wouldn't have expected him to leave his difficulties behind nor did he expect that of me. We always did our best to share our feelings, although admittedly sometimes our best wasn't good enough.

PG: Did you notice any change in Doug after *The Virginian* became a success?

BL: Yes; however, it had nothing to do with the success of the show. Dougie was already successful. After all, he had already starred in two series prior to *The Virginian*.

PG: Did you watch Doug on *The Virginian?* Or did you and Doug watch it together?

BL: Sometimes we watched it at his parents' house. We especially watched the segment his daughter Tané guested on when she was four years old. Actually, I brought her to the set the day she was filming. We were nervous but Tané was fine!

PG: When Doug arrived home from work, is it true he took off his clothes before entering the house?

BL: This makes me giggle when I think about it. *The Virginian* often filmed long hours so, rather than take the time to

Doug McClure and BarBara Luna's wedding day at the McClure parents' family home in Palisades, December 17, 1961 (courtesy BarBara Luna).

change into his street clothes, Dougie would come home in his wardrobe. The problem was, he smelled of horses, and because I was very allergic to horses he would have to undress on our porch and walk into the house naked. Most of the time I sneezed anyway, causing him to laugh hysterically.

PG: Was there ever any conflict with your careers and did it affect your marriage?

BL: I don't think their chosen profession is what affects marriage in a negative way. It's affected by a person's lack of good character, knowledge, understanding and maturity. If you lack any of the above, you won't survive in a marriage no matter what profession you're in or to whom you are married. In fact, I think actors married to each other could be an ideal situation.

An actor and an actress understand what it feels like when they are working and when they are not working and all of the pitfalls in show business. However, one needs to know how to apply the knowledge in order to make it work. I think marriage is basically difficult for most people, particularly where success is involved.

PG: Did your work schedules keep you apart during your marriage?

BL: If you mean travel, no. I turned down films that required going on location.

PG: Why do you think Doug was married five times? Bad luck or bad choices?

BL: Dougie liked to be married, as did I. However, as it is with most people and particularly young people, we didn't know how to be married. When we were having difficulties, it was my choice to end the marriage. At that time I didn't know how to handle the problem. It seems Dougie finally learned how as he was married to Diane for I believe 12 years ... until he passed away.

PG: Faye Brash was Doug's first wife, you were his second and Diane was his fifth. What happened to the other two?

Doug McClure and BarBara Luna at a Celebrity Tennis tournament in Jupiter, Florida, 1970s (courtesy BarBara Luna).

BL: Dougie's third wife was Helen Crane. They had no children. His fourth wife was another Diane. They have a daughter, Valerie. Faye's other daughter Tabor is from another marriage. Diane, whose name I think was Soldani, is perhaps still alive. However, I don't know whatever happened to Helen. At one time, before Dougie, she was married to one of the owners of the famous Luau restaurant, Steve Crane. By the way, I love Faye. She never used Tané as a weapon as some mothers do when there's a divorce.

PG: How long were you married? Actually sharing the same home.

BL: We shared several homes over a period of five and one-half years.

PG: Did your divorce affect you and Doug badly?

BL: Divorce affects everyone badly in one way or another. Hopefully we both learned from the experience.

PG: When he received his star on the Hollywood Walk of Fame, you and three of Doug's ex-wives showed up. How had he changed? I know he was very ill at the time, but did anything surprise you when you met him? Or had you stayed in touch through the years?

BL: When Dougie made his thank-you speech he said, "Well, I guess I didn't piss off too many people. All of my ex-wives are here!" I always loved his sense of humor and he never lost it. Prior to marrying Diane, I saw Dougie around here and there. It was obvious to me and to those who knew him that he was having some rough times. After he married Diane, I saw them intermittently at various events. Dougie appeared to be different. I was happy to see she was a good influence on him.

PG: Was he generally a happy man or did he have a dark side in times of stress?

BL: When we were married, he had no dark side. Mostly he was a sweet country bumpkin.

PG: Tané is very proud of her father and said he was a great dad. What's your lasting impression of Doug?

BL: He was too naive for show business.

PG: I assume that means people in the business often took advantage of him

BL: Unfortunately yes. There are many assassins and victims in show business. Sadly, some actors like Doug were easier prey. But that's a world problem, isn't it?

13

Gary Clarke

Steve Hill

Born Clarke L'Amoreaux on August 16, 1936, in Los Angeles, California, Gary Clarke was a multi-talented youngster, adept at singing, comedy and acting. Performances at the Glendale Center Theatre led to Clarke's first screen roles for American International Pictures. In *How to Make a Monster* (1958) he played a teenage werewolf in a homage to Michael Landon's *I Was a Teenage Werewolf* (1957). A few years later, Clarke appeared in a supporting role on the TV series *Michael Shayne*. The 60-minute crime drama, starring Richard Denning in the lead role, lasted 32 episodes. From 1961–62 Clarke appeared on nine TV shows including *Tales of Wells Fargo, Laramie, 87th Precinct, Wagon Train, The Tall Man* and *Gunsmoke*.

A few months later, he auditioned for the part of Steve on *The Virginian* (1962).

PAUL GREEN: Can you tell us how you got the part of Steve?

GARY CLARKE: It cost me a lot of money, Paul. I had to pay off a lot of people (laughter). Well, first, I was under contract to Universal and I did a bunch of their shows. *The Virginian* came about and everybody and their uncle was testing for it. My biggest competition was Ben Cooper. And it was a closed set so anybody who got to audition would go in and make certain the set was cleared just to be fair to everybody. I had met Doug [McClure] before. We had met socially and become kind of friends. Not drinking buddies but we were friends. So he and I were talking and he was up for Trampas and I was up for Steve.

I had done a lot of preparation for this because I knew there was a bunch of guys up for the same part. So I made up a song about the Virginian. I just did a lot of extra stuff. And then Doug and I got together and we knew we were going to have a little scene together. So we blocked out this thing where at the end of the scene I jumped up into his arms and I had my legs around him and he had his arms under my legs. He threw me up in the air and I did a back flip and I think that was one of the things that got me the part.

PG: So basically the circus act got you the part.

GC: Yes, I think it did help me get the part because it established a nice chemistry with Doug. When I was doing my test, I think one of the powers-that-be wanted Ben Cooper to have the part so he allowed Ben to stay on the stage and watch me while I did it. Which wasn't a cool thing. But it just made me work all the harder.

PG: Did Ben Cooper test with Doug McClure?

GC: I think so. Then we had to wait. That everpresent waiting time. Jere Henshaw

Gary Clarke jumping for joy (courtesy Gary Clarke).

was instrumental, I think, in my getting the part and was also a major force at Universal studios. They were having a party at his house and we still hadn't heard. There was a day or two before we were going to hear. So I went to the party, of course. And when I walked in he said, "Hey, Steve, I mean Gary. How you doing?" So I had an inkling but it wasn't formal. But I got it.

There were a lot of people skeptical about another Western. An hour and a half. No pilot. Not proven yet. And I remember on the first show we were out on the back lot on a big set that represented the town. I think I was standing on the porch of the courthouse or something. There was some PR people and press people who were there and they were talking amongst themselves. As I was just sitting waiting for my turn, I overheard this one guy say, as Doug was doing his scene with Jim, "Well, there's Doug McClure in another show. That's probably a sure sign that this going to bomb too." I went over to Doug and I said, "Doug, if you'd like me to help me throw this guy off the lot, I will be happy to."

Doug went over and grabbed the guy by the scruff of the neck and didn't hurt him, but just said, "Don't ever, ever let me see you on this lot again. If you're on the lot, don't come on this set."

And the guy replied, "Oh, Doug, I didn't mean ... I was just being ..."

"Get out of here."

There was some of that skepticism.

An article came out in *Life* magazine and it showed Doug and me cutting up. I had just put my gun in my holster butt first. And then they had a shot of Jim on his horse and he had this grimace on his face and they talked about a case of hemorrhoids (laughter). It was just so ridiculous. Well, he did have them. He was suffering with hemorrhoids!

PG: Have you read the Wister novel?

GC: When I was up for it, I read it. In the original story Steve gets hung, and I said to the producer, "Are you trying to tell me something here or is this a sword you're going to be holding over my head?"

PG: In the first season, Steve and Trampas were like a double act with you teasing and joking with each other. Did this grow out of your personalities or did you just stick to scripts as they came your way?

GC: A lot of the stuff that Doug and I did was off the cuff. There was one show with Brian Keith and we had a scene in there where it said, "Johnny teaches Steve how to shoot." And all that was ad lib. That scene where he's setting up the can and I'm fooling around and shoot the can out of his hand and he comes over and punches me in the chest. I can't tell you how close I came to knocking him out.

PG: Brian Keith was a big man to knock out.

GC: No. He was stocky but he was a little shorter than me. We had a good time but he caught me unawares and I didn't know he was going to do it. So I just played it.

PG: That was a key episode showing the audience how Steve came to Shiloh. Were you aware it was adapted from a 1950s movie?

GC: Yes. The guy who wrote that script would also play small parts in the various scripts that he wrote. But his father wrote the original script. The one you're talking about which I thought was great.

PG: In the second season, Steve became more mature and serious. Was that your input or just a natural evolution of the character?

GC: I think it was a natural evolution. There was something that happened that I think contributed major league to that. And that was my tongue-tiedness every time I was around Lee J. Cobb. I was just in awe of the man. A brilliant actor. A powerful presence. And I got to work with him.

After about three or so months of shooting, I began to realize that my getting intimidated by Lee was getting in the way of my performing. Especially in scenes with him. I can't tell you how many times I would drop a line in scenes with him. So I decided that I was going to have a conversation with him. Just let him know what was going on. Just get it out on the table at least, and then what he did with it was fine after that. So I told Jim and Doug that the next morning after we were riding out to location at Albertson's Ranch. I said, "If you wouldn't mind, just leave me alone in the limo with Lee." So Jim was in the front seat. Lee was in the back on the right, Doug was in the middle and I was in the back on the left. We got to the location. Jim and Doug got out. Jim took the driver out and there I was sitting with Lee. And he's just looking straight ahead, just kind of calm and nonchalant. He may have suspected something. I don't know. And he took out his ever present cigar. Lit it and let this little curl of smoke go out.

It seemed like it took me a week and a half to get up enough nerve just to say the first words. And that was something like, "Lee, I wanted to talk to you," and I'm stammering, "I just wanted to take a moment of your time and just let you know about a situation ... er ... I would certainly like to ... er ... remedy ... er ... I don't want to put any burden on you or anything. But I thought maybe something like this has happened to you in the past ... because I'm just in awe of you and I'm ... er ... finding I'm tongue-tied and

I can't talk when I'm around you. I'm just wondering, has anything like this ever happened to you before and if so ... er ... how did it work out?"

I finally got it out and realized I was sweating. He took another draw on his cigar and let the smoke curl out of his mouth. And I'm expecting really something profound. Lee J. Cobb, he is going to give me something that will change my life forever. Nothing. Didn't say a word.

And it seemed like ten minutes. I'm getting really antsy and I said. "Well, look, Lee, I don't mean to intrude. I know you're thinking about the day's shoot. There's a lot of stuff we have to shoot. But I just figured we're going to be working together for years, I hope. And this is just kind of getting in the way and I thought there might be something you could say to help me get by it."

Another puff. Another curl of smoke. Nothing. And it seemed like an half-hour this time. He didn't even look at me once. Straight ahead, puffing on the cigar thinking about the tulips in his backyard or something. I don't know.

So I got out of the car and said, "Oh, excuse me. I'm sorry I intruded on your time. And as far as I'm concerned, you can stick this limo up your butt!"

And I slammed the door and walked off and walked by Jim and Doug who were standing by the chuck wagon and they said, "Hey, how'd it go?" and I said. "***!!!!xxx****!"

Ironically, all that day, about 95 percent of everything I had to shoot was with Lee. Of course, it would have to be. We do all the scenes and I'm just ploughing through them. About halfway through the day the director came up and said, "Gary, I don't know what you're doing here but keep it up. It's great."

And I said, "Yeah, well, who asked you?"

So we had about two more shots to go. And this was one that I had with Lee. And he was sitting in his high director's chair and he was smoking his cigar and I was pacing back and forth in front of a horse, getting ready. And I just caught a glimpse of him and he was watching me walk back and forth. And I caught this little twinkle in his eye. And it just hit me like a sledgehammer between the eyes.

I said, "You son of a gun. You did that on purpose."

And he laughed and stood up and gave me the biggest hug. I've never forgotten that. That a fellow actor would do something like that for another actor. I mean, he took a chance. I could've walked off the set. But he stayed with it all day. He let me discover it for myself. As a result, that has probably never happened to me since.

I remember Lee doing a scene with Roberta. She was sick in bed or going to bed or something and he was sitting on the side of the bed just talking to her. I was riveted. Just watching him.

PG: When did you shoot the ride-in sequence?

GC: We shot the ride-in credits on the first or second day. I hadn't spent any time on horses. But when they asked me, I said, "Are you kidding? Of course. I was trained by Gene Autry, Roy Rogers and Tom Mix. C'mon!"

So they believed that I could ride. They gave me the same stunt man that I had on the other shows when I was under contract. Gary Combs. His father Del Combs was the head wrangler. So I figured I could get with Gary and he could show me what I needed to do. But we had other things to do and I kept setting it aside. I was under the assumption that the first stuff we would shoot was going be indoors. But it wasn't. It was back out at Albertson's Ranch. Not only that, but the first shot of the first show on the first day was Jim and then Doug and then me wrangling this herd of about 50 horses. I was pan-icked. I figured, that's it. They're going to find me out.

The way they shot it was, they put the herd of horses together and then on the other side of a fence that you never saw in the shot was the camera car. And then on the other side of the horses was Jim. Jim worked on a dude ranch and he had his own horses.

So they said, "Action!" and they whipped up the horses and then those horses were running full out. And the camera car zoomed in and out on Jim as he was wrangling and doing all that stuff. So there was no way you could fake it.

And Doug did his stint. Doug did rodeo stuff before. He was so at home on a horse. He always looked sensational on a horse. Doug and Jim both. So Doug did his stint and he was terrific.

Meanwhile I was talking to Gary and his dad and I said, "Listen. Just get me through this shot. I know I can get on a horse. I practiced getting on a horse. Hopefully I can stay on. I'm a little concerned about stopping the horse."

And they were laughing and they said, "Don't worry. We gave you a great horse. Her name is Babe."

"Okay, okay. So I want to be friends with Babe right away."

They said, "Now look. At the end of the shot, just aim in toward us. I'll have some wranglers out here and we'll stop the horse. You won't have to worry about it." The assis-tant director said, "Gary, you want to ride up to the start point?"

"No, I'll walk. I'll be right there. I'm getting warmed up."

"Okay."

So they were up there waiting. And I had been practicing this mount where you jump up in the air. While you're in the air, you stick your left foot in the stirrup and swing your right leg over. And I did it and it worked. The director, who just happened to be watch-ing me, gave me a thumbs-up and I gave him one back.

Now I was pleading with Babe, "Oh, Babe, please, don't throw me off. Don't buck me off. And when it comes time to stop, please stop and I'll do everything that I can to stay on your back and be good."

And Babe went, "brrrrrrr" or whatever horses do.

So they said, "Okay. Action!"

They whipped up the horses. The camera car started. I jabbed Babe in the side with my spurs and she was off and running, full out. And I figured that's one of the things that saved my life because I was able to ride away and get in a rhythm with Babe.

And I was going, "Hey, this feels pretty good."

And then I have my left hand holding the reins and I was taking the excess reins and I was giving Babe little swats on the side. And I took my hat off and I was whopping her on the butt. Kind of out of the corner of my eye I see the director going, "Yes, yes, yes!"

At the end of the shot, I aimed Babe toward the wranglers. And as I got there ready to stop, I notice Babe stopping and starting. Stop. Start. Stop. Start. Stop. Start. And finally they grabbed the reins and I jumped off.

The director came over and said, "Gary that was sensational!" and I think I said, "Yeah, well, I told you I could ride."

And then they looked at Jim and Doug, "Why couldn't you guys do it like that?"

After the directors went away, I asked Del and Gary, "How come Babe was doing that at the end? Stop, start. stop, start?"

And they said to me, "When you stop a horse, you pull on the reins. But when you pull on your reins, you don't dig in with your spurs. Because the horse doesn't know what to do."

Later in the day, and this will finish a very long story, Jim and Doug wanted to get even. We had this shot and it was at the bend of a dirt road. Like a hill. We were at the top of the hill. We came down right toward camera and we turned and the camera turned and followed us so the camera would see us running toward it. And then riding away from it.

Jim and Doug were talking, conspiratorially I might add, as I came up. You couldn't get me off the horse. I mean, I ate lunch on the horse. So I rode up there and said, "Okay, let's go."

I was on the outside, which meant I would be closest to the camera when we rode by. This was the first take. "Action!" We came down the hill at the run. We turned right and as we turned right, they were edging over to the left, edging me off the road. It wasn't a drop-off or anything but it was no road. And in front of me there was this big round bush. It looked 12 feet tall. I looked at it and my eyes panicked. No problem with Babe. She just leapt up and over it. And as she went, I somehow kind of leaned forward hoping I'd stay on. And when she landed, I kind of leaned back. And I stayed on. And the director wet himself. He was just so thrilled with it. "Great shot. Cut. Print!"

PG: Can you recall what you and Doug said to the Virginian in the ride-in credits? Did you rehearse it or was it just ad-libbed?

GC: Yeah, it was all ad-libbed. Jim comes along and then Doug and I ride in beside and they identify us and we peel off again and leave.

PG: So you have no memory of what you said to each other?

GC: Probably something obscene. I don't remember.

PG: Can you recall where the credits were shot?

GC: It was out on location. Usually it was Albertson's Ranch. That was down the Ventura Freeway and out beyond Thousand Oaks.

PG: Were you frustrated working on the show? Did you want more episodes focused around you?

GC: Well, yeah, they'd do that for everyone once in a while. They'd do it for Roberta, for Doug, for me. I had a couple like that. I had one with Jack Klugman and the cougar I was tracking. That was a fun show, doing that with Jack.

PG: Did anyone ever ask you to sing on the show? How did your *Virginian* theme single come about?

GC: I was a member of the original *Lettermen* which was Tony Butala (who still owns the *Lettermen*), Jimmy Blaine and I. We started out as *The Fourmost* which belonged to Connie Stevens. And I was dating Connie for about seven years. We almost got married a couple of times, and then Connie went off to do something and we started doing the early stages of the *Lettermen*. I guess somebody heard that or I mentioned it. You know, anybody who's on a series is asked to sing a song. If you put out a song and it clicks, that's great for the show. I think I sold ... I know that I sold nine copies.

There was a time when these guys came on the set and asked Doug where I was. And I just happened to see them around the back lot. And they came up to me and they said, "Gary, congratulations. You've been voted *Photoplay's* Best Newcomer."

I was to receive the award on *The Tonight Show*. Johnny Carson was wonderful. He was just great. I had recorded the theme from *The Virginian* and the producers said, "Why

Gary Clarke learns a painful lesson (courtesy Gary Clarke).

don't you do this on the show?" And they called the Carson show and they said, "Okay, fine."

So I figured, terrific, I can go on and lip-synch it. Oh no! The union wouldn't have it. I had to rehearse and do the song live with Skitch Henderson. I thought, "I certainly hope Skitch will show me what to do here, because I'm in front of 40 to 50 million people." So I get there for rehearsal early and they're rehearsing Della Reese. For two hours they rehearse Della Reese. Which was great. Listening to her sing was wonderful.

She left. My turn. He flipped out the music to all the guys and he said, "Okay. It's got a rock 'n' roll beat." I had five minutes rehearsal with the band.

I said, "But I don't really..."

"Don't worry about it. It'll be fine."

Came the time. "And now we present the most promising actor.... And here he is, Gary Clarke."

I walked out. The music started. I started singing. And Skitch and the band finished about 20 seconds before I did. I turned to Johnny and he waved me over. He had that little grin on his face. The audience was very polite. And I walked over and I was looking at Johnny and he was watching me. It was one of those moments when something had to be said. And I turned around and sat in the chair. And I was tapping my fingers on his desk. And he was tapping his pencil on the desk. And after a long time I looked up and I said, "Well, the award's for the most promising actor. It didn't say anything about singing, as I recall."

I did get fan mail from a young lady. She sent me her picture. A very attractive young lady. She said, "I love watching you on the show. I love watching what Steve does and the problems that he gets into. I never miss it. I just think it's great. But please, don't sing any more."

PG: Did you ever have any hits?

GC: No, not really. How can you have a hit with songs like "One Summer in a Million"? I'll tell you, I sang for just about every major label. RCA, Victor, Decca, 20th Century-Fox, Raleigh Records. They were songs like "Greenfinger" and "I Promised Amelia." You know songs like that. Like my old movie titles.

PG: In season three, you only had guest star status and dropped out of the show early into that season. What happened to cause you to leave so early into the run?

GC: To be perfectly honest with you, I got a little cocky. I had asked for maybe an extra show or two that featured me out of the, maybe, 40 that we did every year. And the producer said, "Okay, we will." And nothing happened. So I went to Lew Wasserman, who was God. I went in and he was just as sweet as can be. I was dumb and I went over my producer's head. That summer following the second year ... and the studio had just lent me, I think, $5,000 to buy a home because I was just getting married. I married Pat Woodell.

After I bought the house, and we were in the house a month or so, I got a call from my agent Lew Weitzman and he said "They didn't pick up your contract, Gary."

"Oh, what happened?"

"Nobody knows really. It's just..."

But I'm sure that's what it was. I wasn't very politically inclined. If it didn't go the way I thought it should go, I spoke up.

PG: Like Jim.

GC: Yeah, Jim was like that. They would tolerate him a little more than me.

PG: What was your reaction to losing your job?

GC: Well, where can I go to work? What can I do? I'd done a little bit of writing before, so I started writing. I wrote a couple of scripts. I tried to use my own format and realized right away that producers weren't interested in how creative I was in my format. They just wanted a good script. So I quickly learned how to do that. I was having lunch with Bill Kiley who was the head of NBC publicity, and whom I had come to know and had become friends with while I was still on *The Virginian*.

He said, "I saw this funny show last night about this bumbling spy," and he told me a little bit about it. And I said, "Gee, I have an idea. Can I run it by you? Can I write it?" And he said, "Absolutely."

So I wrote this thing. It was an half-hour show but I think I wrote an hour-long script. I showed it to him and he said, "This is perfect. Have your agent get it to him."

Well, they weren't taking any unsolicited scripts. My agent at the time said to the producers Buck Henry and Mel Brooks, "You have to read this. This guy is only here for a while out of New York and you gotta read it." So he forced them to read it.

Gary Clarke as Captain Richards in the MGM series *Hondo*, 1967 (courtesy Gary Clarke).

Universal had hired me to do one of those teenage-in-the-snow movies called *Wild, Wild Winter*. When I was doing *Hondo,* I wrote something and gave it to the producer and he took it in his hand and without even looking at it he handed it back. He said, "Gary, you're an actor. You act. Let the writers write."

My impression was, oh, well, he's a big producer here at MGM. Maybe that's the way all producers look at it. "So when I submitted the script I used my real name, Clarke Frederick L'Amoreaux. I turned the script in under C.F. L'Amoreaux and they called me while I was on site in Lake Tahoe and they said, "Clarke, we'd like to see you when you get back. We're interested in your script."

"Wow! Great. Okay I'll be there."

I left both names at the front desk so they wouldn't give me away and tell them I was Gary Clarke. Before I went in, I decided they might recognize me so I parted my hair funny, like in the middle, and wore horned rimmed glasses and just dressed dorky. They said, "Hey, we really like it and we want you to this one and then we'll do some more."

And that was *Get Smart*.

PG: How many episodes did you write?

GC: Oh, 10 or 12 at the most I think. I created the character *Hymie the Robot*. Dick Gautier played the part and thanked me profusely for re-energizing his career. I have to tell you, I was Clarke L'Amoreaux for maybe the first three or four scripts and then I finally said to myself, "Hey, if they're going to fire me just because I'm Gary Clarke, then so be it. I'm gonna tell 'em."

I walked into Buck's office and Mel Brooks was there.

"Excuse me, gentlemen. Have a minute?"

"Sure, Clarke. What is it?"

"Well, I've written three or four shows for you now and I just wanted to tell you, I hope you don't think I got in here under false pretenses, but my name is also Gary Clarke. I'm an actor."

And without flinching they said, "Yeah, we know."

"You *know*?"

"Yeah, we watch TV too, you know."

"Why didn't you say something?'

"We just wanted to see how long you'd carry it out."

PG: Did you continue writing during and after *Get Smart*?

GC: Yeah. I did some stuff for *Ozzie and Harriet*. I wrote a movie called *People Toys* that I know was produced but I've never seen it. I was bouncing around a lot. Working with some friends of mine—one did music and I did the writing and the other was the director. I worked with David Nelson for a while. Another sweetheart. I did a couple of shows and did a couple of movies for him. I just did stuff but nothing major.

PG: You appeared in three or four shows in the third season. How did that come about?

GC: They actually brought me back. My rationale for that is that they'd lent me $5,000. But they paid me much more for those three shows. Almost as much as I did for the whole season. It was just a way to get the money back and to get the books straight. But I was delighted they invited me back.

PG: What did you miss most when you left the show?

GC: Of course you miss being in a regular show. Particularly with a show you don't leave voluntarily. But I kept in touch with Jim and with Doug.

PG: Were you close to Clu Gulager, Randy Boone or Roberta Shore?

GC: Yeah, but more so with Jim and Doug. We'd go out with the wives and things like that.

PG: When you left the show, did you continue to watch it or did it hurt your feelings that it went on for nine years?

GC: It wasn't like that for me. There might have been a little twinge but there was other stuff I could do. I really got interested in writing. Then the series *Hondo* came along. That kept me busy. I remember one time *Hondo* and *The Virginian* were shooting in the same area. I rode over and I saw Jim that day and Gary Combs and his dad Del and just shot the breeze for awhile. That was fun.

PG: And you briefly acted with Doug again in an episode of *Search*. Was it good working with him again?

GC: Yes. I ended up being the bad guy.

PG: In the mid–1970s you dropped out of acting. What did you do?

GC: Around 1975 I just kind of stepped out of the business for awhile and went to work for an organization called "est." It was pretty controversial at the time. It was run by Werner Erhard. It started up in San Francisco and I found it in L.A. It was a two-week seminar. It was about discovering things about yourself. It wasn't "OM" and it wasn't "Scientology," because I checked into that and that scared me.

This one I appreciated. It was like they would hold a mirror up in front of you. Not literally. And seeing areas of your life you hadn't seen. Probably if I had done "est" before I got hired on *The Virginian*, I would have been a little more diplomatic.

PG: What does "est" stand for?

GC: Well, it stands for "It is" and it also stands for "Erhard's seminar training."

Gary Clarke and Sam Elliot take a break between filming on 1993's *Tombstone* (courtesy Gary Clarke).

PG: So basically it's a self-discovery course?

GC: Yeah. I went to work for them and it was an extraordinary five years. I was on staff. And then I came back down to L.A. in 1981.

PG: In 1985 you returned to acting.

GC: Yeah, I did soaps. I did *General Hospital.* I did a new one they were doing called *Bright Promise* that was neither bright nor promising.

PG: And then you did *Young Riders* for three episodes.

GC: Yeah. That's when I came out here to Phoenix. It was filmed in Tucson. I did four of five of those. And I did a movie, *Tombstone.* Wyatt Earp, Kurt Russell, steps off the train and he's looking around. And he looks toward the end of the train and he sees some guy off loading this horse. And the guy smacks his horse with the reins and Wyatt comes over and smacks him with the reins and says, "This hurts, doesn't it?" Instantly after that, two guys walk up, one in a derby, and he asks him to become marshall. So next time you watch it you'll say, "Oh, yeah. Put on a few years that guy."

PG: What do you do today?

GC: I go to North Phoenix Baptist Church. I actually moved out here in 1987 to do a little real estate venture with my ex-wife's [Pat Woodell] husband. We were divorced in 1985 and she married again in '87. I was an usher at their wedding. They were my best friends. He invited me to participate in a real estate venture out here in Phoenix so I moved here.

Then I met my third and last wife in 1991 and we got married the same year. And my daughter Ava came along in '93 and my daughter Natalie came along in 2001. I have three sons from my very first marriage to Marilyn right out of high school. The age difference between my youngest daughter and my oldest son is 48 years. Jeff, Dennis and David are my sons. I have great-grandchildren who are older than my children. I'm not kidding.

PG: Are you officially retired?

GC: No. I'm writing radio spots and TV spots for our church. They hire me, on like a seasonal basis. I keep my hand in. I still have a couple of films that I wrote that I would love to get done. Whether they get done or not, I don't know. Mostly I'm raising my girls.

PG: Do you take your Christianity seriously?

GC: Yes, I do.

PG: Looking back on *The Virginian,* what are your high points and low points?

GC: There weren't many low points. I remember one director I wanted to punch. Dick Bare was his name. He was rude and, in my opinion, not nice. I had to actually walk off the set or I would have punched him. We were shooting a scene out on the back lot. I had an idea—and I always did. But mostly the directors would listen.

I asked him, "Can we do this in this shot? Can I do this? I would think it would be something Steve would do." And he didn't answer. He just walked away. So I went up to him again and I asked him again and he turned and he walked away.

Then I started for him and I guess Doug saw something and he kind of said, "Hey, it's all right. Just stop." So I just walked off. I went back to my dressing room. Took a breather and then came back and I finished it.

PG: Did you ever see Jim lose his temper on the set?

GC: Yeah. We were working with a monkey once. So we were sitting at a table and

Gary Clarke, wife Jerrene, Ava (9) and Natalie (2), December 2002 (courtesy Gary Clarke).

the monkey bit my arm. Didn't do anything, because I had my Levi jacket on and luckily I didn't move. I was just still and flexed my forearm and the monkey stopped. But Jim was furious. He was very protective. He jumped in and he said, "Damn it, can't you get some monkey in here that isn't going to attack people?"

That was the episode with David Wayne. It was interesting because Steve took care of Doug's daughter in the episode. So we had a good time.

PG: So basically you have fond memories of working on the show?

GC: Oh, yeah. Nothing will tarnish that. I got let go, fired, terminated, whatever you want to call it. And it was my own doing.

PG: If you hadn't been released from your contract, would you have been the sort of person to last nine seasons?

GC: I would have gone nine seasons. I'm sure I would have started writing. You can see the past any way you want and this is what happened. Maybe I wouldn't have started writing like I did. I've always had a penchant for it. But necessity is the mother of invention and creation, so...

14

Roberta Shore

Betsy Garth

Roberta Shore was already a seasoned performer when she made her first appearance as Betsy Garth on *The Virginian* in 1962. Born Jimmye Roberta Shourup on April 7, 1945, in Monterey Park, California, she made her professional TV debut on *The Tex Williams Show* from Knotts Berry Farm. *The Pinky Lee Show* (1954) and an early association with Walt Disney followed, appearing with "The Mouseketeers" on *The Mickey Mouse Club* (1955) and in the short-lived Disney serial *Annette* (1957) with Annette Funicello. Billed as Jymme Shore, she played Laura Rogan, a young snob influenced by her mother's social pretensions.

In 1958 she was cast as Joyce Kendall on the popular Robert Young sitcom *Father Knows Best*. Movie roles followed in *The Shaggy Dog* (1959), *Because They're Young* (1960) with Doug McClure and *The Young Savages* (1961).

A busy Roberta Shore, under contract to Universal, also appeared in guest spots on Western shows, including *Zane Grey Theatre, Wagon Train, Laramie, Lawman* and *The Tall Man.*

In 1962, Shore was approached to test for the role of Betsy Garth on *The Virginian.*

PAUL GREEN: Can you describe auditioning for *The Virginian?*

ROBERTA SHORE: I was under contract to Universal at the time and the show I was in, *The New Bob Cummings Show,* only lasted about three episodes. It was really a bad show. And so they asked me if I knew how to ride a horse. Back in those days you said yes to everything and then you went out and took lessons. I basically had one lesson on horseback riding.

Actually I tested with an actor by the name of Tony Young, who has since passed away. I can't remember if I tested with Jim or not. I think I basically got the part because I was under contract. I'm not so sure they tested any other girls for that. To my knowledge they didn't. I thought Tony Young was up for the part of the Virginian, but I did a festival with him years later and he told me he was actually auditioning for the part of Trampas, which was interesting. Tony was very tall and really, I thought, cowboy-looking (*laughter*). And he had dark hair. Doug McClure was just a totally different personality. I guess Doug was probably more suited for what they had in mind. At that time I didn't know anything of the character.

PG: Did Universal provide you with a back story for the Betsy character?

RS: They probably could have. It's been so many years ago I honestly can't remember (*laughter*). Actually, I don't even hardly recall reading a script for that. It was just a part I tested for so I wasn't really sure of the characters and how they were supposed to be portrayed.

PG: James Drury said he was told he had the role on the Friday before shooting started that Monday. Was that the same with you?

RS: You know, I don't think I was even told. I knew I'd be playing the daughter of Lee J. Cobb. As far as the rest of the cast, I didn't have a clue.

PG: Did Universal sign you to a standard seven-year contract?

RS: Yeah, I was under a seven-year contract to Universal that started when I turned 18.

PG: You'd worked in episodic TV and even in regular series roles. But this was a 90-minute format and more hectic than usual.

RS: Oh, a bit more hectic. There were times when we'd be doing two shows at a time. We'd go on one set and shoot one scene, and run to the next set and change our wardrobe and shoot another. Luckily my character didn't involve a lot of heavy acting so I didn't have to change character a lot. I just went from one stage to another.

PG: You had to do a lot of horse riding and you say you only had one lesson on a horse. Were you afraid of horses?

RS: Oh, I was scared to death of horses. We were on location one day doing some things and I was supposed to be running or chasing somebody. I don't remember the scene. And I had a horse that kind of ran away with me. Luckily there was a wrangler that finally was able to stop him. But I would hardly get on a horse after that. It would petrify me.

PG: Did you get used to horses over your period of time on the show?

RS: Well, not really. Jim and Doug were both really good horsemen. In fact, a lot of those guys were. Doug was raised on a ranch, so he knew a lot about horses. But one of the things those guys did was, they had their own special horses they would use and I had a different horse every time I did a show.

I remember riding on Jim's horse one day, and boy there was such a difference on how he rode. I think it had a lot to do with horses and the fact I didn't have a horse I could ever get used to. I think the same with Lee J. Cobb. We were always the jokes of the cutting room floor because there was so much space between us and the horse when we'd be cantering (*laughter*).

PG: What was an average working day for you?

RS: If we were on location I would be in the studio at 5 a.m. If we were not on location I would be at the studio at 6 a.m. Back in those days they curled your hair and you had to sit under the dryer for an hour and then you were in makeup for another hour. Sometimes we'd sit around all day and do nothing, but if I was in at 6 o'clock that meant I had, as I recall, an 8 o'clock call because that would give me a couple of hours to get ready. The filming usually went on until six or seven. I can remember doing a show with Vera Miles and we were going until 10 o'clock at night, because we were on a real tight schedule.

PG: Did that wear you down?

RS: Oh, listen, we would get the giggles we'd get so tired.

PG: So you weren't getting stressed out?

RS: No, it was fun.

PG: Did you wear hairpieces?

RS: Yes I did. Mostly I wore a ponytail and the reason I did is because I had long, but very fine hair. By ten o'clock in the morning, every ounce of curl would be gone from my hair and I was just a hairdresser's nightmare. So that's the reason I wore pieces. And I didn't all the time. When I wore my hair down I didn't, but if I did wear a ponytail I'd sometimes wear a piece.

PG: *The Virginian* included your singing in quite a few episodes. Is it true you started your singing career as a child at supermarket openings with Tex Williams?

RS: Yes, that's how I started out, as a singer. When I was eight years old I sang at my grandparents' fiftieth wedding anniversary. My dad used to play in a little country–Western band with some of my uncles. So somewhere along the line they said, "You need to go around to some of these contests." So they took me around to these contests and there was a time when they were having all these great big supermarket openings and they always had Tex Williams, who was a country–Western singer at that time. He would go to all of these openings and perform. My parents just kind of dragged me around from supermarket opening to supermarket opening and finally they fixed it so I had to get up and sing.

PG: Did you enjoy it?

Roberta Shore, 1963.

RS: Oh, I loved it! Well, I guess I loved it. I was too young to know any different (*laughter*). And then when I was ten years old, Tex Williams had a local TV show from Knotts Berry Farm in California and he put me on his show. And that's kind of how I started out. I went on to *The Pinky Lee Show* and after that is when I started doing Disney.

My maiden name was Schourup so we just shortened it to Jymme Shore. When I was working for Disney and they were getting ready to release *The Shaggy Dog*, whenever they would send out any type of publicity, if there wasn't a picture accompanying the article, they would refer to me as a "he." Walt Disney was the one that suggested I change my name to Roberta. But I've just never cared for the name Roberta. My friends call me Jymme.

PG: Can you describe your impressions of the cast?

RS: Clu Gulager was, as I

recall, very serious. I was kind of the Lone Ranger in there because it was a real guy thing (*laughter*), with Jim and Doug and Clu and all those guys. I was a little bit distanced from them. Jim was the hardest one to get along with and he'll tell you that himself. I think that's when Jim was drinking. I've done lots of festivals with Jim since and he's said, "I was not a nice person back then." And he wasn't (*laughter*). They just partied a lot. They would come to work having partied all night and half the time they'd have these (*laughter*) hangovers.

They would take us out in a limousine to the location, which was about a 40-minute drive from the studio. One morning, Jim and Doug had been partying all night. I was driving in a limo with them and I was very young and had tons of energy and was always singing. I was singing in the limo all the way to the location. And finally those guys just absolutely refused to take a ride with me any more. We were laughing about that at this little dinner we had, and Jim said, "I can remember the name of that song right to this day." It was the song "I Like to Be in America!" from *West Side Story*.

Lee J. Cobb I just adored. He just had this dry wit. He could walk into a set and all tension would just leave. Most of the guest celebrities we had, of Lee J.'s generation, like Bette Davis and Henry Morgan, were the most professional people I had ever worked with.

PG: I've heard Lee J. Cobb was unhappy on the set because of the schedule and some of the scripts. Did you ever get the impression he was unhappy?

RS: You know, I was never aware of that. I found out about that later on. After I left the show, I came back and was visiting my family and had lunch with Frank Price, who was producer at that time. He told me how hard Lee J. was to work with. That was the first I even heard of it. He was very professional on set. In fact, I remember one time we were waiting to shoot a scene and Jim was in it. I don't remember what the circumstances were but Jim was, like, 45 minutes late to the set. And I thought "Oh, brother," because we were all sitting around waiting for Jim. And I just thought Lee J. Cobb was very cool about it. He said, "We've been waiting for you."

When we were doing *The Virginian*, that's when they first started doing the Universal tours. And at that time there was just bus loads of people they would drive around. I know Lee J. Cobb just hated them. Because you could just walk out of the sound stage with your hair in curlers and no makeup and there'd be all these people.

PG: Was Jim often late on set?

RS: I don't think so. The only time our schedule was late was when they'd go out and party. I swear those guys would go out and party all night and come in to the set the next day having not even been home. I don't recall Jim being late other than that.

PG: In the show, you and Doug McClure seemed to get along like brother and sister. Was that transferred to real life?

RS: Well, Doug and I did a movie together called *Because They're Young*. I got my one and only screen kiss from Doug when I was 16. And after we finished that movie he went on to do *Checkmate* and from *Checkmate* he went on to do *The Virginian*. Yeah, Doug I'd just known a long time. He was just an overgrown kid. He was just the cutest guy.

PG: Your relationships with the characters evolved over the three years you stayed with the show. In the first episode, Betsy says she'll marry the Virginian one day. But in later episodes he treats you more like a daughter than a precocious teenager. Any comments?

RS: I don't remember that. No kidding? I'm sure that was said as a joke. It's funny, I don't remember that at all. I don't ever recall any type of romance whatsoever.

PG: It was more like you had a crush.

RS: Oh, I don't even remember that.

PG: Likewise, Trampas and Steve take fun in teasing you. Did your character view them as elder brothers rather than potential boyfriends?

RS: Elder brothers. Not potential boyfriends. There was no romance in it at all.

PG: Was Gary Clarke temperamental?

RS: Well, the only thing that I recall about Gary is that everything kind of went to Gary's head a little bit. Because, this is only what I remember, and I don't know how accurate it is, but he kind of started demanding things. Demanding this and demanding that. The story that I heard was that he kept going in to producers and threatening and saying, "If you don't do this, I'm going to leave," and finally they just said, "Hey, see you later." I think there was a little bit of truth to that, but I don't know how much. I think Gary kind of talked himself out of that.

PG: Who was tight on the set?

RS: Jim and Doug were tight and Gary Clarke was tight with them. I don't think Clu was. I didn't have a lot to do with Clu. One of my favorite people on the set was Randy Boone.

PG: When Randy Boone joined the show, the singing you did with Randy was highlighted. Did Universal have an agenda for promoting you as a singing duo act?

RS: I don't think so. We did a *Virginian* album but they never promoted it. It didn't sell that well. Randy was kind of right off the farm when he came on the show. He was pretty well self-taught on the guitar and everything. So, no, I don't think they had any plans for that.

PG: Randy Boone's character gave you a person of a similar age to work with.

RS: I loved Randy. Randy was just so down-to-earth. Randy and Jim had some really funny stories because Randy used to do a lot of pot, I think. Randy said how he was so stoned one day there was one scene that he just couldn't get and finally he just made up his own thing. And he couldn't believe that they shot it.

Then he talked about some experience where I had gone up to him. He was sitting under a tree smoking or something. And of course, being a real staunch Mormon girl I went up and started lecturing him on his smoking. He said, "She did not have a clue that I was smoking pot" (*laughter*).

PG: So the cast used to tease you?

RS: Well, they used to tease me because of my age and because of my religion. Gary was always trying to give me glasses of orange juice with vodka in. I'd take a lot of ribbing.

PG: So basically it was a man's set and you felt a little like an outsider?

RS: Plus I was raised a very strict Mormon and I had a real strict mother. So I wasn't in the Hollywood set. I would come to do my job and then I'd leave. I was still living at home. My mother was on the set before I turned 18. It was law back then, but not when I did *The Virginian*.

PG: Was there ever a conflict between your Mormon faith and plot lines for your character on the show?

RS: Oh, lots of times. Not so much on *The Virginian.* I remember auditioning for a role for a Burt Lancaster movie called *The Young Savages.* I was a rebellious teenager in the part and I was supposed to smoke. And I told them at the time I was a very strict Mormon and I wouldn't smoke. They said okay but when it came down to shooting the scene they actually tried to get me to do it. And I wouldn't do it. I just absolutely refused to do it.

PG: When did you become a Mormon?

RS: Well, I was born into the Mormon church but you don't basically become a member of our church until you're baptized, which is when you're eight years old. You're born into Mormon heritage, until you're officially baptized, then you become an official member.

PG: You left the show rather suddenly in season three and returned for the marriage episode. Why did you decide to leave the show?

RS: I left the show to get married. And I had told the producers and they actually did not believe that I would do it. When I did, I guess they felt I had to have closure to my character.

PG: How did you feel about leaving the show?

RS: The person I married was very adamant about me being his wife and [he did not want to be] Mr. Roberta Shore. I had kind of mixed feelings. I had so many friends and I'd worked so many years in the industry. But at the same time, I was raised very strict Mormon and when you meet the right one he becomes your life. I don't know if I actually regret leaving.

I remember I had lunch with Lee J. Cobb about a year after I left and he said, "You left at the right time. This industry is changing so much." The only thing I think I regretted was leaving the people I had worked for. They were very nice to me. I moved to Salt Lake City and have remained there ever since.

PG: Lee J. Cobb quickly followed you in leaving the show. Did you ever watch other episodes during its nine-year run?

RS: I just kind of left it. I may have watched the following season to see who they put on to replace me. I don't know who she was, but she only lasted one year. Sara Lane, I guess, lasted. I don't ever know what happened to her.

PG: Did you prefer the first or later seasons?

RS: Probably the later seasons because I was a little bit more aware, I think, of what was going on. The first season I was 18 and they wanted me as a 14-year-old. Basically no makeup hardly, other than a base. At least I got to grow up in and have a bit better clothes in the second and third seasons.

PG: And they gave you some storylines as well.

RS: Yes they did, they gave me some nice storylines. They really tried to feature somebody in a show every episode.

PG: Did you make personal appearances at rodeos like Jim and Doug?

RS: No, I never did. But those guys, I think, made a lot of money doing those things. Mostly because I can't ride a horse. There's no way. I didn't know those guys did them until we had that dinner one night and Jim was telling us about all the things they did.

PG: That's where they made the money.

RS: That's what happened with the people on *The Lawrence Welk Show.* On all the years that Lawrence Welk was on the air, he only paid scale to the people on his show. How they made their money was doing the fairs and stuff on the weekends. Personal appearances.

PG: When you see actors making millions of dollars in sitcoms today, does that annoy you?

RS: It's absurd. Nobody's worth that much money. I'm sorry.

PG: Does that anger you?

RS: Oh, absolutely. That's a real topic of conversation when I do these film festivals with Jim. All the guys like Roy Rogers and Hopalong Cassidy, those guys never made money like that. Roy Rogers made a lot of his money, not from the series, but from the little Roy Rogers lunchboxes and stuff. The merchandising. When you look back, even I remember that Lee J. Cobb was getting $10,000 a show. I thought that was an astronomical amount of money. I just remember saying, "Oh my gosh, that's so much money." Jim and Doug made more money than I did, of course, and it was piddling in comparison to Lee, but I thought they made a tremendous amount of money at the time. And it's nothing compared to what they get today.

PG: I read an interview where Doug said he made no money from *The Virginian*.

RS: You know why? Because Doug was paying all of his ex-wives (*laughter*). In fact, [someone] told me once that Doug was always having to ask for advances for money because he had so much alimony. So if he wasn't making any money, I think it's because it was all going to his ex-wives.

PG: It's just a pity that Doug died so young.

RS: Oh, it's a real shame. And he and Jim were very close. Jim said he'd finally straightened his life out. He was playing tennis every day. But, you know, I think his hard living just caught up with him. He had a drinking problem and was a real heavy partyer.

PG: You had quite a history before *The Virginian*.

RS: I did a lot of recordings with Lawrence Welk. And I also did a show with Ronald Reagan. When we do these festivals we sell photographs and the photographs that I have are photographs that were sent to me by fans. Because I didn't have any. And I finally called Universal Archives to see if I could get some new photographs and the lady who was there, to save me a trip going down to Los Angeles, went through and pulled some photographs.

I was quite surprised how few photographs there were for being on the show for three years. But she sent a couple of photographs to look at that were not me. So I'm not so sure she knows who I am (*laughter*). But I did get a few new ones.

PG: Except for the 1973 short film *Cypher in the Snow* you quit acting after leaving *The Virginian*. Do you miss acting?

RS: No, I don't miss acting. I miss music. That's how I started out, singing. I did a lot of stuff for Disney. In fact, I did the Swiss yodeling in the *It's a Small World* exhibit in Disneyland. When you come to Switzerland, that's me doing the yodeling. My daughter took my grandkids to Disneyland about three weeks ago and she left a message on my answer phone, "Mom, you're still here."

I think I was 16 or 17 years old and to this day I can picture myself in the studio recording that, not knowing for sure what it was for. And then seeing this lady, I can see her to this day. I can't remember her name but she had kind of blond hair and she was little. And they were doing sketching for the ride at Disneyland.

PG: What did you do when you left the show?

RS: I have two daughters. I was divorced from my first husband and I remarried about nine years later. My second husband passed away of a brain tumor at 45. He died very young. And then eight years ago I married a gentlemen who had lost his wife to cancer. I have four little grandsons and a granddaughter. I inherited 15 grandkids so I have a really busy life. I tell you, when you get older you're supposed to slow down, and, boy, we just keep going faster.

My late husband was a furniture rep and after he died I just kept doing what he did and I've been doing it for 20 years. I go to furniture markets four times a year and have three states that I travel. I just love it. It's been the perfect job for me.

PG: So do you find your life more authentic than when you were in show business?

RS: Oh yes. I watch what's going on today in the industry and every other headline is "Britney's pregnant" or "Britney's having trouble with her pregnancy" and I think, who cares about any of that stuff? My husband says it's nothing but a bunch of gossip. I think I would hate to be in the industry right now.

When I was working, they'd didn't have the *Enquirer* or all the paparazzi and all the crap that they have now. We would have movie magazines and the most risqué thing that we would ever do is doing a date layout with Bobby Rydell or Fabian or whatever. I wouldn't even meet Bobby until we'd get there and we'd take the pictures and that was it. I'd never see him again (*laughter*). That was about as racy as it got.

Now it thrives on all the horrible stuff. I do a lot of shows with Dale Robertson, and they all feel the same way. It's not the caliber of people, as far as I can see now, that there were back then. In fact Lee J. Cobb came from the stage. People worked their way to where they got.

PG: You were, in effect, starting a trend, because a lot of musical people, like Fabian, were transferring to acting in the late 1950s and early 1960s. You were at the beginning of that trend.

RS: Yes, I was. And there will never be another generation like that for music. Ever(*laughter*).

PG: Did you work on the *Book of Mormon* movie in 2003? Some sources credit you.

RS: I wasn't in it. Thank heavens. Originally they had asked my husband and me to be in it and we both said yes. But then it took them so long to get going on the movie that I couldn't do it because of my work schedule. Which I'm kind of glad of because it was not a very well-made movie. It didn't do very well and I was quite relieved I wasn't in that.

PG: I know you don't recall individual episodes of *The Virginian* because of the hectic filming schedule, but does anything stand out in your memory from your time on the show?

RS: Probably some of my fondest memories are when I had some really touching scenes with Lee J. Cobb. Most of my scenes were "Hi, Daddy," or whatever. But I did have a couple of shows that I liked. I actually fell in love with Robert Redford in one episode. That was one of the first TV shows that Robert Redford ever did. Also, my most fun times were with Vera Miles. She was the dearest lady in the world. I loved her.

15

Randy Boone

Randy Benton

Born January 17, 1942, Clyde Randall Boone originally intended to make his living as a singer-songwriter. When he made his way across country to Hollywood from his native Fayetteville, North Carolina, he had little idea he would find employment and fame as an actor.

PAUL GREEN: How did you get into acting in Hollywood from your beginnings in North Carolina?

RANDY BOONE: After I graduated from high school in the class of '60 I went to State College in Raleigh, North Carolina, for a really short time because my heart wasn't in it. I had looked forward to getting out of school. I was just going to take the usual couple of years of courses preparatory to choosing a career but didn't know what I wanted to do. It was a problem. My mother didn't want me to get out of the habit of learning. I had started learning to play the guitar and ended up not being a very good student of the books. I spent more time at the college hang house playing guitar and actually started making money. I was being paid to come to the parties and play.

A friend and I rented an apartment and his hobby was photography. He had a really swell car, so he'd drive me to these fraternity parties. I'd play up at Chapel Hill and the university and lots of colleges and places all around Raleigh. Then I realized studying at college wasn't what I wanted to do. What I wanted to do was to see some life and get my service done. Get in the Army and do the two-year hitch. After you did your service, the Army had something like a G.I. Bill and if you put your money into going to school they would match the money and help you. So it was a good plan, and a lot of boys were doing it. And so I figured, well, okay, that does it. I'm going to take my guitar and I'm going to hitchhike around the country and have some fun until the Army drafts me and then I'll let them beat some discipline into me. I couldn't wait to get out of school and have a good time.

I remember I climbed right down off the lifeguard stand in the middle of the day and gave the job to the other guy and by that that evening I was packed and the next morning my mother and my sister took me out to the highway. That's how quick I was going to hitchhike off. I couldn't wait another minute. I said, no, I'm just not going to work another summer and go back to college next year. I'm gonna do it *now*.

I hitchhiked all the way down to Florida and back up to New York and spent a summer on Cape Cod in Massachusetts. Then the kids were talking about California, so I hitchhiked out to California. Playing the guitar was a great way for me to meet people and have fun. It made for easy traveling. A lot of times people would give me a ride more easily if they saw I had a guitar because they'd be curious. Guitars were still a little bit new. It wasn't like it is now. Today everybody plays all over the place. People were rather curious if you played the guitar then. And they'd ask to well play something. I used to meet people all over the place.

I was playing at a little bistro that had real good food. It was called Sid's Blue Beat in Newport Beach. One of the boys that I had met up in Los Angeles at a club there called the Troubadour had tried out for an acting job and he saw that there was a part for a southern boy who hitchhikes into this series, *It's a Man's World* (1962). He asked the producer Peter Tewksbury who they were going to cast. Tewksbury said they were having trouble finding somebody realistic (*laughter*). My friend told him, "Well, I met this kid who hitchhiked into town and he plays guitar."

Anyway, this fellow and Terry Wadsworth got in touch with me down in a place I was playing and said he'd arranged a meeting for me with Tewksbury. They had me do a reading for them and asked me back for a screen test. They said they'd let me know. I didn't really know anything. I didn't have any acting training. I had taken acting courses but I didn't go out there to be an actor. Anyway, I went up to San Jose and got a call from the producer who told me that they'd looked at my film and I was the boy if I wanted the job.

PG: Was that for Universal?

RB: Yeah. At that time it was called Revue Studios. They signed me to a seven-year contract and they put me in *It's a Man's World* in 1962. I'd only been in Los Angeles for about three months before I got that job. Pretty amazing. Just a fluke.

PG: Especially when you think of people in that area going to acting school and you come in from North Carolina and just walk into a job.

RB: I know (*laughter*). I wish, looking back, that I had someone in the family that knew the profession. I was a long way from home and I was really wet behind the ears and didn't realize what a wonderful opportunity I had here as far as earning power to make money.

PG: So you took it for granted?

RB: Yeah. Here I was just playing guitar to meet people and they're putting me on stage and giving me a job. And I'm going from one town to another and having fun. The whole folk music craze is happening. And I just go and meet some other guys and play guitar in Berkeley. And right away they invite me to sleep on the floor or the couch that night and the next day we're over here and over there. It was great up there in San Francisco. They had folk music at the universities. Things were just poppin' all over.

PG: So there was a bigger music scene in San Francisco at the time than in Los Angeles.

RB: Yeah. I just went up to San Francisco and hitchhiked there and back. Even after I got into *It's a Man's World*. I bought a car, and I would go up there to San Francisco and park it and let the police impound it (*laughter*). And I'd have to get it out of the impound after I'd been up there for a week. I didn't care about the money.

PG: So you were living a good lifestyle?

RB: Yeah. Just having the money to do it. And I really was fascinated by the people that played music and folk singers and their stories.

PG: It was a real creative time.

RB: Yeah, it really was. History goes through its pages and I don't think there'll ever be a time like that again. So many young people were just out for seeing what was going on in the world. Just for the experience. And that's when the Love Generation started all that stuff.

PG: Did *It's a Man's World* last long?

RB: No it didn't. After *It's a Man's World,* Universal-Revue loaned me out to several other studios where I did small parts for other shows like *Wagon Train, Combat,* etc. During that time I met a girl who was getting a divorce from Randy Sparks, who started the Christie Minstrels. Her name was Jackie Miller. She knew about the entertainment business and told me, "You want to get a horse, because you've got a seven year contract and with this series going on they're going to put you in Westerns. If you know how to ride, that'll be a big plus for you. You've got to do that." She helped me find a horse to buy and we boarded him at Duncarris stables which is near Griffith Park. We would go out riding and I became a very good rider.

About a year went by and my agent told me, "Go and see Frank Price about your new career." Frank Price was the executive producer at that time on *The Virginian.* He put me in the *Virginian* series and I bought a little ranch. My family came out to stay with me but they weren't here very long. My mother's brother, who had graduated from Annapolis, crashed his private plane and was killed with his wife of several months. It just devastated the family and they all moved back to Fayetteville instead of staying out here with me.

I gave up the ranch because I didn't need a big place for just myself. I talked to Universal and they let me board my own horse at the studio. I said I'd let them use him for free on *The Virginian* show if they let me board him there. So that was a good deal for them.

PG: What was the name of your horse?

RB: Clyde, which is actually my first name too. I remember I went through the papers and paid for him and said, "Oh, does he have a name?" Most times horses don't come to their name as readily as dogs do but they usually *have* a name. And this woman came back out and said, "Yeah, they say he's called Clyde." It was a coincidence or they were just pulling a fast one on me. But I don't think they knew my name was Clyde.

PG: So you used him in the show?

RB: Yeah. It was really fun. You can't always get just the scenes you want. Movie horses are really funny. They stand there and if they hear the director say "Action!" they take off. And when they hear the word "Cut!" they stop right then and turn directly for the food trough or the water trough. I mean, it's amazing. My horse wasn't trained though, because he wasn't a movie horse. He wasn't brought in under rental by the wranglers. He acted very much like a real horse and I got a lot of fan mail about how he didn't stand still. He was spirited. The horse stories among actors were really something. Doug was a good rider. Doug and I did some personal appearances at rodeos. He and James and I all had our own horses. I used to read the scripts and it would say, "One Nd horse." And I'd say, "What's this Nd mean?" And someone told me it means "Nondescript." It means any old horse. Otherwise it would call for James Drury's personal mount, or Doug's or my mount.

PG: So you didn't have to audition for *The Virginian?*

RB: No, I was under contract. What Jackie Miller told me had come true. She said they saw my potential for playing a young cowboy. I had the accent. I was a good rider.

PG: Did Universal provide you with a back story for the Randy character?

RB: I remember sitting in the office with Frank Price and he said, "What we have in mind to get you into the show is, you're sort of a runaway. A young boy. You come passing through the area and get in some trouble. And I'm going to have the Virginian take up for you and then offer you a job on the ranch. And then you'll become the young ranch hand. You'll be Roberta Shore's age and you and Roberta will probably have ... not a real romance ... but there'll always be a kind of a thing where people will wonder. You two being the same age, when they have dances you'll probably be asked to escort her around."

PG: Was it your idea to use the guitar? Or did Frank Price suggest it?

RB: I brought it up first. I said, "Hey, can I use my guitar?" Because one thing from the very first was, I wanted my own recording rights. I thought, gee, this would be great. Not only will I be able to go and play clubs now and sing my songs, I'll also be a TV star. I'll be able to appear as "Randy, of *The Virginian*." I'll have extra clout for a recording career.

So Frank Price said, "Yes, we've thought about that. We think it might be very good. We don't want to make it like that's all you do. We want you to do a lot of things without your guitar." So they included it in.

PG: Was your character brought in as a replacement for Steve? I know you appeared with Gary Clarke but he was written out shortly after your arrival.

RB: I didn't know. They didn't tell me I was replacing anybody. Gary and I worked again in the pilot episode of *Hondo*. That was a short-lived show. I think the principal in that wasn't strong enough. Gary is just a nice man and a good guy. It was really refreshing to see him and work with him again at a Charlotte [North Carolina] Western nostalgia event. He looked great for his age. People told me I was staying young but he really looked like he'd been taking great care of himself. He looked very young. And not only that, he had a picture of his wife and two kids. They weren't very old either.

Gary said, "You could do that if you wanted to," and I said, "I don't think I could! (*laughter*) You're really staying young and strong and moving right along, aren't you?" He was really fun to be around.

PG: Did you socialize with the cast?

RB: Yeah. Doug McClure and I did more things together off screen. James moved in different social circles and he really was one person to be off doing personal appearances and to be gone a lot. But Doug and I got along great. Doug would have parties up at his house and Burt Reynolds would often be there. Doug loved his daughter. He talked about the next time he would get to see her and all that. He was a heck of a guy. Her mother was exotic. She was Hawaiian or she had some sort of island blood. She was a beautiful woman.

Roberta and I did a few things. Not like something you might expect. We'd go grocery shopping together and cook up a microwave dinner at her little apartment. And just talk. She is just one of the most straightforward, good, good, sweet people you just could hope to meet.

Lee J. was one of those special people. Among people in general, there are these people that seem to stand out. That seem to have a life within them and a wisdom and an understanding of what's going around them. And they don't seem to need to be stroked. They don't need all that. But they seem to draw it. And he just had that. He had a stature that we all admired and respected. But at times he would do some of the funniest things. For instance, because I had to do songs, the music department would send a man down with a little keyboard. He blew on one of them in his mouth so he could play the tunes for me and I could get it down to play. Well, this one guy comes down from the music department and he happens to be an old friend of Lee J. Cobb's and he remembers him from back in the vaudeville days.

And there's another guy who starts playing the piano. They grab some canes and little hats out of this bucket that was there for the prop department because it was a party scene or something like that. And they started tap dancing. Running around, locking tap dancing, waving the little straw hats and swinging the canes around. And you couldn't believe it. There's Lee J. Cobb. He could dance, he could sing (*laughter*). Then he stopped as abruptly as he started and put the hats and canes down. And he turned to us and said, "What are you all looking at?" And he would pick the most perfect moments to say the most humorous and precise line and break the entire set-up. It'd crack us up.

The man was a real pleasure to be around and a pleasure to work with. A wonderful thing happens sometimes when you're an actor and that is, you get into a scene and you forget you're acting. You start talking to the other person and you're staging your lines and the scene comes towards the end and the director says "Cut!" It seems like you've forgotten what you were doing. You wake up. And that's when you realize you were really doing some great work. Lee had an ability to do that. You'd forget you were acting. That's a special something for an actor to have and to be able to pull other actors into a scene with him. You always liked to do a scene with Lee J. because you knew you were going to get a chance to do some of your best work.

Clu was good. I remember watching Clu on TV in the state of North Carolina before I ever hitchhiked off. He had this peculiar little way of acting. I just never got to know him very well. And later on when we were doing these nostalgia events, we tried to get Clu a lot of times to come and join us so there would be more of us from *The Virginian*. That would always draw more fans and we'd make more money. I think his wife was seriously ill with cancer and he moved to Oklahoma and just kept taking care of her and became a bit of a recluse.

PG: Was Jim temperamental on set?

RB: Yeah, James Drury was temperamental on the set at times. Even when we were going to these nostalgia events, he was the only guy that I ever saw that would act temperamental. One time he actually blasted out the busboy. I don't know, he did something wrong. He poured the wine before he was asked or something like that (*laughter*). He would act like a typical New Yorker. "Don't you know how to properly serve a meal? Working in a fine restaurant and you don't know your job."

And sometimes he would get on his high horse, so to speak, and act like "I'm the great star and this is how it should be run." He would assert himself. After all, he was the Virginian and this is the *Virginian* series (*laughter*). I think the guy had a heart of gold. He just had his moments when he'd get temperamental. And it was quite irritating at times.

He'd done some big things. He'd worked with Elvis Presley. He was being groomed and I think at times he kind of got a big head. And felt like the big star and let it show. Pretty much to a person, we all felt the star of the show was Lee J. Cobb. He just had the stature and credits. If he was having a problem, he just had a way of handling it. He never let his temper show. He never made a display of anything. He would just handle things.

PG: When Roberta and Cobb left, the show kind of drifted for awhile in the John Dehner-Morgan Starr season. Did you enjoy your last season as much as the previous seasons?

RB: No, I don't think so. Part of the [problem] was, I owned a horse and I really studied up on cowboys and a lot of the particulars about the way they treated their animals and the way they dressed to work. I felt like the *Virginian* series was just a notch or two below *Bonanza* as far as some of the realities. Well, that was worrying. And James Drury, for instance, wore some of the tightest pants (*laughter*). You work all day in a pair of pants that tight, you guys wouldn't be able to walk. But that was just me.

I felt like it could use more realism. And the gun belts they wore didn't tie down. They were examples of the highest gun belt technology of the time. They were stiff and made so that you could fast-draw real easy. It was a lot of little things like that. They just weren't authentic. I thought we might have done a lot better if they'd paid attention to that.

Horse owners all across the country would often ride in and bring their fan mail and they'd talk about things that did and didn't get done by the stars. When you work with a horse on a ranch, you treat them a certain way. Just certain realities and realism that I thought *The Virginian* was lacking.

PG: Did you like your costume?

RB: I liked it really good. I liked the little blazer vest that I wore. I wouldn't have looked right as the kid on the ranch if I'd had a sophisticated-looking hat. The kid with the cap skin vest made me stand out. Plus it had two little pockets. One on each side and it was the greatest way to carry my flat picks to play my guitar.

PG: I believe the filming was hectic. How many takes, on average, did it take to complete a scene? Was there any time for rehearsals?

RB: People probably often perceive the work of an actor as being easy. And they think of them as being pampered. After all, you don't have to work hard. But it *is* hectic. You've got to be ready at any time to be your best. You might be your best and because somebody else isn't on time or hasn't learned their lines, you don't get to exhibit your best because the other character in the other part of the scene isn't coming off well. Schedules would get changed because of the weather.

Actually, Hollywood became the place it is, where movies are made, because the weather was the most predictable. It was less likely that weather would eat into your money. But it was so hectic. And there were moments of genuine danger. Whenever you mount a horse, it's dangerous.

PG: Did you enjoy working with Doug McClure?

RB: Doug was just one of the guys that people loved. He was a guy that liked people. He just had a smile for anybody that was willing to be friendly and he could make you feel at ease. I loved doing rodeo shows with him. Our favorite bit was that he would come riding out and get up on the stage. And I would sing a few songs and I'd tell them Doug was gonna come in. And all of a sudden they'd look out to the arena and Doug would ride around waving his hand. And they'd say, "Here he is, ladies and gentlemen, Doug McClure."

I'd say, "Boy, Doug, that's not a movie pony. That's a real rodeo rider pony there. You ride the heck out of that, man. You must have done some real cowboy work in your day."

"Yes, Randy, as a matter of fact I was raised on a ranch."

"Yeah? Well what was the name of the ranch?"

"Oh, it was the D Bar, Q Double R, Lazy J, Lightning Rod, Target Brand, Triple C Double X Y Z."

"Why, Doug that sounds like a big ranch. Did you have a lot of cattle?"

"Nope. Not many of 'em survived the branding." (*laughter*)

He just had a way of delivering those.

We were up in Petaluma, California, just above San Francisco, where they have a big rodeo every year. It's a real cowboy section of California. After we did our show, a couple of the cowboys said, "Hey, if you go round back of the grandstand you can see the motel where you guys are staying. You can ride the horses over there and we'll just come over with our trailer later and pick 'em up."

We rode our horses all the way over to the motel. I tell you, my horse was a pretty regular horse but he wasn't a trained cow pony like these cattle ponies. And we were riding over there and we came to this little barrier. Probably only about two feet high. I was running toward it and Doug was a little distance from me. He was going around the end of it. And I thought about jumping over it, but I thought I better not jump this guy's horse. For one thing, we were on asphalt and a little rubble mixture. I thought it might hurt the horse. I said, "I don't want to take any chances with somebody else's horse or somebody else's property."

So I decided not to jump and I just lifted the reins a little bit as if I were in a pullback to pull the horse up. Well, those horses are trained to the slightest touch that when I did that, that horse dropped his back legs and dropped his seat right back on there and stopped. Like on a dime. I never stopped so quick. I thought I was just gonna cut myself in half. I went *wham!*! I sat so hard down in the seat of the saddle I actually felt like I blacked out. Like it was a boom! I thought, boy, these cow ponies can really stop and start fast.

PG: Roberta Shore said you were down-to-earth and not like the average affected actor in Hollywood. Did you like the Hollywood scene?

RB: I liked all sorts of places and people. I just wasn't into the Hollywood scene as such. From time to time I would go to some of these parties. Some actors made it their business to attend first-time showings for movies. Anything for publicity. It's good for publicity and it can be very good for your career to be seen. Today I think it's more so than ever. Especially with the periodicals they have. *The Enquirer* and stuff like that. These days they really seem to keep up with that sort of thing more.

Bob Dylan was a friend of mine and when he came into town I would know. I was a little bit more likely to come to a Hollywood party because Glen Campbell, who was a friend of mine, or Bob Dylan was going be there. I just loved the aura of songwriters like Kris Kristofferson. These people amazed me.

I was really interested in the poets and the songwriters of the time. Whereas another actor more or less wouldn't interest me as much. I knew something about songwriting and playing an instrument and performing music in front of a live audience, whereas I didn't know what it entailed to write a script and to produce a movie.

I got along with directors rather well, which was good, but I didn't understand what a tremendous job they had. They had to work with all those different actors and get what they needed out of them. They often had to do twice the work of an actor.

PG: Even though you were a successful actor at the time, did you want to be a success as a singer-musician more?

RB: I really did. I just didn't get to do that. Had I been more formally trained in the workings of show business, I believe I could have prevailed and made the two careers work together. But it didn't seem like Revue Studios or Universal was interested in helping me with the singing and the songwriting and making the records I wanted.

Roberta and I made one record together, "Singing Stars of *The Virginian.*" It was really a record for fans of the *Virginian* series. It really wasn't about me or the songs I was writing. It wasn't helping me or my career grow musically.

PG: I would imagine that a songwriter, like yourself, who had friends such as Dylan and Glen Campbell would feel frustrated singing cowboy songs.

RB: Yeah. Although recently I got a pretty good check from Broadcast Music Incorporated [BMI] because they ran the *Virginian* series in Germany a couple of years ago. I got a big check because somewhere during *The Virginian* they were bringing public domain songs down to the set for me to do because they

Randy Boone publicity shot, 1984 (courtesy Randy Boone).

didn't want to have to pay any royalties to recent writers. They were songs like "You Are My Sunshine."

And I said, "Look. At least let me write some of the songs that I'm doing on set. I tell you what I'll do, I'll sign them over to you so that you can use them for free. But let me write some of the things so I can feel like I'm putting something special into the work." So I did. I wrote a little more than half of the songs that I did in those little spots here and there on the show. And they were supposed to use them for free. Except that, once seven years went by, these new markets came into being.

They hadn't anticipated the CD market and the "go to the store and rent a movie" market. And overseas markets and stuff like that. So after a certain time Screen Actors Guild said they were just going to have to pay me for the time performed for the songwriting that I did on the show. It was a really nice surprise to get that check from Germany.

PG: Why did you leave the show?

RB: Actually, I was let go. They'd changed producers several times on the time I was on there. But the guy who hired me, Frank Price, came back to the show. The show was having its troubles about that time and they were starting to change the characters. They'd already lost Roberta Shore and Lee J. Cobb and then James was trying to get them to pay him more by holding out and saying, "How are you going to make it? I'm the Virginian." And they stopped production until they waited for him to come back in.

I was told that Frank thought I was window dressing and wasn't needed on the show, but I feel that I was needed as much as anybody. I think a show suffers when you make big changes in a show and you lose the actors that caused the people to fall in love with the show. When they go, it suffers. By the time *The Virginian* had turned over to Charles Bickford, I was working over at CBS in a series with Stuart Whitman called *Cimarron Strip*. That was fabulous.

We really went to some locations. We went to Flagstaff, Arizona. We went out to the desert for those scenes. We went out all the way to the Rio Grande. The most we did on *The Virginian* would be to go outside of L.A. We went to Thousand Oaks which is about 30 miles outside of L.A. (*laughter*). Every time we did a scene with cattle, we would go to this ranch that was out there at Thousand Oaks. We'd get up some cows and they'd have us looping forever going, "Yeehaaa, cows. Giddy-up..."

PG: Did you have much rehearsal time or did you go straight into it?

RB: We didn't really have a lot of rehearsal time that I remember. We pretty much went straight into things. There were instances of a couple of scenes that had to be rehearsed and worked out. Rehearsals were pretty easy because by the time they blocked out the scene, for instance, well, the actors didn't need the rehearsal. We'd generally get it in one take. Often if they didn't get it in the first take, it'd be on account of the camera not moving right or a person moving wrong or something like hat. Because we would know our lines.

PG: Did you watch *The Virginian* on TV?

RB: I didn't own a TV set. I quit watching TV. And people used to say, "What do you mean? You got to watch it." Maybe it was unprofessional. Perhaps I should have.

Actually, getting into it almost spoiled TV and movies for me. I looked for the shadows and sometimes you could see the microphone still in the scene or some guy that's supposed to be hiding behind a rock and he didn't get out of the shot in time. It ruined it for me. It took years before I quit looking for those things again. I enjoy TV now and I enjoy movies.

PG: Do you enjoy talking about your role on *The Virginian?*

RB: When I was doing all those shows, who would have thought when I'd get to be 60 years old I'd be sitting on a phone talking to a guy about all those crazy things we did. Actually the most nagging or distressful thing about you talking about it is, so much happened. There's way, way too much to tell. To think back on it's just amazing. But I'm really pleased. I feel that it's a real compliment for you to call to talk to me about it.

When I was touring England, a fellow came up to me and said that he really loved that episode where I sing the song about the inchworm. "Butterfly has wings of gold, a moth has wings of flame, inchworm's got no wings at all but he gets there just the same." He told me he and his friends thought it was so good they fully expected there'd be a record out soon and the song with all the verses would be there. And I thought to myself, that's really what I wanted to do. But I could never get it to happen. Oh, well.

PG: Do you consider yourself fortunate in your acting career?

RB: So many things had to happen for me to fall into that little place and to get into acting. And then all the things that happened to me. They're not so much remarkable in that I did them, they're more remarkable in that I saw them through. That I lived it. Saw a lot of things from a lot of angles that your average person wouldn't get to see. See them from onstage, backstage, seen the lives of other performers. When the Westerns went, a lot of guys' careers went. The last thing I did of any note acting-wise was *The Wild Pair* with Beau Bridges and Bubba Smith, around 1980. Pretty much my career ran through 1962–1975. After that I did a little bit here and there.

I did some blue jeans commercials for some company over in England. I was skinny and had long hair like a hippy then and I played the guitar. I just suited what they had in mind and I jumped around on the stage and threw a sweater all over the place and screamed. I don't even do rock 'n' roll. So I got up there and made fun of them and they thought I was great. They hired me to do another one about six months after that. Good deal. They shot them over in L.A.

PG: Do you miss acting?

RB: Yes and no. More than anything, what really interrupted my acting career was that I wanted to have a family. I wanted to have a wife. A home to come to and my own kids. I wanted to have some children. I got married the first time and it was just a terrible mistake. Actually, nobody ever liked that girl (*laughter*). And then that situation seemed to lead to another marriage that didn't last very long. Then I was single for 10 to 15 years and got married again. And now I'm single again and when I look at performing and acting now, I do, I miss it. I wish I could settle down with somebody and have a family.

Actually, I'm an artistic type. Even in my construction work, I was known for some of the best work (*laughter*). I love doing something really well. I live in an apartment now and I just hate seeing where somebody didn't finish a drywall corner rack or something like that. I mean, I just like doing things well.

Randy Boone in the driveway of his Van Nuys, California, home in 1973 (courtesy Randy Boone).

PG: What sort of things were you constructing?

RB: I did it all. I had a little construction company out in California for about the last 20 years I was out there. I mostly did additions and repairs. I added on another room or especially a bathroom or remodeled a kitchen. And even some landscaping. I could save a person money and go in and do all aspects of it. The plumbing, the masonry, the electrical, glass. The whole addition. And I could pull it all together. As time went on, I know it had a deleterious effect on my back. I began to wake up in the mornings and I couldn't move.

My friends saw me and said, "You just gotta quit and get out of the business or you're going to paralyze yourself." So I finally quit about 1995. I stopped and said, "Well, I'll work on my own house. I'll pull it together and try to get more out of it."

But I really should have cut my losses right then because I kept on going and I ended up having a bad divorce. So I just had to leave it. But I feel good now. Besides the beach here in Wilmington, one of the reasons I came down here is that they have a film industry. They have a sound stage that was built by Dino DeLaurentiis. Now it's called Screen Gems Studio. They shot some good films here and the town is finally getting a life. It's a very historic town. I think they've got to manage to preserve the history that's here and still have a new tourism. And still have a film industry here. You can't stop progress. I worked one day on *One Tree Hill* that they shot in Wilmington. And I've got an agent back here.

PG: Andy Griffith has done lots of filming in North Carolina on *Matlock*.

RB: I worked with Andy Griffith but not on *Matlock*. They had quit making *Matlock* before I moved back this way. But, yes, they did *Matlock* for a while here in Wilmington. And Andy Griffith's one of North Carolina's shining stars. I worked with him out there in California on *Savages* (1974). It was a movie of the week.

PG: What are you doing to keep yourself busy?

RB: I'm studying screenwriting at college. I just finished a script. I've written half-scripts a lot of times but I've finally finished one. I think is really good. It's a nice little story of a father and son who get reunited and go on to chase a bigger dream. It's a sort of family comedy thing and I just feel like it's really well put together. I'm looking forward to doing more of them.

My mother is doing fine. She lives in Fairville. And my younger sister lives there. She's five years younger than me. I'm still active writing songs and performing here and there. On my website I'll be offering up some of these products in the way of songs and CDs. Gradually it's coming together. It's called randyboone.com.

PG: I know you don't recall individual episodes because of the hectic filming schedule, but does anything stand out in your memory from your time on the show?

RB: Yeah. Early in the mornings, especially when we were on locations, we would show up and the cattle and the horses would be moving into place and the men doing their various jobs would be getting into position. It actually, at moments, felt like you were really there in the Old West. And it was tough. You'd be cold and be trying to keep warm. You'd be getting a cup of coffee and holding your horse's reins and you'd be waiting to see where you're supposed to be. And the sun would be coming up. It felt like you were there sometimes.

16

Clu Gulager and Diane Roter
Emmett Ryker and *Jennifer Sommers*

Clu Gulager was rarely satisfied with his working life as an actor. He claimed to find the process "very painful and laborsome." As Deputy Sheriff / Sheriff Emmett Ryker on *The Virginian,* his acting style was in marked contrast to the seemingly relaxed Doug McClure or the laid-back Randy Boone, owing more to the 1950s' Method Acting School, with its deep introspection and often mumbled delivery.

Born November 16, 1928, in Holdenville, Oklahoma, William Martin Gulager was an only child. Part Cherokee, Gulager grew up on his uncle's farm near Tahlequah, Oklahoma. Uncle Chris was an abusive drunk. Aunt Mary was the protector.

Gulager was first introduced to acting through his father John, who had worked as an actor on Broadway. Gulager decided to follow in the same tradition and took drama classes at Baylor University in Texas shortly after completing a two-year stint in the Marine Corps at Camp Pendleton.

A spell in Paris with actor, mime artist and Experimental Theater teacher Jean-Louis Barrault followed before Gulager returned to America and married actress Miriam Byrd Nethery. In 1952 they moved to New York City where he worked on the stage and in live television. Finding opportunities limited for a young actor wanting film experience, Gulager shifted his focus to Hollywood.

In Hollywood, Revue Studios signed Gulager to a seven-year contract. His first regular TV series featured him opposite Barry Sullivan, playing Billy the Kid, in the half-hour NBC Western *The Tall Man* (1960–62).

One of Gulager's most memorable early roles was as a hired hit man in Don Siegel's *The Killers* (1964). Starring Lee Marvin, John Cassavetes, Angie Dickinson and Ronald Reagan in his last film role, the movie was originally planned as the first TV movie on NBC's *Project 120*.

"It was too violent and NBC was afraid of it, so Lew Wasserman let NBC off the hook and did not insist that they accept it and pay for it. He kept it and released it theatrically," said Frank Price.

Gulager made an impact as the cold, calculating killer named Lee, with Lee Marvin winning a BAFTA (British Academy of Film and Television Arts) Award in 1966 for "Best Foreign Actor."

"*The Killers* was the first movie to be done in an experimental project to see if movies could be successfully produced directly for television. Ronald Reagan played a bad guy for the only time in his career in this movie. *Project 120* was later named *World Premiere* and

Clu Gulager, Frank Price and Barry Sullivan, joking on the set of *The Tall Man* (courtesy Frank Price).

I produced one of the first movies in the new attempt in 1966, *The Doomsday Flight*. It got a 47 share of audience and its success helped persuade Universal and Lew Wasserman to go ahead with *Airport*," concluded Price.

Gulager's next role would mark his return to a regular role on a Western television series. Executive producer Frank Price had worked with him on *The Tall Man* and wanted him on *The Virginian*. Gulager had often proved to be difficult but his talent outweighed any temperament problems he might have had.

Emmett Ryker was introduced in the premiere episode of season three. Gulager had appeared twice previously on the show, as outlaw Jack Carewe in "The Judgment" (1:17) and as a deaf mute in "Run Quiet" (2:09). He would stay for three seasons before moving on to the short-lived *The Survivors* (1969) and his own film project.

Released in 1969, *A Day with the Boys* featured his 12-year-old son John. Clu wrote, produced and directed the dialogue-free drama about a group of boys who befriend a black businessman and then bury him in a pit. Controversial for its day, the short film failed to make any impact despite a screening at Cannes.

Another aborted television series, *San Francisco International Airport* (1971), followed. It would prove to be Gulager's final attempt at a weekly ongoing series. In 1971 he appeared on the big screen in Peter Bogdanovich's *The Last Picture Show* with Cybill Shepherd and

Ellen Burstyn. Years earlier, Bogdanovich had visited the set of *The Virginian* and met Gulager. He found an actor with ambition and a need to direct his own movies. *A Day with the Boys* had been a start. Others would follow. None would be completed.

Gulager drifted through the remainder of the '70s and early '80s in episodic TV, movies and mini-series. A new form of television that resulted from the success of *Rich Man, Poor Man* (1977), the mini-series was the perfect vehicle for adaptations of best-selling novels sold in airport lounges to long distance travelers.

Gulager found his career unexpectedly revitalized with the horror movie *Return of the Living Dead* (1985). Graphic violence, sex and humor sit side by side in an odd mixture that found an audience with youngsters. Gulager had discovered a new niche. The remainder of his career would be devoted to horror movies.

Gulager and his family moved back to Oklahoma in 1988 to film personally funded projects. Gulager had become obsessed with extreme violence with his first proposed project based on the notorious serial killer Ed Gein, who literally skinned his victims and wore their skin. His next project in 1992 was initially titled *Kill! Kill! Kill! Kill!* but was renamed *Fucking Tulsa: An Excursion Into Cruelty.* From a script by Gulager, it starred son Tom as a serial killer. The 20-minute promotional film was shot on Super 8 film by John Gulager and shown to potential backers in 1996. There were no takers for the graphic tale of murder and bodily desecration.

Gulager's wife Miriam had serious health problems during this period and was diagnosed with a brain tumor that resulted in loss of sight in her left eye. She passed away in 2003. Gulager's two sons continued producing and filming home-made movies, with some success.

On March 15, 2005, Clu Gulager accepted a Legacy Award from the First Americans in the Arts (FAITA) organization for his contributions to the film industry on behalf of the Cherokee Nation.

Gulager was always a complex man. Often bored with commercial acting, his creative spirit wandered into the dark areas of nightmare that either alienated or thrilled his potential audience. He had little interest in the safe area in between. He once likened his time on *The Virginian* to a horror movie. It's to be hoped he was referring to the frenetic filming schedule and not the quality of the scripts. In any weekly show, the episodes vary in quality. Gulager was lucky to play a character who had his share of good scripts to work with.

"I got to know Clu very well when I produced *The Tall Man,* said Price. "I thought he was a terrific actor. Additionally he became a social friend. However, Clu could be extremely difficult to work with. He took the artistic part of his acting very, very seriously. He was seldom happy doing anything. I'm sure *The Virginian* was no exception. It was probably worse for him because he wasn't the major star in it.

"Ultimately, I came to the conclusion that the more successful Clu became, the more difficult he became. Perhaps, psychologically, he did not want success. His difficult behavior helped get *The Tall Man* cancelled. I was going to cast him in the pilot of *Laredo,* but he became demanding and very difficult about his requirements, so I didn't use him. Subsequently I used him in a pilot called *San Francisco International,* which also starred Pernell Roberts. The network ordered the series without Pernell (another temperamental actor) and replaced him with Lloyd Bridges. Bridges, a canny old star, took charge and made sure Clu had little to do in the series. Clu's career never lived up to the potential that I think he had, partially because he did blow it every time he got close to real success."

Clu Gulager and Don Quine in conversation at *The Virginian* 5th-season wrap party, 1967 (courtesy Frank Price).

Diane Roter had the unenviable task of playing a character that replaced the much-loved Betsy on *The Virginian* in 1966. She was introduced to viewers as Jennifer Sommers, niece to Judge Garth, who agrees to take her in at Shiloh following her parents' tragic deaths in Boston.

"Diane was serious and quiet, but sweet," recalled Joel Rogosin. "More subdued and less exuberant than Roberta and a little nervous at times. But Roberta had set the tone so it would have been difficult for anyone replacing her. Diane's father, Ted Roter, ran a fairly well-known little theater company in Santa Monica. She had very little experience in TV when she joined the show."

Fellow actor Randy Boone, commenting on Roter, said, "She took a little time to fill some pretty perky shoes."

Roter continued her short-lived career in guest spots on *Laredo* (1966) and *Family Affair* (1969) before retiring into private life.

17

Charles Bickford, Don Quine and Sara Lane

John, Stacey and *Elizabeth Grainger*

On February 11, 1936, Charles Bickford's distinctive voice was heard on CBS' *Lux Radio Theatre* in a radio adaptation of Owen Wister's *The Virginian.* Gary Cooper played the Virginian in a repeat of his famous movie role. Bickford gave voice to the villainous Trampas. Thirty years later, Bickford would once again be associated with *The Virginian.*

Born January 1, 1891, in Cambridge, Massachusetts, Charles Ambrose Bickford was the fifth of seven children. As a child he displayed a confrontational temperament that resulted in the shooting of a driver who had run over his dog. He was tried and acquitted of attempted murder at the tender age of nine.

His teenage years were spent lumberjacking, selling bogus real estate, working as a pest exterminator and going to sea, among other things. He even got to spar with heavyweight boxing champion "Gentleman Jim" Corbett. In 1914 he found himself in San Francisco acting in burlesque as a female impersonator. Back in Boston he joined the John Craig stock company. His acting career was in its infancy but he finally had direction to his life.

Bickford's breakthrough year was 1925. He appeared on Broadway as Oklahoma Red in Maxwell Anderson's *Outside Looking In.* The play was a hit and Bickford's stage career was in forward motion. Four years later he

Charles Bickford publicity photograph.

155

would appear in his debut movie, Cecil B. DeMille's first talkie *Dynamite* (1929). Bickford told DeMille the dialogue "stunk." Despite the bad start to their working relationship they became good friends, each admiring the other's candor.

Bickford was under contract to MGM but his temperament didn't sit well with studio executives, in particular Louis B. Mayer, who cast him in "B" pictures for the next decade. Only DeMille continued to cast him in prestige movies such as *The Plainsman* (1936) and *Reap the Wild Wind* (1942). Bickford was offered a contract in the mid–1930s by 20th Century–Fox but an incident with a lion on the set of *East of Java* (1935) left extensive scar tissue on his neck and the contract offer was rescinded.

Bickford settled into character roles throughout the rest of his career, receiving Oscar nominations for *The Song of Bernadette* (1943), *The Farmer's Daughter* (1947) and *Johnny Belinda* (1948). In 1958 he starred in the precursor to all ranch-based TV Westerns, *The Big Country*. The following year he was offered the role of Ben Cartwright in *Bonanza* (1959) but turned it down because he "didn't like the script."

In 1965 Bickford's autobiography *Bulls, Balls, Bicycles and Actors* was published. His former wife, Beatrice Loring, son Rex and daughter Doris didn't receive a single mention.

Bickford was 75 when he agreed to sign up to *The Virginian* in 1966. In a January 1967 *TV Guide* interview with Dwight Whitney, Bickford talked about his feelings for *The Virginian* and TV in general.

"I've got what I want in *The Virginian*. But it wouldn't hurt my feelings if TV sank into the ocean tomorrow."

Bickford's time at Shiloh was short-lived. He died of a blood infection on November 9, 1967, at age 76.

"He was a tough, principled guy," commented Frank Price, "who had never been afraid to show his independence in Hollywood. L.B. Mayer intimidated others, but not Charlie."

Bickford was laid to rest at Woodlawn Cemetery, Santa Monica, California.

Don Quine had the reputation of being hot-tempered. He joined *The Virginian* in 1966 as grandson to the new Shiloh Ranch owner, John Grainger. The show needed a larger youth audience and a 26-year-old Quine was brought in to excite the teenagers.

Quine was born in Fenville, Michigan, in 1939. His father, a neurosurgeon, was killed in an Air Force plane crash in Gunnison, Colorado, when Don was only five. He failed to get along with various stepfathers and quickly became a problem child who had the habit of getting into fights. His rebellious nature ultimately led to six months in juvenile hall when he was 15 years old after being accused of 27 minor burglaries. The experience sobered him up to the consequences of a life of a crime and he decided to express his anger in more creative ways.

In 1957 his poem about alienated youth won Quine a Pegasus Award as "one of the nation's outstanding young poets." After attending New Dorp High School in Staten Island, Quine studied premed at the University of Colorado. After one year he returned to Staten Island and became interested in acting. Before he left for Hollywood, he married talented pianist Carol Kane. Their courtship had lasted five days.

Quine's television career began with guest appearances on *The Detectives Starring Robert Taylor* (1961) and *The Fugitive* (1964). The following year, after a return guest-starring role on *The Fugitive* and an appearance on *Dr. Kildare*, he was cast as Joe Chernak in the nighttime soap opera *Peyton Place* (1965). The role brought him some recognition but only lasted one season before he returned to guest roles on *The Fugitive, Twelve O'clock High* and *The F.B.I.*

In 1966, Quine was approached to play Stacey Grainger on *The Virginian*. Quine replaced Randy Boone as the youth element. He was a hit with the viewers but failed to impress the executives and some fellow actors with his demanding nature and hair-trigger temper. He refused to be reduced to an "image" for public consumption or to be categorized as "the new James Dean." He was his own man and demanded control and respect. Some studio hands thought he had too high an opinion of himself. He had to prove himself first to win the respect he took for granted. Following a mid-season meeting with executive producer Frank Price, Quine reflected on his behavior and agreed to "cool it."

Price commented on Quine's manner. "He was temperamental and difficult once he got the role, but that's not unusual with actors. Sometimes it becomes too extreme. If you are hugely talented, you get away with it. Marlon Brando did. If not..."

In the meantime, Quine's marriage to Carol Kane had collapsed. Quine stayed on *The Virginian* for two seasons before moving to more episodic television. A 1968 guest spot on the TV Western show *Lancer* was soon followed by his departure from acting.

Quine's career took a U-turn when he married Judy Balaban, daughter of Paramount Pictures boss Barney Balaban. In 1975 Don and Judy Quine founded the Professional Karate Association. Quine's three sons from his first marriage had shown an active interest in karate, motivating Don to research into the background of the sport. In 1974 Universal Pictures and ABC were producing an episode about karate for the *Wide World of Entertainment* show. The Quines agreed to organize the event. It was such a success the Quines decided to invest their own money in launching the PKA.

In 1989, Judith Balaban

Don Quine and Frank Price at *The Virginian* 5th-season wrap party, 1967 (courtesy Frank Price).

Quine's book about her friendship with Princess Grace of Monaco, *The Bridesmaids,* was published. Don made a brief return to acting on *Judith Krantz's The Torch Song* (1993). A balding, bespectacled Quine was barely recognizable as the same man viewers knew from the 1960s. In a brief appearance he shared a scene with Raquel Welch. Quine had come a long way from his troubled youth and, like his *Virginian* successor David Hartman, found lasting success outside of his originally chosen profession.

Sara Lane (real name Susan Russell Lane) was born in the spotlight. Henry Fonda announced her arrival, on March 11, 1949, to a Broadway audience as father James "Rusty" Lane hurried to the hospital. He was appearing with Fonda in *Mister Roberts* and was told during his performance at the Alvin Theatre that his wife, Sara Anderson, had given birth to a baby girl.

Lane made her acting debut at the tender age of nine months, in a commercial promoting Ivory Soap. A One-A-Day Vitamin commercial was so successful she was able to buy a palomino quarter horse mare she named Aurora at only nine years old.

"I had seen *The Virginian* first with Roberta Shore when I was twelve and I thought what a wonderful thing to have a show where you can ride horses," recalled Lane.

Four years later she would be a regular on the show. But first she would make her screen debut in the movie *I Saw What You Did* (1965). She had come to the attention of producer/director William Castle after entering a "Miss Teenage" contest. The horror movie about two teenage girls making prank telephone calls to strangers also featured Joan Crawford and John Ireland.

Sara Lane and Frank Price engaged in conversation at *The Virginian* 5th-season wrap party, 1967 (courtesy Frank Price).

"I ended up touring New York with William Castle and Joan Crawford. It was a really interesting experience because Crawford had a really huge audience. Mostly gay, but not exclusively. She was already older and quite idiosyncratic by this time," commented Lane.

The film was a moderate success and the money earned enabled Lane to breed her mare Aurora to a quarter horse named Leo Bar. Aurora gave birth to a palomino filly Lane named Ariel. In 1966 her father's ill health forced Lane to sell her beloved horses, but later that year she was signed to *The Virginian* and was able to buy back Ariel.

Sara Lane played Elizabeth Grainger, granddaughter of Shiloh Ranch owner John Grainger. Lane's character had a playful relationship with Trampas, with her share of teenage crushes on various visitors to Shiloh Ranch. Lane would outlast both Charles Bickford and Don Quine and acquire a new Grainger family in season six through eight.

"As the executive producer, I had considerable contact with her in the first few episodes," remarked Frank Price. "I found her to be a very pleasant, very agreeable person who didn't have the kind of inner conflicts that Roberta Shore had. She gave no one any problems and was a sweet, untroubled girl on the set."

Sara Lane lived with her mother and father in Topanga Canyon. Situated between Los Angeles and Malibu in the Santa Monica mountains, the isolated community became known as "Haight Ashbury South" in the late 60s because of its hippie and arts scene. In February 1969 the area was flooded, with entire hillsides being swept away in the floodwater. Nine days of continual rain had resulted in mud slides and torrents of water ploughing through Topanga Canyon. Lane refused to be evacuated until her four quarterback horses were safe. One of them was trapped in mud at the bottom of a creek. The floodwater was rising dangerously high and Lane was fast losing hope the horse could be rescued. In the meantime her mother and father were being hoisted to safety on a stretcher and cable lift. Her father had suffered a broken leg in a recent accident riding his son's moped.

Just as Lane was losing hope for her horse a bulldozer managed to pull him free with the aid of a rope. The flooding had been traumatic for everyone in Topanga Canyon. Homes were completely destroyed and the peaceful community shattered. It would take time to recover.

Neighbor Renata Casser recalled the floods and her friendship with Sara Lane and her family. Renata, originally from Germany, moved into the area in the late 1960s.

"We called her Russell. We both got badly flooded in 1969 and that's how we became friends. People kept their privacy, but after the flood the whole neighborhood got together. Russell and her family took us in because our house was so badly flooded. It was a nice community at the time.

"I went with her once to the studio and stayed all day. I met James Drury. They spent hours in make-up and doing their hair. The guys got bored and Doug McClure and James Drury, one of them threw a whole bucket of water over the other and they had to do all their make-up again. They were just bored. It was all sitting and sitting and waiting. That's what they did the day I was there."

Following her departure from *The Virginian* in 1970 Sara Lane continued acting as Russell Lane and appeared in *The Trial of Billy Jack* (1974) and *Billy Jack Goes to Washington* (1977) before retiring from acting.

Lane and husband Jon Scott became joint owners of Havens Wine Cellars situated in the Napa Valley in 1984. Lane gave birth to her daughter Sara at the age of 40 and adopted James, an African American, when he was two days old. She has recently returned to social work helping children with mental health and juvenile delinquency problems.

Sara Lane's father, "Rusty" Lane, appeared on *The Virginian* as Ezra Griswold in "The Money Cage" (1:23) and as Sheriff Calder in "Seth" (6:26).

PAUL GREEN: Did you ever take acting lessons?

SARA LANE: I was in *The Virginian* by junior year and I never took drama classes. After the William Castle movie I actually took acting lessons for a month or so in Santa Monica from Diane Roter's father Ted Roter. They are the only acting classes I've ever taken. I also met Clu Gulager at those classes. I actually acted with them way before I was cast in the show and I was in their little acting school when Diane was in *The Virginian*. And by a totally different mechanism I ended up interviewing for the show and getting it. It was a funny thing that I had known them before. I also worked with Lorraine Tuttle who was a wonderful acting coach

PG: Do you recall auditioning for *The Virginian?*

SL: Yes I do. Around the same time I auditioned to be Konkie Johnson for a series of commercials for Johnson's Yogurt. I was pretty sure I'd gotten the yogurt commercial and I was pretty sure I hadn't gotten *The Virginian*. The interview process involved Frank Price. We did a screen test and they wanted to see if I worked well with Don Quine, who was going to be my brother. I think Don Quine was cast before I was, and we did look kind of alike. And I met Charles Bickford at around that time.

I was seventeen. Frank Price hired me and probably kept me when not everyone wanted to. I think I was hired because I came from the business and had a reputation for being no nonsense. And the fact I rode as well as I did made a big difference.

PG: Your original Shiloh family was Bickford and Quine. Any thoughts on why Don Quine left?

SL: They were just wonderful. I don't know why Quine left. We were all easily disposed of in those days. My sense is there was some temperament with Don but I wasn't privy to that kind of information.

Charles Bickford I adored. I come from a very progressive labor family. My Dad had been a shop steward back in the days when they used to take you out of town and leave you there. Charles Bickford was very conservative. We used to have fun arguing because I was pretty articulate. I just loved him and really cherished my time with him.

PG: Was Bickford's death a shock?

SL: Yes. But he was ill. He skin had almost become almost transparent. He was an old man and he wasn't well. It was so hard because I took it so personally when all of a sudden John McIntire and Jeanette Nolan came in. They were lovely people but they did things differently. They were very dear but I really felt like they were my step-parents and I'd lost my grandfather. I missed him terribly.

I learned a lot from McIntire and Jeanette Nolan. They were easier to work with because they were not frail and they were such good actors. But all of a sudden Jeanette joined the show and her character took care of the kitchen and that had been my kitchen before. In the Bickford seasons I was the woman of the house and now I was just the kid.

PG: McIntire, Nolan, Quine and yourself worked well as a family unit.

SL: We did. I was there from 6 o'clock in the morning until 8 o'clock at night. So it was my family. And after that transition it was really fun because there was a lot to learn in the kitchen and about acting from Jeanette. She was a really neat person.

PG: Did you find James Drury and Doug McClure easy to work with?

SL: James could be moody at times. Doug was not moody at all. He was funny and maybe a little casual at times about the show. James Drury took it very seriously. He was the lead. And there were times, certainly, with both of them, when their attention appeared to be somewhere else in addition to the show. But for the most part they were pretty hard working guys.

Both ways of working can be fun and can be challenging. Doug always had wonderful women around. He was just really fun and full of energy. The younger girls would always ask me what Doug was like and older women would always ask me what James Drury was like.

PG: You've always had a love of horses?

SL: I was horse crazy forever. I got my first horse when I was ten or eleven. In the beginning I was anxious to be an actress so I could have the money to buy horses. My parents had been very reluctant to have any of their children act until they were adults because my parents had been in the theater and they were so used to stage brats. And child actors have to be bribed a lot because it's really hard work and everything falls apart if they decide not to do something.

James Drury actually had a well trained horse that I used called Easter Ute. He was a really brilliant horse. The best horse that I ever rode on the show. It was a reining horse, also called a cutting horse. It's important that quarter horses can work with cattle. They turn by tucking their bottoms under and they almost sit down and pivot. And that's the way they stop so they can change directions really quickly. The English equivalent would be like a dressage horse. You just think a thought and the horse responds.

And I rode the white stallion that had started with Cantinflas. It was a specialty horse that came in just for "Beloved Outlaw." I don't remember the name of the big buckskin.

PG: Did you use a stunt woman in many of your scenes with horses?

SL: There were a lot of faraway shots going through locations on "Beloved Outlaw" and because I was a minor at the time I couldn't do a lot of horse riding because they had to save my time on camera.

I showed horses so while I could ride cowboy I had slightly better posture than is typical of people who are self taught riders. And Polly Burson was one of the stunt women who had the same kind of carriage that I did. She was a really neat person. She was probably around 45 at the time we filmed "Beloved Outlaw."

PG: What was it like working with Clu Gulager?

SL: Clu was wonderful. He was a curious man. But quite a fine actor. I was very young and is was hard for me to be part of an ensemble with him. I admired him but I always felt that he might be a little critical of me. He never did anything mean to me but I think he probably found me a lightweight and I was sensitive enough to that kind of thing to not seek him out.

Clu Gulager and Don Quine brought a method sensibility to it. I would be a little nonplused. Those folks were a little harder for me to work with.

PG: Any thoughts on David Hartman?

SL: David and I went out for a while but I don't think we told anybody. And it wasn't very serious. We dated for a little bit. He was very tall and he had just appeared in *Hello Dolly* so I was very impressed with him for that. I used to tease him because he was always reading Ayn Rand, who of course I didn't approve of. He was so intent on learning how to do cowboy things. Which is part of the reason we got together because I was always around the horses. He was learning to rope and to ride. He'd spend a lot of time practicing.

PG: Elizabeth Grainger and Trampas appeared to have a strong brother and sister type relationship in the show. He would kiss you on the cheek or forehead in season seven and appeared to be a little more intimate.

SL: Doug was so charming. His flirtatiousness had the quality of making me look good. Doug McClure and I were never involved. He was probably in love which made him more demonstrative. He tended to be like that. I adored Doug's stand-in Harper Flaherty and would have liked to have been with him but it never worked.

PG: Did you like Tim Matheson?

SL: Yes I did. He was very debonair. Very attractive and cute with a great deal of presence.

PG: Did you find your lack of academic drama school training a hindrance?

SL: I regret that the only time I'd ever acted was professionally. I'd never had a chance to practice and learn academically. It mattered so much that I not only get my lines right but that I could convert a cue so that if somebody else in the cast didn't have their lines down I could still make it work for a shot. And that's an important thing to be able to do. But it's only part of what you should do. And now that I'm older and I can remember all the tentative offers of help I realize that I should have taken those offers.

PG: Did you find it difficult internalizing emotion in scenes?

SL: I found it hard focusing on that. I probably could have tried to get into some kind of a workshop and do some acting to have brought more depth to my acting. There was some times when I was rather interesting and there were times when I was not all. I could have learned to be more consistent.

The role could be kind of deadly as well. I was responsible for an awful lot of the exposition in scenes. I probably did best in the episodes that featured me.

PG: Is it true you won a trip to Africa on a game show during your time on *The Virginian?*

SL: I did. It was *The Celebrity Dating Game.* There was a celebrity guest who would go on and be blindfolded and ask questions of three contestants and get to pick one to go on a date. They would take you to pretty fancy places with a chaperone. So it was publicity for our show. The whole thing was very odd. Here I am, 18 or 19 and so excited to get to Nairobi and all this stuff. It was a kind of a funny experience but Africa was glorious. We had a *TV Guide* photographer with us and he wanted so badly to take animal photos and he didn't realize it takes a huge group to do that. So it was just me, the stand up comic and the chaperone with the photographer trying to get animals to run towards us to get a good picture. It was comical.

PG: Did you enjoy acting as a profession?

SL: I didn't find acting boring. I did find it very difficult to have to reinterview and represent yourself every single part. I may have pretended it was boring but it was more terrifying. I was never part of the social part of the business. My whole life was so separate from it that I wasn't sustained by that. If I were to advise a young person now I would say go to a four year college. Hang out with other actors, do it academically and give yourself the chance to fail.

I never dared fail. I never dared take any risks. Because hundreds of thousands of dollars depended on getting an episode in the can. I'm not going to experiment with something when I got praised for getting it in the can. And yet I think if I'd shown that spark to people like Frank Price and Leslie Stevens they would have pulled me along. They seemed happy enough with me getting the damned thing shot.

I supported my family. I cared about the dynamics of my mom not working anymore. I think if I'd been a little more self involved and a little more driven it would have been better. Because I did have some things that were really interesting about me. Actors have to find a funny kind of balance. Just being popular is not really going to make it for you.

And because I come from the labor background and all that it mattered an awful lot to me what the wranglers thought and what the assistant directors thought. It mattered to me that they respected my workmanlike qualities. And I lost sight of the fact that you have to really be interesting and you have to take some risks.

PG: You enjoyed working with the wranglers?

SL: I had a lot of fun with the wranglers. I was my at most comfortable with them. Some of the wives of the producers and I had a lot of fun too because we were kind of irreverent. We had endless publicity events. Usually I was the one to open supermarkets in the Midwest.

PG: Can you describe your daily working experience on the show?

SL: My father was happy and willing to drive me the studio every morning. I was scared of driving at the time. I would be on the set at 6 a.m. in the morning to start two hours of hair and makeup and I'd actually sleep in the car on my way home. Before I would get home the new pages would come every night. They'd do it by colors. There was so much dialogue in that short a shooting schedule. I'm very grateful that my parents drove me. They had to drive me in my first year because I was a minor. And then they slipped into that. When I turned 17 there was really no life except the series.

We had a shorter hiatus than other shows because of our longer shooting schedule. I pretty well knew where I was on the pecking order. I was used very little outside of *The Virginian* and a couple of times I thought I'd gotten close but I didn't. When we were on break I tended to go open shopping centers in Iowa.

There was a lot that was wonderful about the show. It had a lovely pastoral quality and it was expansive. And there wasn't a mean thing in it. In my first year when you were on the Shiloh Ranch set it felt like you were really on a property. The house had more substance than just a flat facade. The exterior was very authentic. The buildings were made of wood and the fences were real and the steps were actual concrete. It made you feel like it had some depth to it.

I remember when I filmed "Vision of Blindness" I was coming down the steps from the Shiloh house and ended going up and down them. They were pretty treacherous steps.

When the tour buses came through in my second year we quickly got the sense we were there to provide entertainment to the tourists. You had less of the sense of being in the country as things about the tours grew up and were more aware you were on a set. We had to stop filming many times. It became a situation where we felt we existed for the tourists.

PG: Would you describe yourself as a hippie during the 1960s?

SL: I wasn't a hippie. It would be very difficult to work in a series that hard and be a hippie chick. I used to wear a long Muu Muu kind of thing that I made myself. I used to make those because the dresses that we wore were so heavy and hot when we were out on location at ranches. Before I got dressed I would wear this because it covered me from my chin to my feet and it seemed the most comfortable thing to wear. And people speculated about what I had on underneath.

I wore a lot of Doris Day clothes because I had similar proportions to her. Universal at that time was not very extravagant with their budgets and they recycled all their clothes. I think they made one outfit for me during my entire time on the show.

When we got new dressing rooms I had grown up with American antiques. There's a style called "Cowboy Antique." It's not fancy stuff. The oak dresser look. Anyway, they tried to decorate my dressing room in their fancy modern stuff and I asked for permission just to go to the property and I decorated my dressing room in Cowboy Antique. There was a time when it was like my home. It was really fun. It was almost like being *Eloise at the Plaza*. You could run around there and do all sorts of interesting things.

The cast and crew were all very gracious with me. And I wasn't always that easy because this was during the 1960s and I was a political little firebrand. They didn't necessarily agree with anything I said. And I probably wasn't very subtle. I was into the women's liberation and civil rights movement.

PG: What was your reaction when you were told you wouldn't be required for the revamped ninth season?

SL: I was shell shocked. I shouldn't have been. I kind of figured the show might be going off. I was aware that there were problems with the demographics. I think I found out from my understudy rather than from anybody else. When my parents went to pick up my stuff from the lot because I was too sad to go they couldn't get on the lot to clear out my dressing room. They had to go through all kinds of channels. There was no kind of conspiracy. It was just studio policy. It was harsh and when it was over it was over fast.

Had the show gone off the air we would have had some kind of celebration and closure. It was a very small part of John McIntire and Jeanette Nolan's life. And Tim Matheson was just passing through. So I had felt more connected with Doug and James. It was pretty abrupt. Nobody was cruel but it was thoughtless.

PG: Do you miss acting?

SL: I do. I still dream sometimes I arrive on the set without knowing my lines. I don't think there's anybody more generous or real than actors. I think it's a wonderful life. The way you have to put yourself out and the professionalism required.

After the show I went back to school and went to college slowly and went on to U.C.L.A. and studied Women's Studies, Chicano History, African History and Marxist History. I graduated summa cum laude from U.C.L.A. And that was way cool considering I dropped out of high school when I was in the series and then I went back to Community College.

The *Billy Jack* movies were filmed during the time I was in college. I was under contract to Tom Laughlin for a couple of years. It turned out nobody did much because it was such a huge cast. It was such a refreshing and different experience. It was terrifying because they were always on the verge of firing people. On the other hand nobody knew anything and I would help people break down their scripts and wardrobe.

After that I didn't work anymore in acting. I felt so behind the people who had studied acting. I should have gone to school and studied acting and then known whether or not it was something I wanted to do.

When I got of school it looked like I would have an academic future if I wanted. But I became an intern at an Episcopal church for two years at the request of this priest. So I became a community activist in Santa Monica. We had an underground railroad for El

Salvadorian refugees and we started a food bank and homeless shelters. My life's work, rather than acting, was working with schizophrenic street women in Santa Monica. It was at a time when the government in Santa Monica was very willing to help. I did that for ten years and never did get back to school.

During that time I met the people who have become our partners in the wine business. And at this wonderful church we would drink a lot of wine and make wine and protest things we thought were inappropriate. It was just a very exciting time.

18

John McIntire, David Hartman
and Tim Matheson

Clay Grainger, David Sutton and *Jim Horn*

John McIntire's television career followed an unusual pattern: as a replacement for dead actors. First there was Ward Bond on *Wagon Train*. The hugely successful Western series had been an international hit thanks, in part, to Ward Bond as trail master Seth Adams. When Bond died of a heart attack in 1961, McIntire was cast as his replacement. When Charles Bickford passed away in 1967, Shiloh Ranch was suddenly without an owner. Enter John McIntire, rescuing the situation again. And where McIntire went, his wife, Jeanette Nolan, often followed. Shiloh had a new owner and Clay Grainger had a wife. The Shiloh family was intact.

McIntire gained a taste for real-life ranching as a youngster in Montana. Born June 27, 1906, in Spokane, Washington, he was raised in Montana on the family homestead. Graduating from U.S.C., his early career was centered on radio and stage work. His frequent co-star on such radio programs as *The March of Time* and *Cavalcade of America* was Jeanette Nolan. They married in 1935.

McIntire and Nolan both made their film debuts in 1948. Always looking older than his years, McIntire's gaunt, weathered features lent themselves to both authority figures and villains in such movies as *The Asphalt Jungle* (1950), *Winchester '73* (1950), *The Far Country* (1954), *The Tin Star* (1957) and *Psycho* (1960).

He starred in his first regular television series role as Lt. Dan Muldoon on *The Naked City* (1958) but only lasted one season before being killed off. Christopher Hale on *Wagon Train* (1961–65) followed before he joined *The Virginian* in 1967 as Clay Grainger. Charles Bickford was a tough act to follow. McIntire succeeded, although some, including former executive producer Frank Price, thought he didn't carry enough authority for the role. His polite, homely manners and often gruff exterior provided a suitable mix for the new owner of Shiloh Ranch.

Following his departure from *The Virginian* in 1970, he was reunited with James Drury and Doug McClure on the TV special *When the West Was Fun* (1979). The Western reunion show, broadcast on ABC, also featured his wife Jeanette Nolan and nearly 50 TV Western stars. McIntire also appeared in the short-lived series *Shirley* (1979) with Shirley Jones and *American Dreams* (1981) before his retirement in 1989. He died two years later, on January 30, 1991. He was 83.

David Hartman was born May 19, 1935 in Pawtucket, Rhode Island. The Hartman clan had emigrated from Germany to make a new life in America. His father was a Methodist minister who found it increasingly difficult to support his family on a minister's salary. He abandoned the church to become a salesman for the advertising agency J. Walter Thompson.

As a youngster, Hartman studied voice and choral singing and learned to play several musical instruments. These skills helped him land the role of singing waiter Rudolph in Gower Champion's original production of *Hello Dolly*, which premiered on January 16, 1964, at the Saint James Theatre in New York City. Touring with the Harry Belafonte Singers and the road company of *My Fair Lady* followed.

Prior to his first major acting role, Hartman had graduated from Duke University, Durham, North Carolina, in 1956 with a degree in economics and served three years active duty as an officer in the U.S. Air Force, Strategic Air Command.

Universal offered Hartman a seven-year contract, with *The Virginian* being Hartman's first weekly series assignment. Hartman played David Sutton, a tall, awkward-looking man from Pennsylvania, ill at ease in Wyoming. Unfortunately, the introduction of David Sutton failed to boost ratings and Hartman was transferred to another Universal show after only one season at Shiloh Ranch.

The Bold Ones: The New Doctors (1969) would prove to be a better fit for his talents. Set in the David Craig Institute of New Medicine clinic, the series featured Hartman as Dr. Paul Hunter, assistant to neurosurgeon Benjamin Craig (E.G. Marshall). His final TV series work was on the short-lived *Lucas Tanner* (1974).

Hartman decided to quit the insecure acting profession for a daily co-hosting job on ABC's *Good Morning America* starting in 1975. The morning show gave him the high profile and financial success he failed to achieve in his acting career, attracting a morning audience of seven million viewers. Hartman took home an annual salary of $2 million.

When Hartman left *Good Morning America* in 1987 he formed his own New Jersey–based production company, Rodman-Downs Inc., to produce documentaries for television. The successful PBS New York City "Walk" documentaries premiered in August 1998 with *A Walk Down 42nd Street*. Hartman co-hosted with historian Barry Lewis.

David Hartman publicity photograph, 1980's.

His first wife, Maureen Downey, passed away in 1998. They had four children from their 23-year marriage. He remarried in 2000.

As a result of his success on *Good Morning America*, Hartman's acting career has been overshadowed. Always a genial screen presence, Hartman was an unlikely cowboy on *The Virginian*. David Sutton was an outsider who had to adapt to Wyoming and Shiloh to gain acceptance. His own career followed a similar path with acceptance finally coming on a morning news show.

Katherine Crawford, commenting on Hartman, said, "David was a friend of ours after Frank and I were married. We loved him. A gentle, sweet, kind man."

Tim Matheson's first success as an actor was as a cartoon character. Hanna-Barbera, famous for *Yogi Bear* and *Huckleberry Hound* were expanding into the action-adventure genre in the mid–1960s and were looking for a voice for their latest project. Enter Tim Matheson as young adventurer *Jonny Quest* (1964). Matheson followed up his success on *Jonny Quest* with voice-overs on Hanna-Barbera's *Sinbad Jr.* (1965), *Space Ghost* (1966) and *Samson & Goliath* (1967).

He was born Tim Matthieson on December 31, 1947, in Glendale, California. His father, Clifford, worked as a training pilot; his mother, Sally, supplemented the family income working long hours as a bookkeeper and L.A.P.D. dispatcher. They divorced when Matheson was only six years old.

Matheson's mother was a motivating force in his early Hollywood career. He made his debut as Roddy Miller on *Window on Main Street* (1961) starring Robert Young as writer Cameron Brooks. This was followed by guest spots on *My Three Sons* (1962) and *Leave It to Beaver* (1963) and movie roles in *Divorce American Style* (1967) with Dick Van Dyke and *Mine, Yours and Ours* (1968) starring Lucille Ball and Henry Fonda.

A spell in the Marine Corps Reserves was followed by a four-year contract with Universal. In 1969 Matheson joined *The Virginian* playing James Joseph Horn. Matheson was a much-needed fresh face at Shiloh Ranch, but would only appear in the final season of *The Virginian* in its original format.

Matheson joined *Bonanza* as Griff King in 1972, following the death of Dan Blocker. The final season of the long-running Western was an often somber affair with the premature loss of Blocker as Hoss Cartwright still evident. Then Matheson was cast yet again in a Western series, as Quentin Beaudine in *The Quest* (1975). The short-lived series co-starred Kurt Russell.

Tired of what he perceived as typecasting, Matheson became involved in the improvisational comedy troupe "The Groundlings" in 1976. His time with the troupe ultimately led to the role of Eric "Otter" Stratton in *National Lampoon's Animal House* (1978). The film was a big hit and quickly gained an even larger audience following John Belushi's cocaine- and heroin-induced death in 1982. Matheson had been carrying over the "party animal" character into his personal life but was brought to his senses by the premature death of his friend Belushi.

He married for the second time in 1985. His first marriage to actress Jennifer Leak in 1969 ended in divorce in 1971. His marriage to Megan Murphy produced three children, Molly, Emma and son Cooper.

In 1989 Matheson bought *National Lampoon* magazine with business partner Dan Grodnik but sold it in 1991, unable to reverse declining sales. He continued to thrive in numerous TV movies through the 1980s and 1990s, turning increasingly to production and direction.

In 1999 he was cast in the recurring role of Vice-President John Hoynes on NBC's *The West Wing* (1995). He also continued with voice-over work in the animated series *Batman* (1993), *Batman Gothic Knights* (1998) and an updated version of his first success, *Jonny Quest vs. the Cyber Insects* (1995). He also directed for episodic TV, including *Threshold* (2005).

Matheson's time on *The Virginian* led to him being typecast as a young cowboy with a rebellious streak. When he felt stifled by Westerns he consciously changed course into comedy and contemporary roles. It was a move that has kept him constantly employed throughout his long career.

19

Stewart Granger and Lee Majors
Col. Alan Mackenzie and *Roy Tate*

Stewart Granger as Col. Alan Mackenzie was the first English owner of Shiloh Ranch. The English were an often overlooked part of the West and their investment in the relatively new country of America was a prime factor in its expansion—a factor Stewart Granger acknowledged when he created his character for *The Men from Shiloh* (1970).

Granger was born James Lablanche Stewart on May 6, 1913, in London, England. He studied acting at the Webber-Douglas School of Dramatic Art and made his film debut as an extra in 1933. After struggling to gain recognition throughout the 1930s, Granger was drafted into the army during World War II but ended up being demobilized for health reasons. Returning to civilian life, Granger made his breakthrough film opposite James Mason and Margaret Lockwood: *The Man in Grey* (1943). His long association with Gainsborough Studios included *Fanny by Gaslight* (1944), *Madonna of the Seven Moons* (1944) and *The Magic Bow* (1946).

Stewart signed with MGM in 1950 and moved to Hollywood, where he found himself cast in adventure and period costume movies such as *King Solomon's Mines* (1950), *Scaramouche* (1952) and *The Prisoner of Zenda* (1952). He became a U.S. citizen in 1956 but reverted to being a British citizen in 1962.

The 1960s saw Granger moving back to Europe to star in a variety of Italian and German productions such as *Swordsman of Sienna* (1962), *The Legion's Last Patrol* (1963), *Among Vultures* (1964) and *Old Surehand* (1965).

By the late 1960s Granger was finding movie work hard to come by and moved into television. He was approached to appear in the revamped *Virginian* series. He had been a fan of the show and welcomed the prospect of a change of direction in his career. He would play Indian-born Col. Alan Carrie Mackenzie, who abandoned a career in Her Majesty's service to buy Shiloh Ranch. *The Men from Shiloh* only lasted one season. Granger stated he didn't enjoy his experience on the show, claiming the rushed schedule didn't allow for quality. Following its cancellation, Granger played Sherlock Holmes in a TV remake of *The Hound of the Baskervilles* (1972) before returning to movies with *The Wild Geese* (1978) opposite Richard Burton, Richard Harris and Roger Moore.

In his 1981 autobiography, *Sparks Fly Upward*, Granger was his usual candid self, talking about his marriages to Elspeth March, Jean Simmons and Caroline LeCerf and his extramarital affair with Deborah Kerr. Granger's final TV work included the German soap opera *The Guldenburg Heritage* (1987) and a failed Glen A. Larson pilot, *Chameleons* (1989). In 1989 he appeared with Glynis Johns and Rex Harrison in the Broadway revival of *The*

Circle and later went on tour with the play in England.

He died August 16, 1993, of cancer, in Santa Monica, California.

Lee Majors had already made his mark as Heath Barkley on the TV Western series *The Big Valley* (1965–69) when he was asked to join *The Men from Shiloh.* The clean-cut Heath was replaced with a long-haired, mustachioed Roy Tate.

Born Harvey Lee Yeary on April 23, 1939 in Wyandotte, Michigan, Majors was an orphan by the time he was two years old. His father, Carl, died in a work accident a month before he was born. His mother, Alice, died in a car accident when he was still an infant. Majors was taken in by his aunt and uncle and moved to Middlesboro, Kentucky.

Majors was an accomplished track athlete and won an athletic scholarship to Indiana University but only lasted two years before he was expelled for getting into a fight. He moved to Eastern Kentucky College where he excelled at football. Turning down an offer from the St. Louis Cardinals, Majors decided to move to Los Angeles.

Stewart Granger hand-signed publicity photograph.

Studying at the MGM Drama School, he made his film debut in *Strait-Jacket* (1964) starring Joan Crawford. Following guest spots on various TV shows, Majors auditioned for the part of Heath Barkley on *The Big Valley.* His audition was a success and he was hired to work alongside seasoned veteran Barbara Stanwyck. Stanwyck warmed to Majors and taught him the day-to-day craft of working in front of a camera.

The Big Valley ran for four years and brought Majors recognition from fans and professionals in the industry. In 1968 he was cast in the gritty movie western *Will Penny,* opposite Charlton Heston. He was already being typecast as a "cowboy actor"—a fact that attracted the attention of movie director John Schlesinger. Majors was cast in the role of Joe Buck in *Midnight Cowboy* (1969) but had to pass after *The Big Valley* was renewed for a final season. Jon Voight replaced Majors and Schlesinger was named Best Director at the Academy Awards.

The Big Valley was cancelled in 1969, but Majors was only briefly unemployed before he was hired as Roy Tate, a classic loner with a past, on *The Men from Shiloh.* Following the failure of the revamped *Virginian,* Majors was looking for a new series and found it in *Owen Marshall: Counselor at Law* (1971). Majors was an action star and didn't have the temperament for a courtroom drama. His next project would be more suited to his talents. Following three successful 1973 TV movies, *The Six Million Dollar Man* (1974) became a weekly series and a worldwide hit. The mixture of action, sci-fi and hi-tech appealed to audiences and spawned a successful spin-off, *The Bionic Woman* (1976).

Majors' much-publicized marriage to Farrah Fawcett fell apart in the late 1970s. In 1981 he starred in his fourth weekly TV series. *The Fall Guy* (1981) centered around Hollywood stuntman and bounty hunter Colt Seavers. It was another success for Majors and featured the first *Virginian* reunion. In the episode "Happy Trails," James Drury and Doug McClure appeared in their "classic" Virginian and Trampas costumes, but playing themselves. Drury even featured in a new "ride-in" sequence as the Virginian. At one point McClure teased Drury by claiming that he (Doug) carried the show for all those years.

Following the 1986 cancellation of *The Fall Guy,* Majors continued working, with recurring roles, on *Tour of Duty* (1990) and *Raven* (1992). Throughout the '90s he appeared in TV and theatrical movies and continued to be active, despite undergoing single bypass heart surgery and a knee replacement in 2003. He married his fourth wife, Faith Noelle, in 2002 in a simple ceremony in Italy. In 2005 he starred with James Drury in *Hell to Pay*.

20

Familiar Faces

Pippa Scott, L. Q. Jones, John Dehner, Jeanette Nolan and Ross Elliott

The Virginian was populated with a varied supporting cast. Many were respected actors who were listed under "Also Starring," "Co-Starring" or "Special Guest Star." Character actors found employment as residents of Medicine Bow working in various professions, or as ranch hands at Shiloh Ranch.

"We tried to repeat actors in certain erratically reoccurring roles, to give some broad feel of continuity to minor characters in the series," explained Frank Price. "These were actors that we felt would cost too much to put under contract, so they remained free to work on other series. We hired them when they were available."

The daughter of playwright and screenwriter Allan Scott, Pippa Scott was born December 10, 1935. She attended the Royal Academy of Dramatic Art in London before returning to America and her Broadway debut at 19, in Jed Harris' *Child of Fortune*. Good reviews and a Theatre World award led to a contract with Warner Bros. in 1956 and a small role in John Ford's classic Western *The Searchers* (1956). Scott's first regular TV series work was on the short-lived *Mr. Lucky* (1959), followed by *The Virginian* in 1962.

Scott appeared in the first half of season one, as newspaper editor Molly Wood, before a change of executive producer marked the end of her brief stint on the show. In 1964, Scott married advertising executive Lee Rich and co-founded Lorimar Productions in 1969. The company achieved high-profile success with the Emmy-winning *The Waltons* and *Dallas*.

Scott continued to appear in guest spots on various television series throughout the 1960s and 1970s. She eventually found herself in another weekly series, playing opposite Jack Warden on *Jigsaw John* (1976). Scott retired from acting in 1984 and turned executive producer on *Meet the Hollowheads* (1989), a sci-fi comedy drama starring Juliette Lewis.

Increasingly active in politics, Scott formed Linden Productions in 1987 and produced a series of documentaries highlighting human rights abuses. Subjects covered include an award-winning *Frontline* PBS/Channel 4 documentary about the hunt for war criminal Radovan Karadzic, entitled *The Most Wanted Man in the World*.

Scott also developed the International Monitor Institute to create film and video archives of atrocities, genocide and human rights violations for use by various individuals and groups wishing to highlight or seek evidence for such abuses.

An active member of the Women's Commission for Refugee Women and Children, she wrote and co-directed *King Leopold's Ghost* (2005) featuring narration by Don Chea-dle. Adapted from Adam Hochschild's international bestseller, the documentary high-lights the atrocities, still happening in the Congo today, as a result of King Leopold II of Belgium's rule at the turn of the century.

PAUL GREEN: Can you please talk about your audition for the role of Molly Wood.

PIPPA SCOTT: My first role as a very young actress had been in John Ford's *The Searchers*. Charles Marquis Warren and the other producers of *The Virginian* evidently knew that. My agents called me with an offer. I was living in New York and my first response was that I wanted to continue with the freelance work that I had been doing up to that point and I wasn't at all sure that a series would be satisfying. Especially when it was a Western, the leading characters of which were the Virginian and his sidekicks.

But Molly Wood was described to me in tantalizing ways. By being the editor and owner of the *Medicine Bow Banner*, it was suggested to me that she would be capable of getting involved with the politics of Wyoming in that period and I found that interest-ing. A sort of early Katherine Graham. But of course it didn't turn out that way, which is why I chose to leave the show after its first season.

PG: Your character was loosely based on the Virginian's love interest in the Owen Wister novel. Did you approach your role with the idea of being the Virginian's girlfriend?

PS: Yes, that was also true in early discussions and scripts. But it appeared that stalwart cowboys don't have passionate romances during the family viewing hours on television. So Revue kept love affairs at arms' length, including the Virginian's and Molly's.

So in time I became more interested in developing Molly with an eye to her involvement in the publishing business and in the power plays that were going on. With mining ventures or cattle grazing or the fights over land rights then in progress, in which the judge also interested himself.

I felt that Molly could help the Virginian with her newspaper by being persuasive editorially ... or maybe get into a little trouble. Either way was more interesting than standing around doing nothing.

PG: Did you have input into making Molly Wood a strong female?

Pippa Scott photographed by Harry Langdon (cour-tesy Pippa Scott).

PS: I tried to, but the producers weren't very interested in pursuing that tack. So Molly was relegated to a decorative position (great gowns), and I was increasingly unhappy.

PG: Did you get on well with the cast? Any thoughts on cast members?

PS: Yes, always. This was a genial cast, happy to be working with each other and full of antics with lots of clowning around. People like Jim and Doug McClure and Gary Clarke were funny and wisecracking and it was generally a pleasure to be on the lot. And often we were on location where it could be very hot, but beautiful.

I remember one show on location here in California in the San Fernando Valley when it was 110 degrees and I wore a fabulous, heavy white lace form-fitting gown. But we could pour water all over it and it never showed so I could stay soaking wet all day, and lovely and cool and happy.

PG: Did you have much contact with Charles Marquis Warren? If so, what was he like as a person?

PS: My memory of him is that he had great hopes for the well-being of the show and in that way was like the rest of us. We wanted the best for this enormous undertaking.

PG: Why was the character written out of the show after half a season?

PS: I found that the role of Molly never reached her potential because of the direction the producers chose to take her. It was too bad because she could have been a powerfully interesting character, but I think the early 1960s weren't conducive to that kind of thinking on network television. So I asked to leave. And my husband and I (and a lot of other gifted people) made Lorimar Productions.

PG: Were you disappointed or angry?

PS: No. no, it was my choice.

PG: Were you asked to reprise your role for the second season episode in which Molly Wood dies?

PS: No.

PG: Do you have any lasting memories from your time on *The Virginian?*

PS: The memories I have, besides a genial cast, were of gifted directors whom I found interesting to work with or knew already, such as Hersh Daugherty, Leo Penn, Earl Bellamy, Alex Singer, Andy McLaglen, Sam Fuller, etc.

L. Q. Jones offered many moments of light relief as Belden on *The Virginian.* A semi-regular member of the Shiloh bunkhouse from 1964–67, Jones had been a television and movie regular since 1954 when he adopted the name of the character he played in his debut movie *Battle Cry* (1955). Justus McQueen became L. Q. Jones, and developed the screen persona of a wisecracking rascal who could come down on either side of the law.

Born August 19, 1927, in Beaumont, Texas, Jones was an only child who showed an active interest in acting but was encouraged to study law instead. His natural tendency for showmanship displayed itself in a successful stand-up comedian routine that led to acting in Hollywood. L. Q. roomed with future *Davy Crockett* star Fess Parker, who introduced him to the Leon Uris novel *Battle Cry.* Justus McQueen tested for the part of L. Q. Jones and despite intense competition was cast in the movie. When asked why he changed his name to L. Q. Jones, he responded it was author Uris' suggestion. Uris was looking for publicity to revive his career and intended to sue L. Q. for "stealing" the name. Luckily for L. Q., it never happened.

In 1955, L. Q., who was under contract to Warner Bros., was cast in their new Western TV series, *Cheyenne*. He only lasted one season. More movie and television roles followed, including an Emmy nomination for his role in an episode of *The Rebel* (1959) with Nick Adams. In 1962 he appeared in the Sam Peckinpah Western *Ride the High Country*. The acclaimed film also featured James Drury. Two years later they would appear together again in *The Virginian*.

Belden was always a supporting player on *The Virginian*, brought in to liven up the Shiloh bunkhouse. As a result, Jones' varied talents were underplayed. He left the bunkhouse in 1967 (he briefly returned in 1971 on *The Men from Shiloh*) to be reunited with director Sam Peckinpah. *The Wild Bunch* (1969) reinvented the Western for the Vietnam generation. Slow-motion graphic violence and a disenchanted group of outlaws built on the growing anti-hero approach started by Sergio Leone in his Clint Eastwood spaghetti Westerns.

Much like Clu Gulager, Jones was a frustrated writer, producer and director. *A Boy and His Dog* (1975) was his one and only feature. A post–nuclear holocaust tale of a man (Don Johnson) and his intelligent telepathic dog, this adaptation of a Harlan Ellison novella won L. Q. a Hugo award. Jones admits to feeling more comfortable acting than directing and has appeared in over 700 television shows in his career. His final attempt at a weekly role was on the modern Western *Yellow Rose* (1983).

Frank Price recalls working with L. Q. Jones.

"L. Q. was great. He became a good friend. My budget didn't allow me to pay him enough to take him off market or I would have done some regular deal with him. So he worked other acting jobs and I got him if he was available for a particular episode. He added a great deal to any scene he was in. A conscious decision to use L. Q. was brought about by the requirements of the scenes. I always liked to have some humor between the guys, so Trampas did it if he was present, otherwise L. Q. handled it. He always had some humor, regardless."

John Dehner replaced Lee J. Cobb midway through season four. Judge Garth had been appointed governor of Wyoming and recommended Starr to replace him at Shiloh Ranch. Dehner was hired to play Starr, but only lasted half a season before the character and Dehner were replaced by Charles Bickford as John Grainger in season five.

Born November 23, 1915, in Staten Island, New York, Dehner, born John Forkurn, began his career in the art department at Walt Disney studios, becoming an assistant animator after one year. Dehner worked on the Beethoven segment for *Fantasia* (1940) and the owl sequences for *Bambi* (1942) as well as contributing to many of their short animated features. Following service with the Army, Dehner decided to change profession. Although he was skilled as an artist, the work was low-paid. He eventually found his true vocation in acting. Starting as a radio announcer, he drifted into acting, appearing in *Hollywood Canteen* (1944). Dehner's rather stern voice and demeanor often led to villainous or authoritarian roles in numerous B movies of the 1940s and 1950s.

He also featured on many radio shows including the original radio versions of *Gunsmoke* (1952), *Frontier Gentleman* (1958) and *Have Gun Will Travel* (1959), on which he played Paladin, a role made popular on TV by Richard Boone.

Dehner was a familiar face to TV viewers throughout the 1950s guesting on such shows as *Cheyenne* (1957), *Bronco* (1959) and *The Rifleman* (1959). He had regular roles on *The Westerner* (1960) and *The Roaring 20s* (1960).

In 1966 he joined *The Virginian* for a short period on a recurring guest star basis. As Morgan Starr he portrayed an efficient taskmaster whose working methods were sometimes at odds with the Virginian's.

The Doris Day Show (1971) would seem an unlikely vehicle for Dehner's talents but he was a success in one of his few comedic roles as Sy Bennett. Dehner's new reputation as a master of deadpan humor led to another comedy role in the hospital based sitcom *Temperatures Rising* (1974). He returned to the TV Western on *Young Maverick* (1979) as Marshal Edge Troy and appeared on the *Dukes of Hazzard* spin-off show *Enos* (1980). Dehner retired from acting in 1988 and passed away on February 4, 1992 of emphysema and diabetes-related problems.

Jeanette Nolan had an acting career spanning 50 years. Born December 30, 1911, in Los Angeles, California, Nolan began her career at the Pasadena Community Playhouse before moving into radio. Radio was a perfect vehicle for the versatile Nolan who excelled in providing various accents on such shows as *Manhattan at Midnight* and *The Adventures of Mister Meek*.

Her film debut, as Lady Macbeth in Orson Welles' *Macbeth* (1948), was a critical failure and she settled into performing character parts on numerous television shows throughout her career. In 1958 she appeared in the original Screen Gems pilot of *The Virginian* alongside James Drury. Nine years later they were reunited on the Universal version. In the meantime she was a regular on the Western series *Hotel De Paree* (1959) and *The Richard Boone Show* (1963).

Following her three-season stint as Holly Grainger on *The Virginian*, Nolan appeared in a two-part *Gunsmoke* episode playing a character she reprised for the short-lived Western series *Dirty Sally* (1974). Nolan continued to work throughout the 1980s and 1990s and made her final appearance as Robert Redford's mother in *The Horse Whisperer* (1998). It was a fine end to a long career. Nolan suffered a stroke later that year and passed away June 5, 1998. She was 86.

She had a son and daughter from her marriage to John McIntire. Both went into acting. Holly McIntire retired from acting in the late 1960s. Tim McIntire was a promising talent who died of heart failure, following drug and alcohol problems, at the age of 42 in 1986.

Ross Elliott was the type of actor the casual viewer recognized but could never put a name to. Such is the fate of most character actors who populate television and film. Steady, reliable and anonymous, Ross Elliott was known to viewers of *The Virginian* as Sheriff Mark Abbott. Overshadowed by Clu Gulager as Deputy Sheriff Emmett Ryker, Elliott appeared and disappeared from the series on a regular basis but was still present when the show transformed into *The Men from Shiloh* for its final season.

As sheriff of Medicine Bow he was tenacious and often abrasive in his manner. A charming smile could turn into the grim face of the law if he thought a person was guilty. Sheriff Abbott had a job to do and nobody was safe. Not even Trampas or the Virginian.

Born June 18, 1917, in the Bronx, New York, Ross Elliott found his first work with Orson Welles' Mercury Theatre and the infamous *War of the Worlds* radio production, before graduating to such sci-fi cult classics as *The Beast from 20,000 Fathoms* (1953) and *Tarantula* (1955).

He played his first TV Western sheriff on a 1953 episode of *The Lone Ranger*. Nine years later he was playing a sheriff again on *The Virginian*. In early first season appearances he was merely "The Sheriff." When Roy Huggins took control of the show, Elliott's character was finally given a name—Sheriff Mark Abbott. The character appeared infrequently until 1967 when Elliott became a regular fixture in the Medicine Bow sheriff's office.

"Ross Elliott was just fine as the sheriff," remarked Frank Price. "He was always available and was a responsible, pleasant presence. Almost anyone could play the sheriff, but it made sense to have someone the audience had seen before as the sheriff. Again, unless I added someone like Clu Gulager and had the intent of making him a 'star' regular, it would make no sense to pay the money to keep a minor player exclusive. So we took the chance that he would be available."

Elliott continued to work regularly in episodic TV until his retirement in 1986. He passed away, aged 82, on August 12, 1999, a victim to cancer.

Supporting Players:

E.J. Andre (1908–84)—Alex, "Cookie." *"Andre was cast in "Ride a Dark Trail" (2:01), but the scene was eliminated in our final cut."*—Frank Price.

John Bryant (1916–89)—Dr. Spaulding

Eric Christmas (1916–2000)—Parker

Stephen Coit—Various businessmen

Cecil Combs—Cecil, ranch hand

Paul Comi (1932–)—Lawyer Brad Carter

Jimmy Lee Cook—Various ranch hands

Chuck Courtney (1930–2000)—Various cowboys and stunt double for Doug McClure

Royal Dano (1922–94)—Faraway MacPhail. *"I liked Royal Dano, but he was too expensive an actor to use as a bunkhouse regular."*—Frank Price.

Brendon Dillon—Mr. Bemis

Roy Engel (1913–80)—Barney Wingate

Dean Harens (1920–96)—Minister

Harper Flaherty (1920–93)—Harper, ranch hand, and stunt double for Doug McClure. *"A second unit director would take a small crew out and film action sequences, generally without the stars, but using their doubles. This was a cost-efficient way of getting the action done. But the second unit director would get the credit and he wouldn't be a stunt man."*—Frank Price.

Walter Woolf King (1899–1984)—Medicine Bow trial judge

John McLiam (1918–94)—Parker

Stuart Nisbet (1934–)—Bart, bartender

Jean R. Peloquin—Jean, singing cowboy, ranch hand

Dick Shane (1932–)—Dick, ranch hand, and stunt double for James Drury and other actors featured in the series. Technical Advisor, Action Coordinator and Director. *"Stunt men were often very helpful in staging a fistfight or other close-quarters battles. That's when 'Action Coordinator' or some such term would be appropriate."*—Frank Price.

Jan Stine—Eddie, ranch hand

Frank Sully (1908–75)—Danny, bartender

Ken Swofford (1932–)—Seth Pettit

Russell Thorson (1906–82)—Sheriff Stan Evans

Harlan Warde (1912–80)—Sheriff John Brannan

21

Frank Price

Executive Producer

Frank Price spent his early years traveling with his family from state to state as his father sought employment during the Depression. Born May 17, 1930, in Decatur, Illinois, Price lived in Minneapolis, Minnesota, Glendale, California, Texarkana, Texas, Provo, Utah, Knoxville, Tennessee, Ventura, California, and Flint, Michigan, where he attended three years of high school.

During the five years his family spent in Glendale, his mother worked as a waitress in the commissary at Warner Brothers. Young Frank was able to visit the Warners lot.

"The first shooting I ever saw was on the flooded sound stage at Warners," recollected Price, "while I was standing on the deck of the ship used in *The Sea Hawk* [1940]. I saw Edward G. Robinson being filmed across the stage on a different ship for the movie *The Sea Wolf* [1941]. They were laying in fog for his close shot while I watched them film."

After serving in the U.S. Navy from 1948–49, Price attended Michigan State University. He transferred to Columbia University in New York City on the advice of a friendly professor who thought Price had talent. Finding out that he couldn't work full time as a reader in the CBS-TV Story Department and attend the university, he dropped out of university to concentrate on work.

Writing and editing duties on shows such as *Studio One, Suspense* and *The Web* followed before Price made the move to Hollywood. He transferred his reading and story editing skills to Columbia Pictures TV division, Screen Gems, from 1953 to 1957, working on such shows as *Ford Theatre, Father Knows Best, Damon Runyon Theatre, Playhouse 90* and *Circus Boy.*

In 1957, Price became a story editor on NBC's *Matinee Theatre,* an Emmy-winning hour-long drama series broadcast daily in color. The year 1958 saw the cancellation of the majority of live television drama shows, including *Matinee Theatre.* Filmed Western series replaced them with 26 new shows debuting on network television.

Price found work as a story editor on one of those Westerns, produced by independent production studio Ziv-TV. Work on *The Rough Riders* (1958) provided Price with invaluable experience that would serve him later on *The Virginian.*

"*Rough Riders* caused me to focus on the Western, both in its Hollywood history and in the history of the West. And I learned a great deal about producing an action Western. I learned how to save money in production. I also learned where it paid not to save money, where Ziv cheapened its product by insisting on the wrong cost-saving measures."

When *Rough Riders* was cancelled after one season, Price worked on *Lock Up* (1959) starring Macdonald Carey and John Doucette. He was given the task of fixing already produced episodes and producing the remaining segments of the season for little cost. His first season production work on the series went uncredited.

"I thought the series had promise so I worked hard on this and to everyone's surprise I managed to make it into a credible show that got good ratings in first run syndication. It was the only Ziv show that year to achieve a second season order. I had fun turning each show into a verbal battle between a defense lawyer and a conservative police chief. I made a rule for the writers that both characters had to be well-grounded and 'right' in their opinions, right down to the close of the show where Macdonald Carey, the main star, was the one mostly right."

Price left Ziv-TV in 1959 and moved to Revue Productions in November of that year.

"One of the people that I used on *Rough Riders* was Samuel Peeples, who sold a pilot that he developed with my input and assistance to Revue Productions called *The Tall Man*. I had told him while we were doing *Rough Riders* that if anyone could figure out how to do Billy the Kid, it would be an easy sell to a network. He figured out the right approach, making the series about the friendship between Pat Garrett and Billy before events tore that friendship apart.

"Sam desperately wanted me to join him at Revue, since he was going to be the producer of the show and he had never done anything like that. I joined Revue as an associate producer and writer on the series. I wrote about 11 of them. The show did pretty well, but got tagged with the label of 'glorifying a criminal' during a time of sensitivity to such.

"Sam moved on to write *Frontier Circus* [1961], and I produced the second season of *The Tall Man* with Ed Montagne as executive producer. I wrote three *Frontier Circus* scripts, which was ironic because I had explained to Sam and everyone that I thought the concept was a bad idea. Trying to do 'the show must go on' in the Great West seemed like an idea that would quickly fail. It did. Although I did some terrific writing for it. I wrote one called

Frank Price and Katherine Crawford at their wedding reception in the Crystal Room of the Beverly Hills Hotel, May 15, 1965, with Doug McClure (courtesy Frank Price).

'Journey from Hannibal' which was about transporting an elephant from Hannibal, Missouri, to the circus location in the West. It starred Thelma Ritter opposite Chill Wills. It was my version of Wallace Beery and Marie Dressler.

"It was after this that I joined a special unit at Revue, which was in the process of becoming Universal TV. That special unit was New Projects, which was run by Jennings Lang."

Following the third season as executive producer on *The Virginian,* Price worked on the World War II drama *Convoy*

Frank Price photographed by David Hartman, 1960's (courtesy Frank Price).

(1965) for one season before returning to *The Virginian* for the fifth season to restore its ratings. Price decided to move on again after season five. His first job was producing one of the first movies made for television. *Doomsday Flight* (1966), written by Rod Serling and starring Van Johnson, Jack Lord, Ed Asner, John Saxon and Katherine Crawford. It proved to be a ratings winner and paved the way for the TV movie on a regular basis.

Price was asked to take over as executive producer on *Ironside* (1967) following trouble with early Collier Young–produced episodes. Winston Miller, Cy Chermak and Joel Rogosin joined him from *The Virginian.* Around the same time, Price produced a two-hour pilot, *It Takes a Thief* (1968) starring Robert Wagner, which was picked up by ABC for a mid-season order.

"It was a very grueling year, with difficult deadlines and a constant shortage of shootable scripts. I had an additional problem in that Raymond Burr and Robert Wagner were competitive about my time. I had a very good relationship with them both, so I wanted to keep them happy. When the season ended, I went into hospital with exhaustion as the prime cause. While there, I thought my life over. I decided that I no longer wanted to produce shows, but wanted to be an executive in charge of Universal's shows on ABC. I became Senior Vice-President of Universal Television and learned how to function as an executive. I built Universal into ABC's largest supplier, developing hits such as *Marcus Welby M.D.* and *ABC Movie of the Week.* I personally produced the pilot for *Alias Smith and Jones,* which was ordered as a series. I was trying to get stars in the roles because I had Peter Duel and Ben Murphy. Jim Drury and Jeanette Nolan had some name recognition. I was grabbing everybody I could on the lot. Glen Larson, who created the pilot, came up with a brilliant way of doing something fresh on the exploits of *Butch Cassidy and the Sundance Kid.* As opposed to having anything to do with the movie. For instance, *Alias Smith and Jones* was influenced in great measure by *It Takes a Thief.* Basically the format of *It Takes a Thief* is that a thief is pressured into being a good guy. So that's the same thing as *Alias Smith and Jones.* As somebody once said, 'If you steal from one, you're a thief. If you steal from three, you're creative.'"

Price became head of Universal Television in 1973 as executive vice-president in charge of production. He was made President of Universal Television the following year. Hit shows produced under his regime included *Kojak* (1973), *The Six Million Dollar Man* (1974), *The Rockford Files* (1974), *Baretta* (1975), *The Bionic Woman* (1976) and *Quincy* (1976).

In 1977, Price was elected to the board of directors of MCA, Inc., but left for Columbia Pictures in 1978 after 19 years at Universal.

"Part of the reason that I ultimately got out of television and ran Columbia Pictures was because of the whole thing of filling in the gaps in between the commercials with your entertainment bothered me. And I felt that I wanted to be in a position where we made entertainment and people would go out and put their money down to see that. And they wouldn't be interrupted.

"It was hard not to enjoy my time at Columbia because we had films like *Kramer vs. Kramer* [1979], *Tootsie* [1982], *Gandhi* [1982] and *Ghostbusters* [1984]. It was just great to be doing pictures were you had the money to buy the best writers and the best talent. In television, you're doing very low-budget pictures on a schedule. You take 60 days to do a movie as opposed to the eight or nine days I had on *The Virginian*.

"It was a thrill for me to be able to make it possible for *A Passage to India* [1984] to be made by David Lean. Columbia's success led the Coca-Cola Company to decide to buy us. There was a year honeymoon and then they started interfering with marketing, so I left."

Price returned to Universal in 1984 as "President of Universal Pictures" and Chairman of the MCA Motion Picture Group. Hit movies with which he was involved included *Back to the Future* (1985), *The Breakfast Club* (1985) and the Oscar-winning *Out of Africa* (1985) starring Robert Redford and Meryl Streep.

In 1987, Price formed his own company, Price Entertainment, Inc., with financial backing from Columbia Pictures. His first film was Jean-Jacques Annaud's *The Bear* (1988). A writers' strike halted script development for many months and he was tempted back to Columbia Pictures for a second term as president following Sony's buying-out of Coca-Cola. Notable movies

Frank Price at work in the 1970s (courtesy Frank Price).

under his tenure included *Awakenings* (1990), *Boyz N the Hood* (1991), *Prince of Tides* (1991), *Bram Stoker's Dracula* (1992) and *Groundhog Day* (1993).

Price restarted Price Entertainment following his departure from Columbia, making *Shadowlands* (1993) with Anthony Hopkins, and *Circle of Friends* (1995), which was shot in Ireland.

"The last thing I produced was a picture for Miramax called *The Texas Rangers* [2001] which I wasn't happy about. I was much happier with one I did for HBO called *The Tuskegee Airmen* (1995). I keep very active because, in addition to whatever might be going on professionally, I'm Chairman of the Board of Councilors for the USC School of Cinema-Television. I assemble the good board there of Steven Spielberg, George Lucas, Bob Zemeckis, Barry Diller, David Geffen and Brad Grey, among others. The Board consults on the school's teaching mission and helps in fundraising. So that takes an amount of time trying to make sure that's a top school. And I think it is. I was also elected to the Board of Trustees of the University of Southern California."

22

Producers

Creativity in television is a delicate balance between business and art. It may be the most intelligent show on TV but if it doesn't attract the desired audience it will be cancelled. In this atmosphere, it becomes vital that producers are aware of the factors that make a show more likely to succeed. Producers in TV are often good writers and they answer to the executive producer, who realizes the importance of their writing talent in making a show work.

The following listings include selective career credits and are intended as a cross section of the work of each producer.

Cy Chermak

Born: September 20, 1929, Bayonne, New Jersey

Cy Chermak began his TV career as scriptwriter on *Kraft Television Theatre* (1947). Writing credits in the 1950s: *Wanted Dead or Alive* (1958) and *Bonanza* (1959).

In 1962, Chermak joined Universal and stayed for 14 years. During this period he was producer and story editor–writer on *The Virginian,* executive producer and writer on *Ironside* from 1967 to 1974 and executive producer on *The Bold Ones: The New Doctors* from 1969 to 1971.

In 1974, Chermak was brought in as a replacement for Paul Playdon, who quit after two episodes in charge on *Kolchak: The Night Stalker* following disagreements with actor Darren McGavin. Chermak formed Francy Productions with his wife, Francine Carroll, who created *Amy Prentiss* in 1974 to be co-produced by their new company. This was followed by the short-lived *Barbary Coast* (1975) with Doug McClure and William Shatner.

The hit series *CHiPs* (1977) would prove to be his last as executive producer. In 1991 he wrote "The Wounded" for *Star Trek: The Next Generation* (1987) and worked with wife Francine on the animated TV film *Rescuers: Stories of Courage* (1998).

Cy Chermak at the Universal offices in 1965 (courtesy Frank Price).

The Virginian credits: producer in seasons: **2, 3, 5, 6**; story editor in seasons: **2, 3**; writer: **2:22, 3:18, 5:12, 5:15**.

"I liked working with Cy and involved him in some story and script meetings unconnected to the episodes he was producing. His 'story editor' credit allowed me to pay Cy for two different functions and I got additional creative brain power."—Frank Price.

Howard Christie

Born: September 16, 1912, Orinda, California; died: March 25, 1992.

Following graduation from the University of California, Berkeley, Howard Christie began his film career as an actor in 1935 but quickly abandoned it in favor of production and direction. He never progressed above assistant director status, working on *Ghost Catchers* (1944) and *In Society* (1944), among others. In 1945 he concentrated on production duties at Universal and was kept busy on a series of Abbott and Costello and Ma and Pa Kettle movies through the 1950s.

Moving into television in the late 1950s, Christie produced *Wagon Train* (1957) and *The Virginian* (1962) and features including *Nobody's Perfect* (1968), *Journey to Shiloh* (1968) and *A Man Called Gannon* (1969).

Christie retired in 1970 and passed away in 1992 following a long illness.

The Virginian credits: producer in season: **8**.

Warren Duff

Born: May 17, 1904, San Francisco, California; died: August 5, 1973.

Turning from a career on the New York stage to film in 1931, Warren Duff wrote for Warner Bros. from 1932 to 1939. Screenplay credits included *Gold Diggers of 1937* (1938) and *Gold Diggers in Paris* (1938). He was also assigned writing duties on the James Cagney classics *Angels with Dirty Faces* (1938), *Each Dawn I Die* (1939) and *The Oklahoma Kid* (1939).

Duff moved to Paramount in 1940, but only stayed for three years before he settled at RKO. Turning to production, he worked on various B movies including *Lady Luck* (1946) and *Sealed Cargo* (1951).

With a downturn in film production in the late 1950s, Duff joined the exodus to television with production duties on *The Virginian*. He contributed scripts for *Burke's Law*, *The F.B.I.*, *The Invaders*, *Mannix* and *Dan August* before cancer claimed his life in 1973.

The Virginian credits: producer: **1:20, 1:21, 1:24, 1:26, 1:28**

Paul Freeman

Work as producer on *The Virginian* (1962) in 1969–70 was followed by three years on *Rod Serling's Night Gallery* (1970) as executive producer, the 1979 *The Chisholms* miniseries and 1980 series, and *North and South* (1985), among others.

Since 1988, Freeman has been producer on the *Halloween* movies, with the final film to date being *Halloween: Resurrection* (2002).

The Virginian credits: producer in season: **8**; writer: **8:10**.

Herbert Hirschman

Born: April 13, 1914, New York, New York; died: July 3, 1985.

Graduating from the University of Michigan and Yale University Drama School, Hirschman served in the U.S. Navy as a member of the Seabees in the Philippines and New Guinea. Entering the TV industry in the 1950s, he worked as both director and producer. TV shows as director included *Playhouse 90, Dr. Kildare, The Iron Horse, Felony Squad, Hawaii Five-O, Cannon, The Waltons* and *Nero Wolfe.*

As producer–executive producer he worked on *Perry Mason, The Twilight Zone, Dr. Kildare, The Men from Shiloh, The Zoo Gang, Planet of the Apes* and *Mistral's Daughter.*

Hirschman won a number of awards during his career including the Robert E Sherwood Award for live direction on the *Playhouse 90* episode "Made in Japan," the Peabody Award for *Mr. Imagination* and the *TV Guide* Award for production on the third season of *Perry Mason.* In addition to his television work, Hirschman produced feature films and directed for the stage.

The Virginian—The Men from Shiloh credits: executive producer: **9:01, 9:05, 9:07, 9:09, 9:24**; director: **9:07, 9:24**.

Roy Huggins

Born: July 18, 1914, Litelle, Washington; died: April 3, 2002.

After graduating Summa Cum Laude in Political Science from U.C.L.A. in 1941, Roy Huggins worked for the U.S. Civil Service during World War II, followed by three years as an industrial engineer. The year 1946 saw the publication of his first novel *Double Take.* This was quickly followed by *Too Late for Tears* (1947) and *Lovely Lady, Pity Me* (1949). Huggins broke into the movie industry when he was offered a job adapting *Double Take* for Columbia Pictures. Full-time employment ensued in 1952 when he joined Columbia as a staff writer.

Three years later, Huggins moved into the burgeoning television industry, working on *Warner Brothers Presents* (1955) and the drama *King's Row* (1955). *Maverick* (1957) and *77 Sunset Strip* (1958) proved to be his most successful creations at Warner Bros and enhanced his reputation as a producer and writer of note.

A short-lived and controversial time at 20th-Century Fox resulted in Huggins' work on *Bus Stop* (1961) being publicly criticized as violent and degrading. Huggins returned to U.C.L.A. to study for a Ph.D., but when Universal approached him to apply surgery to *The Virginian* in 1963 he accepted, completing his studies by day and working in the evening.

The Fugitive (1963) would be his most successful creation in the 1960s. *Run for Your Life* (1965), with a strong central performance by Ben Gazzara, followed. In 1969 Huggins formed his own production company, Public Arts Inc., with *The Bold Ones, Alias Smith and Jones, Toma* and *Baretta* all co-produced with Universal.

His greatest success in the 1970s was *The Rockford Files* (1974), which he co-created with Stephen J. Cannell. His final TV series, *Hunter* (1984), was another successful collaboration with Cannell. He was also involved in a hit movie adaptation of *The Fugitive* (1993) starring Harrison Ford. In 2000, *The Fugitive* was revived in a short-lived series on which Huggins, although credited as executive producer, served as a consultant.

Huggins passed away in 2002.

The Virginian credits: executive producer: **1:13, 1:15–1:30**; writer (under pseudonyms): **1:16, 1:19, 1:20, 1:22, 1:24, 1:25, 1:27.**

"From the beginning, Roy called me Francis. His Irish background told him Frank was a fake name for me. He pushed himself, and anyone working with him, to achieve a high standard. He was a labor-intensive intellectual. Roy created unusual characters who were outsiders observing society. Alienated, but with a sense of humor. They were Maverick, Fugitives ... running for their lives. I consider Roy to be the best producer of dramatic series in television history."—Frank Price.

"My father would never work on anything he didn't respect. He hated bad drama and The Virginian *was a perfect backdrop for great drama. He believed good drama had to be honest, and always required some humor, and that the best drama had the least talk. Good stories were what excited him. And* The Virginian *had very good stories."—Katherine Crawford.*

Glen A. Larson

Born: 1937.

Producer, writer, musician and director, the multi-talented Larson had a string of major TV successes from 1968 to 1982. His debut as associate producer and writer on *It Takes a Thief* (1968) starring Robert Wagner was followed with *The Men from Shiloh, McCloud, Alias Smith and Jones, The Six Million Dollar Man, Switch, Quincy, Battlestar Galactica, Buck Rogers in the 25th Century, Magnum P.I.* and *Knight Rider.*

In 1983 his formula for success deserted him with a number of failed shows. In recent times he's looked to past triumphs to revitalize his career.

Larson achieved a certain notoriety when James Garner admitted to punching him on the Universal back lot after he took a dislike to Larson's theme music for a new show, claiming it was a *Rockford Files* rip-off.

The Virginian—The Men from Shiloh credits: producer: **9:02, 9:04, 9:08, 9:11, 9:13, 9:17**; writer: **9:04.**

"Glen was the lead singer for the group the Four Preps. They had a big hit with the song "Sixteen Miles." Glen wrote an It Takes a Thief *script during a trip he took to Japan as part of a tour with his music group. We bought it and he ultimately became a producer on the show."—Frank Price.*

David Levinson

Levinson began his TV career as a writer on *McHale's Navy* (1962). He joined *The Virginian* as associate producer in 1967 and in 1971 won an Emmy for producing the Outstanding Drama Series *The Bold Ones: The Senator* (1970).

In the mid–to late 1970s, Levinson produced two hit series for ABC, *Charlie's Angels,* and *Hart to Hart.* In 1985 he was producer on the revived *Alfred Hitchcock Presents* for the USA Network, receiving cable television's ACE award for Best Series.

The 1990s saw Levinson at work on such shows as *The Commish, Hawkeye* and *Two. The Invisible Man* is his last work to date as writer.

The Virginian credits: associate producer–producer in seasons: **6, 7**; writer: **7:16.**

Norman MacDonnell

Born: November 8, 1916, Pasadena, California; died: November 28, 1979.

Starting as a page at CBS, Norman MacDonnell produced and directed a host of radio shows in the 1950s including *Suspense, The Adventures of Philip Marlowe, Escape, Fort Laramie, Have Gun Will Travel* and *Gunsmoke.*

Following the success of the radio version, MacDonnell was approached to produce the TV adaptation of *Gunsmoke.* After a ten-year stint on *Gunsmoke* he joined Universal in the New Projects Division, developing several programs, including production duties on an episode of *Kraft Suspense Theatre.* Taking over from Frank Price in 1965 for one season on *The Virginian,* MacDonnell produced the short-lived Western series *The Road West* before returning to *The Virginian* in 1967. He remained as executive producer until the ninth season when he worked on James Drury episodes on *The Men from Shiloh.*

MacDonnell retired in 1972 and passed away in 1979. Although a major contributor to *The Virginian,* he is still best known for his work on *Gunsmoke.*

The Virginian–The Men from Shiloh credits: executive producer in seasons: **4, 6, 7, 8, 9:03, 9:06, 9:10, 9:12, 9:15, 9:22.**

James Duff McAdams

McAdams made his TV producing debut as associate producer on *The Virginian* in 1965. Dropping "Duff" from his name, James McAdams also worked as producer on *Ironside* but arguably achieved his greatest career success as producer and writer on *Kojak.*

In the 1980s, McAdams was executive producer on the hit series *The Equalizer* with Edward Woodward and revived *Kojak* in a series of successful TV movies starring Telly Savalas.

McAdams cut down on his workload in the 1990s, producing two unsuccessful sci-fi shows, *M.A.N.T.I.S.* (1994) and *The Burning Zone* (1996).

The Virginian credits: associate producer–producer in seasons: **4, 6, 7, 8; wWriter: 4:08, 8:03, 8:17.**

Winston Miller

Born: June 22, 1910, St. Louis Missouri; died: June 21, 1994.

Following his older sister Patsy Ruth Miller into acting, a young Winston made his film debut in 1922 in an acting career that lasted seven years and included roles in *The Iron Horse* (1924) and *Stella Dallas* (1925). With the arrival of sound, he quit acting and studied at Princeton University. He switched from acting to screenwriting on his return to Hollywood in the mid–1930s, finding employment with Republic Pictures. He was put to work on the *Dick Tracy* serial in 1937 and after a series of undistinguished screenplays for forgettable movies wrote the screenplay for the John Ford classic *My Darling Clementine* (1946).

Miller moved into television in the mid–1950s, providing scripts for *Gunsmoke* and *Rawhide.* In 1960 he joined Universal Studios. Producing and writing assignments on *The Virginian* were followed with work as producer on *Ironside, It Takes a Thief* and *Cannon.* In 1974 he produced seven episodes of *Little House on the Prairie* and rounded off his career writing for the short-lived *Barbary Coast.*

He died in 1994 following a heart attack.

The Virginian credits: producer in seasons: **1, 2, 3, 4, 5, 6, 7**; writer (uncredited): **3:05**.

"Winston did the uncredited final polish on Gone with the Wind *under threat that if he ever told anyone, he would be banished from the business"—Frank Price*

Edward Montagne

Born: May 20, 1912, Brooklyn, New York; died: December 15, 2003.

Edward J. Montagne, Jr., began his film career in 1932 as production assistant at Paramount Pictures, graduating to director with RKO–Pathe in 1948. While working on low-budget movies such as *Project X* (1949) and *The Man with My Face* (1951), Montagne ventured into television in 1949 directing *Man Against Crime*. In 1956 he created *I-Spy* and took over production duties on *Sgt Bilko*.

The 1960s saw Montagne working in both TV and movies as producer and director for Universal Pictures on TV's *The Tall Man* and *McHale's Navy* and the feature *The Reluctant Astronaut* (1967).

The majority of the 1970s were spent in TV production on *The Men from Shiloh*, *Quincy* and *Delta House*. TV movies included *Ellery Queen: Don't Look Behind You* (1971) and *The Amazing Spider-Man* (1977).

Montagne retired in 1981 following work on *High Noon, Part II: The Return of Will Kane* (1980) and *The Munsters' Revenge* (1981). He passed away in 2003.

The Men from Shiloh credits: executive producer: **9:14, 9:19, 9:21**.

Arthur H. Nadel

Born: April 25, 1921, New York, New York; died: February 22, 1990.

An editor on such films as *The Man Who Watched Trains Go By* (1953) and *The Littlest Hobo* (1958), Arthur Nadel turned TV producer, writer and director in the late 1950s, working as producer on *The Rifleman*, *Law of the Plainsman*, *The Detectives Starring Robert Taylor* and *The Virginian*.

In the 1970s and 1980s, Nadel became associated with children's TV, beginning with *Shazam!* and *Isis* (both 1975), and culminating in his role as executive in charge of production at Filmation animation studios on *He-Man and the Masters of the Universe* (1983), *She-Ra: Princess of Power* (1985) and *BraveStarr* (1987).

Following the closing of Filmation studios, Nadel passed away in 1990 at the age of 68.

The Virginian credits: producer in season: **4**; director: **4:28**.

Joel Rogosin

Born: October 30, 1932, Boston, Massachusetts.

After attending high school in Arlington and Falls Church, Virginia, Rogosin moved to California, graduating from Stanford University. Starting in the film industry as an assistant film editor, he progressed to producer on the Warner Bros. hit detective series *77 Sunset Strip* (1958). Moving to Universal in the early 1960s, he joined the production team on *The Virginian*, working as an assistant to Roy Huggins. Rogosin later became a *Virginian* producer and remained with the show until 1969. Other Universal production assignments included *Ironside, The Bold Ones: The New Doctors, Longstreet, Ghost Story* and *The Blue Knight.*

In 1982, Rogosin was supervising producer on *Magnum P.I.* before assuming the same duties on *Knight Rider* from 1983–84. Following work as supervising producer and writer on *The New Lassie,* he focused his attention on advanced acting, writing and directing workshops. His personal memoir, *A Writing Life,* was published in 2003.

The Virginian credits: producer in seasons: 3, 4, 5, 6, 7; writer: 4:25, 7:10, 7:22; director: 6:26, 7:14

Joel Rogosin relaxing at home in 1971 (courtesy Joel and Deborah Rogosin).

Jules Schermer

Born: September 15, 1908, Jessup, Pennsylvania; died: March 23, 1996.

Moving to Los Angeles in 1932, Schermer found work as a reporter and film reviewer on *The Hollywood Reporter.* Reviewing films led to producing them when he was hired by Paramount Pictures. His short time with the company was interrupted by World War II, during which he served as a staff sergeant in Culver City's First Motion Picture Unit.

After the war, Schermer worked for Columbia Pictures, followed by a stint at 20th Century–Fox. Moving to Warner Bros. in the late 1950s, he spent six years in the television department as supervising producer working on *Lawman* and *The Dakotas,* among others.

In 1963 he served as a producer on *The Virginian* and provided series presentations and character descriptions for *Laredo.* Schermer resurfaced in 1969 on *A Dream of Kings* starring Anthony Quinn.

The Virginian credits: producer in season: **2.**

Leslie Stevens

Born: February 3, 1924, Washington, D.C.; died: April 24, 1998.

The son of Admiral Leslie Stevens, Stevens began his writing, producing and directing career on Broadway and had a hit with *Marriage Go-Round,* which he adapted for the movies in 1961. Moving to Los Angeles, Stevens' first film work was adapting Gore Vidal's story of Billy the Kid, *The Left Handed Gun* (1958). President of the independent TV production company Daystar Productions in the 1960s, Stevens worked as writer and director on *Stoney Burke* and executive producer on *The Outer Limits.*

Working for Universal in the late 1960s as writer and producer, Stevens' credits included *It Takes a Thief, The Name of the Game, The Men from Shiloh, McCloud, Search, The Invisible Man, Gemini Man* and *Buck Rogers in the 25th Century.*

He also contributed stories and screenplays for the features *Sheena* (1984), *Return to the Blue Lagoon* (1991) and *Gordy* (1995).

In 1995 he was brought in as program consultant on the new *The Outer Limits.* The successful updated revival was still in production when Stevens died in 1998.

The Virginian–The Men from Shiloh credits: executive producer: **9:02, 9:04, 9:08, 9:11, 9:13, 9:17**; writer: **5:19, 5:28, 9:02, 9:08, 9:11.**

Frank Telford

Born: February 2, 1915; died: May 19, 1987.

Producer-writer-director Frank Telford worked in television from the early 1950s on shows such as *Robert Montgomery Presents, The Gulf Playhouse* and *The Stranger.*

In the 1960s Telford was employed as producer on *The Virginian, Kraft Suspense Theatre, Destry* (as executive producer) and the feature *Sergeant Ryker* (1968). He was also provided scripts for TV's *Mannix* and *Hawaii Five-O.*

Telford concentrated on writing in the 1970s and 1980s with work for *Nichols, Police Woman, Wonder Woman, CHiPs* and *Knight Rider,* among others.

The Virginian credits: producer in season: **3**; writer: **3.24.**

"Frank suffered from a mysterious ailment that every afternoon seemed to produce a fever and general weakness in him. Doctors couldn't figure out what was causing it. He was a good producer who approached his work with enthusiasm and dedication."—Frank Price.

Charles Marquis Warren

Born: December 16, 1912, Baltimore, Maryland; died: August 11, 1990.

One-time agent to acclaimed author F. Scott Fitzgerald, Warren spent his early career contributing to *The Saturday Evening Post.* Arriving in Hollywood after serving as a naval officer in World War II, he provided scripts and screenplays for *Beyond Glory* (1948), *Streets of Laredo* (1949) and *Oh! Susanna* (1948).

In 1951 he directed his first feature film, *Little Big Horn* (1951). Scriptwriting duties followed on *Woman of the North Country* (1952), *Springfield Rifle* (1952) and *Pony Express* (1953). In 1955 Warren became producer, director and writer on *Gunsmoke.* He stayed until 1957, returning briefly to B features before tackling his second TV series, *Rawhide.* He continued as executive producer and writer until 1961 when he once again changed TV Western assignments to work on *The Virginian.* His lack of success on the show marked his departure from TV and movies until 1968, when he contributed the story to *Day of the Evil Gun.* His Western film career ended with *Charro!* (1969) starring Elvis Presley.

Following almost two decades away from the film industry, Warren surfaced again in 1986 as executive producer of the 30-minute movie *C.A.B.*

Warren was buried at Arlington National Cemetery in 1990.

The Virginian credits: executive producer: **1:01, 1:05, 1:07, 1:08, 1:10–1:12**; producer: **1:02–1:04, 1:06, 1:09, 1:14.**

23

Writers

Without strong and engaging storylines, any series will fail. Yet the writer is often the last person to receive credit from the public. Actors and directors have been elevated to a status far removed from writers. But actors are often only as good as the words they are given to interpret and directors require a strong story to provide motivation and reaction. A bad story equals a weak episode.

Writers used on *The Virginian* came from all areas. Some had graduated from radio and pulp fiction. Others had an illustrious career, writing screenplays for Oscar-winning movies. Some were novelists. Most had experience of writing for various genres.

The following listings are intended as a cross section of the work of each writer. My listing is selective and doesn't include every writer who worked on the series, but represents those writers whose contribution to the series is noteworthy.

True Boardman

Born: October 25, 1909, Seattle, Washington; died: July 28, 2003.

Former child star True Eames Boardman was the son of actress Virginia Eames and actor True Boardman. Graduating from UCLA in 1934, he worked as head writer for *Lux Radio Theatre* and created shows for the Armed Forces Radio Services during World War II. Continuing in radio after the war, Boardman later moved into television, providing scripts for such 1950s-60s shows as *Gunsmoke, Perry Mason, Bonanza, My Three Sons* and *The Virginian*.

Boardman also resumed his acting career, appearing in small roles in *Perry Mason* and *The Virginian* and, later in his career, a one-man stage show as Ralph Waldo Emerson.

His autobiography *When Hollywood and I Were Young* was published by the Library of Congress Press. In 1993 he received the Valentine Davies Award for lifetime achievement from the Writers Guild of America.

He died from pancreatic cancer in 2003.

The Virginian–The Men from Shiloh credits: **2:28, 3:02, 3:08, 3:10, 3:15, 3:20, 3:21, 3:27, 5:10, 5:11, 5:16, 5:23, 5:29, 6:03, 6:18, 7:12, 9:13; 3:26** (actor), **6:15** (actor).

Howard Browne

Born: April 15, 1908, Omaha, Nebraska; died: October 28, 1999.

Browne left behind a career in pulp magazine writing and editing to move to Hollywood in 1956. Starting his writing career in 1939, Browne had worked as magazine editor for Ziff-Davis publications in the early 1940s on the science fiction pulp magazines *Amazing Stories* and *Fantastic Adventures*. He also wrote a number of detective stories and novels under various pseudonyms including John Evans and Alexander Blade.

In Hollywood, Browne provided scripts for many TV shows produced by Roy Huggins, including *Maverick, Bus Stop, The Virginian, The Fugitive, Kraft Suspense Theatre* and *Alias Smith and Jones*.

His feature film work included screenplays for *Portrait of a Mobster* (1961), *The St. Valentine's Day Massacre* (1967) and *Capone* (1975).

The Virginian credits: **1:13, 1:16, 1:20, 1:25, 1:29, 3:21.**

Borden Chase

Born: January 11, 1900; died: March 8, 1971.

Frank Fowler rose from being a New York taxi driver to a screenwriter in Hollywood, adopting a change of name to Borden Chase en route. His Hollywood screenwriting career got off to a promising start with adaptations of his novels *Sand Hog* and *Hell's Kitchen Has a Pantry*, as *Under Pressure* (1935) and *The Devil's Party* (1938) respectively. In 1944 Chase provided the screenplay for *The Fighting Seabees* (1944) starring John Wayne, and worked with Wayne again on the Western classic *Red River* (1948), for which Chase received an Oscar nomination.

In the 1950s Chase worked on a series of classic Anthony Mann Westerns including *Winchester '73* (1950), *Bend of the River* (1952) and *The Far Country* (1955). TV credits include *Bonanza, Overland Trail, The Virginian* and *Daniel Boone* in the early 1960s. He ended his career with the TV Western movie *A Man Called Gannon* (1969) before a stroke claimed his life in 1971.

The Virginian credits: **2.22, 3.30.**

Frank Chase

Born: 1924; died: July 2, 2004.

Son of Borden Chase and brother of Barrie Chase, Frank Chase was known in the 1950s as a character actor. Mostly resigned to small, often uncredited parts, his appearances include *Winchester '73* (1950), *Bend of the River* (1952), *The Creature Walks Among Us* (1956) and *Attack of the 50 Foot Woman* (1958).

Moving to television in 1959, Chase concentrated on writing, although he did appear on *Bonanza* and *The Virginian*. His writing credits include *Bonanza, The Rebel, Route 66, The Virginian, Branded, Hondo* and *The High Chaparral*.

The Virginian–The Men from Shiloh credits: **1:20, 2:05, 2:24, 2:29, 3:07, 3:23, 4:09, 5:01, 7:23, 9:09**; **2:05** (actor)

Gene L. Coon

Born: January 7, 1924; died: July 8, 1973.

Remembered today for his work as producer-writer on TV's *Star Trek*, Gene L. Coon's career as a writer for TV began in the 1950s on shows such as *Dragnet, Wagon Train, Maverick, Zorro* and *The Rebel*.

In the 1960s he worked on *The Virginian, Laredo* and *The Wild Wild West* before gaining his greatest recognition on *Star Trek*, working under his real name and the pseudonym Lee Cronin. Production and writing duties on *It Takes a Thief* were followed by *The Men from Shiloh, Nichols, The Streets of San Francisco* and *Kung Fu* before his untimely death (lung cancer) in 1973 at the age of 49.

The Virginian–The Men from Shiloh credits: **3:29, 9:19, 9:21**

Frank Fenton

Born: April 9, 1907, Hartford, Connecticut; died: July 24, 1967.

After graduating from Georgetown University, Fenton initially pursued an acting career on the stage. Working as a screenwriter for Fox Studios in the 1930s, he divided time between writing and acting in motion pictures until the late 1950s when he retired from acting.

Screenwriting credits included *The Saint in London* (1939), *A Date with the Falcon* (1941) and *River of No Return* (1954) starring Marilyn Monroe.

In the 1960s Fenton turned to writing for television, working with Roy Huggins on *Bus Stop* and *Kraft Suspense Theatre*. He also contributed scripts to *The Virginian* before his untimely death in 1967 from a pulmonary embolism. He was 60 years of age.

The Virginian credits: **1:26, 2:19, 3:01, 3:22, 5:12**

Morton S. Fine

Born: December 24, 1916; died: March 7, 1991.

The working partnership of Morton S. Fine and David Friedkin went to back to radio, writing for such shows as CBS' *Suspense* (1947) and *Escape* (1950) and *Think/ABC Radio Workshop* (1953), for which they adapted Ray Bradbury stories.

Fine and Friedkin turned their attention to television in the mid–1950s with *Climax*; later credits include *Bat Masterson, The Dick Powell Show, The Virginian* and *The Alfred Hitchcock Hour*.

In 1965 Fine and Friedkin created, wrote and produced *I Spy* and worked in partnership through the 1970s on *McCloud, Banacek, Barnaby Jones, Police Story* and *Kojak*.

The Virginian credits: **1:01, 1:02, 1:14, 1:27**

Douglas Heyes

Born: May 22, 1919; died: February 8, 1993.

The son of actor Herbert Harrison Heyes, writer-producer-director Douglas Heyes worked on various Warner Bros. shows in the 1950s, including *Cheyenne, Maverick* and *77 Sunset Strip*.

In the 1960s he moved to Universal, working on *Thriller, Checkmate, The Virginian, Kraft Suspense Theatre* and *The Bold Ones: The Lawyers*, among others. He also wrote and directed feature films such as *Kitten with a Whip* (1964) starring Ann-Margret and the remake of *Beau Geste* (1966) starring Doug McClure.

In the 1970s and 1980s, Heyes contributed as writer and director on *Alias Smith and Jones* under his pseudonym Matthew Howard, created the short-lived *Barbary Coast* and was responsible for two hit mini-series, *Captains and the Kings* (1976) and *North and South* (1985).

He became disillusioned with television in his final years as creative control became increasingly placed in the hands of network executives and he passed away in 1993 from heart failure.

The Virginian credits: **1:10**

Joseph Hoffman

Born: February 20, 1909, New York, New York; died: May 25, 1997.

A veteran screenwriter before his move into television in the late 1950s, Hoffman started his career in 1935, working for 20th Century-Fox on the Charlie Chan and Jones Family movies. He worked on numerous features throughout the 1940s and 1950s for Monogram, Columbia, RKO and Universal including *China Sky* (1945), *Has Anybody Seem My Gal?* (1952) and *Tall Man Riding* (1955).

Hoffman's television output includes, *Colt .45*, *My Three Sons*, *The Virginian*, *Branded* and *Nanny and the Professor*. He continued writing for feature films, including collaborations on *Sex and the Single Girl* (1964) and *The King's Pirate* (1967).

The Virginian credits: **3:02, 5:09, 5:29, 7:06.**

Jean Holloway

Born: April 16, 1917; died: November 11, 1989.

Starting her career working for singer Kate Smith on CBS radio, Holloway moved to MGM in the 1940s, with co-writing duties on *Till the Clouds Roll By* (1946), *Summer Holiday* and *Words and Music* (both 1948).

Moving into television in the 1950s, Holloway contributed scripts for such shows as *Wagon Train*, *Shirley Temple's Storybook*, *Adventures in Paradise*, *Bus Stop*, *The Virginian*, *Julia*, *The Ghost and Mrs. Muir*, *Nanny and the Professor* and *The Magic of Lassie*.

Holloway briefly ventured into feature films in the 1960s with *Madame X* (1966) starring Lana Turner, based on the play by Alexandre Bisson. The Emmy Award–winning TV remake, *Madame X* (1981), adapted Holloway's 1966 screenplay.

The Virginian–The Men from Shiloh credits: **3:05, 3:11, 7:10, 9:01, 9:05, 9:19**

Don Ingalls

Writer, producer and director of episodic TV, starting on the Western series *Have Gun Will Travel* and concluding decades later with the *T.J. Hooker* spin-off *Blood Sport*. Writer and producer on such shows as *The Virginian*, *Honey West* and *Fantasy Island*, Ingalls also worked as writer on the feature film *Airport 1975* (1974) and contributed scripts to *Bonanza*, *The Big Valley* and *Star Trek*.

The Virginian credits: writer: **1:15, 4:02, 5:04, 7:19, 7:21**; producer: **1:15, 2:18, 2:20, 2:22, 2:26.**

"*Don Ingalls was a good writer of Westerns and I used him when he was available. He never became a regular like Cy, Joel or Winston, though.*"—Frank Price

Roland Kibbee

Born: February 15, 1914, Monongahela, Pennsylvania; died: August 5, 1984.

Starting his career as a radio announcer, Kibbee wrote for Fred Allen and Groucho Marx before turning to movies such as *A Night in Casablanca, Angel on My Shoulder* (both 1946) and *Vera Cruz* (1954).

In 1959, Kibbee provided scripts for the TV Western series *The Deputy* starring Henry Fonda. He also wrote, produced and directed individual episodes of *The Bob Newhart Show, The Virginian, Alfred Hitchcock Presents* and *Bob Hope Presents, the Chrysler Theatre.* In 1967 he created *It Takes a Thief* starring Robert Wagner.

Executive producer of *The NBC Mystery Movie*, Kibbee also worked on *Columbo* and *Barney Miller.* The hard-working Kibbee continued to write for feature films, including *Valdez is Coming* (1971) and *The Midnight Man* (1974), both starring Burt Lancaster; he co-directed the latter with Lancaster.

His final work hearkened back to his start as a radio announcer, providing voiceovers on *Blade Runner* (1982) starring Harrison Ford.

He was a three-time Emmy Award winner.

The Virginian credits: **1:05** (writer, producer and director)

Harry Kleiner

Born: September 10, 1916, Tiflis, Russia.

Russian-born Harry Kleiner decided on a career in screenwriting following his graduation from Temple and Yale in the 1940s. Finding employment at 20th Century-Fox, Kleiner provided scripts for a series of quality movies including *King of the Khyber Rifles* (1953) and *Carmen Jones* (1954).

In the early 1960s, Kleiner worked in TV on *Bus Stop, The Virginian* and *Bob Hope Presents the Chrysler Theatre,* among others. Returning to features in the mid–1960s, he enjoyed success with *Fantastic Voyage* (1966), *Madigan* (1968) and *Bullitt* (1968).

He renewed his working relationship with *Bullitt*'s Steve McQueen on the less successful *Le Mans* (1971) and continued working through the 1980s on *Red Heat* (1988) and *Rambo II* (1988).

The Virginian credits: **1:19, 1:22, 1:28, 1:30, 3:16, 3:24**

Andy Lewis

Best known for his screenplay for the Oscar-winning *Klute* (1971) starring Jane Fonda, Lewis worked in TV during the 1960s on series such as *The Virginian, The Nurses, Twelve O'Clock High, Profiles in Courage, The F.B.I., Dundee and the Culhane, Lancer* and *Medical Center.*

The Virginian credits: **4:25, 5:02, 5:13, 5:25, 6:08** (with David Lewis), **6:12, 7:03**.

Donn Mullally

Working throughout the 1950s as writer on many TV series including *The Cisco Kid, Mr. & Mrs. North, Topper, Science Fiction Theatre, Behind Closed Doors, Law of the Plainsman* and *Bonanza,* Mullally continued writing for TV until the mid–1970s. Other credits include *The Virginian, Stoney Burke, Flipper, The Wild Wild West, Hondo, Mannix* and *Get Christie Love.*

The Virginian credits: **1:08, 1:23, 2:13, 2:15, 4:14, 5:21**

Dean Reisner

Born: November 3, 1918, New York, New York; died: August 18, 2002.

The former child actor Dinky Dean, who appeared with Charlie Chaplin in *The Pilgrim* (1923), is best remembered today (as Dean Reisner) for his screenwriting association with Clint Eastwood on the movies *Coogan's Bluff* (1968), *Play Misty for Me* (1971), *High Plains Drifter* (1973) and *The Enforcer* (1976).

With a writing career dating back to 1939, Reisner, like many of his generation, turned to television in the late 1950s and provided scripts for *Playhouse 90, Lawman, Rawhide, Bonanza, Ben Casey, The Virginian, The Outer Limits, Twelve O'Clock High* and *Slattery's People.*

From 1968 on, he worked in feature films, returning to TV for the mini-series *Rich Man, Poor Man* (1976). His uncredited work as a script doctor in the 1980s included *The Boat* (1981), *Blue Thunder* (1983), *The Sting II* (1983) and *Starman* (1984).

The Virginian credits: **2:08, 2:23, 2:30, 3:12.**

Sy Salkowitz

A prolific writer of episodic TV since the late 1950s, Salkowitz worked on *Perry Mason, The Untouchables, Checkmate, The Virginian, Mission: Impossible, Cimarron Strip, Ironside, McCloud, Alias Smith and Jones* and *The Six Million Dollar Man,* among others.

In the 1970s he was President of 20th Century-Fox TV for a short period before returning to scriptwriting duties on *Jessie* (1984) starring Lindsay Wagner and *Columbo: Grand Deceptions* (1989).

The Virginian credits: **4:18, 5:08, 5:17, 5:26, 6:11, 6:15.**

Gerald Sanford

Writer, producer and playwright, Gerald Sanford began his TV writing career in the 1960s, working for shows such as *The Virginian, Twelve O'Clock High, The Loner* and *The F.B.I.* In 1968 Jayne Mansfield made her last film appearance in an adaptation of Sanford's play *Single Room Furnished.*

Sanford has continued to work steadily from the 1970s to the present day, mainly on TV series such as *Kung Fu, Knight Rider, Bodies of Evidence, Star Trek: Deep Space Nine* and the 2002 TV movie *Cybermutt.*

The Virginian credits: **7:04, 7:08, 7:13, 8:06, 8:08.**

Alvin Sapinsley

Born: November 23, 1921, Providence, Rhode Island; died: July 14, 2002.

After serving on D-Day as a cryptographer, Alvin Sapinsley worked in TV from the late 1940s, writing and adapting material for various drama series often involving live performances, including *The Philco Television Playhouse*, *Tales of Tomorrow* and *The Elgin Hour;* the latter featured Boris Karloff as an elderly Sherlock Holmes in "The Sting of Death."

In the 1960s and '70s, Sapinsley worked regularly on TV shows including *The Virginian, The Man from U.N.C.L.E., The F.B.I., It Takes a Thief, Night Gallery* and *Kojak.* He won the Edgar Allan Poe Award for "Best TV Feature or Mini-Series Script" in 1977 for *Sherlock Holmes in New York* (1976) starring Roger Moore.

Following work on the short-lived TV series *Shannon* (1981) starring Kevin Dobson, he retired.

The Virginian credits: **7:05, 7:09, 8:03, 8:12, 8:20.**

Maxwell Shane

Born: August 26, 1905, Paterson, New Jersey; died: October 25, 1983.

Writer, producer and director Maxwell Shane began his career as a journalist and writer for the pulp magazine *Black Mask* before moving to Hollywood to work in publicity. His first screenwriting credit was *You Can't Beat Love* (1937) followed by a series of B movies including *The Mummy's Hand* (1940) and *Cowboy in Manhattan* (1943). During World War II, Shane contributed to Paramount's *Victory Short* series before turning to directing in 1947 with film noir thrillers such as *Fear in the Night* (1947) starring DeForest Kelley and its remake *Nightmare* (1956) with Edward G. Robinson.

Maxwell spent time in TV starting in the late 1950s on *Thriller, The Virginian* and *The Mod Squad* before retiring from the screen.

The Virginian credits: **1:12, 1:24.**

Robert Van Scoyk

Born: January 13, 1928, Dayton, Ohio; died: August 26, 2002.

After starting as a columnist for the *Dayton Daily News*, Robert Elseworth Van Scoyk progressed through the ranks at NBC in New York to become a scriptwriter on *Kraft Television Theatre, The Imogene Coca Show* and *The Ann Sothern Show.*

Moving to Los Angeles in the 1960s, Van Scoyk contributed scripts to *The Defenders, The Virginian, The Nurses* and *Mr. Broadway*, among others. He became involved in producing in the late 1960s, starting with *The Virginian* and continuing with *Rafferty, Flying High, Young Maverick* and *Murder, She Wrote.*

In his later career, Van Scoyk became associated with crime dramas, writing for *Partners in Crime, Murder, She Wrote* and, in the 1990s, *Columbo.*

He died in 2002 of complications from diabetes, age 74.

The Virginian–The Men from Shiloh credits: **6:20, 7:01, 7:17, 7:20, 7:24, 8:04, 8:17, 8:18, 8:24, 9:06, 9:15, 9:18**; associate producer–producer in seasons: **6, 7, 8.**

Carey Wilber

Born: June 26, 1916, Buffalo, New York; died: May 2, 1998.

Carey Wilber began his career in 1936 as a copy boy. Working for a variety of newspapers, including *The Ketchikan Chronicle* and *Anchorage Times,* in Alaska through the 1940s, he decided to write for TV in the early 1950s and moved to New York City. Early work included scripts for *Studio One, Captain Video and His Video Rangers, Armstrong Circle Theatre, Maverick* and *The Californians.*

The 1960s saw Wilber settle into writing for prime time hit shows such as *The Virginian, Lost in Space, The Big Valley, Star Trek, The Time Tunnel* and *It Takes a Thief.* He also provided the scripts for two *Tarzan* movies.

Wilber's TV credits in the 1970s include detective shows, *Cannon* and *Barnaby Jones.* Wilber passed away in 1998, age 82.

The Virginian credits: **2:03, 2:10, 2:16, 2:17, 2:19, 2:27, 3:03, 3:06, 3:07, 3:19, 3:27**

"I always managed to get good work out of Carey, partially because he argued with me so much that I became his uncredited collaborator, as I would describe the scenes for him or give him the proper dialogue."—Frank Price

24

Directors

The role of the director working in television is markedly different than in motion pictures, where an accomplished director brings together all creative elements into one cohesive vision. In television, the director answers to the executive producer and is hired by the episode, moving between different assignments. Editing is usually out of their control and therefore any continuing creative management on any individual episode is lost. The general public conception of the director as the key decisionmaker wielding considerable power is only true of the movie director. The television director is more limited in his scope and has little real power in relation to the executive producer, who is the person in charge.

The following listings are intended as a cross-section of the work of each director. They don't include every director who worked on the series, but represents those directors whose contribution or career is noteworthy.

Richard L. Bare

Born: August 12, 1909, Modesto, California.

Bare is best remembered today by fans of vintage TV for his record-breaking 167-episode run on the 1960s series *Green Acres*. Among film aficionados, his 1971 book *The Film Director* (Macmillan & Co.) is considered a classic.

Between teaching assignments at USC, Bare wrote and produced the one-reel documentary *So You Want to Quit Smoking*. Warner Bros. bought the film, retitled it *So You Want to Give Up Smoking*, released it in 1942 and hired Bare to produce a series of shorts. The series proved successful and lasted until 1956.

Bare transferred to the Warner Bros. television department in the mid–1950s, directing episodes of *Cheyenne, Sugarfoot, Maverick, Colt .45, Lawman* and *77 Sunset Strip*.

Bare's work on *The Twilight Zone* brought him the attention of sci-fi fans who acknowledged his skill as a director. He returned to Westerns on *The Virginian* and *The Dakotas* before making a lasting mark on the comedy series *Green Acres*.

Following the cancellation of *Green Acres*, Bare directed episodes of *Alias Smith and Jones* and *Faraday and Company* before retiring.

The Virginian credits: **1:20, 1:29, 2:10, 2:27, 3:04, 3:16.**

Earl Bellamy

Born: March 11, 1917, Minneapolis, Minnesota; died: November 30, 2003.

Moving to Hollywood with his family as a young child, Bellamy graduated from Hollywood High School in 1935 and began his film career as an office boy at Columbia Studios. Progressing through the ranks to first assistant director, Bellamy worked alongside noted directors George Zukor and Fred Zinnemann on such films *From Here to Eternity* (1953) and *A Star Is Born* (1954).

In 1954, Bellamy began an association with television that lasted over 30 years. Working as a director, he was employed consistently throughout the 1950s–1980s on numerous popular shows including *The Lone Ranger, Lassie, The Adventures of Rin Tin Tin, Perry Mason, Wagon Train, The Andy Griffith Show, The Virginian, The Munsters, I Spy, The Monroes, The Partridge Family, M*A*S*H, Starsky and Hutch, Fantasy Island, Hart to Hart* and "*V.*"

Bellamy claimed to enjoy the fast pace of shooting television, preferring it to movies (which he described as "long and drawn-out").

He retired in 1986, living in Rio Rancho, New Mexico, from 1991 until his death from a heart attack in 2003. He was 86.

The Virginian credits: **1:04, 1:17, 2:08, 2:16, 2:20, 2:28, 3:30, 4:29.**

Richard Benedict

Born: January 8, 1920, Sicily; died: April 26, 1984.

A former prizefighter, Benedict turned to acting in 1944, appearing in *Streets of San Francisco* (1949), *Ace in the Hole* (1951), *It! The Terror from Beyond Space* (1958) and *Ocean's Eleven* (1960). In the early 1960s he began concentrating on directing episodic TV.

In a TV directing career spanning almost 20 years he worked on many top-rated shows including *Hawaiian Eye, The Virginian, The Fugitive, I Spy, Laredo, Get Smart, Mission: Impossible, The Invaders, The High Chaparral, Alias Smith and Jones, Harry O, Quincy, Fantasy Island* and *240-Robert*.

He died in 1984 following a heart attack.

The Virginian credits: **3:21, 4:11, 9:11.**

Leon Benson

Benson's TV directing career spanned almost 20 years, beginning with the '50s comedy series *Meet Corliss Archer* (adapted from the radio show of the same name). He followed this with *Science Fiction Theatre* and *Highway Patrol*.

Benson also worked on *The Man Called X, Sea Hunt, This Man Dawson, Ben Casey, The Virginian, Ripcord, The Outer Limits, Flipper, Laredo, The Wild Wild West, Mission Impossible, The Flying Nun* and *The High Chaparral*, among others.

The Virginian credits: **3:27, 4:05, 4:09, 4:17.**

Abner Biberman

Born: April 1, 1909, Milwaukee, Wisconsin; died: June 20, 1977.

Biberman spent nearly two decades of his early film career as a character actor in a series of distinguished movies. Usually confined to villainous roles, Biberman appeared in *Gunga Din* (1939), *The Rains Came* (1939), *His Girl Friday* (1940), *The Keys of the Kingdom* (1944), *Captain Kidd* (1945), *Viva Zapata!* (1952) and *Elephant Walk* (1954).

Following an appearance before HUAC, Biberman went under the pseudonym Joel Judge in 1954 for his directorial debut, *The Golden Mistress* (1954). He soon dropped that *nom de screen* and moved into television, directing Warner Bros.' *Maverick, Colt .45* and *77 Sunset Strip*.

Throughout the 1960s Biberman directed numerous TV episodes for various studios, including *Ben Casey, The Virginian, The Outer Limits, The Fugitive, Voyage to the Bottom of the Sea, Gilligan's Island, Laredo, Ironside* and *The Bold Ones: The New Doctors*.

His final credits were acting roles in the '70s on *Hec Ramsey* with Richard Boone and *Kodiak* with Clint Walker.

The Virginian–The Men from Shiloh credits: **5:04, 5:08, 5:13, 5:17, 5:19, 5:22, 5:24, 5:26, 5:28, 6:01, 6:02, 6:04, 6:05, 6:11, 6:12, 6:15, 6:17, 6:22, 6:24, 7:04, 7:10, 8:10, 8:13, 9:05, 9:23.**

Michael Caffey

Beginning his TV career in the 1950s as assistant director on shows such as *The Rebel*, Caffey has since directed hundreds of hours of episodic TV on shows such as *The Virginian, The Wild Wild West, Garrison's Gorillas, Hondo, Ironside, Lancer, Dan August, Wonder Woman, Serpico, Logan's Run, The Amazing Spider-Man, The Dukes of Hazzard, Trapper John M.D., Simon & Simon, T.J. Hooker, MacGyver, Paradise* and *Hawkeye*.

The Virginian–The Men from Shiloh credits:**7:08, 7:18, 7:19, 7:23, 7:26, 8:01, 8:03, 8:20, 9:12, 9:15.**

Thomas Carr

Born: July 4, 1907, Philadelphia, Pennsylvania; died: April 23, 1997.

Former child actor Thomas Carr, the son of director William Carr and actress Mary Carr, moved into direction in 1945 following time spent as a dialogue coach at Republic Studios. He worked mainly on B Westerns such as *Bandits of the Badlands* (1945) and *Wyoming Roundup* (1952) throughout the 1940s and early 1950s.

Carr became associated with the DC Comics character Superman when he directed episodes of the serial *Superman* (1948) starring Kirk Alyn and followed it up with work on the *Adventures of Superman* TV series of the 1950s starring George Reeves.

Throughout this period, Carr was still directing B Westerns and venturing further into TV direction on *Annie Oakley, The Adventures of Champion, Buffalo Bill Jr., Gunsmoke, Wanted: Dead or Alive, Rawhide, Bonanza, The Virginian* and *Daniel Boone*.

Carr briefly strayed from familiar Western territory directing 1960s episodes of *Honey West* and *The Felony Squad* before ending his career on *The Guns of Will Sonnett*.

The Virginian credits: **5:10, 5:15, 5:20.**

Alan Crosland, Jr.

Born: July 19, 1918; died: December 18, 2001.

The son of silent film director Alan Crosland, he worked from 1944 to 1957 as a film editor on such films as *Adventures of Don Juan* (1948), *The Jazz Singer* (1953) and *The Sweet Smell of Success* (1957).

His first TV work was in the 1950s, as film editor on *Sergeant Preston of the Yukon*. Abandoning film editing for directing in the late 1950s, Crosland worked in television for Warner Bros., Universal and 20th Century-Fox, among others. Popular shows he worked on include *Maverick, Peter Gunn, Lawman, 77 Sunset Strip, Rawhide, Bonanza, The Twilight Zone, Checkmate, 87th Precinct, The Virginian, The Outer Limits, Voyage to the Bottom of the Sea, The Wild Wild West, Adam-12* and *Emergency!*.

Crosland received the DGA Award for Outstanding Directorial Achievement in Television for his work as first assistant director on the *Kojak* pilot, *The Marcus-Nelson Murders* (1973). He passed away in 2001, age 83.

The Virginian credits: **1:23, 3:08, 5:07.**

Marc Daniels

Born: January 27, 1912, Pittsburgh, Pennsylvania; died: April 23, 1989.

A graduate of the University of Michigan, Marc Daniels initially worked as assistant stage manager in a New York theater before turning to TV direction on CBS' *Ford Television Theatre*. In 1951 he directed the first season of *I Love Lucy*, helping to master the revolutionary three-camera system that captured the spontaneity of a live performance on film.

In the 1960s, Daniels became best known for his extensive work on *Hogan's Heroes* and *Star Trek*. Other directing work included *The Man from U.N.C.L.E., Mission: Impossible, The Doris Day Show* and *The Men from Shiloh*.

Daniels continued to work steadily throughout the 1970s and 1980s on *Kung Fu, Vega$, Private Benjamin, Crazy Like a Fox* and a final reunion with Lucille Ball in 1986's *Life with Lucy*.

Daniels died of congestive heart failure in 1989.

The Men from Shiloh credits: **9:09, 9:20.**

Herschel Daugherty

Born: October 27, 1910, Indiana; died: March 5, 1993

Working as dialogue director at Warner Bros. from 1943 to 1951 on films that included *Mildred Pierce* (1945), *Life with Father* (1947) and *On Moonlight Bay* (1951), Daugherty turned his attention to television in 1952 and focused on directing shows such as *Biff Baker, U.S.A., Suspicion* and *Wagon Train*.

In the 1960s, Daugherty's credits included *Checkmate, The Virginian, The Man from U.N.C.L.E., Star Trek, Cimarron Strip, The High Chaparral* and *It Takes a Thief*.

He continued into the mid–1970s directing episodes of *Cannon, Emergency!, Banacek, The Six Million Dollar Man* and *Petrocelli*, retiring in 1975.

The Virginian credits: **1:14, 2:09, 2:25.**

Charles S. Dubin

Born: February 1, 1919, Brooklyn, New York.

Graduating from Brooklyn College in 1941, Dubin worked as a stage actor and singer before moving into live television with ABC in 1950.

When Dubin was blacklisted in 1958 following his failure to testify before HUAC, NBC dropped him from the hit game show *Twenty-One*. He remained unemployed for the reminder of the 1950s. The '60s series *The Defenders* marked his return to directing and he worked regularly on prime time network TV until his retirement in 1990.

Dubin directed over 40 episodes of *M*A*S*H* between 1976 and 1983 and was nominated for an Emmy on ten occasions.

The Virginian credits: **4:12, 4:14, 6:07, 7:01, 7:11, 7:15, 7:17.**

John English

Born: June 25, 1903, Cumberland, England; died: October 11, 1969.

English was a master director of the Republic serial. Working in collaboration with fellow director William Witney, his credits include *Zorro Rides Again* (1937), *The Lone Ranger* (1938), *Dick Tracy's G-Men* (1939), *Adventures of Red Ryder* (1940), *Drums of Fu Manchu* (1940), *Adventures of Captain Marvel* (1941) and *Captain America* (1944).

In the early 1950s he began work in TV on such shows as *The Roy Rogers Show*, *The Range Rider* and *Biff Baker U.S.A.* He continued through the 1950s with *The Adventures of Champion*, *Broken Arrow*, *Wagon Train* and *Johnny Ringo*.

He retired in 1966 after working on the 1960s series *Thriller, The Virginian, Daniel Boone, A Man Called Shenandoah* and *Laredo*.

The Virginian credits: **1:25, 2:04, 2:07.**

John Florea

Born: May 28, 1916, Alliance, Ohio; died: August 25, 2000.

Florea worked as a staff photographer for *Life* magazine before he decided to earn his living working behind a movie camera as a producer and director. The feature film *Suicide Attack* (1951), on which he served as producer, was followed by non-stop TV work over the next 30 years, directing episodes of *Highway Patrol, Sea Hunt, Bonanza, The Virginian, Honey West, The High Chaparral, Ironside, Primus, Barbary Coast, The Dukes of Hazzard, "V"* and *MacGyver* (1985), among others.

The Virginian credits: **2:18, 3:09, 3:14, 3:22, 3:24.**

David Friedkin

Born: March 8, 1912; died: October 15, 1976.

A graduate of Juilliard (he was a violin major), writer-producer-director David Friedkin began his film career as an actor. In 1950 the multi-talented Friedkin turned his attention to writing for radio shows (such as Humphrey Bogart's *Bold Venture* in collaboration with Morton S. Fine.

In the mid–1950s he moved to TV, writing, producing and directing *Sea Hunt, The Rifleman, The Virginian, Ironside, Kojak, Barnaby Jones* and *Police Story*. He also co-wrote, in collaboration with Fine, the screenplay of the controversial *The Pawnbroker* (1964) starring Rod Steiger. Freidkin and Fine's most celebrated show from the 1960s was *I Spy* starring Robert Culp and Bill Cosby.

The Virginian credits: **1:01, 1:19, 1:27.**

Samuel Fuller

Born: August 12, 1912, Worcester, Massachusetts; died: October 30, 1997.

Fuller was a screenwriter, novelist, producer, director and World War II hero, receiving the Bronze Star, Silver Star and Purple Heart. He made his directorial debut in 1949 with *I Shot Jesse James*. He became adept at writing and directing low-budget war dramas that often reflected his own war experiences.

In the early 1960s he directed episodes of *The Dick Powell Show*, *The Virginian* and *Iron Horse* and continued his feature film work with *Shock Corridor* (1963) and *The Naked Kiss* (1964).

The war movie *The Big Red One* (1980) was followed by the controversial "racist" drama, *White Dog* (1982). *Street of No Return* (1989) marked the end of his directorial career.

The Virginian credits: **1:09**.

Maurice Geraghty

Born: September 8, 1908, New York; died: June 30, 1987.

Princeton graduate Maurice Geraghty followed his father Tom Geraghty into the screenwriting profession in 1935, working for Republic Studios. Employed mainly on B Westerns such as *Hills of Old Wyoming* (1937) and *The Mysterious Rider* (1938), Geraghty turned to production duties from 1942 to 1945 on RKO's *Falcon* movie series.

In the 1950s he divided his time between B features and TV, writing and directing episodes of *The Gene Autry Show*, *Annie Oakley*, *Buffalo Bill Jr.*, *Tales of the Texas Rangers*, *Panic!*, *Bonanza*, *Thriller*, *Whiplash*, *87th Precinct* and *The Virginian*.

Geraghty provided the script for *Love Me Tender* (1956) starring Elvis Presley.

The Virginian credits: **1:08, 1:13, 2:21, 3:10, 3:19, 3:26**.

Bernard Girard

Born: February 22, 1918; died: December 30, 1997.

Entering the film industry as a screenwriter in the late 1940s, Girard split his time between writing and directing throughout his career with the occasional foray into producing. Concentrating on TV from 1953 to 1963, Girard worked on *The Lone Wolf*, *Playhouse 90*, *Wagon Train*, *Johnny Staccato*, *The Twilight Zone*, *Checkmate*, *The Virginian*, *The Alfred Hitchcock Hour* and *Kraft Suspense Theatre*, among others.

In 1966 Girard had a surprise hit with *Dead Heat on a Merry-Go-Round* (1966). His subsequent work was routine and he retired after directing *Gone with the West* (1975).

The Virginian credits: **1:07, 1:16**.

Darrell Hallenbeck

Died: 31 January 1987.

E. Darrell Hallenbeck is best remembered for his directing work on the '60s spy series *The Man from U.N.C.L.E.* Other work from the 1960s includes *The Virginian*, *The Green Hornet* and *The Girl from U.N.C.L.E.*

He later worked as production manager on *All the President's Men* (1976) and *Baby: Secret of the Lost Legend* (1985).

The Virginian credits: **6:16, 6:25**.

Harry Harris

Born: September 8, 1922, Kansas City, Missouri.

Progressing from editor at Republic Pictures' TV division National Telefilm to director on the '50s series *Wanted: Dead or Alive* and *Naked City,* Harris worked on familiar prime time hits such as *Lost in Space, Land of the Giants, The Waltons, Kung Fu, Dallas, Spenser: For Hire* and *7th Heaven,* throughout the 1960s-1990s.

The Men from Shiloh credits: **9:03, 9:06, 9:22**.

Jeff Hayden

After graduating from the University of North Carolina in Chapel Hill, Hayden moved between NBC and ABC before directing live TV dramas on *The Philco Television Playhouse* beginning in 1954.

From 1957 Hayden concentrated on filmed series work for shows such as *Leave It to Beaver, The Andy Griffith Show, The Virginian, Peyton Place, Batman, Alias Smith and Jones, Quincy, Falcon Crest* and *In the Heat of the Night.*

Hayden also worked in theater where he has directed his wife of over 50 years, Eva Marie Saint.

The Men from Shiloh credits: **9:14, 9:18**.

Herman Hoffman

Born: June 29, 1909, Montgomery, Alabama; died: March 26, 1989.

Writer-producer-director Hoffman began his career as a writer for MGM in the early 1930s. He achieved recognition from the Academy of Motion Picture Arts and Sciences for the political documentary *The Hoaxsters* (1952) and the historical short *Battle at Gettysburg* (1955) before turning to TV direction in the late 1950s on series ranging from *Sea Hunt* to *Flipper.*

He retired in 1977 following the cancellation of the TV series *Monster Squad.*

The Virginian credits: **4:19, 4:24**.

Jerry Hopper

Born: July 29, 1907, Guthrie, Oklahoma; died: December 17, 1988.

Veteran director of numerous TV series, Jerry Hopper started in radio. He progressed from film editor to director for Paramount Pictures, before moving into television in the late 1950s.

Directing credits include *Perry Mason, Naked City, The Untouchables, Overland Trail, The Virginian, The Fugitive, The Addams Family, The Time Tunnel* and *It Takes a Thief.*

He retired following the failure of the Western feature film *Madron* (1970) starring Richard Boone.

The Virginian–The Men from Shiloh credits: **1:15, 9:01**.

Burt Kennedy

Born: September 3, 1922, Muskegon, Michigan; died: February 15, 2001.

Kennedy started his professional life as a member of the family vaudeville act "The Dancing Kennedys." He was awarded the Bronze Star, Silver Star and Purple Heart in World War II. Following the war, Kennedy provided scripts for radio shows and moved into film, helping script a series of classic Budd Boetticher–Randolph Scott Westerns.

Kennedy worked in television in the late 1950s on *Lawman* and continued to direct on *The Virginian* and *Combat!* Among his other big-screen westerns are *The War Wagon* (1967) and *Welcome to Hard Times* (1967). Creating his own niche for comedy Westerns, he achieved his greatest success with *Support Your Local Sheriff* (1969) and *Support Your Local Gunfighter* (1971) both starring James Garner.

In the 1970s, Kennedy returned to directing TV series and movies, preferring to specialize in Westerns such as *The Wild Wild West Revisited* (1979) and *Once Upon a Texas Train* (1988).

He died of cancer in 2001 and was buried in Arlington Cemetery to a 21-gun salute. *The Virginian* credits: **1:02**.

Tony Leader

Born: December 23, 1913, Boston, Massachusetts; died: July 1, 1988.

Anton Leader began his career as a producer and director for CBS Radio in the 1940s, working on *Suspense* and *Murder at Midnight*. In the mid–1950s he started to direct episodic TV and stayed with the medium until his retirement in the early 1970s.

In the 1960s he was often credited as Tony Leader on shows such as *The Virginian*, *Gilligan's Island*, *Lost in Space*, *I Spy*, *Get Smart* and *Star Trek*.

The Virginian credits: **4:01, 4:13, 4:21, 4:23, 4:25, 4:30, 5:02, 6:19, 7:21, 8:06, 8:08, 8:09, 8:11, 8:23**.

Ida Lupino

Born: February 4, 1914, London, England; died: August 3, 1995.

The daughter of British comedian Stanley Lupino, Ida Lupino arrived in Hollywood in 1933 and soon progressed from small parts to a starring role next to Humphrey Bogart in *High Sierra* (1941).

Finding roles of merit increasingly rare through the 1940s, she left Warner Bros in 1947 and started directing, writing and producing low-budget movies. A genuine trailblazer, she was the only woman of that period to direct and only the second woman to be admitted to the Directors Guild.

In 1953 she appeared in *Four Star Playhouse* and began her long association with TV as both an actress and director on such shows as *The Untouchables*, *The Virginian*, *The Fugitive*, *Bewitched*, *Gilligan's Island* and *The Ghost and Mrs. Muir*.

In the 1970s she concentrated on acting in both TV and feature films. The TV work included *Alias Smith and Jones*, *The Streets of San Francisco*, *Columbo* and *Charlie's Angels*.

She passed away in 1995 from a stroke brought on by colon cancer.

The Virginian credits: **5:09**; **1:25, 5:28** (actor).

Russ Mayberry

Starting his career as floor manager on the early TV series *Kukla, Fran and Ollie*, Russell B. Mayberry directed Screen Gems and Universal TV productions through the 1960s with work on *The Virginian, Bewitched, I Dream of Jeannie, Love on a Rooftop, That Girl, The Monkees, Ironside, Marcus Welby M.D.* and *The Brady Bunch.*

Mayberry continued to direct TV series throughout the 1980s and 1990s with credits ranging from *The Partridge Family, Alias Smith and Jones* and *Barnaby Jones* to *Magnum P.I., The Equalizer* and *Star Trek: The Next Generation.*

The Men from Shiloh credits: **9:02, 9:08, 9:17.**

Don McDougall

McDougall began his film career as a script supervisor at Republic Pictures on the Roy Rogers movie *The Far Frontier* (1948). A few years later he was directing Rogers on his TV show.

Working exclusively in television throughout his long career, McDougall was particularly suited to Westerns, and directed over 100 combined episodes of *Wanted Dead or Alive, Rawhide, Bonanza* and *The Virginian*. Other shows McDougall directed include *Jungle Jim, The Man from U.N.C.L.E., Star Trek, Ironside, Kolchak: The Night Stalker, Planet of the Apes, Dallas* and *The Dukes of Hazzard.*

The Virginian–The Men from Shiloh credits: episodes: **2:03, 2:13, 2:19, 2:29, 3:02, 3:11, 3:12, 3:13, 3:18, 3:20, 3:23, 3:25, 3:29, 4:10, 5:01, 5:05, 5:06, 5:12, 5:14, 5:18, 5:21, 5:23, 5:25, 5:27, 5:29, 6:03, 6:06, 6:08, 6:09, 6:10, 6:14, 6:18, 6:21, 7:02, 7:06, 7:12, 7:25, 9:16.**

Bernard McEveety

Born: 1924, New Rochelle, New York; died: February 2, 2004.

Coming from a family of talented directors and producers, McEveety, Jr., worked as assistant director on the cult horror film *The Return of Dracula* (1958) before settling into a lengthy career in television, directing episodes of *The Untouchables, Combat!, The Virginian, The Waltons, The Rockford Files, Trapper John M.D.* and *In the Heat of the Night.*

The Virginian credits: **1:28, 2:06, 2:11, 3:03, 3:05, 3:06.**

Robert Ellis Miller

Born: July 18, 1932, New York, New York.

Former child actor Robert Ellis Miller decided on a directing career following graduation from Harvard University. As an adult he worked behind the camera on many TV shows in the 1950s and early 1960s including *Peter Gunn, The Twilight Zone, Checkmate, Route 66, Dr. Kildare, Ben Casey, The Virginian, The Fugitive* and *Burke's Law.*

Turning to feature films in 1966, he directed *The Heart Is a Lonely Hunter* (1968), *The Buttercup Chain* (1970) and *Reuben, Reuben* (1983) but returned to TV in the 1990s following the failure of *Brenda Starr* (1989).

The Virginian credits: **1:22, 2:02.**

Hollingsworth Morse

Born: December 16, 1910; died: January 23, 1988.

John Hollingsworth Morse began his film career as a casting director for Paramount Pictures and soon progressed to assistant director for George Stevens. Harrowing color footage from his time working with Stevens during D-Day and the liberation of Berlin and the concentration camps is included in *George Stevens: D-Day to Berlin* (1994) with Morse providing commentary.

Following the war, Morse turned to television, directing numerous episodes of *The Lone Ranger* and *Roc Jones, Space Ranger*. In the 1960s Morse directed episodes of *Petticoat Junction, Flipper, The Rat Patrol, The Ghost and Mrs. Muir* and *H. R. Pufnstuf,* among others.

The remainder of his career was spent directing shows such *Isis, Shazam!, The Dukes of Hazzard, Enos* and *The Fall Guy.*

The Men from Shiloh credits: **9:19, 9:21**.

Leo Penn

Born: August 27, 1921, Lawrence, Massachusetts; died: September 5, 1998.

The father of actor Sean Penn, Leo Penn's film acting career was cut short when he was blacklisted in the 1950s. Turning to Broadway and TV, he decided to quit acting in favor of production and direction and began directing TV shows in the early 1960s.

A prolific TV director, Penn worked on numerous prime time shows from the 1960s through the 1990s including *The Virginian, Lost in Space, I Spy, Star Trek, The Name of the Game, Lancer, Cade's County, Little House on the Prairie, Starsky and Hutch, St. Elsewhere, Jake and the Fatman* and *Diagnosis Murder.*

Returning to acting in the late 1970s, Leo appeared with his son Sean and wife Eileen Ryan in *The Crossing Guard* (1995). He died of lung cancer in 1998.

The Virginian credits: **6:23, 7:07, 7:16**.

Joseph Pevney

Born: September 15, 1911.

Originally a stage actor and director, Pevney abandoned acting for a directing career at Universal Studios in 1950. *Away All Boats* (1956) starring Jeff Chandler proved an early success with another hit movie, *Tammy and the Bachelor* (1957), quickly following.

Despite a promising start to his directing career, Pevney drifted into television in the 1960s, achieving his greatest success on *Star Trek*. A prolific director of episodic TV, he worked on many Western shows including *Bonanza, The Virginian, The Legend of Jesse James, Laredo, The Loner, The High Chaparral* and *How the West Was Won.*

Pevney retired in 1985.

The Virginian credits: **8:02, 8:05, 8:07, 8:14, 8:15, 8:19, 8:21**.

Don Richardson

Born: April 30, 1918, New York; died: January 10, 1996.

Although working regularly as a director in theater and television until the mid–1970s,

Don Richardson is best remembered as an acting teacher. His book *Acting Without Agony: An Alternative to the Method* has won admirers throughout the acting community. TV directing credits include *The Defenders, The Virginian, The Munsters, Lost in Space, The High Chaparral, Lancer* and *One Day at a Time.*
   The Virginian credits: **3:01, 4:03, 4:06, 4:07.**

Seymour Robbie

Born: 1920, New York, New York; died: June 17, 2004.
   After directing the game shows *Down You Go* and *The $64,000 Question* in the 1950s, Robbie turned to TV series in the 1960s with *The Virginian, Bewitched, The Green Hornet* and *The Name of the Game,* among others.
   He continued through the 1970s and 1980s with work on *Cannon, Kolchak: The Night Stalker, Wonder Woman, Hart to Hart, Remington Steele* and *Father Dowling Mysteries.*
   He passed away in 2004, a victim of Lou Gehrig's disease (ALS).
   The Virginian credits: **8:04, 8:12, 8:24.**

James Sheldon

Born: New York, New York.
   Working almost exclusively in television since 1950, James Sheldon directed hundreds of hours of prime time TV in a career lasting over 35 years. His credits include *Gunsmoke, The Virginian, The Bing Crosby Show, Batman, That Girl, My World and Welcome to It, Bridget Loves Bernie, Petrocelli, Alice, Knots Landing, The Equalizer* and *Sledge Hammer!*
   The Virginian credits: **1:05, 7:03, 7:05, 7:13, 7:20, 7:24, 8:18.**

Paul Stanley

Entering television in the late 1950s, Paul Stanley worked consistently directing shows such as *Adventures in Paradise, The Untouchables, The Virginian, Combat!, The Outer Limits, The Time Tunnel, The Rat Patrol, Mission: Impossible, The High Chaparral, Cade's County, Kojak, Lou Grant, Vega$, Knight Rider* and *MacGyver.*
   The Virginian credits: **4:08, 4:20, 4:22, 4:26.**

Jeannot Szwarc

Born: November 21, 1939, Paris, France.
   Contracted to Universal from the late 1960s, Szwarc worked initially as a writer and director on *It Takes a Thief* and associate producer on *Ironside.*
   Concentrating on direction, he worked in TV throughout the early to mid–1970s. He directed the feature films *Jaws 2* (1978) and *Somewhere in Time* (1980). The failure of *Supergirl* (1984) and subsequent work resulted in a brief fling with European TV movies before Szwarc returned to America with work on two *Rockford Files* reunion movies and TV shows such as *The Practice, Ally McBeal, Smallville, CSI: Miami* and *Boston Legal.*
   The Virginian–The Men from Shiloh credits: **8:17, 9:10.**

William Witney

Born: May 15, 1915, Lawton, Oklahoma; died: March 17, 2002.

Starting his film career as an extra, Witney worked as editor, writer, actor and assistant director before tackling his first directing assignment on the serial *The Painted Stallion* (1937). Working with directors John English and Spencer Bennet, Witney mastered the art of directing fast-paced action adventure serials such as *Daredevils of the Red Circle* (1939), *Zorro's Fighting Legion* (1939) and *Spy Smasher* (1942).

The tight budgets and fast turnover of serials from the 1930s and 1940s made Witney a natural for the transition to television in the 1950s. He specialized in Westerns, directing episodes of *Tales of Wells Fargo, Wagon Train, Zorro, Frontier Doctor, Bonanza, Riverboat, Laramie, Overland Trail, Frontier Circus, The Virginian, Daniel Boone, Branded, Laredo, The Wild Wild West, Hondo, The High Chaparral* and *The Cowboys.*

Witney authored two books, *In a Door, Into a Fight, Out a Door, Into a Chase* (McFarland & Co., 1996), about his career in serials, and *Trigger Remembered,* before his death following a stroke in 2002.

The Virginian credits: **1:11, 1:18, 2:12, 2:14, 2:30, 3:07, 3:15, 3:28, 5:11, 7:22.**

25

Directors of Photography

The Virginian engaged many of the top directors of photography working in television in the 1960s. At a time when the majority of TV Westerns were still shot in black and white, *The Virginian* was shot in color. This gave the show an obvious advantage, but placed extra pressure on the D.Ps, who had to ensure the quality of the filmed image transferred to television screens. An experienced camera crew was essential.

"All the D.P.s were top-flight. We were lucky in that they all came from extensive motion picture backgrounds of many years," recalled Frank Price. "Remember that during the years 1950 to 1960, television siphoned away the motion picture audience and that created unemployment among motion picture crews; most of them began to work in film shows done for television. We benefited from their great experience. And, since we were an important show—the first 90-minute series—we were able to attract the best. My favorites were Bennie Kline, Bud Thackery, Lionel 'Curley' Lindon and Enzo A. (Tony) Martinelli. All were men I respected greatly. They worked fast and often under difficult conditions, but they achieved great results."

Neal Beckner

Born: January 6, 1906; died: July 23, 1972.

Progressing from assistant camera operator in 1932 to cinematographer in 1952, Beckner worked on TV shows such as *Gunsmoke, Rawhide, Shotgun Slade, Johnny Staccato, Thriller, Combat!, The Virginian, The Great Adventure, The Baileys of Bilboa* and *It's About Time*.

Alric Edens

Born: May 26, 1914, Durant, Kentucky; died: June 10, 1990.

Edens worked throughout the 1960s, 1970s and 1980s on various Universal TV shows and movies, including *The Virginian, McCloud, One More Train to Rob, Kolchak: The Night Stalker, Quincy, Mrs. Columbo* and *Hunter*.

Gerald Perry Finnerman

Born: December 17, 1931, Los Angeles, California.

Son of cinematographer Perry Finnerman, he graduated from Loyola University with a degree in abnormal psychology but chose to follow his father's profession, working as his assistant at Warner Bros. Following his father's early death, at 55, Finnerman worked alongside Harry Stradling, Sr., as camera operator on the Academy Award-winning *My Fair Lady* (1964).

His first TV work was on *Maverick* as camera operator was followed by promotion to director of photography on *The Virginian, Star Trek* and *Mission: Impossible.*

In the 1970s and 1980s, Finnerman worked on *Kojak, Planet of the Apes, Quincy* and *Fantasy Island,* among others, and was nominated for an Emmy for his creative work on *Moonlighting.*

Ray Flin

Born: June 21, 1905, Michigan; died: July 29, 1969.

Cinematographer for the controversial Edward D. Wood, Jr., Flin survived the experience of *The Sun Was Setting* (1951) and *Crossroad Avenger: The Adventures of the Tucson Kid* (1953) to enjoy a relatively brief career in TV in the late 1950s and 1960s.

After working on *Leave it to Beaver, Overland Trail, Checkmate, The Virginian, McHale's Navy* and *Ironside,* among others, Flin died of a heart attack in 1969 at the age of 64.

Ed Wood's *Crossroads at Laredo* (1948), on which Flin served as cinematographer, was finally released in 1995.

Benjamin H. Kline

Born: July 11, 1894, Birmingham, Alabama; died: January 7, 1974.

Benjamin Harrison Kline's career spanned over 50 years, starting in 1920 and working through the 1930s and 1940s on numerous B films and comedy shorts starring the Three Stooges, including *Three Smart Saps* (1942), *Sock-A-Bye Baby* (1942) and *Dizzy Pilots* (1943).

Kline began working in TV in the early 1950s on *Captain Midnight,* and continued with movies such as *Rock Around the Clock* (1956), *Zombies of Mora Tau* and *The Giant Claw* (both 1957). In the late 1950s and into the early 1970s Kline worked full time for Revue–Universal TV, on *Shotgun Slade, Checkmate, Thriller, The Virginian, Munster, Go Home* and *Dragnet.*

His final work was the TV movie *Manhunter* starring Sandra Dee and Roy Thinnes. He passed away two years later in 1974. His son Richard H. Kline continues in his father's footsteps.

Lionel Lindon

Born: September 2, 1905, San Francisco, California; died: September 20, 1971.

Moving through the ranks from lab assistant to camera operator to director of photography, Lionel Lindon worked on many high-profile movies for Paramount Pictures, including *Going My Way* (1944), *Road to Utopia* and *The Blue Dahlia* (both 1946).

Beginning his TV career in the early 1950s, Lindon worked on *General Electric Theatre, Letter to Loretta, Alfred Hitchcock Presents* and *The Deputy,* among others. He continued his movie career, winning an Oscar for his color cinematography on *Around the World in 80 Days* (1956).

Working for Universal in the 1960s, Lindon contributed to many of their top-rated shows, including *The Virginian, The Munsters* and *Ironside*. His feature film work in the 1960s included *The Manchurian Candidate* (1962) starring Frank Sinatra, *Grand Prix* (1966) starring James Garner and *Generation* (1969) starring Pete Duel.

Shortly before his death in 1971, he received an Emmy for his photography on the TV movie *Ritual of Evil* and worked on *Columbo: Ransom for a Dead Man*.

Fred Mandl

Born: July 13, 1908; died: February 21, 1985.

Mandl went from a camera operator on *The Twilight Zone* to an Emmy Award for Best Cinematography in 1974 for the TV movie *Trapped*. His work in between consisted of *Checkmate, McHale's Navy, The Virginian, The Fugitive, The Munsters* and *A Man Called Shenandoah*, among others.

William Margulies

Born: January 5, 1906; died: February 15, 1988.

Margulies began his career as camera operator at Monogram Pictures, working on the Joe Palooka series of movies from 1946 to 1949. Moving up to cinematographer in 1956, he filmed the B movies *Tomahawk Trail, Pharaoh's Curse, Jungle Heat* and *War Drums* (all 1957) before turning to TV to earn his living.

TV credits include *The Virginian, Ironside, Night Gallery, Emergency!* and *The Family Kovack*.

Enzo A. Martinelli

Born: September 29, 1907; died: February 5, 1997.

Moving from Paramount Pictures to Warner Bros. in 1929, Martinelli teamed up with his uncle Arthur Martinelli on *White Zombie* (1932), working as an assistant cameraman.

Spending the 1940s as camera operator for Republic Pictures on such films as *The Streets of San Francisco* (1949), Martinelli moved to TV in the 1950s and rose to director of photography on shows such as *The Virginian* and *Ironside*.

He continued to work regularly for Universal TV on *The Six Million Dollar Man, The Bionic Woman, Gemini Man, Quincy* and *Battlestar Galactica*.

He retired in the early 1980s and passed away in 1997, at age 89.

"Enzo was skillful and easygoing. I thought of him as a good friend."—Frank Price

Ray Rennahan

Born: May 1, 1896, Las Vegas, Nevada; died: May 19, 1980.

Pioneer cinematographer Ray Rennahan perfected the three-strip Technicolor process, filming the first live-action short (*La Cucaracha*, 1934) and the first feature film (*Becky Sharp*, 1935) using the new system. He followed this with Academy Award-winning cinematography on *Gone with the Wind* (1939) and *Blood and Sand* (1941).

In the late 1950s and 1960s, Rennahan worked in TV on shows such as *M Squad*, *The Restless Gun*, *Daniel Boone* and *The Virginian*.

He retired in the late 1960s with one of his final assignments being the *Columbo* pilot movie, *Prescription: Murder* (1968). He passed away in 1980, age 84.

John L. Russell

Starting his career in 1934 as a camera assistant for Columbia, Russell graduated to camera operator and cinematographer on *Macbeth* (1948), *The Beast from 20,000 Fathoms* (1953) and *The Eternal Sea* (1955).

His work on TV's *Alfred Hitchcock Presents* led to his Oscar-nominated lensing of *Psycho* (1960). In the 1960s he worked on *Overland Trail*, *Checkmate*, *Thriller* and *The Virginian*.

Walter Strenge

Born: May 2, 1898, Albany, New York; died: September 2, 1974.

Starting his career at Pathe Exchange in 1929, Walter Strenge entered TV in the early 1950s. He juggled television and movie assignments, among them TV's *Rocky Jones, Space Ranger* and *Wagon Train* and the features *Cry Terror!* (1958), *The Littlest Hobo* (1958) and *Lone Texan* (1959).

Universal TV kept him busy throughout the 1960s and early 1970s with *The Virginian*, *Kraft Suspense Theatre*, *The Munsters*, *Dragnet*, *Marcus Welby M.D.* and a series of TV movies including *Portrait: A Man Whose Name Was John* (1973) starring Raymond Burr as Pope John XXIII.

Strenge's final work was on the TV movie *The Chadwick Family* (1974). In addition to his cinematography, his lasting legacy to the profession was his development of depth of field charts for the film industry and editorship of the American Cinematography Manual.

Bud Thackery

Born: January 31, 1903, Oklahoma; died: July 15, 1990.

Joining Republic Studios in 1934 as a glassman, Ellis "Bud" Thackery worked his way up through second unit cameraman to director of photography. Filming serials such as *Zorro's Black Whip* (1944), *Manhunt of Mystery Island* (1945) and *The Phantom Rider* (1946), Thackery learned the technique of filming under pressure and doing it fast. This experience would serve him well in television.

Working for Revue-Universal on *Tales of Wells Fargo* in 1958, he was offered a contract and stayed with Universal for the remainder of his career. TV work on *Overland Trail*, *Checkmate*, *The Virginian*, *McHale's Navy*, *Ironside*, *Night Gallery*, *Emergency!* and *Bridger* was mixed with cinematography on the features *Beau Geste* (1966) starring Doug McClure, *Tammy and the Millionaire* (1967) and *Coogan's Bluff* (1968).

"*Bud could achieve outstanding cinematography with ease. He wore cowboy boots and a cowboy hat and was an amazing character.*"—Frank Price.

Robert Tobey

Born: October 23, 1904; died: February 8, 1973.

After working on the Harriet Parsons documentary shorts *Meet The Stars* in the early 1940s, Tobey worked briefly in TV in from the late 1950s to the mid–1960s on the shows *Maverick, The Virginian, Bewitched, Gidget, I Dream of Jeannie* and *The Monkees*.

He died following a stroke in 1973 at the age of 68.

26

Composers

The Virginian attracted a wide range of high-profile composers, each with their own individual style. Executive producer Frank Price recalled working with music director Stanley Wilson.

"Stanley Wilson headed the music department. A number of talented people worked with him in his department, as the producers of the various television series coped with scoring individual episodes. Stanley would recommend a composer or composers to the producer and the executive producer would decide. But of course it was a shared decision with the executive producer having the final vote."

Price was involved with the musical process from start to finish.

"Generally I met the composer when we were considering who to hire. Then we sat through the spotting session to determine where the music would be placed and what the nature of the music would be. Next came some consulting between the composer and me when he was developing themes to use in the score. Then came the big day on the scoring stage with the orchestra, often conducted by the composer, which was the only real chance to change anything if it didn't seem to be working."

Price explained his part in the decision to hire composer Percy Faith to score the theme and the first few episodes.

"I met Percy Faith and consulted on the decision to hire him and participated in music decisions on the first few episodes. Those episodes went through a big change of command when Charles Marquis Warren was replaced by Roy Huggins. I had great input in determining the nature of the specific music used since I stated up front to the music department and to the composer what kind of music we needed to enhance our storytelling. Anything that didn't achieve that objective didn't get used. Music is just one more creative element that goes to make a complete story."

Universal Music Library currently has a "closed door" policy regarding research of Universal TV scores, so credits and any cues listed are based on research using available videos and resources.

David Buttolph

Born: August 3, 1902, New York, New York; died: January 1, 1983.

Educated at Juilliard and the Music Academy of Vienna, Buttolph began his musical career as a nightclub pianist in Vienna and Munich before returning to New York in 1927. He became music director for WGY in Schenectady, New York, in 1932.

Moving to Los Angeles in 1933, he worked for 20th Century-Fox until 1947. Buttolph's work at Fox included *The Return of Frank James* (1940), *The House on 92nd Street* (1945) and *My Darling Clementine* (1946).

In 1948 he moved to Warner Bros, composing music scores for Alfred Hitchcock's *Rope* (1948), *Montana* (1950) and *The Enforcer* (1951). In 1955 he was approached by Warner Bros. television department to work on *Warner Bros. Presents*. This led to the title theme for *Maverick* and work on *77 Sunset Strip* and *The Alaskans*. Freelancing again in the early 1960s, Buttolph worked on *Wagon Train* and *The Virginian* before his retirement in 1963.

The Virginian credits: **2:05, 2:06, 2:07.**

Frank DeVol

Born: September 20, 1911, Moundsville, West Virginia; died; October 27, 1999.

Composer, conductor, bandleader and actor Frank DeVol first gained an interest in music from his father, a local bandleader. DeVol learned fast and was his own bandleader on KHJ Los Angeles by the 1940s.

DeVol began his film composing career in 1954 with *World for Ransom*. In the following 42 years he would compose the scores for popular movies such as *Pillow Talk* (1959), *McLintock!* (1963), *The Flight of the Phoenix* (1965), *The Dirty Dozen* (1967), *The Longest Yard* (1974) and *Herbie Goes Bananas* (1980). TV series included *Richard Diamond, Private Detective, My Three Sons, The Virginian, McCloud* and *The Love Boat*.

DeVol worked as a character actor from 1961–1979, appearing in the movie *The Parent Trap* and on TV's *I'm Dickens, He's Fenster* and *Petticoat Junction*, among others. A winner of five Emmys, DeVol was also musical arranger for Tony Bennett, Doris Day, Vic Damone and Peggy Lee.

The Virginian credits: **7:13.**

Percy Faith

Born: April 7, 1908, Toronto, Canada; died: February 9, 1976.

A child prodigy at the piano, Faith studied music at the Toronto Conservatory. He changed direction from pianist to conductor and arranger following a fire that badly injured his hands in 1926. Work for various dance orchestras in Toronto led to employment with the Canadian Broadcasting Company in 1938. Two years later, Faith moved to America; he began working for Decca Records in 1944. His long association with Columbia Records started in 1951 and resulted in 85 albums over a 25-year period.

Faith's first work for movies was *Starlift* (1951). He was nominated for an Oscar in 1955 for *Love Me or Leave Me* and had three hit singles: "Delicado" (1952), "Theme from *Moulin Rouge*" (1953) and "Theme from *A Summer Place*" (1960). The latter was the best-selling single of 1960, spending nine weeks at number one on the American pop chart.

He moved to Encino, California, in 1959 and composed his first TV score for *The Virginian* in 1962.

Faith aficionado Bill Halvorsen recalled a visit to Faith's home following his death.

"Percy Faith was always humble about his work and wanted to leave a complete legacy of his recordings to his grandchildren. Therefore, he spent the last year of his life recording his albums and 78s to cassettes. Cassette tapes were, in 1974–1975, thought to be the best medium for archival preservation of fragile records. However, by 1991 when I visited

Dolly's [Faith's wife] home, Percy's carefully recorded tapes had largely self-destructed. Percy had also bundled packages of his LPs for his grandchildren for when they old enough to appreciate them. Happily, nearly all of his Columbia recordings are available through reissues, digitally remastered in the first decade of the twenty-first century on compact discs.

"Percy Faith would have very much liked to have worked extensively in the field of film scores and television. However, he rarely found himself in the right place at the right time. He did score half a dozen films and Percy's unique theme to *The Virginian* certainly seemed to be part of the fabric of the show itself."

Percy Faith was buried at Hillside Memorial Park in Culver City, California.

The Virginian credits: Theme (1962), 1:01, 1:03

Percy Faith seated at the piano where he did most of his arranging, in his Encino, California, home, 1966 (courtesy Bill Halvorsen).

Ralph Ferraro

A graduate of the Manhattan School of Music, Ferraro's film score credits include *The She-Beast* (1965) and *The King's Pirate* (1967). He also worked as an orchestrator on films such as *Close Encounters of the Third Kind* (1977) and *Star Trek IV: The Voyage Home* (1986).

Television work includes *The Virginian, The Men from Shiloh* and David *Niven's World.* Ferraro has also orchestrated and arranged many Randy Edelman compositions.

The Virginian–The Men from Shiloh credits: 6:04, 6:07, 6:08, 7:05, 7:07, 8:04, 9:03, 9:10.

Sidney Fine

Born: December 25, 1904, Waterbury, Connecticut; died: May 20, 2002.

A skilled pianist, Sidney Fine graduated from the University of Connecticut and studied at the Yale School of Music. Starting as a pianist in silent movie theaters, he moved to Los Angeles in 1937, studying with composer Arnold Schoenberg. Fine found work as a pianist and arranger on radio shows starring Jack Benny, Dinah Shore, George Burns and Gracie Allen.

His feature film work included arrangements for Irving Berlin's *Blue Skies* (1946) and orchestrations for the Walt Disney productions *Melody Time* (1948) and *Lady and the Tramp* (1955).

In the 1950s, Fine worked in television on Disney's *The Mickey Mouse Club* and was nominated for an Emmy for his orchestration of Victor Young's score for *Medic*. A contract with Revue-Universal kept Fine busy from 1960 to 1971, composing scores for *Wagon Train, Laramie, Thriller, Frontier Circus, The Virginian, Tammy* and *The Bold Ones*.

Fine was married for 74 years to Rose Mishkin.

The Virginian credits: **1.28, 2:04, 3:01, 3:02, 3:04, 4:01, 4:02, 4:06, 4:10, 5:03, 5:09, 6:02.**

Russell Garcia

Born: April 12, 1916, Oakland, California.

Garcia started in radio and was soon promoted to staff arranger at NBC. He also taught arranging at Westlake School of Music. This led to his book *The Professional Arranger* which still enjoys steady sales throughout the world.

In his time as staff arranger at Universal Pictures, Garcia worked alongside Pete Rugolo, Percy Faith, Henry Mancini, Benny Carter and Quincy Jones. Film credits include Charlie Chaplin's *Limelight* (1952) as an uncredited arranger, and George Pal's *The Time Machine* (1960).

Garcia's TV credits include *Rawhide, The Virginian* and *Laredo*. He also enjoyed success as a songwriter, trumpeter and conductor, working on albums with Mel Tormé and Louis Armstrong.

He retired to New Zealand, where he does occasional concert work.

The Virginian credits: **4:02, 5:02.**

Dave Grusin

Born: June 26, 1934, Littleton, Colorado.

Grusin's first major job after graduating the University of Colorado was as orchestra leader on the 1960s series *The Andy Williams Show*. He left the show to concentrate on composing for movies and TV. *The Girl from U.N.C.L.E.* and *The Virginian* were early TV assignments, followed by *It Takes a Thief, The Name of the Game*, the *Columbo* pilot *Prescription for Murder, The Men from Shiloh* and *St. Elsewhere*.

He received Academy Award nominations for *Heaven Can Wait* (1979), *The Champ* (1980), *On Golden Pond* (1982), *Tootsie* (1983), *The Fabulous Baker Boys* (1989), *Havana* (1990) and *The Firm* (1993). Grusin won an Oscar for *The Milagro Beanfield War* (1988).

Grusin and business partner Larry Rosen formed their own recording label in 1983 and produced many successful albums including *Mountain Dance, Out of the Shadows* and *Harlequin*. The winner of five Grammys, Grusin has enjoyed a highly successful musical career.

The Virginian–The Men from Shiloh credits: **6:06, 9:7.**

Jack Hayes

Hayes began his film composing career with *The Joker Is Wild* (1957). From the 1960s through the 1990s, he scored and adapted music on such films as *Nevada Smith* (1966),

Hombre (1967), *Butch Cassidy and the Sundance Kid* (1969), *Marathon Man* (1976), *Brubaker* (1980), *Sophie's Choice* (1982), *The Natural* (1984), *Pretty Woman* (1990) and *Maverick* (1994).

He was twice nominated for an Academy Award, for *The Unsinkable Molly Brown* (1964) and *The Color Purple* (1985).

Hayes worked in partnership with Leo Shuken on the *Virginian* music scores.

The Virginian–The Men from Shiloh credits: see Leo Shuken.

Lennie Hayton

Born: February 13, 1908, New York, New York; died: April 24, 1971.

Lennie Hayton started his career in the 1930s as a jazz arranger and bandleader. From 1941 to 1953 he served as musical director for MGM, overseeing classic musicals such as *Ziegfeld Follies* (1946), *On the Town* (1949) and *Singin' in the Rain* (1952). Following his exit from MGM, Hayton concentrated on live performance with his wife Lena Horne.

In the 1960s he returned to composing and musical direction for film with *Jack and the Beanstalk* (1967), *Star!* (1968) and *Hello Dolly* (1969).

Previously an Oscar winner for *On the Town*, Hayton received his second Academy Award for *Hello Dolly*. He retired to Palm Springs and passed away in 1971.

The Virginian credits: **2:01**.

Bernard Herrmann

Born: June 29, 1911, New York, New York; died: December 24, 1975.

After studying at NYU and Juilliard, Herrmann founded the New Chamber Orchestra in 1931. Three years later he joined CBS; he worked on *Orson Welles' Mercury Theatre on the Air*, including their controversial 1938 radio adaptation of H. G. Wells' *War of the Worlds*. An Oscar for his first film score *All That Money Can Buy* followed, plus an Oscar-nominated score for Orson Welles' *Citizen Kane* (1941).

His highly successful Hollywood career also included a long association with Alfred Hitchcock on such films as *Vertigo* (1958), *North by Northwest* (1959), *Psycho* (1960) and *The Birds* (1963). Herrmann scored many fantasy films by Charles H. Schneer, including *The 7th Voyage of Sinbad* (1958) and *Jason and the Argonauts* (1963).

Despite his heavy workload on successful movies throughout the 1950s and 1960s Herrmann found time to compose for the 1950s-60s TV shows *Gunsmoke, Alfred Hitchcock Presents, Have Gun Will Travel, Perry Mason, Rawhide, The Twilight Zone, The Virginian, Voyage to the Bottom of the Sea, Convoy* and *Cimarron Strip*.

In the 1970s a new generation of directors sought out Herrmann for *Sisters* (1973), *It's Alive* (1974) and *Obsession* (1976). Soon after completing his score for Martin Scorsese's *Taxi Driver* (1976), Herrmann passed away in his sleep.

The Virginian credits: **4:08**—Instrumentation—horns, strings and tympany, this score contains 32 cues. **4:09**—Instrumentation—horns, strings and tympany. **6:01**—Instrumentation—woodwind, horns, snare drums and tympany; this score contains 32 cues. **7:16**—Instrumentation—strings and electric bass; this score contains 44 cues including "Last Grave at Socorro Creek" (1:36), "Burden and Virginian" (1:00), "Shiloh Barn" (:31), "Four Eyes" (:45), "Burden in Jail" (:16), "Virginian Rides into Town" (1:16) and "Hanged Burden" (1:34).

The Irish Rovers

Formed in 1963 in Toronto, Canada, the Irish Rovers began as the singing duo of George Millar and Jim Ferguson. The following year they were joined by Joe and Will Millar. A 22-week run at San Francisco's Purple Onion folk club led to a recording contract with Decca Records, the 1966 live album *The First of the Irish Rovers* and 1967's million-selling *The Unicorn.* Guest appearances on the seventh season of *The Virginian* saw them singing a variety of songs from their two albums.

The Irish Rovers appeared on a weekly CBC-TV show from 1971 to 1975 and continued their success throughout the 1980s and 1990s. Will Millar retired in 1995 and original member Jim Ferguson passed away in 1997. The Irish Rovers continue to tour and perform around the world.

The Virginian credits: **7:01** ("Come In, I Don't Mind If I Do"), **7:04** ("Shores of Americay"), **7:17** ("Goodbye Mrs. Durkin," "Black Velvet Band," "Marie's Wedding")

Richard Maltby, Jr.,

Born: December 6, 1937, Ripon Wisconsin.

Son of bandleader Richard Maltby, he often worked in partnership with David Shire. Winner of a Tony award in 1978 as Best Director in a Musical for Fats Waller's *Ain't Misbehavin'*, Maltby has also worked in collaboration with Don Black on Andrew Lloyd Webber's *Song & Dance* (1991), with Cameron Mackintosh on *Miss Saigon* (1992), with Arthur Laurents on *Nick and Nora* (1996) and with Ann Reinking on *Fosse* (1999).

TV and film work with David Shire includes *McCloud: Who Killed Miss U.S.A.?* (1971), *One More Train to Rob* (1971) and *Summertree* (1971).

The Men from Shiloh credits (with David Shire): **9:02, 9:17**—Lyrics to "Take a Look Around."

Jack Marshall

Born: November 23, 1921, El Dorado, Kansas; died; September 20, 1973.

Starting his career as a producer and arranger at Capitol Records, Marshall also performed as a jazz guitarist on solo albums and arranged music for Howard Roberts and Barney Kessel.

His movie composing career began in 1958 on *The Missouri Traveler* and *Thunder Road.* Marshall soon found his niche in TV, working on *The Deputy, The Investigators, It's a Man's World, Don't Call Me Charlie, Going My Way, The Munsters, Karen, Laredo* (1965), *The Girl from U.N.C.L.E.* and *The Debbie Reynolds Show.* He also composed the score for *Munster Go Home* (1966) and *Tammy and the Millionaire* (1967).

Marshall died at the age of 51 in 1973. His son Frank Marshall became a successful screenwriter and director.

The Virginian credits: **7:06**.

Hal Mooney

Born: February 4, 1911, Brooklyn, New York; died: March 23, 1995.

After studying composition with Orville Mayhood and Joseph Schillinger, Mooney arranged for Bing Crosby, Frank Sinatra, Judy Garland, Peggy Lee, Kay Starr and Billy Eckstine. In 1956 he became head of A&R at Mercury Records working alongside noted female jazz singers Nina Simone, Sarah Vaughn and Dinah Washington.

Moving to Universal Studios in the 1960s, Mooney worked as musical supervisor throughout the 1970s on TV movies (including 1971's *Duel*) and the series as *Night Gallery*, *Banacek*, *Columbo*, *The Six Million Dollar Man*, *The Rockford Files*, *Ellery Queen* and *The Bionic Woman*.

He retired in 1977 and passed away in 1995.

The Virginian credits: *The Meanest Men in the West* (1967). Compilation movie featuring a new score by Mooney.

Ennio Morricone

Born: November 10, 1928, Rome, Italy.

Born into a musical family, Morricone graduated with honors from the Accademia di Santa Cecilia in Rome. Performing as a trumpet player in nightclubs, he found regular work composing and arranging for television at RAI. Moving to RCA records in the late 1950s, Morricone arranged songs for stars including Mario Lanza.

His work on Sergio Leone's *A Fistful of Dollars* (1964) would bring him international recognition. *For a Few Dollars More, The Good, the Bad and the Ugly* (1966) and *Once Upon a Time in the West* (1969) cemented his reputation as one of the most original composers working in film. When NBC decided to revamp the *Virginian* format, Morricone was commissioned to compose the theme to *The Men from Shiloh* (1970).

Other film scores of note include *Days of Heaven* (1978), *The Mission* (1986) and *The Untouchables* (1987). One of the most prolific film composers of all time, Morricone has scored over 400 soundtracks.

The Men from Shiloh credits: **Theme (1970).**

Lyn Murray

Born: December 6, 1909; died: May 20, 1989.

In the 1930s, the CBS radio show *Lucky Strike Hit Parade* featured the popular Lynn Murray singers. Murray's success with the singers led to many albums and work with Bing Crosby, Louis Armstrong and Burl Ives.

Murray's movie composing career began in 1947 with and reached an early zenith with Alfred Hitchcock's *To Catch a Thief* (1955). Television would prove to be Murray's main employment for the next 20 years, interspersed with the occasional movie score.

Murray's TV credits include *Gunsmoke, The Twilight Zone, The Virginian, Daniel Boone, Gilligan's Island, The Undersea World of Jacques Cousteau, The Time Tunnel, Dragnet, The Bold Ones: The New Doctors* and *The Men from Shiloh*. He retired in 1978.

The Virginian–The Men from Shiloh credits: **3:06, 7:17, 9:04, 9:08.**

Oliver Nelson

Born: June 4, 1932, St. Louis, Missouri; died: October 27, 1975.

Oliver Nelson was acknowledged as a talented jazz artist before his film composing career began in the mid–1960s. His successful debut album was released in 1959, and the early 1960s saw Nelson working as an arranger for Verve Records.

Nelson's first TV work was as orchestrator on 1964's *Mr. Broadway*. Uncredited work as music arranger on *Alfie* (1966), with saxophonist Sonny Rollins, brought him to the attention of producers and directors.

He worked for Universal TV throughout the remainder of his career and scored music for such shows as *The Virginian, Ironside, Night Gallery, Longstreet* and *The Six Million Dollar Man.*

Nelson's life was cut short by a heart attack at age 43.

The Virginian credits: **8:20.**

Leonard Rosenman

Born: September 7, 1924, Brooklyn, New York.

After studying under Arnold Schoenberg, Roger Sessions and Luigi Dallapicolla, Rosenman made his film composing debut in director Elia Kazan's *East of Eden* (1955). He quickly followed this with a score for another James Dean classic, *Rebel Without a Cause* (1955).

Rosenman's distinctive style was soon transferred to the TV series *The Twilight Zone, The Defenders, The Virginian, Combat!, Garrison's Gorillas, Marcus Welby M.D., Quincy, Falcon Crest* and *Amazing Stories.*

Rosenman received Emmys for Outstanding Music Score for the TV movies *Sybil* (1976) and *Friendly Fire* (1979) and Oscars for Stanley Kubrick's *Barry Lyndon* (1975) and *Bound for Glory* (1976). The two movies featured adaptations of Handel, Schubert and Woody Guthrie folk songs. Rosenman remarked at the irony of receiving Oscars for adapted scores when he told the Academy, "I write original music too, you know."

He continued working in movies until 2001.

The Virginian credits: **6:05, 6:20, 7:02, 7:03, 7:18, 8:02, 8:07.**

Pete Rugolo

Born: December 25, 1915, Sicily, Italy.

Sicilian-born Rugolo moved to Santa Rosa, California, with his family as a child. After graduating from San Francisco State College he studied with Darius Milhaud at Mills College in Oakland.

Composing and arranging for Stan Kenton in the 1940s, Rugolo was hired as East Coast music director for Capitol Records in 1949, working with Nat King Cole and Miles Davis among others. In the 1950s he joined MGM as staff composer and arranger.

TV work included many prime time shows of the 1950s, 1960s and 1970s: *Richard Diamond, Private Detective, Leave it to Beaver, Thriller, Checkmate, Dr. Kildare, The Alfred Hitchcock Hour, The Virginian, The Fugitive, Run for Your Life, Felony Squad, The Men from Shiloh, Alias Smith and Jones, M*A*S*H, Cool Million* and *The Invisible Man.*

Retiring in 1985, Rugolo briefly came out of retirement in 1997 to score *This World, Then the Fireworks.*

The Virginian–The Men from Shiloh credits: **1:20, 2:08, 9:21.**

Hans J. Salter

Born: February 14, 1896, Vienna, Austria; died: July 23, 1994.

Following graduation from the Vienna Academy of Music, Salter worked as assistant conductor at Vienna's Volksoper and the Berlin State Opera and became head of the music department at Berlin's Universum-film Aktiengesellschaft (UFA) film studios. Fleeing Germany's Nazi regime in 1937, he found employment at Universal Studios.

Salter scored over 150 movies for Universal including most of their horror output. *The Wolf Man* (1941), *Son of Dracula* (1943) and *House of Frankenstein* (1944) were followed by the sci-fi boom in the 1950s and music for *Creature from the Black Lagoon* (1954) *This Island Earth* (1955) and *The Incredible Shrinking Man* (1957).

With the growing popularity of TV Westerns in the late 1950s, Salter was assigned work on *Wagon Train, Laramie, Wichita Town* and *The Virginian*. His final work of note before his retirement in 1968 was for the medieval action adventure movie *The War Lord* (1965) starring Charlton Heston.

The Virginian credits: **4:07**.

Nathan Scott

A graduate of UCLA, Scott's Hollywood career began in 1946 with work as an uncredited arranger on the classic *It's a Wonderful Life*. His career fell into something of a rut with work almost exclusively on B movies such as *Angel on the Amazon* (1948), *Trail of Robin Hood* (1950) and *Montana Belle* (1952).

From 1954 to 1978 he worked primarily for TV shows including *Lassie, Gunsmoke, Have Gun Will Travel, Perry Mason, The Twilight Zone, The Virginian* and *Battlestar Galactica*.

His final work was as music adaptor and orchestrator for Steven Spielberg's *The Color Purple* (1985).

The Virginian credits: **1:18**.

David Shire

Born: July 3, 1937, Buffalo, New York.

Son of bandleader Irving Shire, his early work was often in partnership with lyricist Richard Maltby, Jr. They met while studying at Yale University and enjoyed a successful collaboration that resulted in them working with Maureen McGovern and Melissa Manchester. Barbra Streisand recorded five Shire songs on four albums between 1964–69.

Shire ventured into television with work on *The Virginian* and *The Men from Shiloh*. A highly successful movie composing career has included scores for *The Conversation* (1974), *All the President's Men* (1976), *Saturday Night Fever* (1977) and *Norma Rae* (1979); he received an Academy Award for Best Original Song for "It Goes Like it Goes."

He also enjoyed success on Broadway in partnership with Maltby, winning a Tony for the musical *Baby* (1983).

The Virginian–The Men from Shiloh credits: **8:01, 8:03, 8:05, 8:15, 9:02, 9:17**

Richard Shores

Born: May 9, 1917, Rockville, Indiana; died: April 12, 2001.

Shores studied at Indiana University and received his master's degree, under the tutelage of Howard Hanson, at the Eastman School of Music in Rochester, New York.

Serving in World War II, Shores was staff arranger for the Jefferson-Missouri Air Force Base band and was among the soldiers who liberated the Bergen-Belsen concentration camp. Returning to Chicago, he worked in radio and live television and recorded albums with Sue Raney and Johnny Desmond. In 1957 his album *Emotions* received favorable reviews and Shores moved to Los Angeles. Composer David Buttolph set up an appointment with MCA's Abe Meyer and Shores soon found himself working for FourStar on TV's *Richard Diamond, Private Detective*.

From 1960–64 Shores worked for Revue-Universal on *Whispering Smith, Wagon Train, Tales of Wells Fargo, Laramie* and *The Virginian*. Shores admitted he "got sick of Westerns" after scoring 48 episodes of various Westerns in total. In 1966 Norman Felton's Arena Productions hired Shores to work on *Jericho, The Man from U.N.C.L.E.* and *The Girl from U.N.C.L.E.*

Shores continued to work throughout the 1970s on the TV shows *Police Woman, The Quest, Hunter, The Paper Chase* and *The Mississippi*. He retired from television in 1984 but continued composing concert music.

The Virginian credits: **1:18, 1:28, 2:15**.

Leo Shuken

Born: 1906; died: July 24, 1976.

Shuken began his movie composing career on Henry Hathaway's *Go West Young Man* (1936) and was credited with his first score on Laurel and Hardy's *The Flying Deuces* (1939). Beginning as an orchestrator with John Ford's *Stagecoach* in 1939, Shuken's early movie work was often uncredited and it wasn't until the 1960s that he was given the regular credit he deserved.

Shuken's orchestrations covered a wide range of subject material and included *For Whom the Bell Tolls* (1943), *Easter Parade* (1948), *Samson and Delilah* (1949), *Roman Holiday* (1953), *The Ten Commandments* (1956), *The Great Escape* (1963), *The Greatest Story Ever Told* (1965), *Nevada Smith* (1966), *Hombre* (1967), *Camelot* (1967), *Funny Girl* (1968) and *Butch Cassidy and the Sundance Kid* (1969).

Shuken often worked in collaboration with Jack Hayes on his TV scores, including his work on *The Virginian* and *The Men from Shiloh*. Other TV work included *Gunsmoke* and *Riverboat*.

The Virginian–The Men from Shiloh credits: **3:03, 4:04, 5:01, 5:05, 5:06, 5:07, 5:11, 9:01, 9:09, 9:11**.

Fred Steiner

Born: February 24, 1923, New York, New York.

The son of composer George Steiner, Fred Steiner started in radio on *This Is Your FBI* (1945) before turning to television since 1951.

Often credited as Frederick Steiner in the 1950s, he scored numerous TV series themes and episodes including *Father Knows Best, Perry Mason, Have Gun Will Travel, The Twilight Zone, The Bullwinkle Show, The Virginian, Lost in Space, The Wild Wild West, Hogan's Heroes, The Loner, Star Trek* and *Star Trek: The Next Generation.*

His classic *Perry Mason* theme was used on the series of TV movies from 1987–95. *The Virginian* credits: **8:06.**

Morton Stevens

Born: January 30, 1929, Newark, New Jersey; died: November 11, 1991.

Morton Stevens is best remembered today for his Emmy-winning theme for the 1960s-70s teleseries *Hawaii Five-0.* Starting his career as Sammy Davis' arranger and conductor, Stevens moved into television in 1953 on *General Electric Theatre.* Work for Revue Studios included *Tales of Wells Fargo, Thriller, Checkmate* and *The Virginian.* In the 1960s he became music supervisor for CBS. He also scored episodes of *Voyage to the Bottom of the Sea, The Man from U.N.C.L.E., Gilligan's Island, The Wild Wild West, Jericho* and *Cimarron Strip, Police Woman, The Fall Guy, Knight Rider, Matlock* and *Jake and the Fatman.*

Stevens died of cancer age 62.

The Virginian credits: **1.20, 1:28.**

Harry Sukman

Born: December 2, 1912, Chicago, Illinois; died: December 2, 1984.

Hired as a pianist by Paramount Pictures in 1942, Sukman was taught by music director Victor Young how to score, compose and adapt material for film. A long uncredited apprenticeship ended with Sukman's first composing credits for the sci-fi movies *Gog* (1954) and *Riders to the Stars* (1954).

In 1960 Sukman hit his stride, sharing an Oscar with Morris W. Stoloff for *Song Without End.* Despite two more Oscar nominations (for *Fanny* [1961] and *The Singing Nun* [1966]), Sukman spent the majority of his time composing for episodic TV. Credits include *Dr. Kildare, The Virginian, Daniel Boone, The Monroes, The High Chaparral* and *The Cowboys.*

Following work on the Stephen King mini-series *Salem's Lot* (1979), Sukman retired. *The Virginian* credits: **3:08.**

Nathan Van Cleave

Born: May 8, 1910, Bayfield, Wisconsin; died: July 2, 1970.

Composer, arranger and orchestrator Nathan Van Cleave made his Hollywood music score debut in 1947. In the 1950s he became known for his work on the sci-fi movies *Conquest of Space* (1955) and *The Space Children* (1958). Work on television's *The Twilight Zone* continued the sci-fi theme. *Robinson Crusoe on Mars* (1964) utilized Van Cleave's sci-fi music style to full effect in what has become a cult favorite.

Away from sci-fi, Van Cleave composed for TV's *Gunsmoke, Perry Mason, The Richard Boone Show* and *The Virginian.*

His final music score for film was on William Castle's *Project X* (1968). *The Virginian* credits: **3:11.**

Franz Waxman

Born: 1906, Konigshutte, Germany; died: February 24, 1967.

Educated at Dresden Music Academy and the Berlin Music Conservatory, Waxman worked for UFA before Nazi persecution forced him to flee to Paris, France.

A two-year contract with Universal produced scores for *Bride of Frankenstein, Diamond Jim* and *Magnificent Obsession* (all 1935). Moving to MGM in 1936, Waxman's scores included *Captains Courageous* (1937) and *The Philadelphia Story* (1940). Waxman joined Warner Brothers in 1943 and received Oscars in successive years for *Sunset Blvd.* (1950) and *A Place in the Sun* (1951).

Throughout the 1950s Waxman's movie output remained strong with scores for *Prince Valiant, Rear Window* (both 1954), *The Spirit of St. Louis, Peyton Place* (both 1957) and *The Nun's Story* (1959).

Waxman worked in television in the 1960s on such shows as *The Virginian, The Fugitive,* and *Peyton Place.*

The Virginian credits: **5:04.**

John Williams

Born: February 8, 1932, Long Island, New York.

Juilliard-trained Williams began his career as a jazz pianist. A move to Los Angeles led to work at 20th Century–Fox as an orchestra pianist in 1956. Composing work on various 1960s TV shows included Irwin Allen's *Lost in Space, The Time Tunnel* and *Land of the Giants.*

Williams' association with Allen continued into the 1970s on the hit movies *The Poseidon Adventure* (1972) and *The Towering Inferno* (1974). But it would be his collaboration with Steven Spielberg and George Lucas that would cement his reputation as one of the most popular composers of his generation. *Jaws* (1975) was followed by *Star Wars* (1977) which in turn was followed *Close Encounters of the Third Kind* (1977). Scores for *Superman* (1978), *Raiders of the Lost Ark* (1981) and *ET the Extra-Terrestrial* (1982) were equally successful.

In the 1990s Williams continued his association with Spielberg on *Jurassic Park, Schindler's List* (both 1993) and *Saving Private Ryan* (1998) and with George Lucas on a trilogy of *Star Wars* prequels.

Post-millennium Williams was still hard at work on the *Harry Potter* movies and Steven Spielberg's *War of the Worlds* (2005).

The Virginian credits (uncredited): **"Tomorrow"** and **"The Golden West."** Originally scored for the *Wagon Train* episode "The Jenny Tannen Story," the song "Tomorrow" was featured regularly on *The Virginian* as background dance music. "The Golden West" theme, first scored for the same *Wagon Train* episode, was often used on *The Virginian* as piano music in saloon scenes.

Patrick Williams

Born: April 23, 1939, Bonne Terre, Mississippi.

Making his film composing debut in 1968 in *How Sweet It Is!,* Williams has composed over 150 scores in his career, working primarily in television on *The Mary Tyler*

Moore Show, Cannon, The Streets of San Francisco, The Bob Newhart Show, Lou Grant, Columbo and *Monk.*

Williams is a winner of four Emmys, two Grammys and the Pulitzer Prize for Music. *The Virginian* credits: **7:01.**

Stanley Wilson

Born: November 26, 1915, New York, New York; died: July 17, 1970.

Beginning his career as a Dixieland jazz trumpet player, Wilson moved to Los Angeles in 1945, finding work at MGM and Republic Pictures. In his eight-year stint at Republic, Wilson composed, arranged and orchestrated over 80 movies, mostly B Westerns and serials. Titles include *Covered Wagon Raid* (1950), *The Old Frontier* (1950), *Lonely Heart Bandits* (1950) and *Zombies of the Stratosphere* (1952).

In the mid–1950s Wilson joined Universal's television division Revue Studios as music director-supervisor. His work consisted of hiring and often collaborating with composers, arrangers and orchestrators. Shows included *Alfred Hitchcock Presents, M Squad, Leave It to Beaver, Shotgun Slade, Overland Trail, Checkmate, The Virginian, The Munsters, Ironside, It Takes a Thief, The Name of the Game, Adam-12, Marcus Welby, M.D., The Bold Ones* and *Night Gallery.*

Wilson collaborated with composer Juan Garcia Esquivel to write the MCA–Universal television signature theme heard at the conclusion of each Universal show.

After discussing film and television scoring at the Aspen Music Festival on July 17, 1970, Stanley Wilson collapsed and died of a heart attack. He was 54.

In Fred Karlin's book *Listening to Movies,* musical director Sandy DeCrescent said, "Stanley Wilson was the most wonderful, nurturing kind of person ... he was like the big daddy ... always looking and always wanting to help people..."

The Virginian credits: **7:22.**

As Music Director he arranged and adapted many scores using uncredited stock music. The *Virginian* theme by Percy Faith was arranged and orchestrated by Wilson to include acoustic guitar, French horn and horn and string crescendo. Faith's original theme can be heard on his own Columbia Records recording.

Torrie Zito

Born: 1933, New York, New York.

Influenced by the jazz culture in upstate New York, Zito began as an instrumental performer on albums with James Moody and Herbie Mann. He transferred his skills to composing for the orchestra and film, citing Debussy, Faure and Ravel as his influences.

In the 1970s, Zito toured with Tony Bennett, Count Basie and Woody Herman's bands. He orchestrated through the 1980s and 1990s for the shows *The Goodbye Girl* and *Minnelli on Minnelli.* Zito's film and TV work has been sporadic, with orchestrations for *Missing Pieces* (1991), *Frankie and Johnny* (1991), *Seasons of the Heart* (1991) and *Open Season* (1996).

The Virginian credits: **8:11.**

27

Episode Guide

Cast (featured on title sequence)—Judge Henry Garth (1962–66, Lee J. Cobb; Trampas (1962–71), Doug McClure; Steve Hill (1962–65), Gary Clarke; The Virginian (1962–71), James Drury; Emmett Ryker (1965–68), Clu Gulager; Betsy Garth (1962–66), Roberta Shore; Randy Benton (1965–67), Randy Boone; Jennifer Sommers (1966–67), Diane Roter; John Grainger (1966–67), Charles Bickford; Stacey Grainger (1966–68), Don Quine; Elizabeth Grainger (1966–70), Sara Lane; Clay Grainger (1967–70), John McIntire; David Sutton (1968–69), David Hartman; James Joseph Horn (1969–70), Tim Matheson; Col. Alan Mackenzie (1970–71), Stewart Granger; Roy Tate (1970–71), Lee Majors.

First prime time broadcast—September 19, 1962.

Final prime time broadcast—March 24, 1971 (first run).

Network—NBC, Wednesday 7:30—9:00 p.m.

Running time—75 minutes (including credits and end titles). 90 minutes with commercials. 249 episodes.

Production—Revue Studios (1962–64), Universal TV (1965–71).

Format—35mm; Ratio: 1.33 : 1.

Film—Color—Consolidated Film Industries (CFI) (1:01–1:30), Pathe (2:01–4:16), Technicolor (4:17–9:24)

Unit Managers (Production Managers)—Ben Bishop, Ralph Ferrin, Joseph E. Kenney, Henry Kline, Frank Losee, George Santoro, Abby Singer, Willard H. Sheldon.

Assistant Directors—Burt Astor, Donald Baer, Earl J. Bellamy, Jr., Richard Bennett, Les Berke, George Bisk, Ben Bishop, Mel A. Bishop, John Clarke Bowman, James H. Brown, Joseph Cavalier, Chuck Colean, Kenward Cosper, Edward K. Dodds, Jack Doran, Ralph Ferrin, Charles S. Gould, Carter de Haven III, Harry F. Hogan III, William H. Kissel, Henry Kline, Donald A. Klune, Gene H. Law, Richard Learman, Arthur Levinson, Frank Losee, Jesus Marin, Michael Messinger, Wilber Mossier, Wilson Shyer, Roger Slager, Ray Taylor, Jr., Jack Terry, Harker Wade, John M. Walters, Jr., Lou Watt, Kenny Williams, Donald White, Wallace Worsley.

Editorial Dept. Heads and Supervisors—David J O'Connell (1:01–4:30), Richard Belding (5:01–9:24).

Film Editors—Edward M. Abroms, James D. Ballas, Edward Biery, Edwin H. Bryant, John Elias, Howard Epstein, John C. Fuller, Edward Haire, Joseph Harrison, Lee Huntingdon, John Joyce, Bob Kagey, Robert L. Kimble, Danny B. Landres, Larry Lester, Tony Martinelli, Michael R. McAdam, George J. Nicholson, George Ohanian, Robert K. Richard, Milton Schifman, Jack W. Schoengarth, Robert F. Shugrue, Bud Small, Richard

M. Sprague, Douglas Stewart, J. Howard Terrill, Bud Thackery, Ray C. de Vally, Robert Watts, Richard G. Wray.

Musical Supervisor—Stanley Wilson (1:01–9:02, 9:04, 9:08, 9:11).

Sound—Robert Bertrand, Lyle Cain, Earl N. Crain, Jr., John Erlinger, William M. Ford, Roger H. Heman, Jr., Corson Jowett, Theron O. Kellum, Joe Lapis, Tedd G. Mann, Robert Martin, Melvin M. Metcalfe, Sr., David H. Moriarty, Robert L. Post, Roger A. Parish, James T. Porter, John W. Rixey, William A. Russell, Ed Somers, Sr., Richard Tyler, Frank H. Wilkinson.

Art Directors—George Patrick (1–7), William J. Kenney (7–9), Raymond Beal, Edward H. Bryant, George Chan, Howard E. Johnson, William J. Kenney, John T. McCormack, George Webb.

Set Decorators—John McCarthy (1–7), Perry Murdock (7–9), Robert C. Bradfield, Claire P. Brown, John Brown, John M. Dwyer, Hal Overell, James S. Redd, John Sturtevant, Ralph Sylos, James M. Walters, Sr.

Costume Supervisor and **Costumes** (Wardrobe)—Vincent Dee (1:01–6:26, 9:01–9:24), Helen Colvig (4:05, 7:01–8:24), Kay Hayden (4:17), Burton Miller (uncredited).

Makeup—Jack Barron, Leo Lotito, Jr. (1:02–2:18), Bud Westmore (2:19–9:24).

Hair Stylists—Florence Bush (1:01–2:18), Larry Germain (2:19–9:24), Virginia Darcy (4:16).

Production numbers start at 16701 and indicate order of story assignment but not order of shooting. If a script failed to make it to film, the assigned production number would remain, thus accounting for gaps in sequences of numbers in any given season. Preemptions were often a regular part of the schedule to allow the network slots for special programming.

Season One

30 × 75 min. (1962–63)
Executive Producer—Charles Marquis Warren (**1:01, 1:05, 1:07–1:08, 1:10–1:12**)
Executive Producer—Roy Huggins (**1:13, 1:15–1:30**)

Charles Marquis Warren was removed from *The Virginian* before the first episode aired and all of his episodes reedited, with scenes reshot and added. Although he was credited as executive producer, he lost control of his work to Roy Huggins and Frank Price.

Thomas Fitzroy and John Francis O'Mara credits are pseudonyms for Roy Huggins.

THE EXECUTIONERS (1:01) # 16704

Air date: September 19, 1962; Guest stars: Hugh O'Brian, Colleen Dewhurst; Teleplay-Producers: Morton Fine and David Friedkin; Director: David Friedkin.

Following the public hanging of a convicted murderer, his son Paul Taylor Newcombe (Hugh O'Brian) arrives in Medicine Bow to discover the truth about the schoolmarm (Colleen Dewhurst) who denied being with his father the night a woman was murdered.

WOMAN FROM WHITE WING (1:02) # 16706

Air date: September 26, 1962; Guest star: Barry Sullivan; Teleplay: Morton Fine and David Friedkin; Story: Burt Kennedy; Producer: Charles Marquis Warren; Director: Burt Kennedy.

Frank Dawson (Barry Sullivan) arrives at Shiloh Ranch and claims Betsy Garth as his daughter.

THROW A LONG ROPE (1:03) # 16701

Air date: October 3, 1962; Guest star: Jack Warden; Teleplay: Howard Swanton; Producer: Charles Marquis Warren; Director: Ted Post.

The Virginian comes to the aid of alleged cattle rustler Jubal Tatum (Jack Warden) after he is badly injured by local ranchers.

THE BIG DEAL (1:04) # 16708

Air date: October 10, 1962; Guest star: Ricardo Montalban; Teleplay: Winston Miller; Story: Richard Jessup; Producer: Charles Marquis Warren; Director: Earl Bellamy.

Wealthy Colombian Enrique Cueliar (Ricardo Montalban) has a disagreement with Judge Garth over the selling of Shiloh land leased to Garth by Cueliar's father.

THE BRAZEN BELL (1:05) # 16719

Air date: October 17, 1962; Guest star: George C. Scott; Teleplay-Producer: Roland Kibbee; Director: James Sheldon.

Teacher Arthur Lilley's (George C. Scott) courage is tested as two escaped convicts hold schoolchildren hostage.

BIG DAY, GREAT DAY (1:06) # 16720

Air date: October 24, 1962; Preempted: October 31, 1962; Guest stars: Aldo Ray, Michael Shaughnessy; Teleplay: Charles Larson; Producer: Charles Marquis Warren; Director: Harmon Jones.

Traveling to Casper, Wyoming, to pick up an Italian bed, Judge Garth meets up with old friend Frank Krause (Aldo Ray), who is competing in the World Championship of Wrestling. Meanwhile, Trampas is trying to prevent Steve from marrying a saloon girl who reminds him of a former love.

RIFF-RAFF (1:07) # 16709

Air date: November 7, 1962; Guest star: Ray Danton; Teleplay: Jon Booth; Producer: Warren Duff; Director: Bernard Girard.

Trampas enlists with the Rough Riders in San Antonio to impress Molly (Pippa Scott) and is soon followed by Steve and the Virginian. They end up fighting in Cuba at San Juan Hill.

IMPASSE (1:08) # 16712

Air date: November 14, 1962; Guest star: Eddie Albert; Teleplay: Donn Mullally; Story: Bernard Girard; Producer: Winston Miller; Director: Maury Geraghty.

Cal Kroeger (Eddie Albert) stakes a claim to a herd of mustangs that the Virginian and the Shiloh ranch hands have rounded up for delivery to the Army.

IT TOLLS FOR THEE (1:09) # 16714

Air date: November 21, 1962; Guest star: Lee Marvin; Teleplay-Director: Samuel Fuller; Producer: Charles Marquis Warren.

Judge Garth is kidnapped by escaped outlaw Martin Kalig (Lee Marvin), who wants to see if the judge will abandon his high ideals given enough pressure.

WEST (1:10) # 16730

Air date: November 28, 1962; Guest star: Steve Cochran; Story: Irwin R Blacker; Teleplay-Producer-Director: Douglas Heyes.

Trampas seeks fun and adventure with three cowhands, nostalgic for the Old West.

THE DEVILS' CHILDREN (1:11) # 16729

Air date: December 5, 1962; Guest star: Charles Bickford; Teleplay: John and Ward Hawkins; Producer: Warren Duff; Director: William Witney.

Family tensions increase when Tucker McCallum's (Charles Bickford) daughter is accidentally killed after burning down the barn at Shiloh Ranch.

FIFTY DAYS TO MOOSE JAW (1:12) # 16727

Air date: December 12, 1962; Guest stars: Brandon de Wilde, James Gregory; Teleplay: Maxwell Shane and Donald S. Sanford; Producer-Director: Maxwell Shane.

James Cafferty (Brandon de Wilde) runs away from his home and stepfather to join a Shiloh cattle drive. He then meets up with a runaway from the law, Slim Jessup (James Gregory).

THE ACCOMPLICE (1:13) # 16732

Air date: December 19, 1962; Guest star: Bette Davis; Teleplay: Howard Browne and William P. McGivern; Story-Producer: Winston Miller; Director: Maury Geraghty.

Trampas is charged with a year-old bank robbery by spinster Delia Miller (Bette Davis).

THE MAN FROM THE SEA (1:14) # 16723

Air date: December 26, 1962; Guest stars: Carol Lynley, Tom Tryon, Shirley Knight; Teleplay: Morton Fine and David Friedkin; Producer: Charles Marquis Warren; Director: Herschel Daugherty.

Retired sailor Kevin Doyle (Tom Tryon) returns to Medicine Bow to buy a farm and find a wife, and becomes romantically involved with a deeply troubled young woman (Carol Lynley).

DUEL AT SHILOH (1:15) # 16740

Air date: January 2, 1963; Guest star: Brian Keith; Teleplay: Don Ingalls; Based on a Screenplay by Borden Chase and D. D. Beauchamp and the novel *Man Without Star* by Dee Linford; Producer: Don Ingalls; Director: Jerry Hopper.

Steve Hill (Gary Clarke) recalls his arrival in Medicine Bow and the range war that led to his joining Shiloh Ranch.

THE EXILES (1:16) # 16738

Air date: January 9, 1963; Guest stars: Tammy Grimes, Ed Nelson; Teleplay: William P. McGivern and Howard Browne; Story: Thomas Fitzroy; Producer: Winston Miller; Director: Bernard Girard.

Attempting to prove the innocence of Judge Garth following a murder, the Virginian becomes entangled with a saloon singer (Tammy Grimes) receiving threats on her life.

THE JUDGMENT (1:17) # 16741

Air date: January 16, 1963; Guest stars: Clu Gulager, Patricia Barry; Story: Bob and Wanda Duncan; Based on the Screenplay by Lawrence Roman; Producer: Frank Price; Director: Earl Bellamy.

The townspeople of Medicine Bow find themselves intimidated by Jack Carewe (Clu Gulager) and his relatives following the sentencing to death of Carewe's brother by Judge Garth.

SAY GOODBYE TO ALL THAT (1:18) # 16735

Air date: January 23, 1963; Guest star: Fabian; Teleplay: Al C. Ward; Producer: Frank Price; Director: William Witney.

Big John Belden (Charles McGraw) loses the use of his legs in a shooting incident with Trampas—and tells his son Martin (Fabian) to get even for him.

THE MAN WHO COULDN'T DIE (1:19) # 16739

Air date: January 30, 1963; Preempted: February 2, 1963; Guest star: Vera Miles; Teleplay: Harry Kleiner; Story: John Francis O'Mara; Producer: Frank Price; Director: David Friedkin.

Judge Garth finds himself attracted to the woman (Vera Miles) he hires as private tutor to Betsy, little knowing she is a spy for a railway line contractor.

IF YOU HAVE TEARS (1:20) # 16726

Air date: February 13, 1963; Guest star: Dana Wynter; Teleplay: Frank Fenton and Frank Chase; Story: Thomas Fitzroy and Howard Browne; Producer: Warren Duff; Director: Richard L Bare.

Kyle Lawson (Britt Lomond) seeks the help of The Virginian and Trampas after he is accused of murdering the husband of a woman (Dana Wynter) he was having an affair with.

THE SMALL PARADE (1:21) # 16728

Air date: February 20, 1963; Guest star: David Wayne; Teleplay: John and Ward Hawkins; Story: Bernard Girard; Producer: Warren Duff; Director: Paul Nickell.

The Virginian, Trampas and Steve help a group of orphans and a traveling salesman (David Wayne) accused of murder.

VENGEANCE IS THE SPUR (1:22) # 16736

Air date: February 27, 1963; Guest stars: Michael Rennie, Nina Foch; Teleplay: Harry Kleiner; Story: John Francis O'Mara; Producer: Frank Price; Director: Robert Ellis Miller.

The Virginian ventures into the Wyoming Badlands to help a woman (Nina Foch) track down her "husband." He becomes involved in a case of claim and counterclaim regarding the murder of her daughter.

THE MONEY CAGE (1:23) # 16733

Air date: March 6, 1963; Guest star: Steve Forrest; Teleplay: Jameson Brewer; Story: Don Mullally; Producer: Winston Miller; Director: Alan Crosland, Jr.

Con artist Roger "Buster" Layton uses his charm on local banker's daughter Lydia Turner (Bethel Leslie) in an attempt to get Mr. Turner and Judge Garth to invest in an oil drilling scam.

THE GOLDEN DOOR (1:24) # 16745

Air date: March 13, 1963; Guest star: Karl Boehm; Teleplay: Maxwell Shane; Story: Thomas Fitzroy and Maxwell Shane; Producer: Warren Duff; Director: John Brahm.

Judge Garth defends immigrant Karl Rilke (Karl Boehm) and gets him cleared of a murder charge. When Rilke later admits to murdering the rancher in self-defense, Garth is left to ponder his decision to defend the man.

A DISTANT FURY (1:25) # 16748

Air date: March 20, 1963; Guest stars: Ida Lupino, Howard Duff; Teleplay: Howard Browne; Story: Howard Browne and John Francis O'Mara; Producer: Winston Miller; Director: John English.

When an ex-convict (Howard Duff), put behind bars due to Steve's testimony, returns to Medicine Bow, Steve becomes convinced he's out for revenge. He later finds himself accused of his murder.

ECHO OF ANOTHER DAY (1:26) # 16744

Air date: March 27, 1963; Guest star: Bradford Dillman; Teleplay: Frank Fenton; Producer: Warren Duff; Director: William Graham.

Trampas' past catches up with him as and an outlaw (John Dehner) intent on recovering $50,000 in hidden gold arrives at Shiloh Ranch.

STRANGERS AT SUNDOWN (1:27) # 16750

Air date: April 3, 1963; Preempted: April 10, 1963; Guest star: Harry Morgan; Teleplay-Producers: Morton Fine and David Friedkin; Story: Thomas Fitzroy; Director: David Friedkin.

Trapped in a way station in the Montana Badlands, Judge Garth and Betsy are among a group of stage passengers who must decide whether or not to hand over a male passenger to outlaws.

THE MOUNTAIN OF THE SUN (1:28) # 16743

Air date: April 17, 1963; Guest star: Dolores Hart; Teleplay: Harry Kleiner; Story: Louis Morheim; Producer: Warren Duff; Director: Bernard McEveety.

The Virginian escorts three missionary women into Yaqui Indian territory, unaware that the tribe murdered their husbands the previous year. A conflict of interest occurs when the Virginian falls in love with one of the women (Dolores Hart).

RUN AWAY HOME (1:29) # 16742

Air date: April 24, 1963; Guest star: None; Teleplay: Howard Browne; Story: Gene Roddenberry; Producer: Frank Price; Director: Richard L. Bare.

The Virginian and Steve transport $40,000 in cash back to Medicine Bow, pursued by three angry townspeople who lost their money in a bank run.

THE FINAL HOUR (1:30) # 16746

Air date: May 1, 1963; Guest star: Ulla Jacobsson; Teleplay: Harry Kleiner; Story: Ward Hawkins and Bernard Girard; Producer: Frank Price; Director: Robert Douglas.

Trampas, a Polish miner's son (Dean Fredericks) and a local rancher's son (Don Galloway) compete for the affections of a Polish girl (Ulla Jacobsson) and in the process bring racial tensions to the surface.

Season Two

30 × 75 min. (1963–64)
Executive Producer—Frank Price **(2:01–2:30)**

RIDE A DARK TRAIL (2:01) # 23501

Air date: September 18, 1963; Guest star: None; Teleplay: E. M. Parsons; Story: Arthur Browne, Jr.; Producer: Jules Schermer; Director: John Peyser.

The Virginian recalls how Trampas first arrived at Shiloh Ranch looking for the man responsible for the death of his father, Frank Trampas (Sonny Tufts).

MAKE THIS PLACE REMEMBER (2:02) # 23510

Air date: September 25, 1963; Guest stars: Joan Blondell, John Dehner; Teleplay: Harold Swanton; Producer: Jules Schermer; Director: Robert Ellis Miller.

Rosanna Dobie (Joan Blondell) asks Judge Garth to find out the truth behind her son's death by hanging.

NO TEARS FOR SAVANNAH (2:03) # 23517

Air date: October 2, 1963; Guest stars: Gena Rowlands, Everett Sloane, Stephen McNally;

Teleplay: Carey Wilber; Story: William R. Cox; Producer: Winston Miller; Director: Don McDougall.

Meeting up again with former girlfriend Savannah (Gena Rowlands), the Virginian is shocked to find she has been accused of murder and seeks Judge Garth's help in proving her innocence.

KILLER IN TOWN (2:04) # 23515

Air date: October 9, 1963; Guest star: Broderick Crawford; Teleplay: Bob and Wanda Duncan; Producer: Winston Miller; Director: John English.

Trampas fears for his life when bounty hunter George Wolfe (Broderick Crawford) arrives in Medicine Bow.

THE EVIL THAT MEN DO (2:05) # 213508

Air date: October 16, 1963; Guest star: Robert Redford; Teleplay: Frank Chase; Director: Stuart Heisler.

Matthew Cordell (Robert Redford), paroled into the custody of Judge Garth to work at Shiloh Ranch, finds himself distrustful of any offers of friendship.

IT TAKES A BIG MAN (2:06) # 23516

Air date: October 23, 1963; Guest star: Lloyd Nolan, Chris Robinson; Teleplay: Harry Kronman; Producer: Jules Schermer; Director: Bernard McEveety.

Judge Garth's decision to hire the rebellious son (Chris Robinson) of old friend Wade Anders (Lloyd Nolan) results in tragedy.

BROTHER THADDEUS (2:07) # 23509

Air date: October 30, 1963; Guest star: Albert Salmi; Teleplay: William Fay; Producer: Winston Miller; Director: John English.

Reformed convict Willie Caine (Albert Salmi) has to win the trust of the townspeople when he returns to Medicine Bow as a monk.

A PORTRAIT OF MARIE VALONNE (2:08) # 23519

Air date: November 6, 1963; Guest star: Madlyn Rhue; Teleplay: Dean Reisner; Director: Earl Bellamy.

The Virginian meets the beautiful Marie Vallone (Madlyn Rhue) on cattle business in New Orleans, then finds himself trying to discover her whereabouts after she mysteriously disappears.

RUN QUIET (2:09) # 23503

Air date: November 13, 1963; Preempted: November 20, 1963; Guest star: Clu Gulager; Teleplay: Norman Katkov and Ed Adamson; Producer: Winston Miller; Director: Herschel Daugherty.

Steve Hill attempts to prove the innocence of a deaf mute (Clu Gulager) after he is accused of the murder of a gambler.

STOPOVER IN A WESTERN TOWN (2:10) # 23525

Air date: November 27, 1963; Guest star: Dick York; Teleplay: Carey Wilber; Director: Richard L Bare.

Caroline Witman (Joan Freeman) tries to win The Virginian's love by pretending affection for a Shiloh ranch hand (Dick York).

THE FATAL JOURNEY (2:11) # 23527

Air date: December 4, 1963; Guest star: Robert Lansing; Teleplay: John Hawkins; Producer: Winston Miller; Director: Bernard McEveety.

The Virginian poses as an escaped prisoner to track down the killers of *Medicine Bow Banner* editor Molly Wood.

A TIME REMEMBERED (2:12) # 23521

Air date: December 11, 1963; Guest star: Yvonne DeCarlo; Teleplay: Peter Germano; Director: William Witney.

Judge Garth's love for opera singer Helen "Elena" Haldeman (Yvonne DeCarlo) is tested when he has to defend her in a murder case.

SIEGE (2:13) # 23523

Air date: December 18, 1963; Guest star: None; Teleplay: Donn Mullally; Producer: Winston Miller; Director: Don McDougall.

Following a win at the poker table, Trampas returns to Logan, New Mexico, to pay off outstanding debts. There be becomes involved in a town power play with commancheros leader Pedro Lopez (Joseph Campanella).

MAN OF VIOLENCE (2:14) # 23529

Air date: December 25, 1963; Guest star: None; Teleplay: John D. F. Black; Based on a Screenplay by James Patrick; Director: William Witney.

Trampas journeys through Apache territory as he tracks down the men who murdered his uncle.

THE INVADERS (2:15) # 23506

Air date: January 1, 1964; Guest stars: Ed Begley, Beverly Owen; Teleplay: Donn Mullally; Producer: Winston Miller; Director: Bernard McEveety.

Mike Tyrone (Ed Begley) buys a ranch near Medicine Bow but causes tension and hostility when he attempts to expand by purchasing land from local ranchers.

ROAR FROM THE MOUNTAIN (2:16) # 23507

Air date: January 8, 1964; Guest stars: Jack Klugman, Joyce Bulifant; Teleplay: Carey Wilber; Story: Carey Wilber and Franklin Barton; Director: Earl Bellamy.

Steve Hill tracks a rogue cougar into the mountains and encounters conflict and danger when he comes across the Mayhew (Jack Klugman and Joyce Bulifant) homestead.

THE FORTUNES OF J. JIMERSON JONES (2:17) # 23530

Air date: January 15, 1964; Guest star: Pat O'Brien; Teleplay: Carey Wilber; Producer: Winston Miller; Director: Don McDougall.

On a trip to Chicago, Judge Garth finds himself protecting gold prospector. J. Jimerson Jones (Pat O'Brien) from con artists while Betsy has to deal with the advances of a naive newspaper reporter (David Macklin).

THE THIRTY DAYS OF GAVIN HEATH (2:18) # 23533

Air date: January 22, 1964; Guest star: Leo Genn; Teleplay: Mel Harrold; Producer: Don Ingalls; Director: John Florea.

Confronted with his own mortality after he is bitten by a dog feared to have rabies, Gavin Heath (Leo Genn) confronts his past and attempts to overcome his cowardly nature.

THE DRIFTER (2:19) # 23513

Air date: January 29, 1964; Guest star: None; Teleplay: Carey Wilber; Story: Frank Fenton; Producer: Winston Miller; Director: Don McDougall.

The Virginian thinks back to the time he first arrived in Medicine Bow and the tragic events that led to his working at Shiloh Ranch.

FIRST TO THINE OWN SELF (2:20) # 23538

Air date: February 12, 1964; Guest star: None; Teleplay: Les Crutchfield; Producer: Don Ingalls; Director: Earl Bellamy.

A drifter (Randy Boone) is accused of murder after a gold miner (Frank Maxwell) is found dead and his gold nuggets stolen.

A MATTER OF DESTINY (2:21) # 23504

Air date: February 19, 1964; Guest star: Peter Graves, Richard Jaeckel; Teleplay: Al C. Ward; Producer: Winston Miller; Director: Maury Geraghty.

Wealthy Chicago businessman Robert Gaynor (Peter Graves) buys a ranch near Medicine Bow and alienates Trampas when he romances the girl (Jean Hale) Trampas had planned to marry.

SMILE OF A DRAGON (2:22) # 23535

Air date: February 26, 1964; Guest stars: Miyoshi Umeki, Richard Carlson, Frank Overton; Teleplay: Cy Chermak and Don Ingalls; Story: Borden Chase; Producer: Don Ingalls; Director: Andrew V. McLaglen.

Accused of being involved in a series of stage robberies and deaths, Trampas attempts to prove his innocence with the help of a Chinese girl (Miyoshi Umeki).

THE INTRUDERS (2:23) # 23536

Air date: March 4, 1964; Guest stars: Darren McGavin, Hugh Marlowe; Teleplay: Dean Reisner; Director: Charles Rondeau.

Judge Garth and Betsy are held hostage by a group of men intent on killing Sioux Chief Black Feather (Iron Eyes Cody) when he arrives at Shiloh Ranch.

ANOTHER'S FOOTSTEPS (2:24) # 23526

Air date: March 11, 1964; Guest stars: Sheree North, John Agar, Paul Petersen; Teleplay: Frank Chase; Producer: Cy Chermak; Director: R. G. Springsteen.

Following the death of friend Dan Grant (Paul Petersen) in a bank robbery, the Virginian tracks the killers into Montana and becomes romantically involved with one of their wives (Sheree North).

ROPE OF LIES (2:25) # 23542

Air date: March 25, 1964; Guest star: Diana Millay, Peter Breck; Teleplay: Les Crutchfield; Director: Herschel Daugherty.

Beautiful Alva Lowell (Diana Millay) persuades Steve Hill to work as foreman of her Lazy K Ranch, but he soon finds himself going to trial for murder.

THE SECRET OF BRYNMAR HALL (2:26) # 23541

Air date: April 1, 1964; Guest star: Jane Wyatt; Teleplay: Herman Groves; Producer: Don Ingalls; Director: Robert Totten.

Betsy Garth is among a group of people invited to Brynmar Hall by the mother (Jane

Wyatt) of Mildred Brynmar, a young woman killed in a fire and known to all the invited guests.

THE LONG QUEST (2:27) # 23540

Air date: April 8, 1964; Guest star: None; Teleplay: Carey Wilber; Producer: Winston Miller; Director: Richard L. Bare.

When Judith Holly (Ruta Lee) arrives in Medicine Bow claiming her young son from Mary Ann Martin (Patricia Breslin), The Virginian attempts to find out the truth behind the claim.

A BRIDE FOR LARS (2:28) # 23545

Air date: April 15, 1964; Preempted: April 22, 1964; Guest star (co-starring): Katherine Crawford; Teleplay: True Boardman; Producer: Winston Miller; Director: Earl Bellamy.

Trampas is given the task of escorting young Swedish bride-to-be Anne Swenson (Katherine Crawford) from Laramie to her middle-aged fiancé Lars Holstrum (Peter Whitney).

DARK DESTINY (2:29) # 23544

Air date: April 29, 1964; Guest star: Brenda Scott; Teleplay: Frank Chase; Director: Don McDougall.

Billie Jo Conrad (Brenda Scott) is torn between devotion to her father (Robert J. Wilke), wanted for horse rustling, and affection for Randy Benton.

A MAN CALLED KANE (2:30) # 23543

Air date: May 6, 1964; Guest star: Dick Foran; Teleplay: Dean Reisner; Director: William Witney.

Randy's older brother "Johnny Kane" (Jeremy Slate) arrives at Shiloh hiding a past that soon catches up with him, forcing Randy to decide between family loyalty and justice.

Season Three

30 × 75 min. (1964–65)
Executive Producer—Frank Price **(3:01–3:30)**

RYKER (3:01) # 24726

Air date: September 16, 1964; Guest star: Leslie Nielsen; Teleplay: Frank Fenton; Producer: Joel Rogosin; Director: Don Richardson.

Landowner John Hagen (Leslie Nielsen) hires former lawman Emmett Ryker to scare a rancher (Russ Conway) off a ranch he holds the mortgage on. Ryker decides to come down on the side of the law when the rancher is found dead.

DARK CHALLENGE (3:02) # 24710

Air date: September 23, 1964; Guest stars: Victor Jory, Chris Robinson, Katharine Ross; Teleplay: True Boardman and Joseph Hoffman; Story: Joseph Hoffman; Producer: Winston Miller; Director: Don McDougall.

Trampas tries to make amends after he inadvertently embarrasses a disabled girl (Katharine Ross) at a local dance, only to become a prime suspect in the murder of the girl's father (Victor Jory).

THE STALLION (3:03) # 24709

Air date: September 30, 1964; Guest star: Robert Culp; Teleplay: Carey Wilber and Louis Vittes; Story: Carey Wilber; Producer: Frank Telford; Director: Bernard McEveety.

With the help of alcoholic ex-veterinarian Charlie Orwell (Robert Culp), Randy helps tame a stallion after it kills a handler escaping from its cruel owner (Donald Barry).

THE HERO (3:04) # 24712

Air date: October 7, 1964; Guest star: Steve Forrest; Teleplay: Clair Huffaker; Producer: Frank Telford; Director: Richard L Bare.

Betsy becomes enamored with "newspaperman" Jim Templeton (Steve Forrest) but Trampas begins to suspect Templeton isn't as perfect as he pretends to be.

FELICITY'S SPRING (3:05) # 24701

Air date: October 14, 1964; Guest stars: Katherine Crawford, Mariette Hartley; Teleplay (uncredited)-Producer: Winston Miller; Story: Jean Holloway; Director: Don McDougall

The Virginian falls in love with Felicity Andrews (Katherine Crawford) little knowing the secret her sister (Mariette Hartley) and grandfather (Carl Benton Reid) are keeping.

THE BRAZOS KID (3:06) # 24716

Air date: October 21, 1964; Guest star: Barbara Eden; Teleplay: Carey Wilber; Producer: Joel Rogosin; Director: Don McDougall.

The Virginian is mistaken for the notorious the Brazos Kid after a reporter (Barbara Eden) writes a physical description of the outlaw that matches the Virginian.

BIG IMAGE ... LITTLE MAN (3:07) # 24714

Air date: October 28, 1964; Guest star: Linden Chiles; Teleplay: Frank Chase and Carey Wilber; Story: Frank Chase; Producer: Frank Telford; Director: William Witney.

Arrogant millionaire Paul Leland (Linden Chiles) is forced to change his selfish ways when the Virginian hires him on a cattle drive after finding him thirsty and alone in the desert.

A FATHER FOR TOBY (3:08) # 24704

Air date: November 4, 1964; Guest stars: Rory Calhoun, Joanna Moore, Kurt Russell; Teleplay: True Boardman; Story: Tom Seller; Director: Alan Crosland, Jr.

Orphan Toby Shea (Kurt Russell) impresses other boys at the orphanage by claiming Trampas as his father, unaware his real father is a hand at Shiloh Ranch.

THE GIRL FROM YESTERDAY (3:09) # 24713

Air date: November 11, 1964; Guest stars: Mark Richman, Ruta Lee; Teleplay: Mark Rodgers and Louis Vittes; Story: Mark Rodgers; Producer: Frank Telford; Director: John Florea.

Steve Hill reluctantly agrees to go undercover to find out how and when a gold shipment is going to be stolen and to learn if his childhood sweetheart (Ruta Lee) is involved with the outlaw gang.

RETURN A STRANGER (3:10) # 24706

Air date: November 18, 1964; Guest stars: Leif Erickson, Peter Brown; Teleplay: True Boardman; Story: George Slavin; Producer: Winston Miller; Director: Maury Geraghty.

Falling behind in their payments, a mine owner's son (Peter Brown) and his business partner (Whit Bissell) cut back on safety, resulting in an angry community and poisoned cattle.

ALL NICE AND LEGAL (3:11) # 24702

Air date: November 25, 1964; Guest star: Anne Francis; Teleplay: Jean Holloway; Producer: Winston Miller; Director: Don McDougall.

The Virginian is attracted to an attorney new to Medicine Bow, Victoria Greenley (Anne Francis), but soon finds himself at odds with her defense of trespassers on Shiloh land.

A GALLOWS FOR SAM HORN (3:12) # 24721

Air date: December 2, 1964; Guest stars: John Lupton, Edward Binns, George Kennedy; Teleplay: Dean Reisner; Director: Don McDougall.

Following eviction from his land by railroad tycoon John Briscoe (Edward Binns), rancher Sam Horn (John Lupton) kills Briscoe's son Scott (Buck Taylor), setting off a chain of events involving his late son's former girlfriend Peg Dineen (Laurel Goodwin).

PORTRAIT OF A WIDOW (3:13) # 24708

Air date: December 9, 1964; Guest stars: Vera Miles, John Gavin; Teleplay: Tom Blackburn and Lawrence Edward Watkin; Producer: Winston Miller; Director: Don McDougall.

Escaping gambling debts, Charles Baker (John Gavin) poses as French portrait painter Charles Boulanger. He sees an end to his problems when he discovers a valuable painting in the home of the woman (Vera Miles) who commissioned her portrait, but soon is conflicted by his growing affection for her.

THE PAYMENT (3:14) # 24732

Air date: December 16, 1964; Guest stars: Lloyd Nolan, Bruce Dern, Lisabeth Hush; Story: Thomas Thompson; Producer: Cy Chermak; Director: John Florea.

Released from prison, Ryker's stepfather Abe Clayton (Lloyd Nolan) promises to keep out of trouble but Ryker senses he may be planning a major robbery.

MAN OF THE PEOPLE (3:15) # 24705

Air date: December 23, 1964; Guest stars: James Dunn; Teleplay: William Fay and True Boardman; Story: William Fay; Producer: Winston Miller; Director: William Witney.

Settlers find themselves innocent victims of a scandal involving a corrupt government official (Arthur Space) and farming land only fit for grazing.

THE HOUR OF THE TIGER (3:16) # 24718

Air date: December 30, 1964; Guest stars: Cely Carrillo, Tom Tully; Teleplay: Harry Kleiner; Producer: Frank Telford; Director: Richard L. Bare.

Finding his cattle pass blocked by an avalanche, Judge Garth enlists the aid of Chinese coolies to dig a tunnel through the fallen rocks. Local landowner Junius Antlow (Tom Tully) attempts to sabotage the work.

TWO MEN NAMED LAREDO (3:17) # 24722

Air date: January 6, 1965; Guest star: Fabian; Teleplay: Don Brinkley; Story: Don Brinkley and Don Tait; Producer: Cy Chermak; Director: William Hale.

Trampas is baffled when the studious young man (Fabian) who saved his life in a cattle stampede is accused of the murder of local troublemaker Bojo Sanders (Rayford Barnes) and saloon girl Molly Weems (Elizabeth McRae).

HIDEOUT (3:18) # 24738

Air date: January 13, 1965; Guest stars: Forrest Tucker, Andrew Prine; Based upon a Screenplay by Edna Anhalt; From a Novel by Stuart Hardy; Teleplay-Producer: Cy Chermak; Director: Don McDougall.

Betsy is caught in a moral dilemma when the son (Andrew Prine) of a man (Forrest Tucker) wanted for murder helps save her life following a rattlesnake bite.

SIX GRAVES AT CRIPPLE CREEK (3:19) # 24734

Air date: January 27, 1965; Guest star: John Doucette; Teleplay: Carey Wilber; Producer: Winston Miller; Director: Maury Geraghty.

Emmett Ryker distrusts reports that the killer of a rancher and his daughter was in turn killed by Indians. Accompanied by the killer's daughter Lucille Carver (Sheilah Wells), he tracks him to Deadwood.

LOST YESTERDAY (3:20) # 24736

Air date: February 3, 1965; Guest star: Shirley Knight; Teleplay: True Boardman; Director: Don McDougall.

Recovering at Shiloh Ranch from a stagecoach accident, Clara Malone (Shirley Knight) does not recall that outlaws have threatened her life unless she tells them the location of money stolen by her late boyfriend.

A SLIGHT CASE OF CHARITY (3:21) # 24725

Air date: February 10, 1965; Guest star: Kathryn Hays; Teleplay: Howard Browne and True Boardman; Story: Howard Browne; Producer: Joel Rogosin; Director: Dick Benedict.

Trampas becomes embroiled in a complex series of events involving stolen money, a ruby ring, false identity and robbery.

YOU TAKE THE HIGH ROAD (3:22) # 24731

Air date: February 17, 1965; Guest stars: Richard Beymer, Diana Lynn; Teleplay: Dan Ullman; Story: Dan Ullman and Frank Fenton; Producer: Cy Chermak; Director: John Florea.

Acting on behalf of local ranchers, The Virginian gives orders to divert cattle infected with Spanish Fever from Medicine Bow, but rebellious youngster Mark Shannon (Richard Beymer) is intent on getting his cattle to an Army post in Colorado on time.

SHADOWS OF THE PAST (3:23) # 24735

Air date: February 24, 1965; Guest star: Jack Warden; Teleplay: Frank Chase; Director: Don McDougall.

John Conway (Jack Warden) returns from San Francisco with a young woman he plans to marry, but Ryker's concern for the relationship is matched with his concern for the Garr brothers (John Milford and James Beck) who threaten to take revenge on Ryker for the death of their brother.

LEGEND FOR A LAWMAN (3:24) # 24733

Air date: March 3, 1965; Guest star: Adam West; Teleplay: Preston Wood; Story: Frank Telford and Harry Kleiner; Director: John Florea.

Randy Benton, sentenced to hang for a crime he didn't commit, must rely on the Virginian and the aging Marshall Buckman (Ford Rainey) to prove his innocence.

TIMBERLAND (3:25) # 24739

Air date: March 10, 1965; Guest stars: Martin Milner, William Smith, Joan Freeman; Teleplay: Sheldon Stark; Producer: Cy Chermak; Director: Don McDougall.

Tension mounts and relationships are tested when logger Charles Daniels (Arch Johnson) refuses to abandon tree-felling activities that will destroy a watershed area and flood the land.

DANGEROUS ROAD (3:26) # 24740

Air date: March 17, 1965; Guest star: Simon Oakland, Tom Simcox; Teleplay: John and Ward Hawkins; Producer: Winston Miller; Director: Maury Geraghty.

Trampas delivers a murder suspect for trial in Coulter Junction and stays to find out the truth behind the death of his old friend Sheriff Dolan.

FAREWELL TO HONESTY (3:27) # 24728

Air date: March 24, 1965; Guest star: Richard Carlson; Teleplay: True Boardman; Story: Carey Wilber; Producer: Frank Telford; Director: Leon Benson.

Armed with a warrant for the arrest of Major Ralph Forrester (Richard Carlson) for defrauding Judge Garth in a cattle sale with forged deeds, a deputized Virginian is accused of murder after the major is found dead in an alley.

OLD COWBOY (3:28) # 24744

Air date: March 31, 1965; Guest star: Franchot Tone; Teleplay: Gabrielle Upton; Producer: Frank Telford; Director: William Witney.

Taking pity on an old cowboy (Franchot Tone), Trampas offers him work at Shiloh. Resentment grows when Trampas is admired by the man's young grandson (Billy Mumy).

SHOWDOWN (3:29) # 24750

Air date: April 14, 1965; Guest stars: Michael Ansara, Peter Whitney; Teleplay-Producer: Gene L. Coon; Director: Don McDougall.

The Virginian encounters trouble on a cattle-buying trip in Monolith, Arizona, when ill feeling between the Landers (Peter Whitney, Tom Skerritt, Ed Faulkner and Cal Bartlett) and Frome (Michael Ansara and Leonard Nimoy) families results in murder.

WE'VE LOST A TRAIN (3:30)

Air date: April 21, 1965; Guest stars: Ida Lupino, Fernando Lamas, Rhonda Fleming; Teleplay: Borden Chase; Director: Earl Bellamy.

On a trip to Mexico to pick up a prize bull for Judge Garth, Trampas is sidelined in Laredo by Texas Rangers Joe Riley, Reese Bennett and Chad Cooper (William Smith, Neville Brand and Peter Brown) looking for gold and the Mexican bandits who stole it.

Season Four

30 × 75 min. (1965–66)

Executive Producer—Norman MacDonnell **(4:01–4:30)**

Joel Rogosin, uncredited, briefly served as executive producer.

THE BROTHERS (4:01) # 26215

Air date: September 15, 1965; Guest stars: Robert Lansing, Andrew Prine; Teleplay: Dick Nelson; Producer: Joel Rogosin; Director: Tony Leader.

Breaking his younger brother (Andrew Prine) out of jail, Matt Denning (Robert Lansing), his wife (Jan Shepard) and son (Kurt Russell) escape into Sioux territory. There Matt Denning is forced to confront the truth.

DAY OF THE SCORPION (4:02) # 26206

Air date: September 22, 1965; Guest stars: None; Teleplay: Don Ingalls; Producer: Arthur H. Nadel; Director: Robert Butler.

Australian sheep rancher's daughter Reagan Tercell's (Maura McGivney) growing affection for the Virginian creates conflict with her stubborn father (John Anderson), who blames the Virginian for the death of his son Abel (Jon Locke).

A LITTLE LEARNING (4:03) # 26211

Air date: September 29, 1965; Guest star: Albert Salmi; Special guest star: Susan Oliver; Teleplay: Harry Kronman; Producer: Arthur H. Nadel; Director: Don Richardson.

Hired gun Bert Kramer (Bruce Dern) returns to Medicine Bow to win back his estranged wife. When he discovers she may have been having an affair with a man (Albert Salmi) she's been tutoring, he plots to get rid of him.

THE CLAIM (4:04) # 26208

Air date: October 6, 1965; Guest star: William Shatner; Teleplay: Shirl Hendryx; Producer: Joel Rogosin; Director: Bernard Kowalski.

A jaded Trampas decides to leave Shiloh and join up with his friend Luke Milford (William Shatner) in a search for gold in the Dakotas. He learns that the love of gold can destroy friendships.

THE AWAKENING (4:05) # 26218

Air date: October 13, 1965; Guest star: Glenn Corbett, Roberta Shore; Special guest star: John Doucette; Teleplay: Robert Crean; Producer: Joel Rogosin; Director: Leon Benson.

Betsy Garth leaves Shiloh Ranch for Pennsylvania after falling in love with and marrying David Henderson (Glenn Corbett), a minister who rediscovers his faith with the help of a local mining community and the love of Betsy.

RING OF SILENCE (4:06) # 26201

Air date: October 27, 1965; Guest stars: Earl Holliman, Joyce Van Patten, Royal Dano; Teleplay: Barry Oringer; Story: Ruth L. Adams; Producer: Arthur H. Nadel; Director: Don Richardson.

Attempting to escape from a gang of caballeros, Emmett Ryker and several stagecoach passengers hole up in a miner's cabin. They learn that one passenger (Earl Holliman) is wanted by the gang for killing a woman.

JENNIFER (4:07) # 26202

Air date: November 3, 1965; Guest stars: James MacArthur; Teleplay: Theodore Apstein and Rita Lakin; Story: Rita Lakin; Producer: Joel Rogosin; Director: Don Richardson.

Following the death of her parents, Jennifer Sommers reluctantly agrees to stay with her uncle, Judge Garth, at Shiloh Ranch. Blaming Garth for the death of her parents, Jennifer mistakenly places her trust in fugitive Johnny Bradford (James MacArthur).

NOBILITY OF KINGS (4:08) # 26213

Air date: November 10, 1965; Guest stars: Charles Bronson, Lois Nettleton, George Kennedy; Teleplay: Richard Fielder; Story-Producer: James Duff McAdams; Director: Paul Stanley.

Cynical about human nature following a business deal that left him bankrupt, Ben Justin (Charles Bronson) mistrusts the motives of Judge Garth and the Virginian and distances himself from the Cattleman's Association. But a bad outbreak of cattle fever forces him to again place trust in others.

SHOW ME A HERO (4:09) # 26204

Air date: November 17, 1965; Guest stars: Richard Beymer; Teleplay: Frank Chase; Story: Alvin Boretz; Producer: Norman MacDonnell; Director: Leon Benson.

On a stopover in Eagle Rock to treat his injured horse, Trampas becomes involved in a dispute between townspeople and Paul Leland (Ken Lynch), who plans to take over the town with intimidation and gambling.

BEYOND THE BORDER (4:10) # 26205

Air date: November 24, 1965; Guest stars: Thomas Gomez, Joan Staley; Teleplay: Martha Wilkerson; Producer: Winston Miller; Director: Don McDougall.

Struck down by fever on a horse-buying trip to Mexico, the Virginian falls in love with the woman (Joan Staley) caring for him. But near-tragedy makes the woman realize where her true affections are.

THE DREAM OF STAVROS KARAS (4:11) # 26214

Air date: December 1, 1965; Guest stars: Michael Constantine, Louise Sorel; Teleplay: A. I. Bezzerides; Producer: Joel Rogosin; Director: Richard Benedict.

Doubts over an arranged marriage between a wealthy Greek widower (Michael Constantine) and the beautiful Eleni (Louise Sorel) are compounded by a ranch conflict over water rights and advances on Eleni by the rancher's son (Anthony Hayes).

THE LARAMIE ROAD (4:12) # 26212

Air date: December 8, 1965; Guest stars: Leslie Nielsen, Harold J. Stone, Claude Akins; Teleplay: Halsted Welles; Producer: James Duff McAdams; Director: Charles S. Dubin.

Ryker and the Virginian intervene when a woman (Marge Redmond) is murdered and a local mob demands the lynching of hoboes (Leslie Nielsen and Berkeley Harris) thought guilty of the crime.

THE HORSE FIGHTER (4:13) # 26223

Air date: December 15, 1965; Guest star: Harry Guardino; Teleplay: Richard Fielder; Producer: James Duff McAdams; Director: Tony Leader.

An aging bronco buster (Harry Guardino) befriends Randy Benton, resulting in tension between Randy and the Virginian.

LETTER OF THE LAW (4:14) # 26209

Air date: December 22, 1965; Guest star: Simon Oakland; Teleplay: Donn Mullally; Producer: Arthur H. Nadel; Director: Charles S. Dubin.

Chief of railroad security Charles Sanders (Simon Oakland) is convinced of the guilt of Curt Westley (James Best), a man he arrested for robbery. Ryker sets out to prove him wrong.

BLAZE OF GLORY (4:15) # 26216

Air date: December 29, 1965; Guest stars: Leif Erickson, Joan Freeman; Introducing: Michael Sarrazin; Teleplay: John and Ward Hawkins; Producer: Joel Rogosin; Director: Alexander Singer

Facing foreclosure on his ranch, retired sheriff Bill King (Leif Erickson) accepts an offer of stolen gold in return for sheltering an outlaw and becomes trapped in a web of blackmail.

NOBODY SAID HELLO (4:16) # 26203

Air date: January 5, 1966; Guest stars: James Whitmore, Virginia Grey; Introducing: Steve Carlson; Teleplay: Herb Meadow; Producer: Arthur H. Nadel; Director: Alf Kjellin.

Notorious ex–Confederate officer Piper Pritikin (James Whitmore) arrives in Medicine Bow after serving time in prison for cruelty to prisoners, an apparent changed man. But his motives become clear when he threatens to extort money from Judge Garth.

MEN WITH GUNS (4:17) # 26221

Air date: January 12, 1966; Guest stars: Telly Savalas, Robert F. Simon, Brenda Scott; Teleplay: Halstead Welles; Producer-Director: Leon Benson.

Ruthless landowner Col. Bliss' (Telly Savalas) exploitation of the townspeople of New Hope provokes Trampas to lead an armed rebellion, with tragic consequences.

LONG RIDE TO WIND RIVER (4:18) # 26226

Air date: January 19, 1966; Guest star: John Cassavetes; Teleplay: Sy Salkowitz; Producer: Arthur H. Nadel; Director: Paul Henreid.

The Virginian tracks a murderer to an isolated mountain community and is aided by a young Shoshone girl (Pilar Seurat) on his hazardous return.

CHAFF IN THE WIND (4:19) # 26217

Air date: January 26, 1966; Guest stars: Ed Begley, Tony Bill; Teleplay: Joy Dexter; Director: Herman Hoffman.

A family of con artists is offered work at Shiloh Ranch despite the misgivings of the Virginian. The son (Tony Bill) and daughter (Linda Lawson) are changed by their positive experiences at Shiloh and refuse to continue living a double life, causing their father (Ed Begley) to join his brother (Lonny Chapman) in a cattle-rustling scheme.

THE INCHWORM'S GOT NO WINGS AT ALL (4:20) # 26222

Air date: February 2, 1966; Guest stars: Stacey Maxwell, Lou Antonio; Teleplay: Herman Miller; Story: Allan Sloane; Director: Paul Stanley.

A mentally slow teenage girl (Stacey Maxwell), sheltered from the outside world by fearful parents (Anthony Caruso and Angela Clarke), holds the clue to a murder.

MORGAN STARR (4:21) # 26230

Air date: February 9, 1966; Guest stars: John Dehner, Peggie Castle; Teleplay: Herman Miller and Barry Oringer; Story: Barry Oringer; Producer: Joel Rogosin; Director: Tony Leader.

Judge Garth hires old friend Morgan Starr to take over duties at Shiloh Ranch following Garth's appointment as territorial governor of Wyoming. Conflict between Starr and the Virginian is increased when a horde of locusts threatens local herds and Starr's plan for killing the locusts appears to be poorly conceived.

HARVEST OF STRANGERS (4:22) # 26228

Air date: February 16, 1966; Guest stars: John Dehner, Geoffrey Horne, John Anderson; Teleplay: Leon Tokatyan; Director: Paul Stanley.

A group of French-Canadian Indians (Metis) arrive in Medicine Bow awaiting a shipment of money. When Louise Deavers (Barbara Turner) accuses one of the men of sexual assault, trouble flares.

RIDE A COCK-HORSE TO LARAMIE CROSS (4:23) # 26227

Air date: February 23, 1966; Guest star: Nita Talbot; Teleplay: Clair Huffaker; Producer: Arthur H. Nadel; Director: Tony Leader.

Trampas encounters armed pursuers, Sioux Indians and a female card dealer as he escorts the young Gen. Manuel Garcia Lopez (Clint Howard) and his infant sister to Laramie to join up with their mother, banished from Mexico by the youngsters' despot grandfather "El Supremo."

ONE SPRING LONG AGO (4:24) # 26231

Air date: March 2, 1966; Guest stars: John Dehner, Eduard Franz, Warren Oates; Teleplay: Robert Sabaroff; Director: Herman Hoffman.

Sioux Chief Two Hats (Eduard Franz) and his son Tonka (Clive Clerk) are pursued by a bounty hunter (Warren Oates), Morgan Starr and Randy Benton after the Indians steal their horses in pursuit of buffalo to fulfill an Indian prophecy.

THE RETURN OF GOLDEN TOM (4:25) # 26234

Air date: March 9, 1966; Preempted: A **Bald Faced Boy** (4:29)—Air date: March 16, 1966; Guest stars: Victor Jory, Linden Chiles; Teleplay: Andy Lewis; Story: Andy Lewis and Joel Rogosin; Director: Tony Leader.

Returning to Medicine Bow after 35 years in prison, aging outlaw "Golden" Tom Brant (Victor Jory) has to confront the past and come to terms with the dime-novel character he has become.

THE WOLVES UP FRONT, THE JACKALS BEHIND (4:26) # 26233

Air date: March 23, 1966; Guest stars: James Farentino, Jay C. Flippen, Michael J. Pollard; Teleplay: Herman Miller; Director: Paul Stanley.

Attracted to Dulcy Colby (Peggy Lipton), Randy Benton becomes entangled in a Colby family feud involving a "black sheep" (James Farentino) and his apparent intention to kill his brother Ben (Donnelly Rhodes).

THAT SAUNDERS WOMAN (4:27) # 26220

Air date: March 30, 1966; Guest star: Sheree North; Teleplay: Don Brinkley; Story: Edward DeBlasio; Director: William Hale.

Former saloon girl Della Saunders (Sheree North) is blackmailed by a man who knows she served time for murder. When the man is found dead, suspicions once again center on Della Saunders.

NO DRUMS, NO TRUMPETS (4:28) # 26235

Air date: April 6, 1966; Guest stars: Leslie Nielsen, John Dehner; Teleplay: Robert Sabaroff; Story: Robert Sabaroff and Arthur H. Nadel; Producer-Director: Arthur H. Nadel.

Attempting to prevent the assassination of a U. S. senator and a Mexican governor, Morgan Starr finds himself a prisoner of the person responsible for the assassination plan, former Marshall Cleve Mason (Leslie Nielsen).

A BALD-FACED BOY (4:29) # 26224

Air date: April 13, 1966; Guest stars: Andrew Prine, Royal Dano, Andrew Duggan; Teleplay: Jack Curtis; Producer: Arthur H. Nadel; Director: Earl Bellamy.

Fearing released prisoner Jim Claiborne (Andrew Duggan) may seek revenge on Randy Benton for his testimony that put Claiborne behind bars, Randy's older brother Brett (Andrew Prine), Uncle Dell (Royal Dano) and two cousins journey to Medicine Bow. When Claiborne's daughter (Karen Jensen) falls in love with Randy, things become complicated.

THE MARK OF A MAN (4:30) # 26236

Air date: April 20, 1966; Guest stars: Harold J. Stone, Brooke Bundy, Barry Primus; Teleplay: Harold Swanton; Producer: James Duff McAdams; Director: Tony Leader.

Following dismissal from his job at the local saloon, young Johnny Younce (Barry Primus) goes on a rampage and sustains a concussion. The Virginian offers him refuge at Shiloh and slowly unravels the truth behind his job loss.

Season Five

29 × 75 min. (1966–67)
Executive Producer—Frank Price **(5:01–5:29)**

LEGACY OF HATE (5:01) # 27807

Air date: September 14, 1966; Guest stars: Jo Van Fleet, Jeremy Slate; Teleplay: Frank Chase; Producer: Winston Miller; Director: Don McDougall.

The new owner of Shiloh Ranch, John Grainger, receives a hostile reception from neighboring rancher Lee Calder (Jo Van Fleet), who blames Grainger for the death of her husband 25 years ago. With the help of foreman Jim Dawson (Jeremy Slate) she attempts to force Grainger off Shiloh Ranch.

RIDE TO DELPHI (5:02) # 27814

Air date: September 21, 1966; Guest stars: Angie Dickinson, Harold J. Stone, Warren Oates; Teleplay: Andy Lewis; Story: Don Tait; Director: Tony Leader.

The Virginian tracks stolen cattle to sodbuster Ransome Kiley (Bernie Hamilton) but finds himself accused of robbery and murder after drover Wally Buxton (Warren Oates) is found dead.

THE CAPTIVE (5:03) # 27813

Air date: September 28, 1966; Guest stars: Susan Strasberg; Teleplay: Peter Packer; Producer: Winston Miller; Director: Don Weis.

Detained at Shiloh Ranch following a cattle-rustling incident, a white girl (Susan Strasberg) raised by Indians denies she *was* abducted by Indians as a child and resists attempts to reunite her with her birth mother and father (Virginia Vincent and Don Hamner).

AN ECHO OF THUNDER (5:04) # 27818

Air date: October 5, 1966; Guest stars: Linden Chiles, John Anderson, Jason Evers; Teleplay: Don Ingalls; Producer: Cy Chermak; Director: Abner Biberman.

Following a horse drive to Pueblo, Colorado, Trampas looks up old friend Bill Doolie in nearby St. John but ends up trying to uncover the truth behind his murder.

JACOB WAS A PLAIN MAN (5:05) # 27808

Air date: October 12, 1966; Guest star: Aldo Ray; Teleplay: Eric Bercovici; Director: Don McDougall.

A deaf-mute (Aldo Ray) is hired by the Virginian, unaware he is wanted for murder. Ranch hands and a bounty hunter threaten his safety.

THE CHALLENGE (5:06) # 27811

Air date: October 19, 1966; Guest stars: Dan Duryea, Don Galloway, Michael Burns; Introducing: Barbara Anderson; Teleplay: Joy Dexter, Harry Kronman; Story: Joy Dexter; Producer: Joel Rogosin; Director: Don McDougall.

Suffering amnesia following a stagecoach hold-up, Trampas is suspected of robbery and murder when he is found carrying a white-handled gun used in the robbery.

OUTCAST (5:07) # 27810

Air date: October 26, 1966; Guest star: Fabian; Teleplay: Lou Shaw; Director: Alan Crosland, Jr.

Accused murderer Charley Ryan (Fabian) is hired at Shiloh, the Graingers and the Virginian unaware of his jail breakout. But when he uses his charms on Elizabeth Grainger, Stacey and the Virginian become suspicious of his character.

TRAIL TO ASHLEY MOUNTAIN (5:08) # 27822

Air date: November 2, 1966; Guest stars: Martin Milner, George Kennedy, Gene Evans, Steve Carlson; Teleplay: Sy Salkowitz; Producer: Cy Chermak; Director: Abner Biberman.

Pursuing suspected murderer Willy Parker (Steve Carlson) into mountain territory, Trampas must contend with a bounty hunter (Raymond St. Jacques), two gold miners (George Kennedy and Jackie Cooper), a rancher (Gene Evans) and a telegraph operator (Martin Milner); all of whom have their own reasons for wanting to see Parker dead.

DEADEYE DICK (5:09) # 27819

Air date: November 9, 1966; Guest stars: None; Teleplay: Joseph Hoffman; Producer: Winston Miller; Director: Ida Lupino.

A teenage girl's (Marjorie Hammond) infatuation with the Virginian is tempered when the reality of her kidnapping by robbers produces a real-life hero in Bob Foley (David Macklin).

HIGH STAKES (5:10) # 27802

Air date: November 16, 1966; Guest stars: Terry Moore, Jack Lord, Michael Ansara, Dirk Rambo; Teleplay: True Boardman; Story: Mark Rodgers; Director: Thomas Carr.

The Virginian poses as an outlaw in an attempt to capture two brothers (Jack Lord and Michael Ansara) who killed his friend. But bringing them to justice proves more difficult than he imagined.

BELOVED OUTLAW (5:11) # 27809

Air date: November 23, 1966; Guest stars: None; Teleplay: True Boardman; Producer: Winston Miller; Director: William Witney.

Elizabeth Grainger buys an untamed white stallion and trains the horse for entry in the annual Founder's Day race, ignoring her grandfather's well-placed concern for her safety.

LINDA (5:12) # 27803

Air date: November 30, 1966, Guest star: Diane Baker, Teleplay: Frank Fenton, Story: Cy Chermak, Director: Don McDougall.

The Virginian becomes entangled in a series of events involving stolen money, a beautiful woman and a box containing $50,000.

THE LONG WAY HOME (5:13) # 27827

Air date: December 14, 1966; Preempted: **Big Image, Little Man** (3:07)—Air date: December 12, 1966; Guest stars: Pernell Roberts, Michael Burns, Noah Beery, Jr.; Teleplay: Andy Lewis; Story: Ken Finley; Producer: Joel Rogosin; Director: Abner Biberman.

Abandoning his wayward life, Jim Boyer (Pernell Roberts) attempts to impress his son (Michael Burns) by joining him at Shiloh Ranch, but ambition and jealousy threaten to undermine his reformed image.

GIRL ON THE GLASS MOUNTAIN (5:14) # 27816

Air date: December 28, 1966; Guest star: Tom Tryon; Teleplay: Eric Bercovici and James L. Henderson; Story: James L. Henderson; Director: Don McDougall.

A socially ambitious woman's (Pamela Austin) attempts to turn her cowhand husband into a successful businessman seem doomed when he loses his money in a poker game.

VENGEANCE TRAIL (5:15) # 27823

Air date: January 4, 1967; Guest stars: Ron Russell, Mary Ann Mobley; Teleplay: John and Ward Hawkins and Cy Chermak; Director: Thomas Carr.

Seeking revenge for the death of his brother, Toby Williams (Ron Russell) becomes friends with Stacey Grainger during a Shiloh cattle drive, little realizing Stacey is the man he's looking for.

SUE ANN (5:16)—27815

Air date: January 11, 1967; Guest stars: Patty Duke, Edward Binns; Teleplay: Gabrielle Upton and True Boardman; Story: Gabrielle Upton; Producer: Joel Rogosin; Director: Gerald Mayer.

Running from a life of boredom and hard work on her father's farm, Sue Ann McRae (Patty Duke) finds waitressing in a Medicine Bow saloon just as tiring. When her "boyfriend" hands her $200, she sees the chance to fulfill her dreams in San Francisco.

YESTERDAY'S TIMEPIECE (5:17) # 27831

Air date: January 18, 1967; Guest stars: Andy Devine, Stu Erwin, Audrey Totter, Pat O'Brien; Teleplay: Sy Salkowitz; Story: Sy Salkowitz, Al Ramrus and John Shaner; Producer: Cy Chermak; Director: Abner Biberman.

A mysterious watch links Stacey to his tragic past, with a sequence of nightmares and an encounter with a storekeeper's niece culminating in a journey to an Indian reservation in Texas.

REQUIEM FOR A COUNTRY DOCTOR (5:18) # 27824

Air date: January 25, 1967; Guest star: Cloris Leachman; Teleplay: Chester Krumholz and Robert Guy Barrows; Story: Judith Barrows; Director: Don McDougall.

The Virginian endeavors to save Stacey Grainger's life after he is sentenced to hang for the murder of a country doctor and the robbery of money intended for a local orphanage.

THE MODOC KID (5:19) # 27836

Air date: February 1, 1967; Guest stars: John Saxon; Introducing: Harrison Ford; Teleplay: Leslie Stevens; Producer: Cy Chermak; Director: Abner Biberman.

Held hostage by the Modoc Kid's (John Saxon) gang of bank robbers, the Graingers are forced to lie about their predicament to protect their lives. But a perceptive Ryker senses something is wrong.

THE GAUNTLET (5:20) # 27838

Air date: February 8, 1967; Guest star: Mark Richman; Teleplay: Lou Shaw; Director: Thomas Carr.

An injured Virginian becomes a pawn in a wife's (Marian Moses) plan to escape her abusive husband.

WITHOUT MERCY (5:21) # 27833

Air date: February 15, 1967; Guest stars: James Gregory, Lonny Chapman; Teleplay: Donn Mullally; Producer: Winston Miller; Director: Don McDougall.

John Grainger tries to prove the innocence of his grandson Stacey after is framed for the murder of Cal Young (James Gregory), the man who forbade Stacey to date his daughter.

MELANIE (5:22) # 27832

Air date: February 22, 1967; Guest star: Victor Jory; Introducing: Susan Clark; Teleplay: Stephen Lord; Producer: Joel Rogosin; Director: Abner Biberman.

Trampas' romance with the daughter (Susan Clark) of wealthy Jim Kohler (Victor Jory) leads to a proposal of marriage. Melanie Kohler's secret threatens their future happiness.

DOCTOR PAT (5:23) # 27840

Air date: March 1, 1967; Guest stars: Jill Donohue, Mari Blanchard; Teleplay: True Boardman; Producer: Winston Miller; Director: Don McDougall.

Doc Spaulding's new female assistant (Mari Blanchard) has to overcome prejudice after her first operation results in the patient's death.

NIGHTMARE AT FORT KILLMAN (5:24) # 27830

Air date: March 8, 1967; Guest stars: James Daly, Les Crane; Teleplay: John and Ward Hawkins; Producer: Cy Chermak; Director: Abner Biberman.

Accosted by two men, Stacey Grainger finds himself in Army uniform accused of being new recruit Willard J. Thorne and becomes implicated in a case of bribery, deceit and murder involving Sgt. Tom Beale (Johnny Seven) and Sgt. Joe Trapp (James Daly).

BITTER HARVEST (5:25) # 27835

Air date: March 15, 1967; Guest stars: Whitney Blake, Larry Pennell, John Lupton; Teleplay: Andy Lewis; Director: Don McDougall.

Learning that struggling farmer Frank Adams (John Lupton) is being forced off his land by homesteaders, the Virginian intervenes and becomes entangled in a range war.

A WELCOMING TOWN (5:26) # 27848

Air date: March 22, 1967; Guest stars: Robert Fuller, Frank Overton, Carole Wells; Teleplay: Sy Salkowitz; Based on a screenplay by William Talman and Norman Jolley; Producer: Cy Chermak; Director: Abner Biberman.

Family deception comes to the surface when Trampas uncovers the truth behind the disappearance of the woman (Jocelyn Brando) who helped raise him and the violent death of her son.

THE GIRL ON THE PINTO (5:27) # 27812

Air date: March 29, 1967; Guest stars: None; Teleplay: Seeleg Lester and Theodore Apstein; Story: Theodore Apstein; Producer: Joel Rogosin; Director: Don McDougall.

Trampas becomes determined to discover the truth behind the adoption of a girl he met.

LADY OF THE HOUSE (5:28) # 27846

Air date: April 5, 1967; Guest star: Myrna Loy; Teleplay: Leslie Stevens; Producer: Cy Chermak; Director: Abner Biberman.

Mrs. Miles (Myrna Loy) agrees to help old friend John Grainger with the Shiloh household duties and "educate" Stacey and Elizabeth. But her refined manner masks a deep resentment of the Graingers and she plans to break the family apart.

THE STRANGE QUEST OF CLAIRE BINGHAM (5:29) # 27839

Air date: April 12, 1967; Guest stars: Andrew Prine, Sandra Smith; Teleplay: Joseph Hoffman, True Boardman and Winston Miller; Director: Don McDougall.

Mistaken for a long-lost brother by a nurse (Sandra Smith), accused murderer Chuck Larson (Andrew Prine) escapes custody, helped by Bingham, unknown to the pursuing Emmett Ryker.

Season Six

26 × 75 min. (1967–68)
Executive Producer—Norman MacDonnell **(6:01–6:26)**

RECKONING (6:01) # 28523

Air date: September 13, 1967; Guest stars: Charles Bronson, Dick Foran; Teleplay: Ed Waters; Producer: Joel Rogosin; Director: Abner Biberman.

Held hostage by outlaw Harge Talbot (Charles Bronson), Elizabeth Grainger must deliver his wife's (Miriam Colon) baby while the Virginian attempts to secure her release.

THE DEADLY PAST (6:02) # 28504

Air date: September 20, 1967; Guest stars: Darren McGavin, Linden Chiles, Mary Robin Redd; Teleplay: Phyllis and Robert White; Producer: Cy Chermak; Director: Abner Biberman.

Troubled by a letter listing his name, among six others, along with the dates of their deaths, Trampas decides to visit the three remaining living persons on the list and discovers a link to the town of Wicksville.

THE LADY FROM WICHITA (6:03) # 28516

Air date: September 27, 1967; Guest star: Joan Collins; Special guest star: Rose Marie; Teleplay: True Boardman; Producer: Winston Miller; Director: Don McDougall.

Inheriting a ranch near Medicine Bow, Lorna Marie Marshall (Joan Collins) and Belle Stephens (Rose Marie) become subject to blackmail when details of their shady past surface.

STAR CROSSED (6:04) # 28508

Air date: October 4, 1967; Guest stars: Tom Tryon, Lisabeth Hush, Kiel Martin, Brian Nash; Teleplay: Don Tait; Producer: Joel Rogosin; Director: Abner Biberman.

Emmett Ryker assists former outlaw Andrew Hiller (Tom Tryon) in his attempts to start a new life, but a Shiloh ranch hand hampers his efforts by threatening Hiller with blackmail.

JOHNNY MOON (6:05) # 28531

Air date: October 11, 1967; Guest stars: Tom Bell, Ben Johnson, Michael Higgins, Bo Hopkins; Teleplay: Stanford Whitmore; Producer: David Levinson; Director: Abner Biberman.

Canadian Mountie Johnny Moon (Tom Bell), recuperating at Shiloh Ranch from wounds sustained in pursuing a killer across the border, places the Virginian in a moral dilemma when he discovers that Moon is a deserter.

The Masquerade (6:06) # 28517

Air date: October 18, 1967; Guest stars: Lloyd Nolan, David Hartman, Diana Muldaur; Teleplay: Norman Katkov; Producer: Winston Miller; Director: Don McDougall.

Timorous George Foster (David Hartman) poses as sheriff of Medicine Bow to please his unsuspecting father (Lloyd Nolan), an ex-sheriff who believes his son is carrying on his legacy. But Foster is forced to put his masquerade to the test.

Ah Sing vs. Wyoming (6:07) # 28520

Air date: October 25, 1967; Guest stars: Edmond O'Brien, Aki Aleong, Lloyd Bochner; Teleplay: Irve Tunick; Producer: Cy Chermak; Director: Charles S. Dubin.

Denied a restaurant license, Ah Sing (Aki Aleong) opens one in defiance of the law and exposes the racial prejudice of a local justice of the peace.

Bitter Autumn (6:08) # 28518

Air date: November 1, 1967; Guest stars: John Anderson, Richard X. Slattery, Jeanette Nolan, Steve Carlson; Special guest star: John McIntire; Introducing: Shelly Novack; Teleplay: David and Andy Lewis; Story: Ken Finley; Producer: Joel Rogosin; Director: Don McDougall.

Taking over duties at Shiloh Ranch while John Grainger is away on business, Clay Grainger (John McIntire) has to deal with diseased cattle, the accidental death of a woman (Virginia Gregg) and a husband (John Anderson) out for revenge.

A Bad Place to Die (6:09) # 28522

Air date: November 8, 1967; Preempted: November 15, 1967; Guest star: Victor Jory; Special guest star: John McIntire; Teleplay: Judith and Robert Guy Barrows; Producer: Joel Rogosin; Director: Don McDougall.

In a desperate attempt to save his life after he is falsely accused of murder and sentenced to hang, Trampas joins cell mate Luke Nichols (Victor Jory) and two other convicts in a plan to break out of jail.

Paid in Full (6:10) # 28514

Air date: November 22, 1967; Guest stars: James Whitmore, Don Stroud; Special guest star: John McIntire; Teleplay: Richard Wendley; Producer: Winston Miller; Director: Don McDougall.

Disabled after saving Trampas' life in a stampede, rancher Ezra Hollis (James Whitmore) refuses to accept his property deed from Clay Grainger as a reward. But son Frank (Don Stroud) has different intentions, blaming Clay and Trampas for his father's crippled leg.

To Bear Witness (6:11) # 28512

Air date: November 29, 1967; Guest stars: William Windom, Joanna Moore, Malachi Throne; Special guest star: John McIntire; Teleplay: Sy Salkowitz; Producer: Cy Chermak; Director: Abner Biberman.

Trampas is subjected to intimidation after claiming he saw Doc Baldwin (Malachi Throne) at the scene of the murder of a man Baldwin had been in dispute with over property for a new Medicine Bow hospital.

The Barren Ground (6:12) # 28533

Air date: December 6, 1967; Guest stars: Jay C. Flippen, Collin Wilcox; Special guest star: John McIntire; Teleplay: Andy Lewis; Story: Joy Dexter; Director: Abner Biberman.

Killing a young man in self-defense, the Virginian is warned by the man's father to beware of his avenging brother and asked to convince his daughter to return home.

EXECUTION AT TRISTE (6:13) # 28537

Air date: December 13, 1967; Guest stars: Robert Lansing, Sharon Farrell, Burt Douglas; Teleplay: John Dunkel; Producer: Norman MacDonnell; Director: Robert L. Friend.

On a stopover in Triste, waiting for a cattle transaction to come through, Trampas becomes involved in a showdown with legendary gunfighter Lee Knight (Robert Lansing).

A SMALL TASTE OF JUSTICE (6:14) # 28507

Air date: December 20, 1967; Guest stars: Peter Brown, Susan Oliver, John Lupton; Teleplay: Edward J. Lakso; Producer: Joel Rogosin; Director: Don McDougall.

The Virginian comes to the aid of the townspeople of Three Falls, terrorized by a bullying rancher's son (Peter Brown) and a group of ranch hands.

THE FORTRESS (6:15) # 28528

Air date: December 27, 1967; Guest star: Leslie Nielsen; Special guest star: John McIntire; Teleplay: Sy Salkowitz; Story: Sy Salkowitz and W. R. Burnett; Director: Abner Biberman.

Cheated out of $100,000 for cattle delivered to a buyer in Canada, the Virginian attempts to retrieve his money with the help of the beautiful Francoise (Barbara Bouchet).

THE DEATH WAGON (6:16) # 28540

Air date: January 3, 1968; Guest stars: Albert Salmi, Michael Constantine, Tim McIntire; Special guest star: John McIntire; Teleplay: James Menzies; Producer: David Levinson; Director: Darrell Hallenbeck.

Trampas is confronted with his past when the search for an escaped outlaw, believed to be infected with scarlet fever, brings back painful memories of his mother and brothers' death from the disease.

JED (6:17) # 28542

Air date: January 10, 1968; Guest stars: Steve Ihnat, Brenda Scott, Sammy Jackson; Teleplay: Arthur Heinemann; Producer: James Duff McAdams; Director: Abner Biberman.

Jed Matthews (Steve Ihnat) finds his loyalties divided between his feelings for rival farmer's daughter Abby Kiefer (Brenda Scott) and his attempts at stopping a range war.

WITH HELP FROM ULYSSES (6:18) # 28529

Air date: January 17, 1968; Guest stars: Barbara Rhoades, Jill Donohue, Eileen Wesson, Shaggy the dog; Teleplay: True Boardman; Producer: Winston Miller; Director: Don McDougall.

Trampas is accompanied by a shaggy dog called Ulysses as he searches for an old prospector's niece with an identifying birthmark above her knee. Trouble ensues when *two* saloon girls claim to be the niece.

GENTLE TAMERS (6:19) # 28524

Air date: January 24, 1968; Guest stars: None; Introducing: Jean Peloquin; Teleplay: Don Tait; Story: Abe Polsky and Gil Lasky; Producer: Joel Rogosin; Director: Tony Leader.

Hiring three convicts (Val Tussey, Dan Moss and Ira Diller) for a new rehabilitation program, Clay Grainger and The Virginian keep the convict's identities secret until one of them decides to rustle cattle.

THE GOOD-HEARTED BADMAN (6:20) # 28549

Air date: February 7, 1968; Guest stars: Peter Deuel, Jeanette Nolan; Special guest star: John Larch; Teleplay: Robert Van Scoyk; Producer: James Duff McAdams; Director: James Sheldon.

Elizabeth Grainger falls for the charms of handsome "Thomas Baker" (Peter Deuel) as he recuperates from wounds at Shiloh Ranch. When Clay and Holly Grainger discover his true identity, they fear for the safety of Elizabeth.

THE HELL WIND (6:21) # 28509

Air date: February 14, 1968; Guest stars: Patricia Crowley, Ford Rainey; Teleplay: Barbara Merlin and Leonard Praskins; Producer: Winston Miller; Director: Don McDougall.

Taking shelter in an isolated cabin during a wind storm, Trampas, Stacey and Elizabeth Grainger are joined by a banker (Ford Rainey) and his card shark wife (Patricia Crowley), a bank teller and a drifter.

THE CROOKED PATH (6:22) # 28535

Air date: February 21, 1968; Guest stars: None; Teleplay: Robert Presnell, Jr.; Story: Jerry Ludwig; Director: Abner Biberman.

Trampas' childhood friend Kiley Cheever (Kevin Coughlin) is hired by the Virginian and soon causes trouble with his arrogant manner and pursuit of Elizabeth Grainger.

STACEY (6:23) # 28525

Air date: February 28, 1968; Guest stars: None; Teleplay: Douglas Morrow; Producer: Joel Rogosin; Director: Leo Penn.

Stacey Grainger, depressed by an accident that leaves his broken arm paralyzed, is rejected by his new girlfriend (Lee Kroeger). Clay Grainger and the Virginian decide the best cure is a dose of tough love.

THE HANDY MAN (6:24) # 28545

Air date: March 6, 1968; Guest stars: Tom Simcox, Jeanette Nolan; Special guest star: Mel Tormé; Teleplay: Mel Tormé; Producer: Joel Rogosin; Director: Abner Biberman.

A handyman comes to Trampas' aid when a neighboring rancher's son resorts to violence to gain control of Shiloh land and Trampas is accused of killing their top hand.

THE DECISION (6:25) # 28554

Air date: March 13, 1968; Guest stars: Kenneth Tobey, Monica Lewis, Steve Carlson, Ben Murphy; Teleplay: Richard Carr; Producer: David Levinson; Director: Darrell Hallenbeck.

A selfish wife forces Sheriff Dan Porter (Kenneth Tobey) into a change of career, but learning ranching at Shiloh only opens up old wounds between himself and Trampas.

SETH (6:26) # 28527

Air date: March 20, 1968; Guest star: Michael Burns; Teleplay: Reuben Bercovitch; Producer-Director: Joel Rogosin.

Finding a starving youngster (Michael Burns) alone in mountain country, Trampas offers him a job at Shiloh. But the youngster is torn between a new life at Shiloh and returning to his uncle and an outlaw life.

Season Seven

26 × 75 min. (1968–69)
Executive Producer—Norman MacDonnell **(7:01–7:26)**

THE SADDLE WARMER (7:01) # 29218

Air date: September 18, 1968; Guest stars: Ralph Bellamy, Chris Robinson, Quentin Dean, Tom Skerritt; Teleplay: Robert Van Scoyk; Producer: James Duff McAdams; Director: Charles S. Dubin.

Trampas and the Shiloh ranch hands give newcomer David Sutton a hard time after he ropes and tames a wild Appaloosa meant as a surprise gift to Elizabeth Grainger.

SILVER IMAGE (7:02) # 29213

Air date: September 25, 1968; Guest stars: James Daly, Bob Random, Geraldine Brooks; Teleplay: Don Tait; Story-Producer: Joel Rogosin; Director: Don McDougall.

A woman's (Geraldine Brooks) decision to sell her ranch to an oil speculator and risk the chance of destroying grazing land causes concern in Medicine Bow.

THE ORCHARD (7:03) # 29215

Air date: October 2, 1968; Guest stars: Burgess Meredith, William Windom, Brandon de Wilde, Ben Murphy; Teleplay: Andy Lewis; Story: Ken Finlay; Producer: James Duff McAdams; Director: James Sheldon.

Struggling farmer Tim Bradbury (Burgess Meredith), former partner to Clay Grainger on a thriving Texas ranch, feels Clay owes him from years back after a cattle deal left him broke. The actions of his two sons add to his troubles until he is forced to accept change in his way of thinking.

VISION OF BLINDNESS (7:04) # 29226

Air date: October 9, 1968; Guest stars: John Saxon. Ben Johnson; Teleplay: Gerald Sanford and James Menzies; Story: Gerald Sanford; Producer: David Levinson; Director: Abner Biberman.

Recently released convict (John Saxon) comes across Elizabeth Grainger, blinded following a stagecoach accident. He has ulterior motives for her safe return to Shiloh, seeking revenge on Trampas for the death of his brother.

THE WIND OF OUTRAGE (7:05) # 29209

Air date: October 16, 1968; Guest stars: Ricardo Montalban, Lois Nettleton, Lawrence Dane; Teleplay: Alvin Sapinsley; Producer: James Duff McAdams; Director: James Sheldon.

Exiled from Canada, a Metis revolutionary (Ricardo Montalban) faces tough decisions when fellow Metis ask him to return and fight for his Indian homeland, forcing him to leave his fiancée (Lois Nettleton) behind.

IMAGE OF AN OUTLAW (7:06) # 29222

Air date: October 23, 1968; Guest stars: Don Stroud, Amy Thomson; Teleplay: Joseph Hoffman; Producer: Winston Miller; Director: Don McDougall.

Refused a bank loan, Rafe Judson (Don Stroud) capitalizes on his strong resemblance to infamous outlaw Wally McCullough, posing as McCullough to rob a stage. But the real McCullough (also Stroud) learns of the imposter and plans his revenge.

THE HERITAGE (7:07) # 29207

Air date: October 30, 1968; Guest star: Buffy Sainte-Marie; Teleplay: Stephen Lord; Producer: Joel Rogosin; Director: Leo Penn.

A Shoshone girl (Buffy Sainte-Marie) returning from a school in the East finds her people intimidated by a local rancher (Jim Davis) and his men over the right of way of his cattle herd.

Ride to Misadventure (7:08) # 29220

Air date: November 6, 1968; Guest stars: Joseph Campanella, Katherine Justice; Teleplay: Gerald Sanford; Producer: James Duff McAdams; Director: Michael Caffey.

Waiting for vaccine for anthrax-infected cattle, Clay Grainger is told by a bounty hunter (Joseph Campanella) that the Collen gang stole the stage carrying the vaccine. The Virginian and David Sutton attempt to track the gang but the presence of the bounty hunter and his hostage (Katherine Justice) complicates matters.

The Storm Gate (7:09) # 29216

Air date: November 13, 1968; Pre-empted Air date: November 20, 1968; Guest stars: Susan Oliver, Burr DeBenning, Scott Brady; Teleplay: Jerry McNeely and Alvin Sapinsley; Story: Jerry McNeely; Producer: James Duff McAdams; Director: Richard A. Colla.

Discovering old friend Jason Crowder (Burr DeBenning) intends to cheat the townspeople of River Oaks out of farming land and sell it to the railroad, Trampas confronts him and ends up the target of Crowder's anger.

The Dark Corridor (7:10) # 29204

Air date: November 27, 1968; Guest stars: Judith Lang, John Smith, Paul Winchell; Teleplay: Jean Holloway; Story: Jean Holloway and Joel Rogosin; Producer: Joel Rogosin; Director: Abner Biberman.

Taking an unconscious girl to a friend's cabin in the woods to recover, the Virginian becomes the object of her affections. But her amnesia causes growing concern when a stranger, who appears to know her, arrives at the cabin.

The Mustangers (7:11) # 29228

Air date: December 4, 1968; Guest stars: John Agar, James Edwards, Don Knight; Teleplay: Norman Jolley; Producer: David Levinson; Director: Charles S. Dubin.

An aging cowboy resorts to horse rustling to help send his son through school. But his plans hit trouble when his unappreciative son is hired at Shiloh.

Nora (7:12) # 29223

Air date: December 11, 1968; Guest stars: Anne Baxter, Hugh Beaumont, Tim McIntire; Teleplay: True Boardman; Producer: Winston Miller; Director: Don McDougall.

Clay Grainger's old girlfriend Nora Carlton (Anne Baxter), captured by Comanche Indians, sees a chance to exploit the situation and enhance the career prospects of her Army officer husband (Hugh Beaumont).

Big Tiny (7:13) # 29231

Air date: December 18, 1968; Preempted: **Silver Image** (7:02)—Air date: December 25, 1968—Preempted: January 1, 1969; Guest stars: Julie Sommars, Roger Torrey; Teleplay: Joy Dexter and Norman Katkov; Story: Joy Dexter; Producer: Winston Miller; Director: James Sheldon.

A bull-buying trip to Durango by Trampas and David Sutton becomes complicated when Sutton agrees to pose as the fiancé of Martha Carson (Julie Sommars) in the hope of keeping an unwelcome suitor at bay.

Stopover (7:14) # 29201

Air date: January 8, 1969; Guest stars: Jay C. Flippen, Herb Jeffries, Douglas Henderson, Kevin Hagen; Teleplay: John Kneubuhl; Producer-Director: Joel Rogosin.

Guilty consciences surface when hired gun Frank Hammel (Herb Jeffries) comes to Medicine Bow and townspeople fear they could be his target.

DEATH WAIT (7:15) # 29229

Air date: January 15, 1969; Guest stars: Harold J. Stone, Sheila Larkin, Murray MacLeod; Teleplay: Gerald Sanford; Producer: David Levinson; Director: Charles S. Dubin.

Following the killing of Case Buchanan (Clyde Ventura) in self-defense, David Sutton must face Buchanan's father (Harold J. Stone) and brother (Murray MacLeod), both set on revenge.

LAST GRAVE AT SOCORRO CREEK (7:16) # 29212

Air date: January 22, 1969; Guest stars: Kevin Coughlin, Steve Ihnat, Lonny Chapman, James Wainwright; Teleplay: Stanford Whitmore, Nathaniel Tanchuck and David Levinson; Director: Leo Penn.

The Virginian's attempts at finding the truth behind the lynching of a friend are hampered by a violent killer and the dead man's son, who wants reparation.

CRIME WAVE IN BUFFALO SPRINGS (7:17) # 29232

Air date: January 29, 1969; Guest stars: Yvonne DeCarlo, Carrie Snodgress, Ann Prentiss, James Brolin, Gary Vinson, The Irish Rovers, Tom Bosley; Teleplay: Robert Van Scoyk; Producer: James Duff McAdams; Director: Charles S. Dubin.

Trampas and David Sutton become caught in the middle of a feud between banker Nat Trumbull (Tom Bosley) and saloon owner Imogene Delphinia (Yvonne DeCarlo).

THE PRICE OF LOVE (7:18) # 29221

Air date: February 12, 1969; Guest star: Peter Deuel; Special guest star: James Gregory; Teleplay: Dick Carr; Producer: David Levinson; Director: Michael Caffey.

Denny Todd (Peter Deuel) is reunited with Clay and Holly Grainger, who took him in as a child in Texas. But a dispute over water rights sees Todd accused of murder.

THE ORDEAL (7:19) # 29205

Air date: February 19, 1969; Guest star: Robert Pine; Teleplay: Don Ingalls; Story: Merwin Gerrard; Producer: Winston Miller; Director: Michael Caffey.

Scott Austin, the pampered son of Clay Grainger's wealthy friend, is hired at Shiloh to toughen him up. But when negligence results in the death of Elizabeth Grainger's prize colt, he runs away. The care of a badly injured Virginian finally forces him to accept responsibility.

THE LAND DREAMER (7:20) # 29230

Air date: February 26, 1969; Guest stars: James Olson, Cloris Leachman; Special guest star: Don Francks; Teleplay: Robert Van Scoyk; Producer: James Duff McAdams; Director: James Sheldon.

Fleeing after killing a crooked businessman, Hosea McKinley (James Olson) is brought back to Medicine Bow for trial by the Virginian, Trampas and Sutton. Now he is confronted with a lynch mob.

EILEEN (7:21) # 29202

Air date: March 5, 1969; Guest stars: Debbie Watson, Richard Van Vleet; Teleplay: Don Ingalls; Producer: Winston Miller; Director: Tony Leader.

A young girl stays at Shiloh, allowing time for her romance with boyfriend Peter Bowers (Richard Van Vleet) to cool down. But when Bowers turns up at Shiloh his true feelings are revealed when he kidnaps her as ransom to pay off a gambling debt.

INCIDENT AT DIABLO CROSSING (7:22) # 29214

Air date: March 12, 1969; Guest stars: Gary Collins, Kiel Martin, Lee Kroeger, Steve Carlson, Bernie Hamilton, Anthony Caruso; Teleplay: Margaret and Andrew Blanc and Joel Rogosin; Story: Margaret and Andrew Blanc; Producer: Joel Rogosin; Director: William Witney.

A missing government payroll box becomes the focus of attention of a group of stagecoach passengers, stranded at the Diablo ferry crossing.

STORM OVER SHILOH (7:23) # 29203

Air date: March 19, 1969; Guest stars: None; Teleplay: Frank Chase; Producer: Joel Rogosin; Director: Michael Caffey.

Taking shelter from a storm, Elizabeth Grainger is trapped in an abandoned mineshaft following a cave-in. The Virginian, Trampas and the Graingers put their lives at risk to rescue her.

THE GIRL IN THE SHADOWS (7:24) # 29206

Air date: March 26, 1969; Guest stars: Jack Albertson, Brenda Scott; Teleplay: Robert Van Scoyk and Phyllis and Robert White; Story: Phyllis and Robert White; Director: James Sheldon.

A young woman in a mind-reading act (Brenda Scott) claims to be the daughter of Clay Grainger's late brother in order to cheat Elizabeth Grainger out of half her inheritance.

FOX, HOUND AND THE WIDOW MCCLOUD (7:25) # 29219

Air date: April 2, 1969; Guest stars: Victor Jory, Troy Donahue, Jean Inness; Teleplay: Judith Barrows; Producer: Joel Rogosin; Director: Don McDougall.

Fugitive Luke Nichols (Victor Jory) drops in on his old friend Trampas. A pursuing bounty hunter (Troy Donahue) forces Nichols into hiding at a local widow's farm.

THE STRANGER (7:26) # 29208

Air date: April 9, 1969; Guest star: Shelly Novack; Teleplay: Mel Goldberg; Producer: Joel Rogosin; Director: Michael Caffey.

When a quiet ranch hand (Shelly Novack) is convicted and sentenced to hang for robbery and murder, the Virginian attempts to prove his innocence.

Season Eight

24 × 75 min. (1969–70)
Executive Producer—Norman MacDonnell **(8:01–8:24)**

THE LONG RIDE HOME (8:01) # 30004

Air date: September 17, 1969; Guest star: Leslie Nielsen; Teleplay: Richard Fielder; Director: Charles S. Dubin.

Drifter Ben Stratton (Leslie Nielsen) has plans to buy a ranch. When his money is stolen, Stratton sets out to find the culprits responsible. Meanwhile his teenage sidekick, Jim Horn, decides to stay on at Shiloh Ranch.

A FLASH OF BLINDNESS (8:02) # 30020

Air date: September 24, 1969; Guest stars: James Whitmore; Introducing: Pamela McMyler; Story: Edward J. Lasko; Producer: Paul Freeman; Director: Joseph Pevney.

A fall from his horse results in blindness for the Virginian. He must now also contend with a man (James Whitmore) and his two sons who intend to kill the Virginian to conceal their horse-rustling activities.

HALFWAY BACK FROM HELL (8:03) # 30003

Air date: October 1, 1969; Guest stars: William Windom, John Dehner, Susan Howard, Murray MacLeod; Teleplay: Alvin Sapinsley; Story: Alvin Sapinsley and James Duff McAdams; Producer: James Duff McAdams; Director: Michael Caffey.

A reluctant Trampas takes over as foreman at an Arizona prison rehabilitation ranch after the original foreman is killed. But local townspeople and Marshall Teague (John Dehner) are hostile to the ranch and wary of its motives.

THE POWER SEEKERS (8:04) # 30005

Air date: October 8, 1969; Guest stars: Barry Sullivan, Andrew Prine, Davey Davison; Teleplay: Robert Van Scoyk; Producer: James Duff McAdams; Director: Seymour Robbie.

Clay Grainger accepts an offer to run for Wyoming's territorial legislature and comes up against a ruthless candidate (Andrew Prine) willing to sacrifice land promised to the Arapaho Indians and spread lies about Grainger's integrity.

THE FAMILY MAN (8:05) # 30023

Air date: October 15, 1969; Guest stars: Darleen Carr, Frank Webb; Teleplay: Arthur Heinemann; Producer: Paul Freeman; Director: Joseph Pevney.

Caring for a young woman (Darleen Carr) and her newborn baby, Jim Horn falls in love with the woman. But a request sent by her fugitive husband (Frank Webb) to join him threatens Horn's happiness.

THE RUNAWAY (8:06) # 30013

Air date: October 22, 1969; Guest stars: Guy Stockwell, Peter Whitney, Jan Shepard, Johnny Whitaker; Teleplay: Gerald Sanford; Producer: Norman MacDonnell; Director: Tony Leader.

Running away from a home for wayward boys, Hoot Bayo (Johnny Whitaker) finds refuge at Shiloh and seeks his birth father (Guy Stockwell), who unbeknownst to him is the local town drunk.

A LOVE TO REMEMBER (8:07) # 30008

Air date: October 29, 1969; Guest stars: Diane Baker, Fred Beir; Teleplay: Ben Masselink; Producer: Paul Freeman; Director: Joseph Pevney.

The Virginian's romantic feelings for Boston artist-reporter Julie Oakes (Diane Baker) are frustrated when she becomes fascinated with businessman Ord Glover (Fred Beir), a man she suspects of killing her husband and young son.

THE SUBSTITUTE (8:08) # 30026

Air date: November 5, 1969; Preempted: November 21, 1969; Guest stars: Dennis Cooney, Beverlee McKinsey; Teleplay: Gerald Sanford; Producer: Norman MacDonnell; Director: Tony Leader.

Trampas is arrested for the murder of a small town doctor and positively identified by a saloon waitress. But Trampas pleads his innocence and has his own suspicions about the real identity of the murderer.

THE BUGLER (8:09) # 30015

Air date: November 19, 1969; Guest stars: Michael Burns, Morgan Woodward, Alan Hale, Jr.; Teleplay: Jeb Rosebrook and Jerry Day; Story: Jerry Day; Producer: Howard Christie; Director: Tony Leader.

Learning that Private Toby Hamilton (Michael Burns) deserted his Army post after receiving punishment for refusing an order, Clay Grainger arranges a meeting between the youngster and his Army officer father.

HOME TO METHUSELAH (8:10) # 30033

Air date: November 26, 1969; Guest stars: Audrey Totter, John Anderson; Teleplay: Jack Miller; Story-Producer: Paul Freeman; Director: Abner Biberman.

Invited on a hunting trip to the Teton Mountains, the Virginian soon realizes his old friend Sheriff Seth James (John Anderson) isn't interested in hunting game but is hunting two men responsible, in part, for deaths caused by dynamite at a bank.

A TOUCH OF HANDS (8:11) # 30010

Air date: December 3, 1969; Guest stars: Michael Constantine, Belinda Montgomery; Teleplay: John Dunkel; Producer: Norman MacDonnell; Director: Tony Leader.

Peg Halstead (Belinda Montgomery) goes ahead with plans to wed Trampas, despite her sick father's (Michael Constantine) attempts at bribing Trampas to postpone the marriage.

JOURNEY TO SCATHELOCK (8:12) # 30022

Air date: December 10, 1969; Guest stars: Burr DeBenning, Anne Helm; Teleplay: Alvin Sapinsley; Producer: James Duff McAdams; Director: Seymour Robbie.

Following a saloon girl's (Anne Helm) advice to place $4,000 in a hotel safe, Jim Horn ends up pursuing the girl and her accomplice into Canada to retrieve the stolen cash.

A WOMAN OF STONE (8:13) # 30017

Air date: December 17, 1969; Preempted: **Crime Wave in Buffalo Springs** (7:17)—Air date: December 24, 1969; Guest stars: Bethel Leslie, Charles Drake, Tim Holt; Teleplay: Gerry Day; Producer: Howard Christie; Director: Abner Biberman.

Cath Contrell's (Bethel Leslie) plans for revenge on her husband for abandoning her to Shoshone Indians in a raid many years ago come into conflict when she learns her daughter is about to be married.

BLACK JADE (8:14) # 30025

Air date: December 31, 1969; Guest stars: William Shatner, James A. Watson, Jill Townsend; Teleplay: Herb Meadow; Producer: Paul Freeman; Director: Joseph Pevney.

Trampas recognizes a photo of a friend's wife in a pocket watch. Prejudice and bigotry surface when he tracks the "owner" of the watch, Cobey Jade (James A. Watson), to a ghost town and encounters a gang of Southern outlaws.

YOU CAN LEAD A HORSE TO WATER (8:15) # 30027

Air date: January 7, 1970; Guest stars: Strother Martin, Elizabeth Hubbard, Noah Beery, Jr.; Teleplay: Lois Hire; Producer: Howard Christie; Director: Joseph Pevney.

When Mary Marshall (Elizabeth Hubbard) is robbed of $2000 in a stagecoach robbery, Trampas, Marshall and a horse trader (Strother Martin) set off in pursuit.

NIGHTMARE (8:16) # 30030

Air date: January 21, 1970; Guest stars: Joan Crawford; Teleplay: Gerry Day and Bethel Leslie; Director: Robert Gist.

Ill fortune trails the recently married Stephanie White (Joan Crawford) after her husband is left paralyzed and her home destroyed in a fire. But even worse is to come when she's accused of manslaughter.

HOLOCAUST A.K.A. THE SHILOH YEARS (8:17) # 30029

Air date: January 28, 1970; Guest stars: Tony Franciosa, Harold J. Stone; Teleplay: Robert Van Scoyk; Story-Producer: James Duff McAdams; Director: Jeannot Szwarc.

Clay Grainger faces financial ruin: The Shiloh Ranch burns to the ground following a rift with the Cattleman's Association over the falling price of beef.

TRAIN OF DARKNESS (8:18) # 30035

Air date: February 4, 1970; Guest stars: Dennis Weaver, John Larch, Kaz Garas, Charlotte Stewart; Special guest stars: Barbara Werle, Gerald S. O'Loughlin; Teleplay: Robert Van Scoyk; Producer: James Duff McAdams; Director: James Sheldon.

Clay and Elizabeth Grainger and Jim Horn find themselves among an ill-assorted group of passengers on the night train to Medicine Bow. A young farmer (Patrick Tovatt) wants the man who murdered his brother, hired gun Judge Harker (Dennis Weaver), to receive justice at the hands of a lynch mob who wait to ambush the train.

A TIME OF TERROR (8:19) # 30024

Air date: February 11, 1970; Guest stars: Joseph Cotten, Shelly Novack; Teleplay: Edward J. Lasko; Director: Joseph Pevney.

Clay Grainger's friend Judge Will McMasters (Joseph Cotten) is invited to Shiloh, unaware that two men (Shelly Novack and Phillip Afford) and their sister are holding the Graingers captive and laying a trap for the man they blame for their father's death.

NO WAR FOR THE WARRIOR (8:20) # 30006

Air date: February 18, 1970; Guest stars: Henry Jones, Charles Aidman, Charles Robinson, David Sheiner; Teleplay: Alvin Sapinsley; Story: Robert Earll; Producer: James Duff McAdams; Director: Don McDougall.

A sympathetic Jim Horn helps a captured Indian (Charles Robinson) escape from jail, then ends up in jail himself. The fugitive Indian must decide whether to return and help his friend or escape into Canada.

A KING'S RANSOM (8:21) # 30019

Air date: February 25, 1970; Guest stars: Patrick Macnee, Jackie DeShannon; Teleplay: John D. F. Black; Producer: Paul Freeman; Director: Joseph Pevney.

Ambushed and held for ransom in an abandoned mine shaft, an Australian gang threatens Clay Grainger with death and Medicine Bow with destruction unless they receive $20,000.

THE SINS OF THE FATHER (8:22) # 30031

Air date: March 4, 1970; Guest stars: Robert Lipton, Tim McIntire; Teleplay: David P. Harman; Producer: Howard Christie; Director: Walter Doniger.

Clay Grainger plays a waiting game when a newcomer (Robert Lipton) to Shiloh proves to be a troublemaker. Clay is aware the boy has come to Shiloh to seek revenge on him for the death of the boy's father, Josh Randall, 25 years ago.

RICH MAN, POOR MAN (8:23) # 30028

Air date: March 11, 1970; Guest stars: Jack Elam, Patrick Morrow, Michael Larrain; Teleplay: Arthur Heinemann; Producer: John Choy; Director: Tony Leader.

When downtrodden farmer Harv Yost (Jack Elam) receives $10,000 reward for the recovery of stolen money, he squanders his good fortune on self-indulgence and a ranch he can't afford in an attempt to prove himself better than Clay Grainger.

THE GIFT (8:24) # 30036

Air date: March 18, 1970; Guest stars: Tab Hunter, Julie Gregg, Frank Marth; Teleplay: Robert Van Scoyk; Producer: James Duff McAdams; Director: Seymour Robbie.

A saloon singer (Julie Gregg) and former girlfriend of Trampas becomes romantically involved with Jim Horn and the focus of attention of an outlaw looking for stolen money.

Season Nine—The Men from Shiloh

24 × 75 min. (1970–71)
Executive Producers—Norman MacDonnell, Herbert Hirschman, Leslie Stevens, Edward J. Montagne
Main Title Design— Jack Cole

THE WEST VS. COLONEL MACKENZIE (9:01) # 31712

Air date: September 16, 1970; Guest stars: Elizabeth Ashley, Martha Hyer, Don DeFore, John Larch; Teleplay: Jean Holloway; Executive Producer: Herbert Hirschman; Director: Murray Golden and Jerry Hopper.

Following the hanging of an alleged cattle rustler, Col. Mackenzie, new owner of Shiloh Ranch, becomes involved in a dispute with the Cattleman's Association.

THE BEST MAN (9:02) # 31715

Air date: September 23, 1970; Guest stars: Desi Arnaz, Katy Jurado, James Farentino; Teleplay-Executive Producer: Leslie Stevens; Producer: Glen A. Larson; Director: Russ Mayberry.

Trampas becomes involved in a family feud involving a border town chieftain (Desi Arnaz), his daughter and two suitors.

JENNY (9:03)

Air date: September 30, 1970; Guest star: Janet Leigh, John Ireland, Charles Drake; Teleplay: Arthur Heinemann; Executive Producer: Norman MacDonnell; Director: Harry Harris.

The Virginian's ex-girlfriend Jenny Davis (Janet Leigh) hides a secret that puts their lives in peril when they find themselves hiding in the desert from outlaws.

WITH LOVE, BULLETS AND VALENTINES (9:04) # 31710

Air date: October 7, 1970; Guest stars: Art Carney, Tom Ewell, Deborah Walley, Jack Albertson; Teleplay-Producer: Glen A Larson; Executive Producer: Leslie Stevens; Director: Philip Leacock.

After losing his riverboat to Trampas in a poker game, Capt. Skeet (Art Carney) becomes involved in a silver bullion heist.

THE MYSTERIOUS MR. TATE (9:05)

Air date: October 14, 1970; Guest star: Robert Webber, Dane Clark; Teleplay: Jean Holloway; Executive Producer: Herbert Hirschman; Director: Abner Biberman.

Col. Mackenzie rescues Roy Tate from a lynch mob and offers him a job at Shiloh Ranch.

GUN QUEST (9:06) # 31722

Air date: October 21, 1970; Guest stars: Joseph Cotten, Brandon de Wilde, Anne Francis, John Smith, Agnes Moorehead, Neville Brand, Rod Cameron, Monte Markham; Introducing: Sallie Shockley; Teleplay: Robert Van Scoyk; Executive Producer: Norman MacDonnell; Director: Harry Harris.

The Virginian tracks down a hired gunman after escaping a hangman's noose.

CROOKED CORNER (9:07)

Air date: October 28, 1970; Guest stars: Susan Strasberg, Kurt Kasznar, Walter Koenig, Brock Peters; Teleplay: Harry Kronman; Executive Producer-Director: Herbert Hirschman.

German immigrants come under double jeopardy when night riders and the gunmen hired to protect both them threaten the settlers.

LADY AT THE BAR (9:08) # 31717

Air date: November 4, 1970; Guest stars: Greer Garson, E. G. Marshall, James Whitmore; Teleplay-Executive Producer: Leslie Stevens; Producer: Glen A. Larson; Director: Russ Mayberry.

A female barrister (Greer Garson) defends Trampas after he is accused of killing a mine owner.

THE PRICE OF THE HANGING (9:09) # 31708

Air date: November 11, 1970; Guest stars: Tom Tryon, Lew Ayres, Jane Wyatt, Edward Binns, Patricia Harty; Teleplay: Frank Chase; Executive Producer: Herbert Hirschman; Director: Marc Daniels.

Tate works to free a local doctor (Edward Binns) accused of killing a gambler.

EXPERIMENT AT NEW LIFE (9:10) # 31718

Air date: November 18, 1970; Preempted: November 25, 1970; Guest stars: Vera Miles, Sue Lyon, Ralph Meeker; Teleplay: Lois Hire; Executive Producer: Norman MacDonnell; Director: Jeannot Szwarc.

The Virginian becomes involved with a settlement attempting to enforce communal marriage.

FOLLOW THE LEADER (9:11) # 31728

Air date: December 2, 1970; Guest stars: Frank Gorshin, Tony Franciosa, Kate Woodville, Noah Beery, Jr.; Teleplay-Executive Producer: Leslie Stevens; Producer: Glen A. Larson; Director: Richard Benedict.

Outlaw Ritter Miley (Tony Franciosa) attempts to frame Trampas for a murder.

LAST OF THE COMANCHEROS (9:12) # 31725

Air date: December 9, 1970; Preempted: December 16, 1970—Preempted: **The Mysterious Mr. Tate** (9:05)—Air date: December 23, 1970; Guest stars: Ricardo Montalban, James Gregory, Beth Brickell, Carlos Romero; Teleplay: Don Tait; Executive Producer: Norman MacDonnell; Director: Michael Caffey.

Col. Mackenzie attempts to free a woman writer for the *New York World* (Beth Brickell) held hostage by Comancheros demanding $25,000 for her release.

HANNAH (9:13) # 31706

Air date: December 30, 1970; Guest stars: Lisa True Gerritsen, J. D. Cannon, Susan Oliver, Peter Breck, Warren Stevens; Teleplay: True Boardman; Executive Producer: Leslie Stevens; Producer: Glen A. Larson; Director: Jack Arnold.

Hannah (Lisa Gerritsen) enlists the aid of Trampas to help find her "lost" mother.

NAN ALLEN (9:14) # 31730

Air date: January 6, 1971; Guest stars: Diane Baker, E. G. Marshall; Teleplay: Dick Nelson; Executive Producer: Edward J. Montagne; Director: Jeff Hayden.

Col. Mackenzie has to contend with a jealous brother after falling for businesswoman Nan Allan (Diane Baker)

THE POLITICIAN (9:15) # 31714

Air date: January 13, 1971; Guest stars: William Windom, Diana Muldaur, John Ericson; Teleplay: Robert Van Scoyk; Story: Michael Fisher; Executive Producer: Norman MacDonnell; Director: Michael Caffey.

The Virginian becomes a suspect in the slaying of an ex-saloon girl.

THE ANIMAL (9:16) # 31735

Air date: 20 January 1971; Guest stars: Chuck Connors, Rudy Ramos, Katherine Crawford, Andy Devine, Leon Ames, Edd Byrnes, Scott Brady, Jack Ging; Teleplay: James Menzies; Producer: John Choy; Director: Don McDougall.

Tate rescues a deaf-mute Indian boy pursued by a posse for an alleged homicide.

THE LEGACY OF SPENCER FLATS (9:17) # 31731

Air date: January 27, 1971; Preempted: February 3, 1971; Guest stars: Bradford Dillman, Carolyn Jones, Ann Sothern, Edgar Buchanan; Teleplay: B. W. Sandefur; Executive Producer: Leslie Stevens; Producer: Glen A. Larson; Director: Russ Mayberry.

Trampas is mistaken for an escaped convict by a group of eccentrics living in a ghost town.

THE ANGUS KILLER (9:18) # 31727

Air date: February 10, 1971; Guest stars: Van Johnson, Dina Merrill, Ruth Roman, Stephen McNally, Chill Wills, Slim Pickens, Andrew Parks; Teleplay: Edward De Blasio and Robert Van Scoyk; Producer: John Choy; Director: Jeff Hayden.

After discovering a poisoned herd of cattle, the Virginian becomes embroiled in a homicide.

FLIGHT FROM MEMORY (9:19) # 31741

Air date: February 17, 1971; Guest stars: Burgess Meredith, Tisha Sterling, Robert Fuller; Teleplay: Jean Holloway and Gene L. Coon; Executive Producer: Edward J. Montagne; Director: Hollingsworth Morse.

Col. Mackenzie finds a bride-to-be who fled her wedding unconscious in the wilderness.

TATE, RAMROD (9:20) # 31734

Air date: February 24, 1971; Guest stars: Sally Ann Howes, Peter Mark Richman, Rex Allen, Michael Burns, Craig Stevens, Alan Hale, Jr., Jo Ann Harris; Teleplay: Arthur Browne, Jr.; Producer: John Choy; Director: Marc Daniels.

Tate becomes involved in a dispute over a barbed wire fence.

THE REGIMENTAL LINE (9:21) # 31740

Air date: March 3, 1971; Guest star: John Saxon; Teleplay: Gene L. Coon; Executive Producer: Edward J. Montagne; Director: Hollingsworth Morse.

Col. Mackenzie overcomes warring Indians and rough terrain to pursue a man he believes deserted his regiment in India.

The Town Killer (9:22) # 31719

Air date: March 10, 1971; Guest stars: Peter Lawford, Howard Duff, Brenda Benet, Lloyd Bochner; Teleplay: Elroy Schwartz; Executive Producer: Norman MacDonnell; Director: Harry Harris.

The Virginian confronts an outlaw (Peter Lawford) who controls a frightened community.

Wolf Track (9:23) # 31729

Air date: March 17, 1971; Guest stars: Julie Harris, Arthur O'Connell, Clint Howard, Pernell Roberts; Teleplay: Arthur Browne, Jr.; Director: Abner Biberman.

Col. Mackenzie tracks a wolf responsible for the slaughter of Shiloh cattle.

Jump-Up (9:24) # 31726

Air date: March 24, 1971; Guest stars: John McGiver, Jan Sterling, John Astin, Madlyn Rhue, Rick Jason; Teleplay: Ron Bishop; Executive Producer-Director: Herbert Hirschman.

Sentenced to hard labor after being framed for murder, Tate escapes and seeks justice.

28

Afterthoughts

"One does not know the rigors of a big-time television series unless you go through it. Seventy-four minutes and 30 seconds of film. We shot it in eight days. And we did it for nine seasons. You don't expect to get any sleep. You're working all the time. You get up at five in the morning and get down there at seven and you don't get home until ten, maybe 10:30 at night and you're up again at 4:30 to five in the morning. There's no time to do anything else. You have to be totally committed to it."—James Drury

"I think *The Virginian* succeeded because it was a good show. It was well-cast with appealing stars. And I think that our approach, trying to make our episodes as movies, helped us succeed. We did fully developed and plotted sketches which contained important thematic underpinnings. Many television shows did character sketches stretched to an hour."—Frank Price

"For me personally, *The Virginian* was near and dear to my heart, not only because my two favorite men, my father and Frank, worked on it, but because it was so fateful in my life. It began my career, and more importantly, it put me together with Frank. That Frank might become his son-in-law one day had never crossed my father's mind and it did take quite a while for Frank and me to recognize what we were to each other. But it all began there, in those offices at Universal.

"*The Virginian* was a wonderful blend of talents. Actors, producers, directors, writers and the crew, all made it what it was. That doesn't always work. One wrong piece and it can all go wrong. A 90-minute weekly show requires everything from almost everyone. It's almost miraculous that it could be done. And so well. They should all be remembered."—Katherine Crawford

Appendix: *The Virginian* Memorabilia

The following list is not definitive but includes a representative selection of collectible items available through Internet auction sites and dealers.

Albums

Presenting Randy Boone and Roberta Shore—Singing Stars of The Virginian (Decca DL 74619) 1965.
Shadow Mountain (Boone), Anything Love Can Buy (Shore), Medicine Bow (Virginian's Chorus), Tennessee Stud (Boone), Walk by the River (Duet), The Cattle Call (Virginian's Chorus), I Love My Willie (Shore), Banks of the Ohio (Boone), Pretty Saro (Shore), Yonder Mountain (Shore), Just Waitin' (Boone), Lonesome Tree (Boone).
The Film Music of Bernard Herrmann (Cine Sound Records) 1975.
"Last Grave at Socorro Creek"—Side One—The Werzburg Radio Orchestra, conducted by Klauss Kuse.
The First of the Irish Rovers (Decca 74835) 1966.
The Unicorn—The Irish Rovers (MCA 15) 1967.

45 RPM Singles

Gary Clarke—Theme from The Virginian—Lonesome Tree (Decca 31511) 1963.
Stanley Wilson and his Orchestra—The Virginian Theme (Decca 31529) 1963.
Tim Morgon—Take A Look Around (MCA) 1973. Also known as *Trampas' Theme*, folk singer Tim Morgon recorded the song in front of a 110 piece orchestra on the Universal sound stage. The song was also included on the 2003 CD release *Tim Morgon's Greatest Hits* (CDB0143780052) released by Tmfink.

Books

The Men from Shiloh—Lone Trail for the Virginian (Paperback novel) by Dean Owen (Lancer Books, New York, 1971)

Comic Books

Classics Illustrated: The Virginian—Owen Wister No.150 (Gilberton Co., May 1959)
The Virginian No. 1 (Gold Key, June 1963)—TV series—James Drury photo back cover.
MAD Magazine. (December 1965)—"The Virginiaham."
TV Tornado No.63 (March 1968 England)—Trampas—Doug McClure cover art.

Miscellaneous

The Virginian Game -Adventures at Shiloh Ranch (Transogram Company Inc., New York 1962).
The Virginian Movie Viewer (Chemtoy Corporation, Chicago 1966)—TV series.

The Virginian TV series Trading Cards—Estrellas de la TV (Ediciones Este, Spain 1967)—Printed on paper.
The Virginian TV series Trading Cards—Rostros Populares de la TV (Ediciones Este, Spain 1968)—Printed on paper.
The Virginian TV series Trading Cards—set of eight (Editorial Juventud, Mexico 1969)
Trampas Pin Back Button (Fort Madison, Iowa Rodeo, September 1969)

Videos & DVDs

Classic TV Westerns Volume 1: The Virginian. Throw a Long Rope, The Executioners, Woman from White Wing (2000 Universal Playback UK—Color VHS PAL)
Classic TV Westerns Volume 2: The Virginian. Impasse, Echo of Another Day, The Mountain of the Sun (2000 Universal Playback UK—Color VHS PAL)
Classic TV Westerns Volume 1: The Men From Shiloh. Hannah, The Mysterious Mr. Tate, The Price of a Hanging (Universal Playback UK 2000- Color VHS PAL)
Classic TV Westerns Volume 2: The Men From Shiloh. The Best Man, Tate, Ramrod, The Legacy of Spencer Flats (Universal Playback UK 2000—Color VHS PAL)
The Meanest Men in the West (1967)—Charles Bronson and Lee Marvin (Goodtimes Home Video 1989—Color NTSC—DVD Region 1). Compilation of "It Tolls for Thee" (1962) and "The Reckoning" (1967)
The Bull of the West (1971)—Charles Bronson and Lee J. Cobb (Goodtimes Home Video 1995—Color NTSC VHS). Compilation of "Duel at Shiloh" (1962) and "Nobility of Kings (1965)
The Virginian (1929)—Gary Cooper (Specialty Video Company 1989—NTSC VHS)
Universal Western Collection: The Virginian (1946)—Joel McCrea (Universal Studios 2002—NTC VHS). Available on DVD in Europe
The Virginian (2000)—Bill Pullman, Diane Lane (Turner Home Video 2001—NTSC VHS)

Bibliography

Published Sources—Books

Andrews, Wayne, ed. *The Autobiography of Theodore Roosevelt.* New York: Charles Scribner, 1958.

Brown, Dee, et al. *The Wild West.* New York: Warner, 1993.

Cobbs, John L. *Owen Wister.* Boston: Twayne, 1984.

Dawidziak, Mark. *The Night Stalker Companion: A 25th Anniversary Tribute.* Beverly Hills: Pomegranate, 1997.

Fischer, David Hackett. *Albion's Seed: Four British Folkways in America.* New York: Oxford University Press, 1989.

Forbis, William H., et al. *The Cowboys.* New York: Time-Life, 1973.

Larson, T. A. *Wyoming: A Bicentennial History.* New York: W.W. Norton, 1977.

Payne, Darwin. *Owen Wister—Chronicler of the West, Gentleman of the East.* Dallas: Southern Methodist University Press, 1985.

Quinn, Arthur Hobson. *American Fiction: An Historical and Critical Survey.* New York: Appleton-Century-Crofts, 1964.

Smith, Christopher, ed. *American Realism: The Greenhaven Press Companion to Literary Movements and Genres.* San Diego: Greenhaven, 2000.

Spiller, Robert Ernest, Willard Thorp, Thomas Herbert Johnson and Henry Seidel Canby, eds. *Literary History of the United States.* New York: Macmillan, 1959.

Vorpahl, Ben Merchant. *My Dear Wister—The Frederic Remington-Owen Wister Letters.* Palo Alto: American West, 1972.

Wister, Fanny Kemble, ed. *Owen Wister Out West.* University of Chicago Press, 1958.

Wister, Owen. *The Virginian: A Horseman of the Plains.* New York: Macmillan, 1902.

_____. Preface. *The Virginian.* By Wister. Library of the University of Wyoming, Laramie. New York: Macmillan, 1928. vii-xv.

Published Sources—Periodicals, Newspapers, Archives

Aaker, Everett, and Janette Hyem. "Alias L.Q. Jones." *TV Scene* 4 n.d.: 28–30.

Amedeom Marco. "Doug McClure: The Fan Letters I Answer First." *Movie Land* July 1970: 14+.

Austin, Emma Lee. "Stewart Granger." *TV Scene* 6 n.d.: 16–17.

Coon, Chuck. "The Virginian." *American Cowboy* March-April 2002: 36–39.

Croft, Nancy. "Earning Their Belts as Promoters—Don and Judy Quine." *Nation's Business* May 1984.

Dean, Jan. "Virginian Star Sara Lane, Saved From Death in the Floods!" *TVR* n.d.: 44+.

Dern, Marian. "Is It True Blond Cowboys Have More Fun?" *TV Guide* July 18–24, 1964: 6–9.

"Do You Remember." *The TV Collector* March-April 1990: 14–29.

"Do You Remember." *The TV Collector* May-June 1990: 5–28.

"Do You Remember." *The TV Collector* July-Aug 1990: 9–25.

"Do You Remember." *The TV Collector* Nov-Dec 1990: 29–33.

"Doug McClure—Barbara Luna, Look What Marriage Can Lead To." *Motion Picture* Aug. 1962: 36–37.

"Faithful Sons and Big Daddies." *BBC TV Radio Times* Oct. 30, 1968.

Fields-Meyer, Thomas & Ulrica Wihlborg. "Pippa Scott, War Stories." *People Magazine,* April 19, 1999: 93–96.

"The Gang from Medicine Bow." *TV's Top Ten* (1963): 44–51.

"The Gang from Medicine Bow." *TV's Top Ten 4* (1963): 44–51.

Hyem, Janette. "Doug McClure, Tears of a Clown." *TV Scene* 1 (1982): 16–17.

_____. "James Drury, Is He Still the Virginian?" *TV Scene* 4 n.d.: 38–39.

_____. "Randy Boone, Mr. Personality." *TV Scene* 6 n.d.: 42–43.

Johnson, Jean Lamont. "Biography of Everett Cyril Johnson." *Glenbow Museum Archives, M-4018* 1967: 70.

Judd, Peter. "Last Days of *Virginian* Hero." *Globe* Feb. 21, 1995: 4.

MacMinn, Aleene. "Pluses for Girl Next Door." *The Washington Post Weekly TV Magazine* June 2–8, 1963.

Maloney, Martin. "*The Virginian* Review." *TV Guide* Aug. 19, 1967: 14.

Marshack, Laddie. "The Indian Uprising of '68." *TV Guide* Aug. 10, 1968: 9–11.

Morgan, Brendan. "Jeanette Nolan, Tribute." *TV Guide* Aug. 29, 1998: 7.

Press Release, Universal Studios. "Dick Shane—A Special Breed." n.d.

Pivirotto, Peg. "Television's Cowgirl." *The Western Horseman.* March 1970: 66+.

Publicity Brochure, Universal Studios. "*The Men from Shiloh.*" MCA TV 1970.

Raddatz, Leslie. "Her Skirts Cover Her Knees ... and that's not the only difference between Sara Lane and most starlets." *TV Guide* June 24, 1967: 24–26.

_____. "Rebirth of an Actor." *TV Guide* Oct. 26, 1963: 18–20.

Seldes, Gilbert. "*The Virginian* Review." *TV Guide* Oct. 27, 1962: 14.

Sloane, Judy. "Poker Face." *Film Review Special* Video Movie Guide 1994: 29–32.

Smith, Cecil. "Drastic Face-Lift for *The Virginian.*" *Los Angeles Times* March 25, 1970: 22.

_____. "Stewart Granger: Not so bloody sure about Shiloh series." *Los Angeles Times* Aug. 30, 1970.

Tracy, Kathleen. "Hollywood Cowboys Say Farewell to Doug McClure." *Globe* Feb. 28, 1995: 14.

"*Virginian* TV Star Selected Acting Over Athletic Career." *Grit.* Family Section. Jan. 2, 1966.

Whitney, Dwight. "Cantankerous Charlie Bickford." *TV Guide* Jan. 14, 1967: 14–18.

_____. "The Garbo of the Sagebrush." *TV Guide* May 4–10, 1963: 18–21.

_____. "You've Got to Play the Game. *The Virginian*'s rebellious Don Quine..." *TV Guide* Oct. 21, 1967: 19–23.

Wister, Owen. "Balaam and Pedro." *Harper's New Monthly Magazine* 524 (Jan. 1894)

_____. "Em'ly." *Harper's New Monthly Magazine* 522 (Nov. 1893)

_____. "Hank's Woman." Harper's Weekly 36 (Aug. 1892)

Internet Sources

Authors and Creators. "Roy Huggins." <http://thrillingdetective.com/trivia/huggins.html>

Burlingame, Jon. "Richard Shores Remembered." *The Film Music Society.* <http://filmmusicsociety.org/news_events/features/2004/020604.html>

The Classic TV Archive "The Virginian." CTVA Western. <http://aa.1asphost.com/CTVA/US/Western/Virginian/V-homepage.htm>

Duke University News & Communications. "David Hartman to Lecture at Duke Feb. 25." <http://www.dukenews.duke.edu./2004/02/hartman_0204_print.htm>

Entertainment Insiders. <http://www.einsiders.com>

Everett C. Johnson: "The Virginian." <http://www.ucalgary.ca/~dsucha/virginian/html>

Film Score Rundowns. "The Television Works of Bernard Herrmann." <http://www.filmscorerundowns.net/herrmann/index.html>

First Americans in the Arts. "FAITA 13th Annual Awards." <http://www.firstamericans.org/13th%20annual.html>

Internet Broadway Database. <http://ibdb.com>

Internet Movie Pro Database. <http://pro.imdb.com>

The Irish Rovers <http://www.irishrovers.info/history.htm>

The Life of Carey Wilber Sr. <http://www.tuppers.com/pop>

LookSmart's Find Articles. <http://www.findarticles.com>

MBC. The Museum of Broadcast Communications. <http://museum.tv/home.php>

Mikulan, Steven. "Beautiful Dreamers." *LA Weekly* 52. Nov. 21–27. n.d. <http://www.gulager.com/laweekly>

MSN Movies entertainment. <http://movies.msn.com>

National Cowboy & Western Heritage Museum. "Western Heritage Award Winners." <http://www.nationalcowboymuseum.org/e_awar_winn.html>

The New York Times Movies Biography. <http://movies2.nytimes.com>

NationMaster.com. "Encyclopedia: Stewart Granger." <http://www.nationmaster.com/encyclopedia-

/Stewart-Granger>
NNDB. <http://www.nndb.com>
OTRCAT.com. Old Time Radio Show Catalog. "Gunsmoke, About the Radio Show." <http://www. otrcat.com/gunsmoke.htm>
Percy Faith Pages. <http://www.percyfaithpages.org>
Space Age Pop Music <http://spaceagepop.com>
Valle, David Del. "Clu Gulager." *Psychotronic Video* 36. n.d. <http://www.psychotronicvideo.com/wow/ inner_views/gulager/gulager.html>
A Walk Around Brooklyn. "About the Program—David Hartman Bio. " New York: Thirteen/WNET. <http://www.thirteen.org/brooklyn/a-hartmanbio.html>

Interviews

Boone, Randy. Telephone interview. April 23, 2005.
Casser, Renata. Telephone interview. September 14, 2005.
Clarke, Gary. Telephone interview. April 26, 2005.
Crawford, Katherine. E-mail interviews. August 21 to October 21, 2005.
Drury, James. Telephone interview. April 20, 2005.
Halvorsen, Bill. E-mail interview. September 16, 2005.
Kibbee, Meredith. E-mail interviews. August 1 to 29, 2005.
Lane, Sara. Telephone interviews. April 8, 11, 12, 2006.
Luna, BarBara. E-mail interviews. August 2 to 26, 2005.
McClure, Diane. Telephone interview. October 19, 2005.
McClure, Tané. Telephone interview. April 7, 2005.
Perry, Elizabeth. E-mail interview. August 4, 2005.
Price, Frank. Telephone interview. April 25, 2005.
_____. E-mail interviews. April 26 to October 21, 2005.
Rogosin, Joel. Telephone interviews. October 2, 4, 2005.
Saxon, John. E-mail interviews. September 14 to October 13, 2005.
Scott, Pippa. E-mail interview. August 22, 2005.
Shore, Roberta. Telephone interview. April 23, 2005.

Index

Page numbers in *bold italics* denote photographs

275